THE
BUSINESS
GUIDE TO
LAW

THE
BUSINESS
GUIDE TO
LAW

Creating and Operating a Successful Law Firm

KERRY M. LAVELLE

AMERICAN BAR ASSOCIATION
Solo, Small Firm and
General Practice Division

Library of Congress Cataloging-in-Publication Data

Lavelle, Kerry M., author.
  The business guide to law : creating and operating a successful law firm / Kerry M. Lavelle.
      pages cm
  Includes index.
  ISBN 978-1-63425-236-2 (softcover : alk. paper) -- ISBN 978-1-63425-237-9 (e-book)
1. Law offices--United States. 2. Practice of law--Economic aspects--United States. 3. Law offices--United States--Management. I. Title.
  KF315.L36 2015
  340.068--dc23   2015015638

To my mom and dad, Martin and Patricia Lavelle, for demonstrating to me my first example of an endearing partnership;
To my wife, Lyn, the greatest partner one can ever have; and
To Tim Hughes, Ted McGinn, and Matt Sheahin, my first law partners, for believing and buying in (both figuratively and literally) to these disciplines, principles, and concepts that are required to build a great law office.

Contents

Preface   xvii

Acknowledgments   xxi

Introduction   xxiii

Section 1
The Start-Up   1

Chapter 1
While Still in Law School   3
   Expand Your Network   4
   Mentors   6
   Research Assistant   7
   Publishable Quality Writing   8
   Bar Association Activities   9
   Social Media   9

Chapter 2
General Thoughts on the Hours Required   13

Chapter 3
Working *on* Your Business and *in* Your Business   19

Chapter 4
The Five-Tool Attorney   25
   Provide the Highest-Quality, Thorough Legal Work   26

Meet Production Goals   26
Marketing and Civic Involvement   28
Being a Leader, Training Young Associates   29
Participate in Running the Business   30

Chapter 5
Core Decisions   33
Do I Need Experience?   33
Solo or a Partnership?   34
Incorporation or Sole Proprietorship   37
Should You Practice with Your Spouse or Other Family Members? 38
Income During the Start-Up Year   39
Working as a Contract Attorney   40
Naming Your Law Firm   41
Domain Names   42
Insurance   43
The Argument against Growth   45

Chapter 6
The Necessities   47
Bank Accounts   47
Computer, Computer Equipment, and Software   50
Printer   52
Letterhead   53
Supplies   54
Office Furniture   55
Law Library   56
Telephone Systems   59
Website   61
Miscellaneous Equipment, Dictation Machines, Postage Meters   65
Billing and Accounting Software   67
Hiring an Accountant   68

Chapter 7
Finding Office Space   71
Practicing Out of Your Home   71
Traditional Office-Finding Methods   72
Potential Referral Sources   73
Retail-Type Space   75

Practicing in a Cooperative Suite   76
Location of Office   77
Setting Up an Office Within a Law Firm   78

Chapter 8
Departments in Your Law Office; Law Office Management   79
Banking and Bill Paying   79
Billing and Accounts Receivable   80
Payroll   84
Human Resources   85
Marketing   86
Technology   87
Office Manager   87
Managing Legal Work   88

Chapter 9
Billing   89
Hourly Billing   91
Keeping Track of Your Time   95
Hourly Rates   98
Flat Fee Cases   99
Contingency Fee   100
The Monthly Retainer   102
The Hybrid Billing Methods   103
Value Billing   103
Miscellaneous Notes on Billing   106

Chapter 10
Collections   107
Create Detailed Specific Bills   108
Have the Client Sign a Contract and Deposit a Retainer Check   109
Focus on the Thirty-Day Delinquency List   110
Payment Plans   114
Handling Client Complaints About Bills   115
Should We Sue a Former Client for Fees?   119

Chapter 11
Specialist versus Generalist   123
Pick Your Concentration Cautiously   127

Chapter 12
Social Media Networking   129
How to Get the Message Out   130
E-mail Blasts   131
Notes on Legal Advertising   132
Website   133
General Notes on Your Digital Footprint   134

Chapter 13
Traditional Networking   135
Get Connected with People   135
The Marketing Mindset   136
The Elevator Speech   138
The First Meeting   138
The Follow-Up   141
Do Your Research   142
The Subsequent Follow-Through   144
Sometimes You Need to Ask for the Sale   145

Chapter 14
Clients   147
How Do I Add Value?   149
Second Place Is the Next Best Place to Be   151
Respect Your Clients   152
The Things That Clients Hate   154
Clients on Which to Take a Pass   159

Chapter 15
Best Practices   165
New Clients and Initial Meetings   166
Client Communication and File Documentation   172
Client Files   174
Litigation   175
Transactional and Commercial Real Estate   178
Estate Planning and Estate Administration   179
Family Law and Divorce Matters   180
Tax Controversies   181

Chapter 16
Checklists and Document Library   183
   Document Library   184
      Document Directory   186
         Categories/Folder   186

Chapter 17
Perils of Being a Solo Practitioner   199

Chapter 18
Ethical Rules and Avoiding Disciplinary Action   203
   The Lawyer-Client Relationship   203
   Counselor, Advisor   205
   An Advocate   205
   Advertising   206
   Money   207
   Miscellaneous   207

Section 2
Growing a Law Practice   209

Chapter 19
General Concepts in Growing a Law Practice   211

Chapter 20
Hiring Support Staff   215
   Your First Administrative Assistant   217
   Hiring Help for the Accounting Department   219
   Clerks   222
   Incentives and Bonuses for Support Staff   223

Chapter 21
Hiring Attorneys   225
   Base Salary   227
   Compensation Incentives   228
   Hiring out of Law School versus Laterals   231

Chapter 22
Hiring the Right People   235
   Recognition   237
   Managing the Process   239
   Keep an Open Mind   242
   Year-End Reviews   243

Chapter 23
Leadership   245

Chapter 24
Building the Business Plan   253
   Setting the One-, Five-, and Ten-Year Plans   254
      The One-Year Plan   255
      The Five-Year Plan   256
      The Ten-Year Plan   256
   Audacious Goals   257
   Pay-to-Play Requirements   259
   Annual Firm Meeting   260

Chapter 25
Firm Management   261
   How Will We Become What We Are Not?   263
   Organizational Charts   266
   Creating a High-Performance Environment   266
   Operating Manuals   267

Chapter 26
Marketing and Lead Generation System   269
   Referral Sources   272
   What Is Your Franchise?   275
   Yellow Pages Advertising and Internet Searches 278
   Marketing Letters   280
   Public Relations   282
   Public Speaking   282
   Community Development   283
   Branding   284
   Billboards, TV, and Radio   287
   Building Loyalty   288

Build a Marketing Culture   292
Marketing Additional Services to Existing Clients   293
Tracking the Firm's Marketing Efforts   296

Chapter 27
Lead Conversion   301

Chapter 28
Client Fulfillment and Satisfaction   309
Exceed Expectations   309
Naming the Relationship Manager   311
The Client Fulfillment Process   313

Chapter 29
More Than Profits, You Need a Winning Culture   315
So What Is a Core Purpose or Ideology?   316
Why Does Your Law Office Exist?   319
How Does Your Firm Behave and Act?   321

Chapter 30
Building a Winning Culture   325

Chapter 31
Segregating Practice Groups and Management Work   329
Law Office Management   329
Managing Legal Work   331
First Year Out of Law School   332
Two- to Five-Year Associates   332
Six- to Ten-Year Associates   333

Chapter 32
The Income Partner   335
A Big Decision   337

Section 3
The Succession Plan   341

Chapter 33
The Succession Cycle   343
  Options   345
  Why Sell Off at All?   350
  Buy-in and Sell-off Cycle   352
  Ownership Enquiries   354

Chapter 34
What Are You Really Selling? The Valuation Analysis   357
  What Is Your Correct Salary?   359
  What Is Your Valuation Formula?   361
  What Does This Valuation Matrix Mean to You?   364
  What Does the Valuation Matrix Mean to the Buy-in Partner? 365
  Discounts and Premiums   368
  The Unspoken Dark Side   369

Chapter 35
The Preliminary Disclosure; Testing Interest   371
  Expression of Interest   371
  Initial Percentage Sold   372
  Due Diligence   374
    Financial Statements   374
    Marketing Information   374
    Human Resources   374
    Client Problems   375

Chapter 36
Financing   377
  Bank Financing   377
  Seller Financing   381
  Miscellaneous Notes on Financing and the Transition   382

Chapter 37
The Agreement   385
  The Company Valuation Formula   386
  Restrictions on Transferability   386

Call Options 387
Put Option 388
Sales Queue 388
Involuntary Transfers 389
Upon the Death of a Shareholder 389
Termination of Employment Other Than Death 390
Nonsolicitation Duty of Loyalty 391
Retirement 392
Governance and Operations 393
Business Expenses 394
New Client Bonuses 395

Chapter 38
The New Management Team 397
How Often Should You Meet? 401
Reiterate the Message 402

Chapter 39
Are You Really Ready to Sell Below 50%? 33%? 405

Chapter 40
Fixing the Mature Practice 409
Five-Tool Attorney 415
Support Staff 417
The Business Plan 418
Opportunities for Improvement 420
Conclusion 421

Chapter 41
The Small Firm Merger 423
Purpose 423
Process 425
The Economics 434
The Report of Merger 437

Appendix 439

Index 495

Preface

What intrigued me about writing this book? I recently visited a local bookstore and checked http://www.Amazon.com to see what other books exist on starting and growing a law practice. Initially, I was shocked by the amount of material that was out there for an individual wanting to start his or her own law practice. I took the time to review the books that I have used over the years and also investigated the new books that are on the market for growing a law practice.

In a very short period of time, I was energized by the vision I had for this book as being very different from anything available in the marketplace.

Over twenty-five years ago, I purchased a copy of *How to Start & Build a Law Practice* by Jay G. Foonberg,[1] and that wonderful book provided me guidance and inspiration at the time I needed it most. However, after the jumping off point of starting my own practice, I found myself learning as I went along, reading not only law practice books but also business books that provided a completely different insight on how to run a business, which also happens to be a law firm.

There are many outstanding books written by law professors, judges, and many young lawyers who started a law practice that provide guidance and methodology for answering many of the initial questions that a young practitioner would have: Where do I set up my office? How do I best take advantage of social media? What business entities do I use to structure my practice? How much time and economic analysis go into the office design and furnishing? How much money do I spend on technology?

This book is completely different.

This is a business book. While it will answer all those necessary questions (and more) that are important in creating and growing a unique business known as a law firm—I am a lawyer who started and grew a law practice—this book goes through in great detail the time needed by you, and how best to spend it, to grow your own law firm.

You need to understand early on in the progression that a law firm is, in fact, a unique business enterprise (I guess many professional service businesses would argue that they, too, are unique). A law firm business model is unique in that most of the marketing that you will be doing will be promoting individual lawyers, *including yourself*, and yet you need to spend enough time managing your law firm, or as we will more frequently refer

---

1. Jay G. Foonberg, How to Start & Build a Law Practice, 4th ed. (American Bar Association 1999).

to it, working "on the business." Doing this involves a difficult mix and blend of your time, all on top of practicing law.

It is not by accident that this book is divided into three specific sections.

The first section, The Start-Up, touches on the topics that are discussed in many books about priorities and provides some conclusions as to the best ways to structure your start-up. It focuses on associated costs and how to make core decisions, secure office space, establish billing and collecting procedures, create your entrepreneurial model, develop marketing strategies, and offer guidance for key decisions.

The second section, Growing a Law Practice, takes a successful solo practitioner or small partnership and lays the foundation for adding a second, third, fourth, or even tenth, and possibly twentieth, lawyer to the firm. It is difficult, but not impossible. If you create the correct foundation in your early start-up years, the growth of a law firm is a natural progression. The progression is systematic, but it still takes a certain amount of fortitude to add payroll, infrastructure, support, and other third-party contractors to help you be as efficient working *in* the law firm, as a productive attorney, and working *on* your business to help grow the business.

The third section is The Succession Plan. You work your whole career to build up your law practice to presumably transfer it to your children. However, given their young age, you do not know if they will ever go to law school. The intent of this book is to build up a first-class, grade A, competitive law firm in your community that will meet and exceed client expectations and that will ultimately beat competition and, quite possibly, change the world.[2] In order to do that, your succession plan has to be more sophisticated than passing your law firm business along to your children. You may end up passing your ownership interests to your children, but that should not be the predetermined plan. Only the best and brightest attorneys and leaders will elevate themselves to being your equity partner. Remember, this is a business book. It is not about operating a small family business. Your legal community is stacked with bright, often brilliant, practitioners competing against you for clients, to win cases and get an advantage on you and every business deal you document. Thus, the transition from a sole practitioner to having multiple shareholders is a delicate but necessary one that must be done in an honest, ethical manner of which only honest and ethical people partake.

Under ideal circumstances, you start your law office, and through your law school and prelaw school connections are hired by many clients on a regular basis. Not too many the first month; not too many the second month. However, over time, the number of clients

---

2. This reference to the purpose of this book, which is to provide the foundation and architecture to build a great law firm, is made regularly. You, the founding partner, will help define what a great law firm is. Great may not be defined as the law firm with the most attorneys, nor will it be defined as the law firm that makes the most money. Depending on your focus, whether it is with respect to offering certain client services, being the greatest place to work in your community, improving your community, or changing and improving the lives of Americans throughout our country, this book will provide the blueprint. Do not be afraid to change the world.

continues to grow because you have performed the work in an efficient manner and have established an environment in which all clients pay on time.

Next, you hire an assistant or paralegal, and while your overhead is growing, clients continue to pay on time and the breadth of work and diversity of clients continues to increase. You may hire a part-time bookkeeper and possibly sometime thereafter your first attorney to work on cases with you. Again, all problems are solved with clients paying on time; the clients providing good, fulfilling work; and revenues always staying out in front of your expenses and overhead.

All that changes when clients delay payment 60 days, 90 days, and sometimes beyond 120 days. Your assistant, paralegal, and first attorney need to be paid on a regular payroll cycle. There is no time for delay. When one client starts to hire you for more and more projects, and that one client starts to make up 20%, 30%, even 50% of your business—you become in effect an "employee" of that client. If that client's accounts receivable builds up and, ultimately, payment is delayed or not paid at all, you will have your first tragedy.

This pressure, combined with the needs and realities of your home and family life, makes the dream of owning your own firm look like a nightmare. To the underprepared or unprepared, this disaster is bound to derail your law firm and could potentially derail your personal life.

Why do you think so many law firms stop growing at two or three attorneys? Another stopping point is somewhere between six and ten attorneys. The rigors of making timely payments to vendors and employees and the grind of working on collecting receivables curtails growth. Moreover, some firms find themselves in a very vulnerable position when too many of the revenues are derived from one client.

Despite these concerns, all is not lost. This book sets forth the foundation and the stepping stones to progressive growth.

I wish that coming right out of law school I had had a platform on which to practice law the way our firm does, subscribing to the principles discussed in this book. If I had, I would never have started a law practice, and this book would probably never have been written.

This book is not intended to lay out a false sense that there is a simple and easy path to success. It is not intended to lay out a blueprint for a "get rich quick" scheme. This book provides a blueprint for a sustainable, aggressive growth plan for a law office that desires to be the best in its marketplace.

Acknowledgments

A project of this magnitude cannot possibly be completed by one person. I am a true believer in team efforts and "partners" that make it all happen.

First, I thank my wife, Lyn, for being my lifelong cheerleader, because without her, this book could not have possibly be written.

Secondly, to my assistant, Izabela Gorska, whose necessary work (although sometimes mundane) of typing, proofing, and editing was done in the spirit of producing the best possible product. She helped make the project fun and energizing.

To my close friend from high school, Jim Mitchell, who took it upon himself to set the project on the right course and in the right tone, and who provided encouraging words when it was most necessary and believed in the project in his first review. Without him, the book had no theme, pace, or continuity.

To Tim Hughes, Ted McGinn, and Matt Sheahin, in any order. Teams matter. When a team functions properly, it is greater than the sum of its parts. There is no doubt that there is a part of their DNA throughout this book as policies, principles, culture, and unwavering pillars have been created to build a foundation on which this law practice is built. My partners believe in these principles, and through a team effort, assisted in achieving something of which we are very proud.

Thanks to everyone involved in the summation of the nuances required to build a successful law practice—this book.

Introduction

Years ago, before relocating the Lavelle Law Ltd. office, I was very proud that we were growing at a rate of about one to two attorneys every other year. Then, after reading some material about systemizing businesses, I took a new approach to our marketing efforts and client satisfaction experience at our office, and I instituted many changes that, looking back, created a seismic shift in the way we did business and the way we thought about delivering legal services. As a result, we added sixteen attorneys in the last eleven years. It has been quite a run, and through my trials and errors, we have developed as a team, a system, and disciplines that I believe can help you, too, create a successful law office. It seems to have happened so rapidly, and the path has not always been smooth, but as I look back on the history of the firm, it is an enjoyable path on which to reminisce.

I handled a variety of clients when first starting out. During the early years, I tried to add one new attorney every other year and always emphasized my experience and knowledge of tax law. I began to build a support staff working out of a Chicago Loop office. Through exceptional work, the firm continued to expand, with additional attorneys joining to handle the growing demand.

In one of the first signs that the firm would take a path that was unique and innovative, a conscious effort was made in the early years of the firm to be aggressive in marketing and promoting the firm in a variety of ways. I was a frequent speaker throughout the community, providing seminars on tax law, business law, real estate, and other pertinent topics at libraries, chambers of commerce, senior centers, and other organizations. Similarly, our team members focused on relationship building with other professional service providers and have been staunch advocates of supporting that network through trusted referrals. As such, the Lavelle Law attorneys are often asked to speak at events for CPAs, insurance professionals, real estate agents, and other professional groups with whom they have built supportive relationships. The majority of our clients come from referrals from other attorneys or professionals, as well as from existing clients.

As a growing firm, Lavelle Law has accepted responsibility to exhibit leadership within the legal profession. The attorneys not only are involved in a number of professional organizations but have held key positions within them. At area bar associations, we have served on corporate counseling, federal tax, estate planning, health care, commercial litigation, commercial finance and transactions, and corporation and business law committees. Various attorneys from the firm have served as chair or vice-chair of the federal tax and the practice and procedure federal tax committees. Others have served as arbitrators in hearing procedures in the State of Illinois Circuit Court of Cook County Court–Annexed Mandatory Arbitration and on the board of directors of the Corporate Law Association at The John Marshall Law School. Our attorneys and I have served as adjunct professors at John Marshall Law School, and several of our attorneys have also taught classes at a local junior college.

Today, the firm includes twenty-one attorneys and a support staff of fourteen. With six partners now in place, the firm evaluates growth on an annual basis and uses profits to build the resources of the company through expanded office space, improved technology, and additional support staff and to contribute to the community. As the head of the firm, I have initiated the compensation package set forth herein for Lavelle Law attorneys that encourages them to be active participants in the marketing and growth of the firm but also rewards them for their individual and the firm's overall success.

While the firm has not ventured far from its roots in providing tax law services to individuals and businesses, it has grown to include a number of additional practice groups. The planning of the firm called for new practice groups to slowly be added with the intention of not only attracting new clients but also eventually cross-pollinating the services they provide to existing clients from one line of business to others. Today, Lavelle Law has specific practice groups in tax, business law, commercial real estate, estate planning, criminal law, health care, small business, gaming law, bankruptcy, corporate formation, family law, litigation, grocery law, employment law, residential real estate, and in keeping with its forward thinking view of serving all potential clients, lesbian, gay, bisexual, and transsexual (LGBT) law. It has become one of the largest law firms in the suburbs of Chicago and has rolling five- and ten-year plans for continued growth and business development.

As part of the vision for growth, we developed a long-term strategy for public relations, marketing, and advertising. Since the earliest days of the practice, the firm has provided a regular series of press releases to local and national media on a wide range of relevant and time-sensitive matters. The firm has also executed a measured advertising philosophy, testing and evaluating a variety of tactics, including direct mail, television advertising, billboards, radio campaigns, and print advertising.

Not all advertising has been done just to promote the firm. Several years ago, Lavelle Law took out ads, distributed press releases, and devoted podcasts alerting the public about unscrupulous firms that were calling themselves "tax specialists" and preying on uninformed and vulnerable consumers. Lavelle Law was compelled at least to have a voice in the professional community about the unethical practices of these firms. While our actions had little national impact, today many of those unethical firms are out of business through government intervention, and we have made an important statement by taking a stand on behalf of consumers across the country.

Lavelle Law has been an early adopter of various social media, including Twitter and LinkedIn, and has carefully managed a Facebook presence as well. In the early 1990s, we ventured into television, hosting a topic-oriented talk show in the Chicago market, *Newsmakers*. The show was independently produced by our team and featured in-depth discussions of key social, legal, and economic topics.

We have always looked for ways in which to bring innovation to the legal profession, such as developing a weekly podcast series, *Chicago's Legal Latte*. In the series, the attorneys from the firm each contribute topics that they review in a fifteen-minute discussion available via Blogtalkradio, iTunes, and the firm's website, http://www.lavellelaw.com. The series provides general, casual conversation about current legal topics that may be of interest to individuals and businesses. Some recent topics have included "Credit Scores," "Illinois Civil Unions," "Avoiding Foreclosure," "Tax Planning for the Self-Employed," and "Life Insurance Considerations in Estate Planning." The firm has produced over 250 individual episodes of the series, all available for free, which are often based on topics submitted by clients or listeners.

In June of 2003, the firm made another revolutionary move—literally. We made the uncommon decision to relocate from a prestigious Chicago Loop address to a new location in the suburbs. The move was driven by a desire to be in a location that allows for greater access to a wider range of clients, but more important, allows the firm to establish roots in a community where it can play a more active role than it could have in Chicago. To that end, Lavelle Law collectively and the attorneys and staff individually have become significant contributors to the local community. In adhering to the objective of being involved and supporting other professions, the firm is an active participant in numerous chambers of commerce. Through their commitment to the business community, Lavelle Law Ltd. was recognized as Business of the Year in 2009 by the Palatine Chamber of Commerce.

Our commitment to the community extends beyond being passive participants who simply write checks and sponsor youth teams. More than a decade ago, Lavelle Law initiated a community food drive for the holidays. Calling on our many clients in the food and grocery industries, the firm collected significant donations while also inviting local residents to help address the growing issue of hunger in the suburbs. That initial food drive gathered so much food that the recipient, the Palatine Township Food Pantry, had to secure additional storage space to house the donations. The annual event has grown over the years and continues to provide extensive contributions to the Food Pantry. As a result, the Palatine Township Board provided Lavelle Law Ltd. with a special commendation in 2010 for the firm's efforts on behalf of the Food Pantry. That year, the food drive also branched out to a second community, with donations from that drive being directed to another food pantry. Ours remains one of the largest food drives in the suburban area.

For a number of years, the firm has also organized and run an annual flag football game. The event, which pits Lavelle Law and other area business leaders against members of the local police and fire departments, has served as a significant fundraiser for various individuals and organizations in need.

Lavelle Law served as a major sponsor for a theater that enhances educational and artistic efforts for all groups, including young children, seniors, and especially developmentally disabled individuals. Their contributions allowed programs to provide outstanding outlets for education and artistic expression to a wide variety of special groups throughout the suburbs. In 2013, Lavelle began a three-year agreement to serve as the primary sponsor of an annual event that brings together more than one thousand community members for healthy and fun 5K and 10K runs.

Many of the partners, attorneys, and staff members have accepted positions on boards for a variety of local service agencies. In recent years, we have had representatives on the boards of directors for the Society for the Preservation of Human Dignity, Catholic Charities, Shelter Inc., Palatine Senior Citizens Council, Palatine Township Food Pantry, Chicago Planning Council, Countryside Association for People with Disabilities, Palatine Zoning Board of Appeals, Village of Streamwood Plan Commission, and others.

Lest one think that our firm is recognized only for its success and growth, it should be noted that we are also a recipient of the Al Knox Award for Ethics in Business. While practicing law is the central focus of the attorneys at Lavelle Law, we recognize our obligation to share our knowledge and skills with those who may not be able to afford quality legal services. For those in need, we volunteer countless hours to the Clinic for the Disabled and Elder Law (CDEL) and other legal aid organizations and host regular lunchtime discussions at the Palatine Senior Center to hear the concerns of senior citizens.

In 2010, we received the prestigious Spirit of Life Award from the Society for the Preservation of Human Dignity for our efforts within the community.

In 2011, we worked with Illinois state senator Matt Murphy (27th District) on establishing a new law in Illinois that removes outdated, offensive terms such as "mentally retarded" and "crippled" from state laws and replaces them with more contemporary and appropriate terms.

In 2012, the firm was recognized with a highly selective Award for Business Excellence in the small business category.

In 2014, seven of the attorneys were recognized as Super Lawyers or Rising Stars in Illinois by *Super Lawyers Magazine*, a distinction that is handed out to less than 5% of the practicing attorneys in the state.

In 2014, I was fortunate enough to be recognized by the Palatine Chamber of Commerce as Business Leader of the Year for contributions to the community.

Please enjoy the book as much as I have enjoyed writing it.

Section 1

The Start-Up

Chapter 1

While Still in Law School

The best time to plant a tree is twenty years ago. The second-best time is now.

—Proverb

At the time this book is being written, the national economy is rebounding from six very difficult economic years. Although, by definition, the country has not been in a recession for five or six years, it sure seems like it when you read stories about unemployment, a discouraged workforce, the national debt, falling real estate prices, and other problems associated with hard times for the citizens of the United States generally and, probably, of your community specifically. As a result, it is a fact that many law students are coming out of law school with very limited job prospects with established law firms and are faced with the reality of starting their own law practice right out of law school. While the situation is not optimal, it is the brutal reality of today's economic picture.

In the last six years, many attorneys who have been out of law school for over twenty years have been terminated from the largest law firms in the country for many reasons. One of the primary examples involved the almost instantaneous drying up of investment banking money and available credit in banking markets, affecting law practices that have depended solely on mergers and acquisitions. Layoffs from these and similar law practices resulted in high-end, highly skilled attorneys, many of whom had been partners in the large law firms, looking for jobs in an already crowded marketplace.

In addition, many suburban and small town lawyers who had made a very comfortable living practicing in real estate, most notably residential real estate, suffered a similar disastrous loss in business beginning in 2008 during the real estate crash. The economy dried up real estate activity for over four years. These lawyers, who relied on real estate transactions to make a living, have migrated to other areas of law, including criminal law, business transactions, and estate planning, although many have left the practice of law altogether. As a result of this surplus of lawyers, many law students just coming out of law school are faced with a real prospect of not having a job and yet still needing to satisfy a burning desire to practice law (and to get student loans paid off).

If you are in law school, there are a few things that you could be doing to prepare yourself for the possibility of starting your own law practice.

Expand Your Network

There are volumes written about rainmaking and networking for lawyers and other professional business people. These topics are specifically addressed later in the book in Chapters 12, 13, and 26, but you need to know these topics while you are in law school, when the time is right to expand your networking base as broadly as possible.

Your networking base includes four categories of people:

1. All of your law school and law-related contacts;
2. Any business-related contacts you may have had at a young age, including people you have worked for, or with, in the past, such as a colleague (at the mall or at a campus job);
3. Personal social contacts; and
4. Your parents' personal and professional contacts.

> With respect to all of your law school colleagues, please remember, these will be future lawyers you will know who will send you business over time.

All four of these categories will be approached differently when the time comes to develop a networking strategy.

With respect to all of your law school colleagues, please remember, these will be future lawyers you will know who will send you business over time. Will it happen immediately? Maybe it will, maybe it won't. It does not matter because these are the easiest people for you to connect with throughout your career, and they will be a natural business and social networking group with which you can stay connected. Referrals from lawyers will be a significant part of your business if the path set forth in this book is followed. Do not lose sight of the importance of the connectivity to other lawyers.

Some of your colleagues from law school will eventually get jobs with large firms, or they may migrate to large firms and become partners. Those large firms cannot afford to handle small- or medium-sized cases. They will always be looking for an outlet for those cases, and you should position yourself to be that outlet.

With respect to other business-related contacts you have had since a young age, find them on social networking websites and connect with them. They may have been supervisors, retail clerks, librarians, or construction workers. It does not matter. The fact is that you were working at jobs in high school and college and those people saw you, or will soon see you, and your drive to move forward. Depending on how you left the relationship, there will be some respect that they will give you as you further yourself through higher education. As you will find out in Chapters 12, 13, and 26 on marketing, you should make sure you become a resource for them. In becoming a resource for them, you will further your connectivity to them and eventually be their resource for simple legal issues, and perhaps for complex issues as well, that may confront them, their friends, and their family members. These connections will turn into paying clients.

Cultivate those relationships now while you have an opportunity and not too much time has passed between your work with them and your pursuit of a law degree. Keep in mind that depending on where you worked as a high school and college student (and for that matter, your first job out of undergraduate school if you worked for a few years before going to law school), those coworkers may not have anybody within their social circles who is a lawyer. This is exactly the type of group that you need to cultivate as a source of future clients. If you are the only lawyer within those social circles, you will grow your business over time through the connections you have made.

With respect to your personal social contacts, again, evaluate whether within those social circles you might be the only lawyer. Your personal contacts may be friends from grade school, high school, and undergrad. Even if there are lawyers in some of those groups, believe it or not, it is probably highly unlikely that they practice in the same area of law that you do. Evaluate your neighborhood and other people you have kept in touch with through your circle of friends. These are all groups to cultivate and keep in touch with through your social media connections and also face-to-face interactions.

I encourage you to connect with all of your parents' personal and professional contacts. You do not want to be intrusive and a burden with respect to your parents' social circles, but you can convey information that may add value to their lives. Through social media networking and ultimately marketing through traditional networking, you will provide these contacts with valuable information on a regular basis, for which they should be appreciative. Would your parents' friends hire you as a lawyer right out of law school? Maybe, or maybe not. But you should take the time to plant those seeds; for over time, these individuals may have a legal question that they ask at a family function or a social gathering, where you could easily talk to them about their legal issues and convey valuable information to them.

Know the practical aspects of connecting with your parents' social network. If you are in your mid- to late twenties and graduating from law school, members of your parents' social circle are likely in their late forties and fifties. They may be in their prime earning years and have a strong social network of high-level professionals around them that includes lawyers. That is understandable and completely fine. But as they age and you continue to gain valuable experience, you may find work coming your way from them in ten, fifteen, or twenty years. These seeds take a long time to germinate, but remember, you are in the practice of law for a career. In addition, those people may refer their children to you (if you already do not know them) when they need legal assistance in purchasing their first home, for example, or preparing a will with guardian provisions as they start families.

Remember, the perfect time to plant a tree is twenty years ago. The second-best time to plant a tree is today.

Mentors

Begin building up your mentor network. Please consider as a mentor any adjunct faculty members you may have in law school. These are usually practitioners who teach night classes at law schools. Most adjunct faculty members are always delighted to help out students at any point in their careers. Their willingness to help you does not necessarily mean that they will offer you a job after law school. You are not looking for a job at this point, and approaching them on that level may create some resistance in an adjunct's receptiveness.

> Remember, law school professors are lawyers. If you stay connected with those professors postgraduation, they may refer business to you.

Existing full-time faculty members are also potential mentors for life. Full-time faculty members have a constant turnaround of students in front of them if they are career professors. It will take an effort of yours to stay in front of them after graduation and touch base with them as your career builds. Remember, law school professors are lawyers. They live in nearby communities and are often actively engaged in their communities. People will gravitate to your law school professors to ask them legal questions. If you stay connected with those professors postgraduation, they may refer business to you. If they wanted to practice law full time, they would be practicing, not teaching at your law school.

Within the community, law school professors have the highest degree of understanding in clearly defined substantive areas of the law. Those honorable and brilliant law school professors who dedicate their career to teaching law students are exceptional lawyers and are usually passionate and energetic about the classes they teach. So whether it be a class in sales, the Uniform Commercial Code (UCC), bankruptcy, business organizations, or wills and trusts, the more passionate the professors, the more they keep up on the current state of the law and the more they understand how the law in their particular field has developed over the years. Having them as a resource for the substantive area of the law is valuable beyond comprehension.

When starting your own practice right out of law school, you will have a terrible disadvantage if you do not connect with these potential mentors during law school. You need to have someone to run substantive legal questions by, practice related questions, and field new theories and ideas to see if they "pass the smell test." As you become new in the legal community, you will see that someone with an extraordinary amount of experience in substantive areas of the law can, often without citing laws or cases, set you on the right track about how the law works in a particular area. These connections will be very valuable to you.

Other places to find mentors as you are going through law school could be from some of the part-time work you have done over the summer at various law firms. If you have worked as a law clerk or a summer associate with a particular law firm but did not get an invitation to stay at the law firm through the school year, or if you are a third-year law student and did not get an offer of employment, that does not mean the law firm did not like you, did not think highly of your work, or did not think you would be a successful lawyer. The firm may not have had the economic resources to bring on another lawyer at the time, or perhaps you simply got beat out for a job by someone's brother-in-law.

Do not take it personally.

Keep in touch with the people you work with at that law firm. The partners may have been the face of the rejection, but at that firm there may have been associates with whom you need to stay in touch. The actual networking and rainmaking from such contacts will be discussed in great detail later in Chapters 12, 13, and 26. But for right now, you are in law school, and you need to be conducting yourself in a planned fashion in order to best position yourself for success as a solo practitioner.

Research Assistant

There is a chapter in this book on whether you should be a generalist or a specialist as a solo practitioner. The issue requires a complicated analysis and is thoroughly covered in Chapter 11. However, you need to start thinking about the issue in law school. Find a

> Becoming a research assistant will allow you to study deeply in a particular subject matter, an opportunity otherwise lost in a regular classroom environment.

professor in the field of interest to you and offer to be his or her research assistant, even if only as a nominal arrangement without remuneration. First, becoming a research assistant will allow you to study deeply in a particular subject matter, an opportunity otherwise lost in a regular classroom environment. Second, it would be a step toward building a mentor relationship with that professor. Research assistants work very closely with law school professors. This may seem like work dedicated to the elite students, but remember that many elite students are on law review and involved in other interests, including probably high-paying summer associate jobs. If you intend on starting your own law practice, this is about substance and not show. You really do need to dive deeply into law books to research for a professor, and as you assist that professor, understand how complicated the nuances of the law have become. Many professors are always in the process of writing a paper, law review article, or book. There are always legal issues that need to be researched. The time that you take working for a professor in law school will be part of your résumé and bio that you will talk about for the rest of your career.

Publishable Quality Writing

Not every student qualifies to be on his or her school's law review, but there are many other law publications now published by law schools. Getting published while you are still in school, or shortly thereafter, is a tremendous feather in your cap.

There are plenty of publications in the legal field that need content. Do not under any circumstances be hesitant about writing an article through fear of not having it published somewhere. The most sophisticated publications, like law reviews, are at one end of the spectrum, and at the other end are monthly newsletters from local bar associations. Industry publications, as well as committees from large or metropolitan bar associations, constantly look for content, and a well-researched paper will be published. You can view the project of writing a law school–quality paper in two categories.

> You need to understand that creating a foundation for a winning law firm is not easy, but with the right foundation, the building blocks of success remain firmly in place and you have no place to go but up.

First is a dissertation on what the law should be (i.e., when there are dissenting opinions in different circuits on a particular legal issue, and your thorough research will, you hope, bring that issue together to at least determine a more thoughtful resolution of the issue).

The second category is known as a "survey on the state of the law" article. Survey articles just explain problematic areas of the law, what the statute provides, and what the nuances of the cases interpreting the statute provide. These are very helpful in practice periodicals and will almost always be published. Writing articles that are not published is still a good experience, and you will, over time, create an inventory of articles to post on your website.

If it were easy, everyone would do it. You need to understand that creating a foundation for a winning law firm is not easy, but with the right foundation, the building blocks of success remain firmly in place and you have no place to go but up.

If it were easy, everyone would do it.

Bar Association Activities

While you are in law school, you will find that many local bar associations offer discounted rates to be members of the student chapter of their bar association. They may even allow students to sit in on regular bar association committee meetings at no charge. You need to make an effort to investigate the differences between various bar associations in your area. The American Bar Association (ABA) is a wonderful, large association with fantastic publications, including the student lawyer magazine, e-newsletters, and books on areas of the law. Join the law student division of the ABA and get involved in their events and competitions.

Your state bar association and local bar associations have similar opportunities. Join them to meet the administrative governing men and women, as well as peer groups that will help in your social marketing and networking for law-related topics. Invest the time, and you will be pleased that you did.

Social Media

You should start expanding your networking contacts now. With respect to digital media, the leaders are Facebook, LinkedIn, Twitter, and Pinterest. These, by no means, are the only necessary players in social media.

Clearly, the statistics are undeniable. Facebook has over 757 million active daily users on average.[1] We have never witnessed a time where that number has decreased. Facebook has over 1.23 billion active monthly users, and most impressively, approximately 1 billion users are active on mobile devices.[2] LinkedIn has over 277 million members worldwide, including executives from every Fortune 500 company.[3] LinkedIn is emerging as a leader in professional networking.

Other active communication platforms include Twitter and Tumblr. Twitter in particular has over 241 million active monthly users,[4] and over 500 million tweets are sent

---

1. Facebook Company Info, http://newsroom.fb.com/company-info (last visited Apr. 16, 2014).
2. *See id.*
3. LinkedIn, http://www.linkedin.com/company/linkedin (last visited Apr. 16, 2014).
4. Twitter About, https://about.twitter.com/company (last visited Apr. 16, 2014).

per day. Interesting to note is that 76% of Twitter users operate on their mobile devices.[5] Many students are mandated to connect to teachers' and coaches' Twitter feeds to obtain information on school and extracurricular activities. Similarly, businesses are migrating to Twitter, especially retail businesses, as a means of conveying information to customers who sign up for their Twitter accounts.

In comparison, Tumblr has approximately 125,000 new sign ups per day, every day, and there are 180 million different blogs with 82.7 billion posts on Tumblr.[6]

The takeaway from this overwhelming data with respect to social digital media is that the number of users is growing, people are active on these platforms, and information is being conveyed. Nearly 20% of individuals now look at Facebook to obtain information about a brand or product.[7] As we get into this topic in Section 2 of the book, you will see that more individuals are focused on these platforms for obtaining information about service providers, reviews of service providers, and endorsements from their peers and experts.

The context of this discussion on social networking is to explain the significance and importance of *expanding your network*. These platforms give you an easy system for reaching out and connecting to new people who will eventually become referral sources or clients. Add contacts at every opportunity.

> Potential clients and referral sources see social media as a very nonintrusive way to gain knowledge about you and your firm, understand the law, and read commentary on predominant cases that have been followed in the media, and they truly appreciate a content-driven message.

As described in greater detail in Chapters 12 and 13, getting your message out that you are in business and readily providing content and information to your network is exactly the best use of the social media platforms. Potential clients and referral sources see social media as a very nonintrusive way to gain knowledge about you and your firm, understand the law, and read commentary on predominant cases that have been followed in the media, and they truly appreciate a content-driven message. All of those clients, potential clients, and referral sources do not appreciate being inundated with special offers and requests to act immediately on a marketing pitch. But through the proper use of these platforms, you can relay your message, explaining the area of law in which you

---

5. *See id.*

6. Tumblr, http://www.tumblr.com/about (last visited Apr. 17, 2014).

7. 2012 Digital Influence Index Shows Internet as Leading Influence in Consumer Purchasing Choices (2012), *available at* http://www.fleishmanhillard.com/2012/01/news-and-opinions/2012-digital-influence-index-shows-internet-as-leading-influence-in-consumer-purchasing-choices.

specialize,[8] and add value, i.e., add valuable information—to each one of your clients, potential clients, and referral sources.

Understandably, it is very difficult to ask the same people to connect with you on multiple social mediums. Be judicious in determining whom you ask to join you on Twitter, LinkedIn, and Facebook. It appears that LinkedIn is the most business friendly and the platform on which you should try to be very active, but all platforms have business and social value, so manage your presence accordingly.

---

8. Understandably, you cannot "specialize" except as provided under the Code of Professional Conduct, but these are the areas of the law in which you will concentrate your practice. See Chapter 11 for a full discussion on specializing.

Chapter 2

General Thoughts on the Hours Required

Many of you probably have read many business books, including books on starting and growing a law practice. Quite frankly, some of those books talk about how to make $100,000 a year and yet only work under fifteen hours per week, which is quite amusing. There exists no credible game plan to build and grow a great business by only working part-time. You made a decision (or potentially were involuntarily pushed by circumstances) to start a law practice. Did you do so because you are passionate about the law? Because you enjoy practicing law? Or because understanding law is the highest-level skill you possess? Jay Foonberg says that there are only two reasons why you start a law practice: (1) you want to or (2) you have to.[1]

The reasons are no different for the gardener who wants to start his or her own landscaping company, the insurance professional who wants to be independent of his or her insurance agency, or the team that put together the better mousetrap (or in the modern version, built a better computer or better app for a smartphone). Because you have a marketable high-level skill, you are then bitten with the entrepreneurial bug.

Most people who do start their own business, more specifically, their own law practice, are probably great students who have the ability, in a very short period of time, to be wonderful technicians (i.e., lawyers), but they need to be forewarned that the path set forth

> The path in this book is about building a business, a law firm.

in this book does more than trade an existing job for a new job working for yourself. The path in this book is about building a business, a law firm. As a result, you need to be prepared, possibly for the rest of your career, to wear two hats—that of the technician (i.e., the lawyer who produces high-quality legal work) and that of the business owner or entrepreneur, namely, the person managing and growing the business. Note the Michael

---

1. Jay G. Foonberg, How to Start & Build a Law Practice, 4th ed. (American Bar Association 1999).

Gerber distinction between working *in* your business versus working *on* your business.[2] There truly is a profound difference.

All too often, the attorney technician goes to work in his or her business every day, doing everything he or she could do to survive by practicing law. Your own somewhat blurry vision of your future regarding high-status clients, attorneys working for you, and financial independence are very difficult to realize when you are in the grind of practicing law every moment of every day. When you are doing this, you are not running a business; you are working at a job, which is no different than getting a job and working at a law firm. This pattern develops among all too many attorneys, where the entrepreneurial attorney decides to hang out at his or her proverbial shingle. Then, already equipped with the skill set to attract clients and get clients, he or she opens up the practice and work starts flowing in.

After the first year, the attorney feels like a success; he or she has made enough money after expenses to declare this entrepreneurial idea a success and begins to hire one, two, or more paralegals, attorneys, and support staff to support his or her ability to practice law. Once the overhead starts to build, the attorneys start to recognize the ongoing expense of running a law practice. Bills have to be paid on time, regular payroll cycles need to be met, rent needs to be paid monthly, utilities regularly, and other necessary expenses on time. A few slipups where clients begin to pay slowly, beyond thirty, sixty, and ninety days, and ultimately default on their payment obligations to the attorney begin to put the attorney in a cash-strapped position. Remember, in a project that bills $4,000 in legal fees but you collect only $3,000, you have now worked for only 75% of your hourly rate. You have overhead (which would include attorneys' W-2 income—or more) that may cause all of the profit to be lost out of that project.

> Remember, in a project that bills $4,000 in legal fees but you collect only $3,000, you have now worked for only 75% of your hourly rate.

The delays in getting paid by clients, as well as the risks of not getting paid by clients, could overwhelm the entrepreneur by the end of year 1, year 2, and further on if the business is not managed properly. The economic realities take over when the entrepreneurial attorney begins working relentless hours training people, doing bookkeeping, reconciling bank accounts, billing, recording timekeeping data, interviewing potential clients, managing conflicts in the office, managing the myriad nonlegal work involved in the business, and then, ultimately, when time is remaining, practicing law.

---

2. MICHAEL E. GERBER, THE E-MYTH MASTERY (Collins 2005).

In addition, with all the foregoing occurring in your business life, issues involving your personal life are layered upon your work life. Whether you are single, married, with or without children, family issues are woven between your personal and work life.

Some people think that every business starts as a family business.[3] If you have a family, your spouse, mother, father, brother, or sister may, within the limits of confidentiality, be working in some capacity at the firm to assist you. All this interweaving of personal life and business can lead to a lifestyle that feels as if 100% of your waking moments are consumed by the law office.

The story is not intended to scare you away from pursuing the path of starting and growing your own law practice. It is intended for you to make a decision based on informed consent of the entrepreneurial draw to the practice of law. The following are a few of the tasks that you will be required to do, besides practicing law:

- Making bank deposits a few times per week;
- Paying your bills at least one time per week;
- Balancing the checking accounts (you will have several accounts, but once per month minimum);
- Billing once per month;
- Ordering supplies;
- Creating paper files (regularly);
- Scanning documents for electronic files (regularly);
- Purchasing computer and software (once per year);
- Working on computer glitches, with or without an information technology (IT) professional (somewhat regularly);
- Dealing with law library issues;
- Negotiating with online law library search engines;
- Converting banking information into financial statements (monthly);
- Working with an accountant (quarterly and annually);
- Dealing with payroll issues (every two weeks);
- Dealing with the landlord on lease issues (at least a few times per year);
- Marketing and networking for new clients (almost daily);
- Making nonbillable telephone calls (daily);
- Writing law review articles or monthly periodicals (at least monthly);
- Participating in bar association activities (monthly);
- Participating in other chamber of commerce events (monthly);
- Participating in trade association activities (monthly);
- Updating your website (regularly);

---

3. Michael E. Gerber, Et Al., The E-Myth Attorney (Wiley & Sons 2010).

- Posting on social media sites;
- Conducting nonbillable client interviews and consultations; and
- Attending continuing legal education seminars.

The foregoing list is intended to be a wake-up call as to the amount of work that will go into properly preparing your law office for success before $1.00 is generated in a day practicing law. Plan on spending about twenty to thirty hours per week on the activities listed above, for these are needed to support the law practice.

Note that if you are at a law firm with significant support staff, some of these functions are being performed by support staff, and you would probably only be required to practice law and potentially do some marketing (the question remains as to whether you will be compensated for bringing in clients for the law firm at which you work; many times you are not). As a result, be prepared that the minimum time that you will need to put into creating a competitive, winning law firm will be approximately sixty to seventy hours per week: twenty to thirty hours per week managing the firm, and another forty hours per week practicing law.

> Be prepared that the minimum time that you will need to put into creating a competitive, winning law firm will be approximately sixty to seventy hours per week: twenty to thirty hours per week managing the firm, and another forty hours per week practicing law.

While that sounds like an enormous amount of time to dedicate to starting your own practice, please keep in mind that scoring a magnificent job at one of the largest law firms in a large municipality is the goal of many law students, but those jobs require almost the same number of hours. Therefore, if you want to be successful, in the early years of your career, those are the hours you will need to work. That is the bad news.

The good news is that you will departmentalize your time and delegate certain uninterrupted hours of your time to certain categories of work. Certainly Monday through Friday between 8:30 a.m. and 5:30 p.m. will be dedicated to your practicing law, keeping your timesheets up to date, making nonbillable telephone calls, conducting nonbillable client interviews, and servicing clients. Then, a few times a week, before office hours and after office hours, you will do your banking deposits, bill payments, and other systematized financial management of the firm. Once a month, on a Saturday or Sunday, you will block out a large period of time to reconcile bank accounts, conduct final reviews of bills, send out bills, and complete month-end accounting issues. On other weekends, you will engage in some research and writing and preparing articles for website postings. Further, in the evenings, you will be participating in business trade association activities, chamber of commerce events, and other bar association activities. As you can see, discipline and organization are critical to being able to move through the days, weeks, and months in a productive fashion.

The worst that can happen is that you start to blend in all this work in a desperate effort to manage it on a day-to-day basis with no rhyme or reason or synchronization with the priorities of your daily schedule. Every expert in day planning and organization tells you to set aside time for certain tasks. That is the conveyance here. It is absolutely the most efficient way to manage your law office. Schedule a time and stick to that schedule. Always remember, between 8:30 a.m. and 5:30 p.m., Monday through Friday, clients come first. You will, on occasion, need

> Clients come first Monday through Friday, 8:30 a.m. to 5:30 p.m.

to expand your scheduling to accommodate clients either early in the morning, in the evenings, or on the weekends, but that needs to be fit in between your work that does not involve the practice of law. Clients come first Monday through Friday, 8:30 a.m. to 5:30 p.m. Other than those hours, do your best to accommodate clients, but do not go off your schedule of managing the other components of your business. Remember, those other hours are to work *on* your business, not necessarily *in* your business.

Those are long days and sometimes long, hard weekends. It does not mean that those hours last the rest of your career. It will take that many hours to build the appropriate foundation for the firm in order to establish your reputation and beat the competition. It is exciting but demanding. Note that almost all new businesses are family businesses, whether intentionally or by default. As a result, make sure affected family members understand and are willing to share your commitment.

Last, the most important rule is the old Chinese proverb "If you cannot smile, do not open shop."[4]

---

4. PETER F. DRUCKER WITH JIM COLLINS, PHILIP KOTLER, JAMES KOUZES, JUDITH RODIN, V. KASTURI RANGAN & FRANCES HESSELBEIN, THE FIVE MOST IMPORTANT QUESTIONS YOU WILL EVER ASK ABOUT YOUR ORGANIZATION 33 (Jossey-Bass 2008).

Chapter 3

Working *on* Your Business and *in* Your Business

Lawyers are an unusual breed of person. Often the attorney's ego is virtually uncontrollable. As a result of their education, lawyers are extraordinarily qualified in some of the most complex sets of laws, rules, and regulations in the country, which is a testament to their intelligence. As a result, some attorneys tend to have a false sense of confidence, a sense that the world is somewhat egocentric and that no one can do what they do better than they do it. Confidence is a good thing. Too much confidence could be blinding and skew the attorney's vision of reality and self-analysis. Further, bright, but not fully alert to the entrepreneurial challenges, attorneys believe that being a good technician is a recipe for success.

It is not.

In fact, an attorney even with a great sense of confidence and ego, successful at a large law firm, believes that his or her ability to manage people and the high degree of technical skills, which he or she possesses, combined with a degree of management ability, is a recipe for success.

Again, completely false.

The concept of working *on* your business versus working *in* your business was introduced in The E-Myth books by Michael E. Gerber.[1] The point cannot be emphasized enough in the practice of law.

The ability to manage people, along with a high level of technical skills, is not sufficient to build an outstanding law firm. It takes more. It takes the ability to work *on* your business, and not just *in* your business. Managing people is still working *in* your business.

Sometimes it is appropriate to disclose the conclusion before building a model that takes you to the conclusion. The conclusion of this chapter is that you need to stay over

---

1. MICHAEL E. GERBER, THE E-MYTH MASTERY 8 (Collins 2005).

your business in an entrepreneurial way in order to stay ahead of the problem curve that will constantly move toward you.

Will you be able to manage every problem in every case? Absolutely not. However, an entrepreneurial attorney working on his or her business thinks about the next software the law office will need to be better in the future when the existing software is working perfectly well. The entrepreneurial attorney will work on the next marketing program even though the existing marketing programs are bringing clients in at a comfortable pace. The entrepreneurial attorney will be thinking about a better way to reassign support staff, allocate work, group work tasks, and realign management roles in the company when the existing workflows tend to be working adequately at the present time. Logically, an attorney working *on* the law firm will be thinking about the next practice group to open, when the law firm is a successful law firm in one or two practice areas.

The list can go on with forward thinking strategies that you need to review on a regular basis. You cannot possibly do this work and have all of your waking hours buried in contracts, briefs, pleadings, legal research, payroll, accounting, and technology.

> You need to stay over your business in an entrepreneurial way in order to stay ahead of the problem curve that will constantly move toward you.

You need to change the way you think, embrace where the future of your firm will be,[2] and begin to manage your law practice in a way that will put it ahead of the competition and be the prevailing winner in your marketplace. It is highly likely that your dominant personality is that of a technician, i.e., the attorney. As such, an attorney wants to practice law. We all went to law school with the dream of being of a lawyer and practicing law. It is where you are because it is your passion. Many of you may have a family legacy of lawyers and grew up with the dream and ideal of practicing law. That passion is nothing to be ashamed of and should be embraced. If all you want to do is practice law, maybe you would be better suited to getting a job at a law firm. If you do not take the advice of this chapter but continue solely to nourish the technician part of your personality, you will never be free to manage your law firm. It takes a different mindset, way of thinking, and it can be introduced to you only by viewing the future of your law firm, to be free from an eternity of technical, detailed legal work to which the technical side of you willingly succumbs.

The managerial part of your personality will put the moving parts in place within reasonable time constraints to make next month seemingly similar to the previous month, and the month before that, and every month going forward. However, it takes the *entrepreneurial*

---

2. STEVE ZAFFRON & DAVE LOGAN, THE THREE LAWS OF PERFORMANCE: REWRITING THE FUTURE OF YOUR ORGANIZATION AND LIFE (Jossey-Bass 2009).

personality to see the future, anticipate the future, and put the building blocks in place to build the future that is your vision.

It is the entrepreneurial personality that seemingly "floats" above all the noise and activity such as dealing with client issues, engaging in case management and case strategy sessions, doing legal research, balancing checkbooks, paying bills, and billing clients, watching all the activity from a distance. The entrepreneurial viewpoint watches, makes adjustments, documents, and makes changes in the business plan. It keeps an eye on the ultimate finish line, the future, where growth and prosperity operate without an investment of sixty to seventy hours per week, and working *on* the business. Truly going to work *on* your business is the key to success and building a winning law firm.

It is easier said than done.

It is a skill that needs to be learned and developed. It will not happen overnight. It has nothing to do with the core work of the technician that you already possess as an attorney. It has to do with thinking differently and acting as an entrepreneur. Of course, the first step is passion. If you are about to embark on this incredible commitment to build a winning law firm, you have to have the passion to do it, almost blind faith and irrational passion. Clearly see your future. Again, because many of you come from families with a legacy of lawyers, your passion may be inherent in your DNA. But, like every child whose Christmas gifts get old, passion will fade. Adults start many projects around the house only to see them wither away over days, weeks, and months. Every adult has them, closets that need to be cleaned, basements that need to be organized, old furniture that needs to be dumped and replaced; passion is a fire that needs to be constantly stoked.

> It takes the *entrepreneurial personality* to see the future, anticipate the future, and put the building blocks in place to build the future that is your vision.

> If you are about to embark on this incredible commitment to build a winning law firm, you have to have the passion to do it, almost blind faith and irrational passion. Clearly see your future.

Character and purpose are the necessary virtues needed to elongate passion. There is nothing wrong, to some small degree, with equating survival with purpose in the beginning.

In fact, the motivational guru Zig Ziggler gave you the four "*S*'s" in his four-step process. The first *S*, Survival, relates to operating with a sense of necessity, and desperation, for the foundation of your business. Such desperation is good. It will energize you to work (in a methodical business-like fashion) long, hard, purposeful hours in building the foundation for success.

The second Zig Ziggler *S*, Stability, will be achieved as you transition out of the survival mode, even as a sole proprietor. Stability will include a sense of systems, of disciplines, and will over time establish best practices that will become the cornerstone of your law firm. Stability is building a repetitive disciplined approach to marketing, systems, business operations, transformations, change, and tasks such as office management and the like. Stability is truly the launching pad to success.

The third *S* is Success. When success, depending on your definition (the relentless pursuit of your worthwhile goal) is achieved, the establishment of a competitive winning law firm in your marketplace is established.

The last Zig Ziggler *S*, Significance, comes with building a large law firm with the proper culture and the proper civic commitment to altruistic, humanitarian, and philanthropic goals.

Does this seem out of reach?

It is quite an undertaking, but it is not out of reach. You need to start where everyone needs to start—at the beginning.

> The difference between what you are doing now and how you will be doing it ten to fifteen years from now is dramatic.

Right now, you will first start a law practice because you need to pay your bills—many law firms were started under that exact foundation of passion, desperation, and purpose. That is okay; you are in survival mode. Times will be difficult, challenges will come up, but the purpose and your character must be fueled relentlessly to keep the passion for running your business adequately stoked. Again, if it is just about practicing law—get a job.

There is a certain degree of "freeing yourself" from the daily rigors of practicing law that needs to happen to allow you to be free to maintain your passion so that you can grow the business. It is a new and different way of thinking, and you must always find time to float above the noise and think clearly.

You need to do this outside of the office, while you are working out or reading books on great companies. Then, stop to contemplate the applicability of what you have read to your law office. In the entrepreneurial spirit of running the office, you need quiet time to think—regularly think about the business. If you do not change who you are and how you manage this dichotomy, it will be very difficult for you to grow the business.

Here is the secret about the practice of law that will make this chapter maddening for you to synthesize, understand, and appreciate. As attorneys, you will always need to work *in* your business. Surprised? Yes, as attorneys you will always need to work *in* your business because if the client calls and wants *you* to work on a case, you need to be ready to work on the case. There are no shortcuts in this process to being anything less than a great lawyer. Embrace it and be ready for it. You cannot fake it.

The difference between what you are doing now and how you will be doing it ten to fifteen years from now is dramatic. Currently, you will be all things to your business. You will be the lawyer, secretary, paralegal, clerk, administrative assistant, and bookkeeper. In ten or fifteen years, you will manage and oversee far more cases than the cases you will individually and solely handle. You will not be writing all the briefs; you will be reviewing them. You will not be drafting all the contracts; you will be reviewing them. You will not be doing the banking, supply ordering, or accounting work. You will be checking on and auditing the people who do that work for you. Throughout this book, as throughout the life of your law firm, your role will change. But the two truisms that will remain from the day you hang out your shingle to the day you retire are these:

1. Every day you need to work *on* your business, not only *in* your business; and
2. You will work *in* your business every day you are an attorney.

Chapter 4

The Five-Tool Attorney

Have you heard about a five-tool baseball player? The tools, known as the tools of importance, are recognized by professional baseball scouts using the pro-scouting scale when evaluating players. The five tools are

1. Running speed;
2. Arm strength;
3. Hitting for average;
4. Hitting for power; and
5. Fielding.

As you can see, a baseball player possessing all five tools will be greatly valuable to a professional baseball team.

Attorneys also need to have five tools. They are

1. Provide the highest-quality, thorough legal work;
2. Meet production goals;
3. Learn how to market, network, and be civic minded;
4. Show leadership, be a leader, and train young attorneys; and
5. Participate in managerial and entrepreneurial thinking.

As you can see, you need to hire five-tool attorneys, although it can be difficult to do so. What you will try to do is to find individuals who can *develop* into a five-tool attorney. The tools should be developed in the progressive order listed. It is a progression, and no one out of law school possibly possesses tools four and five, unless they understand and adopt the principals in this book. As such, following are the skills associated with each tool.

Provide the Highest-Quality, Thorough Legal Work

Unfortunately, there is no room in the legal profession for A/B+ work. All work produced by lawyers who are well-trained, hard workers must be A+-quality work. There is a continuum on which all IQs lie, and law schools and undergraduate schools contribute to the disparity (as well as your own DNA makeup). We are not all endowed with the same intelligence quotient. However, whatever you lack in pure IQ, you can make up for in hard work. Some attorneys with a higher intellectual quotient than you may file a case against your client, but through hard work, research, drafting, and redrafting, you can level the playing field, if not get ahead, based on your work ethic.

This cannot be emphasized enough in a multitude of ways. You, and any attorney who follows you as a subsequent hire, need to possess and develop the highest-quality, thorough legal work product. Doing this is difficult. It cannot be compromised. Quite frankly, you are in the wrong business if B+ work sounds as if it would be sufficient. It is not. It is not sufficient to hire other attorneys that provide only B+ work. Through long hours in the law library, engaging in long hours of online research, and continuing legal education classes (many of which can be done online), a young attorney can gain valuable information and meaningful skill sets in the practice of law by him- or herself, and as always, the help of mentors greatly benefits this requirement.

> You need to possess and develop the highest quality, thorough legal work product. Quite frankly, you are in the wrong business if B+ work sounds as if it would be sufficient. It is not.

Meet Production Goals

When just starting out, you want to be as productive as possible, and you may not have a goal per se, but there will come a time where you believe you will need to bill at least twenty hours per week, thirty hours per week, or thirty-five hours per week. If these are goals, and they fit your business model, these goals need to be met. As you grow the practice and you hire additional attorneys (discussed in Section 2), you will need to hold future attorneys to a very rigid standard to meet production goals. As long as the work is flowing in, production goals must be met. It does you, the business owner, no good to have the brightest legal mind working for you if he or she cannot meet production goals or bill his or her time properly and fairly.

If there is no work, how could they meet production goals? Simply stated, they can't. But when work is flowing in at a proper work rate, attorneys need to bill appropriately for their work based on the standards set forth by you. This may seem like an incredible notion to you because you would think everyone would bill accurately so that all their time is captured on your time-billing software. It does not happen that way.

Young attorneys are intimidated by the billing process and do not believe their time has value, nor do they want to disclose that a project that, in their mind, should take one hour actually took them four hours. As such, their time is edited *by them,* not by you, and written down before you even have a chance to see the amount of work that went into the project.

The same goes for you.

There is a natural progression through your legal experience, the number of years that you have been practicing, and the value of your skills. Billable rates start low when attorneys are just out of law school but increase thereafter. One of the reasons for that is because younger attorneys need to spend more time on projects than do more experienced attorneys. As a result, there is sound logic in accepting that a $500-an-hour attorney can handle a project more quickly, than the $150-an-hour attorney. Another reason that a young lawyer's rate is lower than an experienced lawyer's rate is depth of knowledge. A young lawyer cannot be expected to handle a merger between two publicly traded companies, for example. The nuances and level of scrutiny and regulations necessary to document that merger are well beyond the scope of a new attorney; indeed, it is often beyond the scope of a very experienced attorney, which is

> It needs to be made very clear that the most brilliant mind in the practice of law does no good if the individual has not accurately and honestly billed for his or her time and met production goals.

why a team of attorneys at large law firms work on these types of transactions. So, without overstating the obvious, the higher billable rate for an experienced attorney also captures the breadth of understanding of complex legal issues, all of which will allow the more experienced attorney to handle or, in a more practical sense, have access to a legal team with skill sets sufficient to manage that project efficiently and with high-quality results.

Your billable rate will reflect your experience, and so you and any subsequent associate must accurately account for your time and meet production goals. In subsequent chapters, there is a discussion on billing and time tracking. However, it needs to be made very clear that the most brilliant mind in the practice of law does no good if the individual has not accurately and honestly billed for his or her time and met production goals.

The same goes for you.

Marketing and Civic Involvement

The third part in your progression as a five-tool attorney is marketing and civic involvement. Being civic-minded means acting in a way that is productive for your community. The most obvious path toward this civic mindedness for a lawyer is activity in local and municipal bar associations. You must be active in them. Even as early as your law school years, you should be involved in the student bar associations or the sections of professional bar associations for students and young lawyers.

The marketing activities and civic mindedness that are required of lawyers are the externalities of the practice of law. They are done outside of the law office and are necessary for your personal growth, growth and improvement of your communities, and growth of your law practice. The externalities are the third tool of the five-tool attorney.

In addition to engaging in the activities involving bar associations, civic-minded lawyers need to be involved in their local church groups, parent-teacher organizations, the school district, and not-for-profit organizations in the community. Civic-minded lawyers are involved in youth sports, whether at the coaching level or the organizational level, high school activities with students, toy drives, food drives, clothing drives, or recycling. All of these externalities add up and contribute to you as a developing professional and benefit the community at large.

Is your purpose just and true? Absolutely. It is your responsibility to help better your communities, and in doing so, you will better yourself and better your law practice. Will clients come from this activity? In time, yes. But the true purpose of being involved is for the betterment of the community and for the betterment of the perception of the practice of law. A very significant concept of this book, known as creating the right culture for your law firm, is discussed in Section 2. Your involvement will always yield connections, relationships, and yes, ultimately clients. But your purpose must be true—to better your community and profession. There is no doubt that the externalities of law create time constraints that in many cases are difficult to manage. Nonetheless, it is an absolute requirement of the complete attorney.

The second externality, which is another draw on your personal time, is marketing.

There are several chapters in this book dedicated to law office marketing, and library shelves of books are dedicated to marketing for professionals. This, too, is more difficult than you may think. Lawyers go to law school, watch movies on practicing law, watch television shows on the practice of law, and often believe that they are magnificent professionals whose services individuals and businesses need and want and will break down doors to hire them.

Nothing can be further from the truth.

It is a competitive marketplace out there. You need to understand that you are building a law practice to compete in the marketplace and to win. What many lawyers do not understand is the level of competition in the marketplace for client work. Be prepared, and consider yourself forewarned that you are competing for the same business on which your neighboring lawyers are working. This will all be done in a professional manner, and your systems of lead generation, closing, and performing legal service will work in unison to provide an A+ experience for all clients.

The notion that after graduating from law school an attorney must now learn how to be a salesperson could be incredibly disturbing to some new graduates. The fact of the matter is that selling legal services is a reality of the law profession.

"Salesperson" is not a derogatory term; in a business sense, it means that you must be able to go out in a professional manner, talk freely and proudly about your practice and profession, and explain how you can help people either through your services or through your connections and contacts. Again, you are here to help people. Not all of that help will generate income, but if you are planning on staying in this profession for the long haul, i.e., your entire career, it is important that you adopt that philosophy early on in your career. Your time and effort spent on marketing yourself and your practice will be extensive. It will happen at trade shows, lunches, and dinners; on the golf course; at weddings you attend, bar mitzvahs, communions, chamber of commerce events, and trade group meetings.

> The fact of the matter is that selling legal services is a reality of the law profession.

To some degree, until selling your professional services becomes natural, you are always "on." It will not always be that way because you will hit your stride and feel very comfortable in social circumstances knowing that eventually someone will approach you with a legal question, a short story, or short vignette about his or her experience with a lawyer.

Be prepared, and be forewarned—marketing and civic involvement are part of being a five-tool attorney. There is no substitute for these activities, and every young attorney must be acculturated very early in his or her career at your office. Again, it is third in the sequence. There is no sense talking about marketing until the attorney is providing the highest-quality, thorough legal work and also meeting his or her production goals. Once you hit a stride with an attorney meeting the first two tools, you then engage and introduce marketing and civic involvement into the job requirement.

Being a Leader, Training Young Associates

The fourth tool is phasing into a senior associate role, which begins approximately five years out of law school. If things are going well, you as the entrepreneur may think of hiring an attorney within two years of starting your own practice. With that being the case, you will need to show leadership and engage in management and training at an earlier point in your career.

The fourth tool is a mindset that an attorney needs to understand that it is not all about you. When working in a team environment (i.e., a law firm), you need to understand that you need to give back to the law office and to your associates. The four-tool attorney takes the time to train young associates regarding best practices such as favorite law books for getting certain answers promptly, online research tricks, site checking, and other drafting techniques. This is how you build a team.

There is no substitute for training.[1]

This is the fourth tool that you must build into your growth program for your firm and even for yourself, individually, so that you are ready to be a leader, to show leadership, and to train young attorneys.

Participate in Running the Business

At some point in time you will begin to allocate business-related responsibilities to senior associates, to income partners, and eventually to equity partners. (These titles and elevations are described much later near the end of Section 2, and Section 3 is dedicated solely to the equity partnership track.) As set forth in

> You, the founder of the firm, will progress into the managing partner role, but your other partners are absolutely necessary to assist you in these various departments.

Chapter 2, to run a law office requires over twenty functions common to running a business in general. Some of these functions can, and should, be allocated to other senior attorneys at the law office and, when possible, administrative staff. Although these functions are involved in managing the business, they are not yet integral to the entrepreneurial thought processes. These are the nitty-gritty tasks of running a law practice. Typically, one attorney greatly assists and largely manages the marketing efforts of the firm and all of the attorneys. Another attorney handles human resource issues, another attorney handles billing and collecting, and yet another attorney works with some of the banking issues. All of these departments have support staff below the attorney managing these issues that do

---

1. I believe this wholeheartedly, and on my first job out of law school (a job I started as a third-year in law school) I received wonderful training from patient and bright attorneys who helped me provide high-quality, thorough legal work. My colleagues from Martin, Brown, Sullivan, Roadman & Hartnett, Ltd, and I still keep in touch regularly and work together on many cases. I was fortunate to have mentors who took the time to train me for my career. Similarly, I spend a large part of my days training young attorneys. I enjoy it, I owe it to the firm, and I owe it to the next generation of lawyers.

a lot of the day-to-day work, but the buck stops with the partner or associate handling that business-related department.

While you have heard and understand the concept of a managing partner, you certainly will be the managing partner for a long time, but move cautiously if you are considering naming another person. It would be difficult to name a managing partner to run and manage *all* the other departments in the law office.

In the case where a managing partner is dedicated solely to managing the business, the cost of that role to the firm is not just his or her salary, but also it includes the lost billable hours doing client-related work. Further, if the managing partner is truly the firm's number 1 "rainmaker," you will have a difficult balance between managing the company, meeting with clients, assigning work, and managing cases and files. You, the founder of the firm, will progress into the managing partner role, but your other partners are absolutely necessary to assist you in these various departments. Moreover, departmentalizing management responsibility begins the process for building a unified coalition and core management group for the growth of the business.

In order for the business to truly grow, like a real business, it cannot be a dictatorship. It requires a cohesive management team.

> A five-attorney office runs differently than does a ten-attorney office; a ten-attorney office runs much differently than does the twenty-attorney office—and those changes continue to escalate as the firm grows.

As a result, the more practical role the managing partner plays in a small and growing law firm is that of a hybrid, a cross between the rainmaker, the leader of the organization, and a practicing attorney. With the help of partners, the management team grows as the law office grows.

Many times there is a separation of personalities as you get into the fifth tool. A very well-rounded four-tool attorney can be very productive, meet production goals, and assist young attorneys and staff members around the office. However, that can all be done with minimal time that barely cuts into his or her billable hours. In time, you need to start transitioning the mindset of the senior associate into a partnership-level thinker (i.e., a person who runs the business) by asking that person to subordinate his or her own billable hours to help make the company a competitive law firm that will win in its marketplace. There are no direct monetary benefits for this that show up immediately. It is a long-term strategy where everyone gains if everyone has this mindset.

Keep in mind that at this point in time, individual goals distance themselves from the bigger picture of the profitability of the firm. In order to build a high-quality firm, the five-tool lawyers need to invest time in running the law firm as a business. These five-tool attorneys will be your partners. This is done by putting the business first above the individual goals, economic benefits, bonuses, and all other individual accolades and awards.

Everyone wins when the law office wins. With respect to the five-tool attorney, the law office comes first.

Once your senior associates, income partners, and equity partners are assisting you in the management of the business, you have five-tool attorneys surrounding you and the business should run like a well-oiled machine.

That is not to say that the entrepreneurial duty is over.

The entrepreneurial requirement still means taking an overview of the business, in a quiet place, making sure things are running as efficiently as possible, and anticipating the next adjustment. A five-attorney office runs differently than does a ten-attorney office; a ten-attorney office runs much differently than does the twenty-attorney office—and those changes continue to escalate as the firm grows.

Remember, follow the tools in order and master the previous tool before you go onto the subsequent tool. It is hard work, but it is the reality of the growth of an attorney in any law firm.

Chapter 5

Core Decisions

Now you have a general understanding of what is required of you when starting and running a law practice, general thoughts on the hours required, and the dichotomy of working *on* your business and working *in* your business. Further, you now know what tools are required of a complete attorney. You passed the bar exam and have now made the decision to start your own law practice.

Do I Need Experience?

Of course, experience is preferred before you start your own law practice. Whether it is just two or up to five years, there is no substitute for learning on the job and being mentored and taught by experienced, high-level professionals.

For the sake of emphasis, repeat, there is great benefit to being taught by high-level associates and partners. Bad training is not beneficial at all. It may buy you time to learn on your own, but you can learn on your own at your own law firm. In a perfect world, being trained by high-quality professionals is optimal. It is also very difficult, but part of the reason you have purchased this book and are reading it is because possibly you do not have a job opportunity and you are on your own. This book is filled with alternative solutions to having the opportunity to be trained and mentored.

Remember, as an alternative to formal training at a law firm as an associate, you are taking all the steps necessary to be mentored by law school professors, perhaps working for them as a research assistant, doing any type of high-level legal research that you can, and producing thorough work product wherever possible. If the opportunity to get a job and learn on the job is impossible, you have no other choice, therefore, but to forge ahead without the requisite practice training.

Notwithstanding the suggestion on gaining experience, all is not lost if experience is not easily available to you. The one substitute for experience is hard work. Utilize all books in law libraries such as casebooks, books on the substantive areas of the law, and practice books. Practice books are usually state specific and teach you about the practice of law in that particular geographical area as well as provide some substantive information on the law. Exhaustive research on the substantive areas of the law, cases regarding the issues that you are facing, and practice books to help you navigate through the legal process are all time intensive and will help you make up for your shortfall on experience. Hours in the law library, bar associations meetings where you talk to experienced professionals, and even telephone calls to law professors all help in this manner.

With respect to litigation attorneys, sometimes you need to spend a morning in the judge's courtroom where you will be appearing to find out how the judge deals with routine motions and contested motions and see the interplay between the judge and the judge's clerks. These all fall into the category of hard work and time, and with the investment of hard work, you pick up experience that previously eluded you.

Last, so there is no slippage on the learning curve, this book highlights the necessity and the requirements of checklists, documenting systems, document libraries, and systemization for certain practice groups. All of these items are used with the sole intent of one goal—never to make the same mistake twice. If you are building a document library, checklists, and systems, your experience curve will increase exponentially, and you will lay the foundation for all future paralegals, administrative assistants, associates, and partners.

> With respect to litigation attorneys, sometimes you need to spend a morning in the judge's courtroom where you will be appearing to find out how the judge deals with routine motions and contested motions and see the interplay between the judge and the judge's clerks.

Solo or a Partnership?

This question is raised quite a bit. Is it beneficial for new attorneys, with no experience, to come out and start a partnership with a friend, classmate, or a respected colleague, because they could then leverage on each other's successes and build from there?

Proceed very cautiously when engaging in a new, inexperienced partnership. These relationships do work on occasion but often do not.

At a law firm, you break up the practice into practice groups by the substantive area of law. For example, taxation, business law, mergers and acquisitions, commercial real estate, litigation, family law, personal injury, class-actions, and employment law, to name a few. You could generally split up a law office into two groups—litigation (which involves dispute resolution attorneys) and transactional lawyers. A perfect blend of a partnership right out of law school would be one lawyer desiring to pursue litigation as a career path and another being the transactional lawyer. Almost all practice groups could fit neatly into those two areas.

However, since you do not know where your business will come from, it is hard to determine which practice group would be fed business early and which will starve later.

The economy also has an influence on which practice groups are called on more often. In a robust economy, business transactions tend to go up, and transactional lawyers are busier. In a recession, clients tend to fight over collections on bills, work product, and foreclosures from banks, where clients need litigation assistance.

There is no doubt that this system could work over time, but like a marriage, there are a lot of personality issues involved in a successful law practice, as well as work ethic and the adoption of the same type of commitment that you will see in Section 2 and Section 3 of this book regarding culture, goals, civic mindedness, marketing, and all the other externalities of law on which partners need to be aligned.

Feeding off each other's energy and success and building connectivity between each other, each other's contacts, each other's clients, and each other's passions is great synergy. However, all those elements must stay aligned and on the same track in a perfectly synergistic manner. Once there is a breakdown on one partner's level of passion, and one partner's involvement exceeds the other, trust will begin to erode, and the partnership will begin to fade.

> Feeding off each other's energy and success and building connectivity between each other, each other's contacts, each other's clients, and each other's passions is great synergy.

There is a story about musicians sitting in a class clearly among other wonderfully skilled musicians. The professor talks about students coming to class wanting to form bands and become highly successful. The professor addresses that issue by stating, "Everyone has an idea for the next great band. The problem is that it breaks down when one guy gets married, the next guy has children, the next guy has addiction issues, and the other guy takes a full-time job out of town." He then emphasizes that the only thing that you can control is yourselves and your own skills. He says it in the context of music, stating that the musicians must each develop their skill set on their own and that any arrangement in a band, i.e., a partnership, is secondary and is just a bonus once your own skill sets are developed. Remember this story when you think about the many nuances that could break down a partnership.

All of these ideas raised by the music teacher are only a small fraction of the ways a law partnership can break down. That is why as you get into Section 2 and Section 3 of the book and analyze your potential hires under the five-tool principles, you will develop associates and partners who are like-minded individuals with the same goals, commitment, and skill sets that you have. The chances of finding that individual right out of law school are slim, but not impossible.

The more common path to success in two-, three-, or four-attorney partnerships is when the partners leave an existing law firm, quite often a large law firm, to set up their own law firm. This model seems to work in boutique firms with experienced attorneys. These attorneys possess many of the technical skills to be successful. Certainly, they provide the highest-quality legal work, and they meet production goals. If they have been fed an incredible number of clients and much business working for a large firm, they may not yet know how to market, network, and be civic minded, though they probably do show leadership and train young attorneys quite well. Also, they probably have a certain level of skill with respect to managing some of the aspects of the business and people. Whether they are entrepreneurial thinking is yet to be determined.

These partners, no doubt, need the continual growth and foundation set forth in this book. Admittedly, being senior associates or young partners in a large law firm is very different than creating the law firm that is envisioned in this book. However, each one of those partners needs to establish the foundation and principals in this book to build upon, and to grow, the business from its initial inception. Make no mistake about it, this is a very favorable start to a law practice. Several like-minded individuals already primed with clients and a "book of business" set up shop to provide the same legal services that were provided in the larger law firm, most likely at rates and fees that are at a fraction of the cost. Clients appreciate this migration, and the attorneys providing the services are often very successful.

Generally, partners from the same department in a large law firm create a one-dimensional "boutique firm" offering services in one specialty area. This is a wonderful start and consistent with a specialty that is necessary to attract business from other lawyers. When leaving the existing firm, if done in a professional, transparent manner, those lawyers often obtain work and get referrals from their colleagues from their former law firm. Nonetheless, as a new partnership, they aggregate as one entity. Each partner in the law firm, every subsequent lawyer, and each subsequent partner needs to adopt the individual skill sets described in this book to continue to grow the law firm.

All of the skills in this book are designed as individual skill sets that need to be developed by you, the originating partner, and every associate and partner to follow. It does not necessarily mean the skills set forth in this book could be developed faster if two people are working on them independent of each other. They are individual skills, and they progress on their own path for each attorney. Two people cannot get there twice as fast as one person. Each person is developing his or her own path for these skill sets that are required of the successful attorney, a successful law firm, and ultimately, a successful partnership of equity partners.

Incorporation or Sole Proprietorship

There are a lot of things that this book is not. One of them is a discussion on the different forms of entities in which to run a business. However, in your jurisdiction, you probably understand that the general forms of business are sole proprietorships, corporations (S corporations and C corporations), partnerships, limited liability companies, and limited liability partnerships. As lawyers, you are liable and responsible for your own errors and malpractice and are not insulated by the corporate shield from malpractice.

That said, consider organizing as some entity that would shield you from nonpractice liabilities, for example, slips and falls in your office and other types of liabilities from a non-employee malpractice practicing in your suite. Organizing as a corporation or a limited liability company seems like a general, good recommendation for any practitioner.

Our peers in the federal tax area remind us regularly that sole practitioners, attorneys who report their income and expenses on a Schedule C of a personal 1040 tax return, are more closely scrutinized by the IRS than are other attorneys; in reality, though, if you are doing everything correctly, that should have no bearing on your decision to be a sole proprietor.

Check the Model Code of Professional Conduct in your jurisdiction. See if there are any limitations that you need to be aware of and if there are recommendations in terms of organization.

> Organizing as a corporation or a limited liability company seems like a general, good recommendation for any practitioner.

Later in the book, and by virtue of the growing business, you will find that operating as a corporation or as limited liability company would provide benefits and safeguards that you would otherwise not have as a sole proprietor.

The last call to make on this subject would be to obtain advice from a trusted accountant. Ask questions relating to your pro-forma income regarding worst case, moderate projections, and a best-case scenario. Ask the question as to whether FICA taxes apply to all the income of the business or just a portion of the income. Ask about segregating your income, a portion of which would be W-2 income (which is required) and another portion as profit from the business. These tax strategies may have a bearing on your choice of entity, based on a few scenarios.

As you go along, if you intend on being a transactional lawyer, this is exactly the advice you will be giving to potential business owners in your jurisdiction, so it will be an excellent investment in time in terms of your analysis. Spend the time to review the business corporation act and the limited liability company act in your jurisdiction. This is all material that would make for wonderful newsletter articles and information to share with other potential clients.

If in doubt, incorporate and make an S corporation (i.e., S-Corp) election. It is a traditional way for a personal service business to operate, and it is also forward thinking in terms of the needed entity as the business continues to grow.

Should You Practice with Your Spouse or Other Family Members?

Throughout the country, there have been newsletter articles and publications written on whether to practice with a family member. Whether to do so is a very personal decision, one that should be made only among the spouses, siblings, parents, and children potentially involved. If you are acculturated to working together and understand each other's strengths and weaknesses in an objective sense, there should be no problem whatsoever.

As a practical matter, without getting into the psychology of working with a family member, you need to objectively determine whether this partnership is the optimal use of each other's time, considering your long-term goal. In the case of spouses, maybe one spouse should try to find a job while the other spouse begins to build the family law practice. If the two family members are skilled and schooled in the same skill set and practice group, you might have the makings of a small boutique firm in one specific type of practice area. It is rare to see a successful example where husband and wife or siblings open up a general practitioner firm and become a "jack-of-all-trades" partnership. The two spouses or siblings must objectively talk through their skill sets, the tasks that have nothing to do with the practice of law (as set forth in Chapter 2), and how to allocate that work. There needs to be a true distribution of work *and* responsibility. For example, with respect to the banking and bank balances, the responsibility should be on one of the spouses who executes on that responsibility.

> There needs to be a true distribution of work *and* responsibility.

These seem like rudimentary business issues with respect to segregating work, responsibilities, and the allocation and ownership of those responsibilities to a particular partner, but if these issues are not discussed before the partnership is established, the law partnership, as well as the marriage or family relationships, could dissolve.

The objections you will hear from other attorneys is that the separation between family life and work life can become very blurry and sometimes nonexistent. This admonition is not intended to be a dissertation on the psychology of the separation between work life and family life, but it does seem that leaving your work issues at the office and enjoying your family is a very healthy balance in life. This can occur with spouses as partners if rules are developed between each other regarding the issue of balance.

The relationship between the parent and a child, and among siblings when children are working for the parents in a law office, is quite different than it would be were the children not involved in the family business, and it changes the paradigm dramatically. Usually, in such cases, parents are delighted to have their children step into the law practice, with the intent of transitioning the running of the family business, the law office, to their children. If that is the case, and it usually is, a litany of problems and concerns with such a strategy may result; these are set forth in great detail in Chapter 33 of Section 3. Unless unusual steps are taken, a family-run law office creates its own boundaries and limitations on the law office being a successful, winning law firm in its own marketplace.

Income During the Start-Up Year

The general consensus among various authorities, including individuals who started a practice, is that you need to have approximately one year of necessary living expenses in the bank in order to float your personal living expenses during the first start-up year. This may sound pretty discouraging for someone coming out of law school with law school loans, but it is a reality if you have no other source of paying your necessary living expenses. For many of you starting your practice, having a working spouse who is able to pay the necessary household expenses, along with some small savings, will allow you to get through the first few difficult years of the start-up.

> The general consensus among various authorities is that you need to have approximately one year of necessary living expenses in the bank in order to float your personal living expenses during the first start-up year.

The ability to accumulate cash may delay the start-up of a law firm, but it is a necessary and practical consideration. Also, for reasons discussed in Chapters 9 and 10, it is safe to say that during the first year of practice, you will not make "zero." You will make money; the question is just how much. So hope is not lost on the start-up risks. There will be income, and you will probably have resources to help you float your personal expenses during the start-up.

Another issue that comes up is whether to continue in another business or another endeavor as you start your law firm on a parallel path with your existing nonlegal job. This occurs with attorneys who have previously been mortgage brokers, insurance professionals, manufacturing reps, bartenders, retail clerks, and tradespeople. As a matter of survival, this parallel track may be a necessity, not an option.

As you could deduce after reading Chapter 2, the endeavor of starting and growing a law practice is more than a full-time job; it's almost two full-time jobs. Time spent doing anything but practicing law is detrimental to the growth of a law firm. If at all economically possible, 100% of your effort and time needs to be spent on building and growing your law practice. How could it be done another way? You understand the necessities of life and the economics required to pay your minimum living expenses, but any time spent on anything other than the requirements set forth in this book will slow down the potential upward growth path of the law firm.

Working as a Contract Attorney

A good opportunity to gain experience is contacting lawyers and small law firms in your area to work as an hourly contract lawyer. This endeavor is hit or miss, however. You need to catch the lawyer with your letter and follow-up telephone calls at a time when he or she is overwhelmed in a particular case, transaction, or dispute and may need a set of hands to assist.

Many law firms hire contract lawyers for brief writing and agreement drafting. Brief writing, which requires extensive research and writing ability, is especially time consuming. A contract lawyer could earn fees that would be between 25% and 50% of the billable rate for the law firm under which you are working. In other words, you are selling your services at a wholesale rate and a law firm purchasing your services is billing the client at a retail rate.

When contracting with another law firm or group of lawyers, get a good understanding of how you will be paid and also the deliverable expected of the law firm. Does the law firm want you to draft a brief? A memorandum in support of a motion? An employment contract? An asset purchase agreement? Did the law firm disclose the client name to you? Sometimes firms do not want you to steal their clients and will not disclose the client name to you. Will there be any ancillary documents, such as exhibits, schedules, certain technical drawings, affidavits? What is your deadline? What is the status reporting date? What is the court-ordered filing date?

Thoroughly vet questions between you and the hiring law firm to find out the technical expectations of the deliverable. If the deliverable is a pleading, should it be jurisdiction specific? Should you know the local court rules? Does the presiding judge have certain courtroom rules?

If you engage in contract lawyer work, make sure the agreement is well set forth so that you will be paid your "wholesale rate" for all the time you put in on the project, and not just after editing and write-downs, resulting in the number of hours the hiring lawyer wants to pass through to the client. As a contract lawyer, you should be guaranteed payment for 100% of the hours put in on a project. Your fees should not be contingent on the hiring lawyer getting paid by the client. Keep in mind that the hiring law firm will most likely keep you separated from the client. Therefore, as you do work for the hiring law firm, you will have no client contact and no ability to collect against the client because there is no privity of the contract between you and the real client; your privity of contract is between you and the hiring law firm. Your only ability to get paid would be to take an action against the law firm, not the client. As such, you have no control over the client paying and no ability to call the client to request payment or to sue the client. Basically, your client is the hiring law firm, and your only recourse is against the hiring law firm.

> As a contract lawyer, you should be guaranteed payment for 100% of the hours put in on a project. Your fees should not be contingent on the hiring lawyer getting paid by the client.

In order to get this type of work, you will need to go to one of your local bar associations or law schools to get a listing of law firms and solo practitioners that you would like to approach. It is necessary, if your mailing is to the small law firms, to find the managing partner of the small office. Send your letter directly to the lawyers of the firm. Remember, sole practitioners and small law firms get inundated with work and may need you too, not just the large firms.

However, if you intend on sending letters for contract work to larger firms (firms in excess of twenty to twenty-five lawyers), you should send them to a managing partner or to the head of practice groups if that is ascertainable on the website. Once the letter is sent, you are not done. You will need to follow up with multiple phone calls with the lawyers to see if work is available. They need to immediately understand in the phone conversation (and the original letter) that you are willing to take short-term assignments and small assignments and that you have had experience (e.g., as a research assistant for a law school professor) in certain areas where you think you could add value.

Naming Your Law Firm

The trend is now moving away from traditional attorney names on the letterhead to marketing names such as Debt Relief Counselors, The Real Estate Lawyers, or Business Law Inc. Be careful with the message that these names convey. From a business standpoint, target marketing will convey the solution necessary for the target clients' problems. You understand and agree with all of that. But you may still be thinking about those names as being a long-term solution for a growing law firm.

During the evolution of the law office, there might be a migration in the growth of the law office to practice areas different from those in which the firm first engaged. Therefore, a name that pigeon holes you into one practice group may be regretted in the future. (This issue is discussed in more detail in Chapter 11, on specializing versus a generalist law practice.) Keep in mind that the name you choose, though it could be changed later in the life cycle of the law firm, will have an impact on your early practice and your clients' perception of your practice.

Further, the name of the practice will have an effect on branding your practice and your professionalism. Again, while such branding might be a good business idea for solving certain client problems, the branding that you need to be developing is for you, the professional, and your name. For that reason, at the early stages in your career (and, of course, your subsequent associates' careers), your name matters, your associates' names matter, and those names need to be put out into the public domain and broadcast. Moreover, putting your name on the letterhead is appropriate, though somewhat conservative, but consistent with a perception of the professionalism of the practice of law.

> The name of the practice will have an effect on branding your practice and your professionalism.

It is misleading for a sole practitioner using the name "John Smith and Associates," for example, if there are no associates. Such an attorney probably has informal "of counsel" relationships with other attorneys and associates and therefore does not necessarily mean that W-2 wage earners are associates with that particular law firm. It is still slightly misleading nonetheless. This type of business name would probably need to be checked with your local jurisdiction's rules on professional conduct.

Whatever your business name, please make sure it is a secured, reserved name with the secretary of state in the state in which you practice; do the same with the domain name on the Internet. Make sure the name is available in a form that you feel comfortable using before going forward.

Domain Names

There is a more sophisticated domain name strategy for you to consider. Specifically, I suggest you visit http://www.godaddy.com and http://www.networksolutions.com to see the ease with which you can reserve domain names. Adding more domain names in the areas of concentration under which you would like to focus your practice will be beneficial to driving traffic to your website.

Names such as "debt relief attorneys" and "real estate attorneys" can be reserved as domain names and directed to your website that may simply be http://www.johnsmithlaw .com. This way, there is a chance that search engines will pick up your domain name simply by a potential client typing in "debt relief attorney" in a search engine. The strategy here is to attempt to lock in a few additional domain names other than your actual law office name in order to attract more hits, even if by happenstance, to your website. Further, these names should, at least at first, be connected to the concentration of your practice. For example, if you are to be a personal injury lawyer, try to reserve domain names that have to do with car accidents, workplace injuries, or medical-related injuries. Do not go overboard, but this is a way to broaden your marketing efforts. Further, even though you will try to brand the name of your office and any artwork associated with your office, you can always further define your concentration by putting your specialized domain name on all advertisements relating to your law firm.

Whether those potential clients click on that domain name is somewhat irrelevant. The domain name conveys a subtle message to the person reviewing that advertisement that this is your specialty.

Insurance

Whether to purchase malpractice insurance is not an issue at all. Purchase malpractice insurance. Notwithstanding the possibility

> Whether to purchase malpractice insurance is not an issue at all. Purchase malpractice insurance.

that you will never need it, purchasing insurance goes to the fact that you are a consummate professional who runs your business properly. Also, given the sensitive nature of your work and the high level of emotional charge in our profession's work, malpractice insurance is a necessity.

Due to the statute of limitations on malpractice cases, malpractice insurance is relatively cheap for someone right out of law school. There is no trail of work that could result in claims against you. Malpractice insurance premiums per attorney tend to increase for approximately five years, and without any claims being filed against the insurance, the cost will level out after that period.

Call bar associations and ask for referrals and seek your own bids. Obtain bids from at least three different carriers and find out if the agent or broker you are talking with is an independent agent and if he or she will actually bid your needs out to three or four carriers known as markets in the insurance business. You want to make sure that you are obtaining the best insurance at an affordable premium. As a first-year law student, $500,000 to $1 million coverage seems reasonable, and the lower your deductible, the higher your premium will be. Buy what you can afford, but by all means have malpractice insurance.

Last, when selecting your insurance, be aware that there are two types of policies, claims-made policies and occurrence. Claims-made policies cover you at the time the claim is made for the purported malpractice action. The occurrence may happen in November 2012, but the claim (and your notice of it) could be made in June 2013. In a claims-made policy, you will have insurance for a claim that was filed in 2013 if the 2013 policy is a claims-made policy. As you can see, if you had an occurrence-based policy in 2012 and the occurrence happened in 2012, that occurrence policy would pick up that liability and you would be covered.

Based on this explanation, you can see that at some time you could have two policies covering the same incident—for example, if you had an occurrence policy in 2012 and a claims-made policy in 2013. Or, if you flip-flop between different policies annually, you could have no coverage at all—for example, if you had a claims-made policy in 2012 and an occurrence policy in 2013. The *claim* did not happen in 2012, and therefore the 2012 policy would not cover you; and the *occurrence* did not happen in 2013, and therefore you will have no coverage on the 2013 policy. Be aware of these possibilities as you ask the hard questions about your malpractice policy. It is best to find one type of policy and stick with that policy throughout your career.

As you change carriers, make sure that the new carrier understands your previous history of coverage, and make sure there are no gaps in coverage. Some new insurance companies can provide "gap coverage" if necessary.

Investigate whether you as the customer have settlement approval, and find out what exclusions to coverage exist. Make sure there are no exclusions if you sue clients for failure to pay their legal bills.

If you are leaving an existing law practice and starting your own, talk to your insurance carrier about the necessary insurance for you. You may be able to obtain malpractice insurance as a new law firm by excluding prior action coverage that is, presumably, covered by the law office you are leaving.

Last, if you are, in fact, practicing in an office suite with other lawyers, while those questions should be asked on the application, please let the agent know about your colleagues to make sure you have coverage for their malfeasance and malpractice. Logically, you should have no exposure whatsoever, but confirm that you have coverage for their bad acts.

In addition to securing malpractice insurance, make sure you speak to your casualty insurance carrier to ask about general liability insurance for your law office. If a client comes into your office and slips and falls on the carpeting or injures himself on the edge of a file cabinet, you could face a claim for general liability. Make sure you are covered for those types of actions.

Next, since you are just starting your law office, inquire as to the costs for disability insurance. Since you are self-employed, if you were to become disabled, whether in your job or through some unrelated accident, your income would be reduced to zero and you would have no way of supporting yourself or your family. For that reason, ask about the cost of disability insurance. In order to bring the premium down to an affordable level, you might have to settle on a sixty- or ninety-day waiting period to qualify for coverage. In other words, the insurance payments would not take effect unless you are unable to work until the end of the wait period. The shorter the wait period, the more expensive the premium. Nonetheless, you are looking for coverage in a disastrous-disability scenario, wherein you may need coverage for the rest of your life. If the disability insurance is affordable, it is advisable to purchase.

Finally, and related to succession planning (see Section 3 of the book), is preparing a death plan. Although the possibility of you dying sounds harsh, if you support a family and have no succession plan in place because you are a sole proprietor, you will need to buy life insurance to hedge against income replacement for your family. Even as your law office grows and you have more associates, if you were to die without a succession plan in place, your family would receive very little because the law allows your estate to recover only for the fixtures and furnishings of the law office and the accounts receivable. In reality, and as a practical matter, there is no ability for your estate to recover the goodwill you have generated as you built up your law office with a team of qualified associates. Therefore, in that case, the only real death plan you have is purchasing life insurance. It is highly recommended that you do purchase it.

How much life insurance should you buy? That topic should be taken up with an insurance professional, but it is usually enough to pay off all of your debts and create a pool of money that will, on being invested prudently, generate enough income to replace your income lost due to your untimely death until your youngest child has completed college. That is simply a rule of thumb, and you can certainly buy more or less depending on affordability.

The Argument against Growth

This book is built on one fundamental principal: you want to build and grow a law firm to be the biggest and best in its marketplace. That may be a twenty-, thirty-, fifty-, or one hundred-attorney law firm. Certainly, bigger does not necessarily mean better, and how big your firm needs to be in order to be the best is dependent on your marketplace.

However, using sound logic, you may think that staying small could provide a very good lifestyle for an attorney. For example, if a lawyer bills approximately two-thirds of his time during the year, he or she will bill approximately 1,475 hours in a year and at $200 per hour, his or her revenues can be approximately $300,000. This amount minus overhead, which will probably be around 50%, would leave approximately $150,000 net at the end of the year for that attorney. In ten years, if the attorney's billable rate increased at $300 per hour, the gross revenues for the same amount of billing time in the year (approximately 67% of maximum) will be about $440,000 per year less overhead, still leaving a nice lifestyle. As you can see, if you continue to do the math, as the attorney's billable rate increases, even at $10 per hour per year, he or she will pick up about $15,000 per year in revenue, and presumably with no other changes, his or her overhead would not increase the same amount; thus, the attorney's net take-home pay increases year to year. Compound this further by adding an associate and other revenue-generating attorneys, and even at a small level, the income of the attorney will continue to increase. A nice lifestyle? It certainly can be.

Contrary to the argument against growth, the purpose of this book is to build a dynamic, aggressive, top-quality law firm. This generally cannot be done with a one- or two-person firm. It probably cannot be done with a law firm of five or six attorneys. Marketing to bigger clients, seeking larger revenues, civic involvement, and philanthropy are more easily achieved with a larger firm. More clients will yield higher revenues, which yield more growth and civic involvement. Growth and profit is a good thing, not something bad. This book is intended to take you on the path of survival, stability, success, and also significance, namely, profits, civic involvement, and philanthropy.

Chapter 6

The Necessities

There are items that are necessary to set up your law office. This chapter will give you an opportunity to comprehensively cover all of the items that you need to think about, order, purchase, lease, or otherwise obtain.

As discussed in Chapter 7 on leasing office space, some of these items may be available to you in your already-established office arrangement. For example, if you are leasing space in an existing law office, you may be able to make an arrangement to pay a fixed amount for each copy made on the landlord's large copy machine, for potential use of the landlord's postage machine, and for furniture. These are all things you need to think about in terms of the ordinary operation of the law office that may or may not be provided to you by your landlord or lessor. Notwithstanding your potential for obtaining this equipment through your lease, this chapter discusses the items that you need to think about obtaining with or without the help of other attorneys.

Bank Accounts

Do not, under any circumstances, jointly open bank accounts with attorneys who are not part of your law office. Again, you are opening your first law office, and you need to open bank accounts for the purpose of operating your business.

Consider three accounts: your operating account, your client trust account (referred to as your IOLTA, which stands for "interest on lawyers trust accounts"), and an ordinary trust account for money that you receive for or from closings and other clearinghouse transactions.

The first account, your ordinary operating account, is the in-and-out account (i.e., the checking account for all of your income and expenses). There is no statute that requires a separate account for payroll, so all of your expenses, including payroll, should be paid out of your operating account. Recall the discussion on banking in regular intervals, such as weekly, for the payment of your bills and probably a few times a week for the deposit of incoming checks; all of these transactions happen in and out of your ordinary operating account. It is an account that you deal with the most to deposit your income and to pay your bills.

Contact your bank or banks and negotiate with them to open your business accounts. Find out what fees will be associated with your account, whether interest on this account will offset fees, or whether the bank will waive fees in general. These are all fair questions, and it is important that you understand the cost of setting up this account.

The money deposited into your checking account is your firm's money. It has been earned by you and is not subject to disgorgement (except for fraud or defalcation) for any operational reason. Needless to say, this account, along with the other accounts, needs to be reconciled monthly.

The second account, the client trust account, most frequently referred to as an IOLTA account, is an account that holds client money. These are not your funds; these are funds specifically belonging to the client. If you have ten clients, or one hundred clients, you do not need ten or one hundred separate IOLTA bank accounts; one IOLTA bank account is sufficient, but each client has to have an accounting of his or her own funds in the IOLTA bank account. You will give the client a monthly balance on every bill indicating what client funds are remaining in the IOLTA bank account. The client's balance being held in trust is an accounting "account" provided monthly to the client as an attachment to his or her bill. Your law office billing software should be able to provide this. In addition to that, your own internal record keeping should track the sum balance of all funds in the IOLTA account and indicate a breakdown of funds for every client who has money in the IOLTA account. However, the actual money is in the IOLTA bank account at your bank.

> Consider three accounts: your operating account, your client trust account, and an ordinary trust account . . . for money that you receive for or from closings and other clearinghouse transactions.

No one in your office should have check-signing authority over the IOLTA account except for you.

The single purpose of the IOLTA account is to put retainer amounts, prepaid deposits by a client, unearned, into a separate account whereby the client has the authority to seek reimbursement of those funds in the event the client has a change of heart about hiring you as a lawyer, moving forward on the litigation, or closing a particular transaction. The funds will become the property of the attorney once appropriately billed and notification is sent to the client that there has been a transfer of the client's money out of the IOLTA account and into the lawyer's operating account. Always remember to notify the client every time money flows in and out of the account. You do not need to call the client about this, but by virtue of your monthly billing or statements, you will demonstrate to the client his or her IOLTA account balance at least monthly.

Never comingle your operating account with client funds. This purpose is the reason you set up a separate IOLTA account. Do not pay any personal or office expenses out of the IOLTA account under any circumstances. You need to take the banking steps necessary to create the proper paper trail before you pay your law office bills. At the end of every month, when your billing is completed and your time is properly accounted for, you will move the appropriate money out of the IOLTA account and into your operating account in one transfer. Then, out of your operating account, you pay your law office bills.

Incredibly, in 2012, the Illinois Attorney Registration & Disciplinary Commission (ARDC) received 421 notices from banks reporting that a lawyer's trust fund account was overdrawn. It seems impossible that attorneys would overdraw on moneys they did not own. That act immediately triggers an ARDC investigation. As a result of those 421 notices, the Illinois ARDC opened almost three hundred additional investigations during 2012 to determine whether a lawyer mismanaged client funds. A majority of the investigations were closed because the ARDC was satisfied that the lawyer understood the ethics rules regarding the safekeeping of client funds but made an innocent mistake. Note that your IOLTA account should clearly state on the checks "client trust account," and you should never use the client money as your own money. It seems like a fundamental rule, but though trust account violations make up but a small percentage of complaints against lawyers, they seem to make up a large percentage of disbarments. Take this matter seriously, for any mismanagement of a client IOLTA fund could put you at risk of being disbarred.

> No one in your office should have check-signing authority over the IOLTA account except for you.

Sometimes using client funds is an act of desperation, and some misuses are conducted as a pattern of theft. You will hear or read of reported instances of client funds flowing through the IOLTA account that were intended to stay in the IOLTA account for months, but as payroll gets tight, bills pile up, attorneys have, out of desperation, "borrowed" money from the IOLTA account to pay their business debts and, in some far worse cases, personal bills. Doing this is, and should be, the quickest path to disbarment.

Last, as you would do with the operating account, make sure you reconcile the IOLTA account monthly. Because you are personally responsible for the funds in this account, you need to take personal responsibility for the balancing of this account. As part of the balancing of the IOLTA account, through the billing software or manually, you need to make sure that the account of every client with funds in the IOLTA account balances to the penny. The balances between the individual client balances and the aggregate total must properly tie every single month.

Always remember to return client funds when requested to do so by the client. If the funds are in the IOLTA account and the client asks for a refund of his or her money, the money must be refunded immediately. Any unexplained delays will trigger a call by the client into your jurisdiction's Attorney Registration & Disciplinary Commission, which will then trigger an investigation into your client trust account. If you have done everything correctly, delays should not be a problem, but they will be a distraction for you and your business. Avoid delays and take the high road with respect to client funds, even if doing so means bending over backward to satisfy a departing client.

The third account is a traditional trust account that does not necessarily hold client retainer funds, but rather it acts as a clearinghouse when you are asked to hold security deposits or deposits for a business or real estate closing. Although you should avoid handling money for clients, handling money tends to be inevitable in the legal profession. Therefore, consider opening this third account, which is a traditional checking account with a bank, and hold yourself to the standards of the IOLTA accounts.

When large deposits come into this trust account, the same temptations occur to some attorneys who are cash strapped and short on funds. It is not their money, yet some try to "borrow" money against this account of funds that do not belong to them. Again, as with the IOLTA accounts, using other people's money to pay your own bills is a quick path to suspension and, ultimately, disbarment. Do not do it.

Similar to the IOLTA, this account needs to be reconciled monthly not only with respect to the bank balance but also with respect to tying the funds in the account to the particular closing and transaction for which you are holding these funds. Sometimes closing receipts get deposited immediately on closing, but because of postclosing issues, there are times that the money gets disbursed weeks and sometimes months later. In addition, sometimes the funds get disbursed in partial payments over a long period of time. As you can see, this particular trust account requires great diligence and detailed record keeping. Unlike the IOLTA, where the account balances can be determined electronically on a good billing system, there is no software system that will necessarily balance a checking account that has funds from five to ten different business deals that are partially closed and partially ready for funds to be disbursed. It takes good old-fashioned record keeping and diligence to make sure this account is regularly balanced.

Computer, Computer Equipment, and Software

Whenever you engage in a conversation about various businesses and various barriers to entry into other businesses, whether manufacturing, service, or retail, it will strike you that opening your own law office has an incredibly low barrier to entry. At a bare minimum, a computer, printer, and some paper is all you need to open a law office. The cost of a high-grade machine with a large flat-screen monitor can be had for approximately $1,000, including all licensing fees for your software.

The industry standard for word processing has moved from Word Perfect to Microsoft Word. The only reason that this move is important is because of the need to find and hire skilled people educated on particular software packages. Most law offices run the Microsoft Office integrated suite, which includes Microsoft Outlook, Excel, and Word. It is pretty close to industry standard. The software components will regularly be used by everyone in the office and are integrated very nicely into a package. Further, the Microsoft Outlook module includes e-mail, calendaring, contacts, and tasks, all of which you will regularly use. This is not intended to be any endorsement for particular software, because Apple also has an outstanding competing integrated system for the needs of the practicing lawyer, which includes e-mail, calendaring, and contacts.

Attorneys rely on the contacts module in computers and on their smartphones. Needless to say, you input all necessary information such as work, home, and cell phone numbers, complete addresses, with complete proper spellings of everyone's names, and e-mail addresses into your Outlook contact list or smartphone.

You will find that the Microsoft Office integrated suite is sufficient for your everyday operation. However, there are practice groups that have specific software packages you will eventually look into as your law practice expands into certain practice areas. For example, there is software for bankruptcy petitions, simple and basic estate-planning shelf document forms, sophisticated estate-planning annuity trust and charitable trust tax calculation software, and corporate forms. The basic word-processing software is what you need to get going. Other software, beyond the scope of this book, is available to you and should be investigated through various law book publishers and legal research databases such as Westlaw and LexisNexis.

> Whenever you engage in a conversation about various businesses and various barriers to entry into other businesses, it will strike you that opening your own law office has an incredibly low barrier to entry.

E-mail has virtually changed the practice of law in the past ten years. Large documents are transferred in moments electronically compared to what used to take hours by messenger in the downtown metropolitan areas and a half day to the outlying rural and suburban areas elsewhere. Measures need to be put in place to ensure the security of the transmission of the confidential client documents and information. Talk to your IT consultant about virtual private networks that, subject to the proper encryptions and passwords, make the transmission of electronic documents safe and secure. These security devices need to be coordinated not only among WiFi transmissions within the office, between the office, and outside of network locations, but also through smartphones and tablet devices.

Also, e-mail transfers of large documents have replaced the time, energy, and sometimes hours attorneys and administrative assistants spend standing in front of fax machines feeding large documents to be faxed to other locations. Even as fax machines evolved into digital format where a single feeding of one large document could then be transmitted to three, four, and five different locations, nothing compares to the electronic mailing of large documents.

Since you are in the service business, scheduling is critically important. What started as a diary calendar kept in every attorney's briefcase and on his desktop twenty-four hours a day has evolved into electronic diary systems for both the law office and your personal work schedule. These electronic systems, input one time into your work computer or your smartphone, share information with each other and are synced without any other further docking stations and, further, could be accessed at home, at the office, or while on vacation. You can share your electronic calendaring system with your assistant, who has access to scheduling appointments and is responsible for knowing your whereabouts on a regular basis. This setup completely avoids the mistakes of forgetting your diary booklet at the office and being at home in the evening wondering where you have to be at 9:00 a.m. the next day. The information is all accessible and available.

> Measures need to be put in place to ensure the security of the transmission of the confidential client documents and information.

Printer

In addition to having a computer with the appropriate operating software, it is critically important to buy a high-quality printer.

As your first foray into the law office setup, consider a high-quality four-in-one machine that copies, prints, scans, and faxes. As your law firm grows, you may invest money in higher-quality items just for one of those functions. You may find you have access to a copy machine through your landlord. But there is no doubt that you will need the ability to copy documents on a regular basis, print from your computer, fax (although it is a dying function), and scan documents.

Soon, scanners will continue to improve to the point of being faster and more accurate with better feeding mechanisms; as a matter of course, you will scan in all your documents and save these to your system.

Letterhead

You need to order high-quality letterhead for your law office. Engraved letterhead was once the only way you could go to be perceived as a high-quality, serious law office. Currently, thermographic imaging is a type of postprint process that is achieved by traditional methods coupled with thermographic machines. The three-section process includes as a first step applying an embossing powder made from plastic resins to the paper, the second step takes away the excess thermographic embossing powder in the uneven areas, and the third is to run the paper through a heated oven that actually raises the letterhead. This process is far less expensive than engraving, but some folks would say that to the expert eye, the difference can be noticed. Before modern technology, running thermographically raised letterhead through a hot and heated printer would reduce the raised letters of the letterhead. In any case, today's processors of the thermographic print say it works well and is far less expensive than engraving.

The next issue is the art of the letterhead. Your letterhead is the most important marketing piece that you will design. It sends a message with every letter and with every correspondence with opposing counsel, whether fax, letter, or e-mail. There are traditional, simple looks for letterhead stating your law office name on the top, followed by your address, telephone numbers, and e-mail address. Other designs include artwork layout across the top of the page, which might also include a bottom portion of the front page of all letters and even laterally along the left margin. First, determine whether you want a more artful, modern look versus a more traditional look. Then, go to a graphic artist to lay out your design concept. Traditionally, you rely on professional printers to lay out your letterhead with a few choices. Finding a qualified artist with an eye toward design is better than using a traditional printer.

You need to convey the tone of your law office and whether you are a traditional law office or a more modern office with up-to-date ideas and systems. The type of law you practice may have a bearing on your approach. Many people believe that in the entertainment law and art law world, an embellished letterhead is the preferred method of dealing with clientele. In reality, many high-powered entertainment lawyers use a very traditional approach. This is a critical issue to understand in formulating your marketing approach to your audience, customer, and client. After all is said and done, and you have examined the subsequent chapters of this book about marketing and aligning yourself with your clients' attitudes, remember that people still want to hire a great lawyer who acts like a lawyer, thinks like a lawyer, and wins cases like a great lawyer. They do not necessarily want to hire a great singer or songwriter who is also an attorney. They want to hire a great lawyer.

Make sure the sizing of the secondary fonts (such as your address, phone number, and e-mail address) is legible when reproduced for fax machines and e-mail. This all needs to be thought through consistently for your full marketing effort. Make sure your letterhead includes your name, the firm's name, the firm's address, telephone numbers, fax number, website, and e-mail address. As part of the letterhead process, think through whether you want to create a reproducible logo for marketing purposes.

A logo is more than just your name typed across the top of the letter. There are design elements that can be reproduced in different types of advertisements, marketing pieces, e-mail blasts, and other information blasts to your market. In Section 2 of this book, there is a discussion about branding, and since the logo is important in branding, it should be involved in the process of letterhead creation.

If you determine that a logo should be designed at this stage, whether it is complimentary to the letterhead or used directly on the letterhead, make sure it reproduces properly in black-and-white print, as well as color print when applicable.

Any design elements that are found on your letterhead should be repeated in either a complementary or an identical style on your business cards. Again, all the necessary information must be on your business cards as it appears on your letterhead: name, address, phone number, fax number, website, and e-mail address.

Similarly, think about an announcement card, which is usually sent out on the opening of a law office. This should be part of the marketing discussion regarding your law office, but the stylistic elements of your letterhead and business cards should be found on your announcement card, which should be sized at approximately 4" × 6". The announcement card should be sent out to every person in your contacts lists, such as your law school friends and contacts, the business-related contacts you had before law school, your personal and social contacts, and your parents' personal and professional contacts. This mailing list should be the broadest scope of contacts that you have in your mailing systems. In addition, you should ask for an electronic version of this announcement so that you can send it electronically to all your e-mail contacts and post it on all of your social media sites.

Again, the point of this discussion is that your letterhead, business cards, and initial announcement should all tie in, in terms of artwork, image, and brand consistency.

Supplies

Purchasing office supplies is easier today than ever. There are very competitive big box retailers out there that provide tremendous pricing on everyday supplies you will need to run your office. You may need to run to the store to purchase a "starter kit" of all of these items as you begin practicing. The costs are nominal. As your practice grows and as you purchase more of these items, you will be able to go to distributors to bring your pricing down slightly, but it is probably not worth the effort initially. Purchasing through online sellers might save you the time of going to the store on your way home from the office, purchasing items, and then bringing them to the office the next morning. Delivery is nominal and sometimes free, and you can have the deliveries made directly to your office Monday through Friday from 9:00 a.m. to 5:00 p.m.

Office Furniture

With any luck, you have found an office space to rent that has an old desk, guest chairs, and your chair on which to operate. If the office is presentable, that is wonderful; if it is not, go through the Yellow Pages or online to find a furniture repair service person who will come out to your office to clean up, restain, and refinish your office desk and chairs. Basically, it is very inexpensive to get the furniture looking good in your office. It is completely acceptable to buy used furniture for your initial office furnishings. Used furniture is often sold at retail sale prices of about 25% of the new price of office furniture. Sellers of used furniture enjoy a high profit margin even at these bargain basement prices because they go into abandoned offices, buy out all the furniture at fractions on the dollar, and resell the furniture at a low price. Because you are trying to furnish only one office, you are a perfect buyer for a small setup of office furniture. If your office is large enough, a forty-two-inch round table with a few chairs around it would be a benefit, or a small sofa that makes the office seem a bit homier.

> Do not overpay for expensive furniture to convey a "successful lawyer" image.

Again, if you could get a great deal on used furniture that appears to be slightly bumped and bruised, just hire a furniture repair person to come and make the furniture look close to new again. Add a few file cabinets, a desk, a comfortable attorney chair, and a couple of client chairs, and you are off to the races. Make sure your desk is comfortable, has adequate drawers, is at least six feet wide, and has an overhang in the front so that the clients can use your desktop as a writing space.

In addition, over time you may want to hang some of your diplomas and certificates in the office. Also, possibly some artwork could be bought from law office art websites or a used furniture store, and some family pictures can be hung, all which will make the office comfortable.

With respect to all diplomas and certificates, make sure they are framed in a professional style with glass fronts. Do this to convey that you are proud of the documents and that they mean something significant, as well as to ensure that all clients will have the same understanding of your background and qualifications.

Do not overpay for expensive furniture to convey a "successful lawyer" image. This is a place where you will be spending fifty to sixty hours per week; therefore, it should be comfortable and pleasing to you as well as to your clients, since it will literally be your second home.

There is a lot written on conveying a particular image for a lawyer, but you will never read in this book about being something that you are not. You are a new, young, aggressive lawyer or perhaps an experienced lawyer starting off your own law practice. Either way, conveying the sense of your practical use of funds will never hurt you in the client's eyes.

Law Library

A fundamental expense that you will have in your new practice is the access to a law library.

Formerly, a very inexpensive way to have access to a law library was just to use the law library at the local law school or the one found in the courthouse. This strategy is still a very good way to have access to the law. If you are just coming right out of law school, there is no doubt that you are probably versed in research methods and have a very good handle on the accessibility to the local law library or the law library at your law school. If you are practicing law away from your law school and do not have access to familiar law libraries, you will need to do some research to find an accessible law library that you will be able to visit regularly.

However, it should be no surprise that legal research has largely moved online. The two major players in this field are still Westlaw and LexisNexis. There is no reason to believe that this situation will change in the near future, but as Internet systems and websites have developed over the years, you will come to the conclusion that there is more and more free information available on the Internet for performing legal research. Now, through simple Google searches, it is incredibly easy to be able to find governmental regulations, the code, and government forms in just a few simple keystrokes. Notwithstanding the availability of free information, you will still need primary access to current information and a true law library. The new search features of the leading online law libraries are incredibly easy to use, and the ability to cut and paste cases and sites into briefs has never been easier. Most of these features do not exist in the theoretical free law materials that you find online.

In addition to the traditional Westlaw and LexisNexis services, they also provide access to practice books and other items that you need as a practical matter for practicing law. Certainly, many jurisdictions have local practice books that are found online. Again, if you are fortunate enough to have gone to law school in the jurisdiction where you are practicing law, you are probably very familiar with the practice books available in your state.

With respect to purchasing law books, consider going to local libraries or researching ads in the local bar association newsletters for sales on used law books. Although it is critical that you keep up on the law, it is probably not necessary for you to buy new law books immediately. Do not make the investment in any casebooks because the volumes are tremendously large, and unless you want to make a substantial investment in your law library, you will never have a comprehensive set of casebooks, nor will you probably have enough space to shelve them properly.

Used books are always on the market, and sometimes it is a good investment to buy a few practice books, especially books in your practice area if you can get them affordably. Quite honestly, a nice set of books looks impressive to the clients if they are in a visible location in your office, but the point is the substance of the books and not window dressing for clients.

It is probably obvious that you need a copy of *Black's Law Dictionary* and other jurisdiction-specific books and directories to navigate you through various government agencies in your jurisdiction. These are always helpful to have near your desk.

If you are a litigator, find a form book that is jurisdiction specific with respect to pleadings in the area of the law that you will practice. It will be of great help and assistance to you to be able to understand the formatting of pleadings and understand the necessary requirements for pleadings in your jurisdiction. If, under unusual circumstances, that book is not available, you need to budget more time in your day to go to the courthouse to look at other files to see the way pleadings are formatted in your locality.

> If you are a litigator, find a form book that is jurisdiction specific with respect to pleadings in the area of the law that you will practice.

In addition to Westlaw and LexisNexis, there are other services such as Jurists Search, Loislaw, and Findlaw. Invest the time to meet with representatives of these companies and have them make competing proposals for your needs. Please be careful executing long-term contracts that they will want you to sign. Of course, you will be practicing law for many years, but do not commit to any one service for more than a year or two unless you are certain this is the system that you were trained on in law school and that you want to use only one system. Also, do not let the representative know that you are predisposed to only one system. Let them bid against each other to earn your business.

Finally, many times practice books provide CD-ROM disks with documents on those discs. They form the basis for a very good document library, as discussed later in Chapter 16. Do not hesitate to spend a little more money to get the add-on for the CD-ROM discs. It is a very good investment in building your document library.

One final word on traditional law libraries and paper books.

In order to keep your law library current, you will be looking at a significant financial investment in pocket parts, new page inserts, and similar updates that will cost money and time for upkeep. If you have a commitment to keep a particular set of practice books or annotated statutes, codes, and ordinances updated, you need to know what doing so will cost going forward. The law library, if unmanaged, could become very expensive to maintain. Please know what you are getting into before you have the inability to pay for the upkeep. Again, an investment in a certain number of practice books is a great idea, but because most of your research will be through your online service, that cost must be clearly defined in the contract for the libraries you purchase.

If you have an odd research issue that will take you out of the library you purchased online (e.g., a research project on a state law issue in another jurisdiction that you did not purchase), you will incur additional costs for that research. Note that online services have a very good system for allocating your research time to clients and client numbers. Again, this online research expense is a cost that directly benefits clients, and so if you feel comfortable, it is a legitimate cost to pass directly to the clients that are benefited in furtherance of the clients' goals and the case. Some attorneys may view this as an overhead cost that should not be passed along to clients—an understandable position. Nonetheless, your time spent in doing legal research online or in a library is legitimate billing time. The exception to the rule is when you take on a new case and you are getting yourself up to speed on a new area of the law.

> Your time spent in doing legal research online or in a library is legitimate billing time. The exception to the rule is when you take on a new case and you are getting yourself up to speed on a new area of the law.

There are a few other considerations on publications and information. In the legal profession, there are many newsletters that go out from various government agencies, bar associations, and other organizations associated with the law. Without being inundated with information, you certainly should subscribe and sign up for good, content-driven newsletters that help further your practice and your knowledge of the law. These are available through the ABA, the state bar associations, and probably even your local bar association. These are wonderful ways to stay on top of the law, and currently many bar associations are indexing their articles online so that you can go back to find the articles in the future.

Also, consider Google Alerts for timely information. Google Alerts can be set for keywords so that you can gather up-to-date information on certain areas of the law. It may be information just picked up in the mainstream media, but if you hold yourself out as a practitioner in a particular area of the law, you need to know what's being reported in the news so you can advise your clients on the latest developments in the law covered in the media with respect to a particular legal issue. Also, at a very low charge you can also get electronic newsletters from your state capitol on pending legislation, and those newsletters can become a great basis for your article writing for your clients.

In summary, your law library will largely consist of your online services but also practice books that you will accumulate in your office. Further, your law library will also include regular monthly publications of informative, content-driven information in your particular practice area. Keep this information organized and readily accessible so that you can be on top of the changes in the law as it develops in your practice area.

Telephone Systems

A majority of attorney contact with clients is over the telephone. Cell phones and smartphones have changed the way people conduct their personal lives and are beginning to change the way lawyers conduct their law practices. Nonetheless, having an excellent landline system is necessary for the operation of the law office. In a perfect world, if you are fortunate enough to rent space with a phone system, you will have to research whether or not the system could be used to meet your functional requirements.

To start, you need to reserve certain telephone numbers that you will have for the rest of your career. This is a critical initial step to starting your law office. As you talk to people at the telephone company about obtaining telephone numbers, make sure you can take those numbers with you to different areas of your state or to different states (with different area codes of course) so that you will have the numbers for the rest of your career. Also, ask if you could retain the number and area code even without an office in the area, because if you move far, you will want to keep the same number, with the area code, and have it permanently forwarded to your new location.

Whether you are working off an already existing phone system or are looking to purchase a phone system solely for you, consider the features that you need to discuss thoroughly with your vendor or your landlord providing the phone system to determine whether it will be adequate for your use. Ask these questions about the features you need:

- Will your phone system accommodate several lines to roll over if you are on a phone call so that the caller does not get a busy signal?
- Will your system have voicemail for the calls being directed specifically to you?
- Will your system accommodate the addition of an administrative assistant and additional attorneys who will require additional telephone numbers?
- Will you have the ability to forward calls to your cell phone?
- Can your system accommodate caller identification features?
- Is your system accessible from an outside location so that you can call in to obtain your voice messages?
- Will your system be able to automatically copy messages to your e-mail? Many times it is difficult to balance between communications that are incoming on the telephone and via e-mail. This way all calls coming in that are not answered live are recorded and sent to e-mail. You can click on your e-mail to listen to the call or message, and,

if necessary, forward the call to your assistant or to another attorney in your office without having to go to the phone.

- Do you want all calls going into a voicemail system prompting the caller to various extensions, including your own extension, or will you have all your calls answered by a live person? Of course, depending on your budget at the beginning of your practice, economic realities may dictate your options. Make no mistake about it, if possible, all calls should be answered by a person during regular business hours. More on that issue in Chapters 15 and 27.
- Do you need to have an outside service answering calls during off hours? If you do, how will that service contact you in an emergency?
- Check to see if your system will accommodate "direct dial numbers" so that in addition to a phone number that will be the law office's main number forever, you will have a number that will ring right at your desk.
- Is there a system that exists to translate oral communications left on a voice message system to a memorandum in a written form?
- Does the system allow you to change recorded messages easily? In other words, if you are out for the day or on vacation, is it easy to change the message that you leave behind as clients call you but you are not available?

> It is best to seek out a telecommunication firm that is small and that will help you with your needs.

- Will your system be able to accommodate any emergency calls, and will there be a button to forward emergency messages to cell phones during off hours?
- Will your telephones accommodate speaker phones at least for the conference room, and how does the system work as a practical matter? Make sure it is tested so that ambient noises are not a distraction on speaker phone calls. You will need a speaker phone for your office, too. Many times, while talking to the client, you will be reviewing documents and taking notes.

As you can see, a telephone system is a very important part of the law practice. This is not something to purchase on your own. It is best to seek out a telecommunication firm that is small and that will help you with your needs as you talk through the bullet points above with the service provider. It is important that your system is affordable but good, and where you can add on features in order for you to have a system that works well and accommodates the functionality that you need when you open and grow your law practice. But moreover, be sure this system is expandable so that as you grow and add assistants, administrative support, and bookkeepers, the system will accommodate more numbers and more users.

Sometimes a facsimile is the only way you have to move a document quickly from a client's home or office to your office. Make sure you thoroughly research the ability to have a telephone system with a fax number that will receive faxes directly to your computer screen. The ongoing cost will be an additional telephone line directly to you, dedicated to facsimiles, but those incoming faxes will come directly to your computer screen without the need to clog up the additional fax machine in the common area of your law office. Consider this as a cost-effective add-on for your phone and computer systems for communicating with clients.

Website

Certainly it is not a new concept, but you need to be prepared to invest time and money in the development of a website. Again, there are many inexpensive software packages and templates you can use to develop a functional website. This is a very difficult analysis in terms of cost-benefit that you as a new attorney will derive from a high-quality website.

> Make sure your site is adaptive for mobile technology and that it reformats to your liking.

You need a website; there's no doubt about it. The challenge to you is how much money to spend to develop a website that will attract business to you. Depending on affordability, early on you should develop a website using available templates and software, to the extent that you are computer savvy, and find an inexpensive host for your website on a server. Make sure your site is adaptive for mobile technology and that it reformats to your liking. You could have your website hosted on sites like web.com or wix.com for a monthly fee as low as $5. If you want to use a vendor's combined web hosting service, plus templates for your web design, you might pay approximately $15 per month. Please be sure that you own your own domain name so that if these services ever fail, they cannot hold your domain name hostage.

There are four important components that you should look at separately when developing the website.

First, look at the art of the website and its design elements. With respect to the art and art development, it might be wise for you to hire a graphic designer to develop the look of the landing page and the subsequent information pages of the website. Most web developers do this for you, including the landing page layout in their development and design package. If the web developer does not have a background in graphic art, however, is he or she qualified to develop a website that ties in with your letterhead art and logo? The website will help you later with the branding of your law office, your image, and as a result, it needs to look consistent with all of the other messages you send out to the marketplace, such as your business cards, letterhead, announcements, and newsletters.

The second element is programming. As you interview programmers for your website, you should also be talking to your graphic artist about suggestions for the desired look for the website. Remember, the programmer of websites is not necessarily a graphic artist. Many times, programmers may have that skill set, but you are paying them for the programming elements of the website as well as optimizing the hits on your website.

Early on in the creative process you must decide how you will emphasize any particular areas of law in which you will concentrate your practice. Make sure during the development of the website that the site has the ability to grow. You may be starting your own law firm as a personal injury lawyer, estate planning lawyer, corporate lawyer, or criminal defense lawyer, but eventually your practice groups will expand and you will be able to service your clients in additional areas as your experience grows or as you add new attorneys with different skill sets. It is wise to have your specialty area be the main focus of the website and then have sections of the website that include other areas of law in which you also practice. As discussed in Chapter 11, you will balance between coming across as a generalist and as a specialist in a particular area of the law, and the website needs to reflect that image.

The preparation of the website should be done in two stages. The first stage is the artwork, where your graphic artist designs the look and art of every page of your website. The design should have a consistent look and convey your office culture. After it is presented, tweaked, redone, and fine-tuned, then, and only then, will you take the finished product to a website programmer for programming. Explain your wants for the functionality of the website and make decisions as to the icons and the navigation of the website before going to the programmer. The programmer will then incorporate your design elements with a clear understanding of the navigation of the website and begin working.

The third element is content. As you can see from the early sections of this book, all attorneys, especially you as a new attorney starting your own law practice, need to produce publishable quality content on a regular basis. This product will form the basis for the content of your website. Generally, original content is generated by attorneys in a law office. Understand that this work takes an enormous amount of attorney time that can otherwise be directed to billing clients on client projects. However, in order to have a commitment to original content, you must accept the responsibility of producing articles, podcasts, and other original content for your newsletters, e-mail blasts, and the website.

Some content links to important websites can be programmed into your site to accommodate clients and displayed on a separate page. To begin to collate, organize, and produce this content is the responsibility of you and the law office.

With the proper initial setup and programming, you should be able to download content to the website, change pictures, revise bios, and regularly update your website without any programmer involvement. You want to retain the ability to add art, news articles, articles authorized by you, press clippings, pictures, and notes on community events. It is important for you to maintain and constantly update your website with timely and relevant content because that is the best way to keep your site fresh, and that freshness will maximize hits to your website.

The fourth element of web design and functionality is search engine optimization. How many people can really claim to understand the complexities of search engine optimization? Clearly, there is some science behind the concept of optimizing the hits you will get on your website based on certain features of your website. A client told a story that for over fifteen years his website barely and rarely if ever received quality hits that he could convert to clients. A recent reworking of the website with a focus on adding metatags, new programming features, and fresh, new, and up-to-date information to the site has changed this situation dramatically, and he now gets hits and requests for information that eventually convert to paying customers on a regular basis. Keep in mind that these are not paid-for inquiries on this website. At this stage, he has invested no money in Google AdWords and other paid websites that drive traffic to his website. These are all purely organic searches on search engines that drive traffic to his website.

> It is important for you to maintain and constantly update your website with timely and relevant content.

The moral of that short story is that search engine optimization is valuable when programmed and set up properly by your website programmer. If you work in a small town, you should use keywords relating to the nearest large municipal center in the area in which you work because searches relating to "lawyers, hometown, USA" will help drive traffic to your website. Of course, the more keywords you include relating to your practice area, the town in which your law office is located, and other unique characteristics of your practice, the more traffic will be directed to your website.

Whether or not you come to the conclusion that the website is necessary for finding new clients, it is absolutely necessary for clients to research you and your law office before your first meeting. A search engine inquiry to look for lawyers is the equivalent of going to the Yellow Pages to find a lawyer. That may be their first point of contact with you. But even if potential clients do not find you with a search engine inquiry, once you have been referred to them, or they've seen your name in advertisements, or heard about you at the VFW hall, they will check you out by visiting your website. Of course, there are other ways they will do research on your reputation beyond examining your website. They will look into Facebook, LinkedIn, and other social digital media that are easily found, as well as the media clippings they may find with a simple inquiry on a search engine. But the landing page they will spend the most time on to learn about you and your firm is your website.

The last issue you need to understand is that your website must be content driven. If it consists of just pictures and headlines, your potential client will not spend much time on your website reading your words and understanding your view on the law. For that reason, every piece of work you prepare for newsletters, articles, and press clippings, and indeed every other writing that you do, must be included on your website. A section on "articles" or "attorney Smith in the news," for example, must be easily navigable within your website so that people can find your content and read it. The longer they stay on your website, the more connected they will become with you, which heightens the chances that they will hire you in the long run. It is critically important for you to spend the time on a regular basis, as suggested earlier, producing publishable-quality legal articles. New postings on a website are captured by search engines far more easily and frequently than are old, stale websites that never change. There is a programming element to posting these articles in a way to maximize hits from search engines, and you need to enquire about those issues. But make no mistake about it, it is in your best interest to publish as much information as you can and post it on your website to demonstrate to all potential clients that you are a lawyer who stays on top of the law and provides quality information to the public.

> Every piece of work you prepare for newsletters, articles, and press clippings, and indeed every other writing that you do, must be included on your website.

Last, if your budget does not allow for an extensive workup on your website, you can go to a hosting site or purchase a software package that will provide a hosting site and then create a website from templates that are provided. Something is better than nothing. As your business grows and as your budget grows, you can improve your website. Even your programming skills using the website software will continue to improve; as a result, you should be able to add new pages, content, and practice groups, all with the goal of making a better presentation to potential clients. Remember, no matter how many clients you gain or do not gain from your website, treat the site as a place where every single potential client will review your content and review your story before meeting you for the first time. If the website is sharp, content driven, and current, your potential new client will be sold on you before ever meeting you face to face.

Miscellaneous Equipment, Dictation Machines, Postage Meters

Quite a bit of the discussion that you will engage in on purchasing additional office equipment will be a function of where your office is and what is available from the landlord. For example, if you locate in an office suite with other lawyers, some of the equipment, such as a copy machine, will be readily available. In such office suite environments, in order to ensure that you pay your fair share for copies, the machines are usually equipped with a mechanism to punch in the user code (which is you) and a client number for billing purposes.

These upgrades on large-scale office suite copy machines are very good for fairly and equitably allocating the cost of the operation of the machine. If you need to bear the expense of a separate copy machine other than the "four-in-one" printer mentioned earlier, do your research, talk to various vendors, and be careful about distinguishing between the contract rate of copies and the additional cost of copies over and above the contract estimate. In other words, for copies you make above the contract rate estimate, you will pay more for each copy. These large-scale copy machines are usually not bought but leased. These types of leases are usually capital leases, sometimes known as dollar-out leases. What that means is that after you make all the payments under your three-, four-, or five-year lease, you own the machine. If cared for properly, the machine will have a useful life after the capital lease. However, the leasing agent

> It is fact that no matter how fast a young attorney can type, he or she can always dictate faster.

will also want to sell you a new machine in order to get into a new lease with new functionality, upgrades, and higher speeds. This is an economic decision you will make at the time, but remember that with the proper care, the copy machine will last well beyond the capital lease term. However, after the capital lease term, you will still probably enter into some sort of maintenance contract to keep the machine running or pay on an as-needed basis.

With respect to the status of your law office, you may be a sole practitioner with an administrative assistant who does your typing for you, or you may choose to do the typing yourself. Young attorneys who have grown up in front of computer screens are very fast typists and tend to want to do all their typing on their own. This is a terrible mistake from an objective standpoint.

It is a fact that no matter how fast a young attorney can type, he or she can always dictate faster. The counterargument to this is that young attorneys who type their own letters, agreements, and briefs can think as they type, and they can construct and structure their documents better as they see them on the computer screen. Dictation is a skill that you can develop, like riding a bike. It takes time, but you can certainly become good enough to save a lot of time rather than doing all your own typing. The downside to this is that the administrative assistant transcribing your dictation will cost money and add another layer of expense to your practice.

This advice is relevant only in the context of whether or not to have dictating equipment. You need to have some dictation equipment because eventually you will need it. A transcription machine for your administrative assistant will cost a little over $100, and a simple battery-operated dictation tape recorder is less than $50. You will start to use it regularly for all documents, agreements, and letters. When preparing a long document, whether it be an extensive agreement, a lease, or a brief, just sketch out an outline on a pad of paper before you begin dictating. If necessary, dictate "blanks" where you need to cite to authority and go back and fill those in later. You will get to a point where, when you need to prepare extensive briefs and memoranda in support of motions, you will literally dictate the brief with twenty or twenty-five law books opened up on your desk staged as to where those cases fit into the brief. Dictate as you follow your outline. If you simply do not have the ability to type a twenty- or thirty-page brief on your own, dictate everything. Remember, no matter how fast you think you can type, you will speak faster than that. Dictation is a very efficient time management tool and is a skill that you need to learn.

If you are interested, consider testing voice-operated dictation software. A large part of this book is being prepared and written by voice-activated dictation. The sections that have not been prepared with voice-activated dictation software have been dictated into tapes and transcribed by my assistant.

You will be stunned as well as pleased with the dictation capabilities of the new Apple products in the newest Apple iPhones. However, after seeing the quality and exactness of the Apple iPhone dictation system, you will see that mainstream, everyday use of this technology is on the horizon. The technology will not make administrative assistants obsolete because they currently contribute so much more than just transcribing tapes, but it will make your ability to communicate with clients, other attorneys, and employees far better because you will have a greater ability to lay out more extensive memos at your fingertips (or, at the tip of your tongue).

You should start using voice-activated dictation software for your e-mails. Again, because you are not typing e-mails, you will find your e-mails to be far more extensive and comprehensive, with more detailed explanations. If you are a slow typist or a somewhat challenged typist, voice-activated software might be a good investment for you. The cost is approximately $250 with a high-quality microphone, and it may be the best solution for a person who does not type very well.

Also, as you try voice-activated software, you will have the ability to dictate into your smartphone and send that transcribed file to your computer or to your administrative assistant's computer. This could, in the practice of law, save enormous amounts of money and better serve your relationships with clients. As discussed later in the book with respect to client relationships, clients need to be informed of everything that is going on in their case on a regular basis. So as you walk out of court, with the court order in hand, you can dictate the cover letter to your client as you are walking to your car, send it to your assistant, and when you return to the office, that dictated file could already be on your computer ready to be sent in a letter format to the client with a copy of the court order.

Imagine that.

With respect to postage meters, you have to determine whether the cost of leasing is worth the postage meter savings. Please keep in mind that every postage meter salesperson will tell you that you will more than make up the cost of leasing the postage meter with the savings you will have by not overstamping parcels to be delivered. Nonetheless, stamps are easy to obtain to avoid the cost of the postage meter. Plan on using stamps at least for the first year of being in business. You can buy stamps in various denominations, and with a very inexpensive scale, you simply put the correct amount of postage on every parcel and envelope being mailed. While a law office's postage expenses have gone down as electronic mail has increased, postage meters and the U.S. Postal Service are still necessary for the operation of the law office. Note that as a practical matter, most law offices do not charge clients postage for regular local mail. However, as an allowable client reimbursable expense, you will pass along postage costs for certified mail, registered mail, and overnight mail charges that are necessitated by the client's matter.

> As you try voice-activated software, you will have the ability to dictate into your smartphone and send that transcribed file to your computer or to your administrative assistant's computer.

As your company begins to grow, you will invest in a postage meter and other mailing systems, making it faster in terms of putting correct postage on every envelope and parcel.

Billing and Accounting Software

Another investment in software that merits its own discussion is in your billing software. Depending on the kind of law office you will run, you might have different demands from your billing software. As a practical matter, law offices are generally run on a time and billing system. At a minimum, invest in an inexpensive time and billing software system for your office. Basically, you keep track of your time as you work on client matters and then bill the client for your time. Time and billing systems are very inexpensive and can be purchased at the big box stores. Templates are available with software systems whereby you can format the bill to look similar to your letterhead and make it part of your every-day system in order to input your time.

The time and billing systems have various fields that you input to accurately track your time, such as the date, client number (if the client has more than one case going on, you can break it up into matter numbers), the amount of time spent on the project, and a description of the work done. As your day progresses, you will have tracked your time and will not need to do the necessary math by adding up the number of hours and multiply-ing by your billable rate to send out a client bill—the software does all the work for you.

The next upgrade would be an accounting system integrated with your time and bill-ing software. These integrated systems have modules that will include a time and billing system, a general ledger, a balance sheet, an income statement, and other reports necessary to run a more sophisticated law office. These other reports include account receivable bal-ances, reports that track the origination of clients (if that data field is input by you), and other important reports. Since these types of software programs are not widely known to general accounting practices, you need to know if your accountant (if you have one) is well versed in this software. Otherwise, the accountant will have to learn to use this soft-ware and understand how it integrates into your billing system.

> As a practical matter, law offices are generally run on a time and billing system. At a minimum, invest in an inexpensive time and billing software system for your office.

Your accountant may want you to operate your accounting function on a software sys-tem called QuickBooks or some other similar widely used accounting software, and he or she will integrate your time and billing system with the QuickBooks software. In either case, an investment in a billing system is mandatory.

Hiring an Accountant

In addition to all of the necessary items needed to be taken care of in this chapter, unless you have an accounting background, I suggest you talk with some local accountants for assistance for the outside accounting function of your law office. You will certainly not need to hire the biggest accounting firm in your area, but you should find an accounting firm or a solo accountant who prides himself or herself with working with small businesses, preferably professional service entities that will give you the attention that you need. Your office will be a cash-basis business, not an accrual basis business; you need to understand that you must account for all your income from clients who pay you for your services and must offset such income with your allowable business expenses. You should feel like you are an important client to the accountant you intend on hiring. If the accountant constantly talks about his or her clients and suggests that he or she is doing you a favor by taking on your business, that accountant will not be a good fit for you. You should not feel that your work is an intrusion on the accountant's work schedule; rather, you should feel free to reach the accountant with a telephone call with an accounting question or to make an appointment (or schedule a call), and have reasonable access to your accountant.

Discuss the time and billing software, as well as the accounting software, that you plan on purchasing for your law office. Make sure the accountant is familiar with that software and is able either to remotely access the software and easily assist you with your monthly or quarterly financial reports or to explain to you how to e-mail reports from the accounting software to him or her to review for your business. As you will see in subsequent chapters of this book, staying on top of financial management of the firm is critical to your success, and having an accountant available to provide unbiased, critical commentary as to the financial health of your law firm is a necessity.

Chapter 7

Finding Office Space

A critical component in your decision matrix is where to locate your office.

A story I tell about my experience as a young tax and business lawyer is about the success I had when I found a large accounting firm that had available space. I made a deal with the firm to rent an office from them on a monthly basis. My first office as a sole practitioner! It was brilliant! A desk was already there. I bought a computer, had my letterhead printed and delivered, worked with the phone company to have my own phone lines brought in, and on Monday morning, I was in business. Things could not have been better. I sat behind the desk, started working the phones to make connections and let my peers know about my new location. Further, I actually had some projects to work on as I had developed contacts and sought work during my short gap after leaving my previous law firm and starting on my own.

That was Monday.

On Friday, the managing partner came into my office and told me the other partners had just met and the accounting firm was going to dissolve. They would be vacating the building within the next two weeks. Wow, that hurt.

I immediately started scrambling for plan B, which completely derailed my first few weeks of practicing law on my own. There are several threshold issues that you need to vet as you make the decision to set up your own law practice.

Practicing Out of Your Home

With all due respect to the economic realities of life, avoid practicing out of your home. Overhead, which largely includes your rent and employee costs in a law office, is a major expense for running a law office. Nonetheless, advising you not to work out of your house is not to be taken lightly, nor is it to ignore the realities of the financial burden of building a law office. You need to understand clearly that in order to build the type of law practice contemplated in this book, working out of your home is completely counterintuitive and counterproductive to that final goal.

That said, if you have no choice but to work out of your home, separate yourself from all noise and people and treat that separate space in your home as though is it is an office in a high-rise building. In your work environment, have very little contact with family members about matters unrelated to your law practice. When such contact does occur, it should only be business related, with little or no socialization.

You should not hear audible sounds of children playing, dogs barking, and vacuum cleaners operating. None of those audible sounds help build a winning law firm. Clients will, at many levels, measure and compare you to their expectations of what a lawyer should be. Under no circumstances are the sounds of children playing in the background or dogs barking among those expectations. First impressions are powerful, and how you are perceived will be determined by a potential client's first connection with you.[1] You cannot necessarily put lawyers in the same category as doctors, who may deal with life-and-death situations during many parts of their day; but clients still hold lawyers in high regard as professionals and will measure you against your competition in terms of professionalism.

Clearly, with the advent of computerized research, law libraries are probably not a hindrance to your practicing out of your home. Given the drawbacks versus your personal needs, however, you need to come to the conclusion of what is best for you.

With respect to practicing outside the home, which is greatly preferred, there are several ways in which to approach your search.

Traditional Office-Finding Methods

There are realtors who specialize in renting commercial space. Those realtors are called "tenant reps." They represent the interests of tenants in large office buildings. Generally, they know the availability of the office buildings, the locations, the general rental rates, and the availability for small office spaces. Also, they are usually tuned in to sublease opportunities where large office space users have sufficient capacity and availability and are interested in renting to a solo practitioner. A very good starting point is to meet with a tenant rep to find out market rates for rental in your locality and availability of office space. In a very short period of time, you will have a great deal of market knowledge in terms of what to expect to pay and the quantity of space you would be expected to rent. Notwithstanding the answers from one tenant rep, investigate thoroughly to drill down to the amount of the space that you require so that you do not lease more than you need.

---

1. STEVE ZAFFRON & DAVE LOGAN, THE THREE LAWS OF PERFORMANCE: REWRITING THE FUTURE OF YOUR ORGANIZATION AND YOUR LIFE (Jossey-Bass 2009); MALCOLM GLADWELL, BLINK: THE POWER OF THINKING WITHOUT THINKING (Little, Brown 2005).

Another method is to go on websites, including Craigslist, to find availability. If you want to make it known to the marketplace that you are a solo attorney looking to rent a single office in a suite, run an ad. In a very short time and after answering a very short number of responses to your ad, you will understand the marketplace much better and be able to make an intelligent decision as to the availability of office space.

Also, look in the classified ads of newspapers, local bar association magazines, publications of CPA organizations and societies, and other financial professional magazines.

Be careful with respect to the way the rental amount is quoted to you. Generally, there are three parts of commercial rental costs: base rent, property taxes, and common area maintenance (CAM). Leases that break out base rent, property taxes, and CAM are called *triple net leases*. If you pay one flat fee to the landlord, which clearly includes base rent, property taxes, and CAM, that is called a *gross lease*, and there will be no additional charges for property taxes and CAM. One type is not necessarily better than the other; these types are highlighted here only for your information on the assumption that you have had no previous experience negotiating leases. Know that the details matter and that the calculation of your total rent will always be a combination of base rent, property taxes, and CAM. Last, if you sign a triple net lease, be aware that taxes are set forth separately, so make sure that the tax bills that you are paying throughout the term of your lease are either as billed by the county or an estimate that will be trued up when the tax bill is actually issued. In many counties, bills are due one year subsequent to the tax year. In other words, many counties issue the actual tax bill about nine or ten months after the close of the year. If this is the case, you may still owe money to your landlord nine months after the termination of your lease. Check the tax clauses in the lease carefully. Ask these questions and vet this issue thoroughly in the preliminary stages of the lease negotiations. Do not wait until the documents are being exchanged.

> Generally, there are three parts of commercial rental costs: base rent, property taxes, and common area maintenance (CAM).

Potential Referral Sources

Within a reasonable distance to the community in which you live or want to work, contact every professional service provider who may be a source of business for you, such as accountants, insurance professionals, money managers, union halls, banks, and financial advisors, to see if they have an overcapacity of available space they would be interested in renting to you. Many times, you may be able to find a furnished office with some tired, older furniture that would work well for you and mean that you would literally have little or no expense for the furniture. Look through the Yellow Pages; send letters to the managing partners or the owners of the business to ask them if there is available space. Follow up those letters with telephone calls. See what is available. Remember, those service providers may believe that you would be a great tenant for them and would, therefore, engage you in conversation about renting office space from them.

Check your applicable code of professional conduct to find out what restrictions you need to have in your office to maintain client confidences and confidential information. These service providers are not lawyers, and so certain documentation and security might be required to keep client documents confidential. Make sure you follow these procedures accurately.

Remember, you will not need a lot of space. A single office with access to a conference room is a wonderful start. As a perk, ask if there is potential growth space for a secretarial cubicle somewhere in the office suite. It would be nice to know if you hire an assistant, potentially soon, your assistant would be able to have a cubicle to work very close to your office. There would probably be an additional charge for the cubicle, but have this conversation with the landlord. Then, ask if you can put your name on the door or place a plaque outside the door. Your name on or near the door will look impressive.

> Your office expenses and (future) employees are the two largest expenses in running a law office.

It is difficult to judge the fair rental rate for such an office arrangement, but remember, like the office arrangements discussed later in this chapter, your office expenses and (future) employees are the two largest expenses in running a law office. Remember that rent has a "legacy" or annuity feature to it. It's hard to reduce once you establish your tolerance. You need to be careful about how you spend your money: the more affordable the office space, the better. Depending on your market, it would be very difficult to get an office for less than $500 per month; but if you can, you should take it. Again, depending on your rental market, be leery of the office offered in excess of $1,000 per month. That cost may be excessive for someone just starting his or her practice. Of course, office space for a partnership with support staff and common areas will far exceed these parameters.

With respect to the various types of service providers you may lease from, each may be able to provide different types of referrals. Obviously, insurance salespeople or finance professionals who may be encouraging their clients to document their estate plan may be a good fit if you will be an estate planning lawyer.

Potentially, renting an office on the second or third floor of a bank building in your community might, for example, provide you with the ability to network with service providers who are also renting space from the local bank, or you may link up with the bankers themselves, who are talking to customers every day about financial information, disputes, growth in their business, and other financial matters.

Ask those service providers who their customers are. Remember, in an office complex with other service providers, you will not get the benefit of having your name and sign outside of the building. You will not necessarily have a retail presence. That is fine for your early start-up. You may need to compromise to be able to get out of the house and start practicing law in a professional office environment. Keep in mind that you need to have access to a conference room or an office that is somewhat presentable and professional enough to bring clients in to talk to them around your desk or around a small table in your office. The clients will take conscious and subconscious snapshots of your professionalism based on how you conduct yourself in your office. You need to get it right the first time. Remember the old cliché, "you only have one chance to make a first impression."

Retail-Type Space

Whether renting space with service providers or finding your own space, you may want to be on the first floor of a busy municipal street that has street-level frontage. This retail look can be good, and consumers (and business owners, for that matter) will see you at street level, and you will increase your chances for walk-in business. This is a fine strategy if your clientele includes individuals such as Chapter 7 bankruptcy clients, immigration clients, estate planning clients, or personal injury clients. If your professional practice is in pursuing these clients, a retail presence might be very good.

> You may want to be on the first floor of a busy municipal street that has street-level frontage.

You need to determine whether you can afford to rent a retail storefront on your own or sublet space from a similar service provider, as set forth in the earlier discussion. The difference between being in a mid-rise or low-rise office building versus a retail presence is that at the retail street-level, you will have exposure to clients and will potentially over time start building your brand (discussed in great detail in Chapter 26) through the visibility of your name to consumers who pass your office regularly. This strategy is worth pursuing based on your practice group. Look into it and evaluate its benefits.

Practicing in a Cooperative Suite

Years ago, a business model emerged that was rather ingenious. Landlords or business-minded tenants would build out a large office suite with ten to twenty private offices, with a series of about five to ten cubicles, and then rent each office to professionals at a rental rate that included the private office and the pro rata share of common area. They would also charge for services a la carte, such as the use of the conference room on an hourly basis or use of the receptionist.

These office suites work well and may be a little more expensive than the solutions articulated above. Many office suites are dedicated to the practice of law. In other words, these arrangements are set up where you can rent a private office and have your peers working around you. There are significant advantages to these arrangements, and you need to investigate those if they are available in your area. As set forth later in Chapters 11, 12, 13, and 26, lawyers will become a significant part of your referral network. You need to understand that early in the life cycle of your business.

In an office suite of lawyers, it would be beneficial if you were the only personal injury, criminal, real estate, or business lawyer in the suite. Understand the benefits of differentiated practice areas when sharing an office with other lawyers. Agree to go forward with such a rental arrangement only if there appear to be potential synergies. Do not agree to go forward if you are a real estate lawyer in an office suite full of real estate lawyers. The chances for conflict work to be referred to you might exist in that arrangement, but not enough on which to build a practice. Ideally, you want to be in an office suite of attorneys where you have a concentration or an expertise that no one else has. If possible, make sure your lease includes a prohibited practice group clause prohibiting the landlord from leasing to other lawyers practicing in your practice area.

Also, you need to evaluate whether your office suite has benefits and luxuries that really benefit you, or mean nothing to you but are included in your rent. Those perks might include

- A professional looking office surrounded and occupied by other lawyers and professionals;
- A person answering your phone;
- A nice, presentable conference room;
- A well thought through and organized phone system, which provides other services of call forwarding, and a nonattendant recording system;
- A small kitchenette that includes coffee for you and your clients;
- Other office equipment that you may not have, including high-speed scanners, copy machines, fax machines;
- Availability of renting office furniture that you otherwise cannot afford;

- Flexibility of lease terms (i.e., you may be able to rent month to month);
- Availability of built-in temporary secretarial service and other assistant services; and
- Potential for referral work from your peers.

The disadvantages are these:

- Generally high rents because you may be paying for items that may be unnecessary for you;
- Personalities of unknown professionals;
- Unknown and rotating practice mix of attorneys and other professionals in your suite; these suites tend not to be stable with consistent tenants;
- Lack of cooperation from your fellow suite members. Know that these are not your partners or associates, and everyone is independent. There is a chance that no one will work for any common good whatsoever. Therefore, you may be struggling against your own peers for conference room space, common courtesies, use of secretarial help, and finding the missing file.

In short, shared office suites are available and should be investigated to determine if sharing is the right option for you.

Location of Office

Have you ever noticed how many lawyers have offices in buildings near the courthouse? It takes attorneys many years to recognize this obvious phenomenon. Whether by coincidence or design, the fact remains that many lawyers set up an office near the courthouse in their area. It is interesting, in a strange way, that clients perceive this arrangement as being very favorable. They think "an attorney who has an office near a courthouse must be a real attorney!"

Whether this location has any bearing on the quality of legal work you provide (obviously it does not), client perception must be weighed in this regard and put on a scale of benefits versus your other office alternatives. For example, an office in a rural or suburban area near the courthouse, if everything else falls into place, is preferable to an out-of-the-way office.

However, if you are in a large municipal area or large city and want to capture the individual clients and want a retail presence, you will not necessarily be able to have your office near the courthouse. You would want to be in the neighborhoods and among your potential clients. Analyze all things that need to be weighed, but there is a perception among clients that being near a courthouse makes you a more active lawyer. Although this may seem an obvious point to make, access to public transportation, expressways, and expressway on-off ramps and exchanges all matter to clients. Remember, as you give your potential clients directions to your office, you will express the directions in a matter of minutes before you express them in a matter of miles, and having accessibility to your office is important.

Also, being near high-traffic areas, restaurants, and other social venues will help you entertain clients to enhance your visibility and professionalism. Certainly in the downtown area of a suburb, a train station, restaurants, and the proximity to an expressway are very valuable perks. In rural areas, there are usually commercial areas dedicated to power centers where people will shop for food, clothing, and other provisions; these area increase traffic and accessibility to your law office. Consider all of these things in the location analysis of your office.

Setting Up an Office Within a Law Firm

As you would do when setting up in an office suite, as discussed earlier, you can send out letters to all small- and medium-sized law firms within your municipality to see if they have the capacity and vacant offices they will rent to you. If a law office is downsizing, the ability to collect some rent off of vacant offices might be very appealing to the firm. Do not be afraid to send letters and make follow-up telephone calls to the managing partner. Certainly, if you are a business lawyer and this law firm solely does insurance defense work, the lawyers of the firm will not see you as a threat and your inquiry could lead to a very open conversation about synergies. If you are practicing in the same area of law, however, it may be problematic, and any arrangement simply would not work out. Nonetheless, practicing among experienced lawyers might be a very good idea for you if you need the mentoring and experience, having the established lawyers available to bounce ideas off when dealing with practice-related issues.

This is how I started. After the accounting firm had collapsed around me, I sent letters out to all the small- and medium-sized firms in the downtown area, followed up with phone calls, and met with two partners of a small law office, whom I now consider life-long friends.[2] We still refer cases to each other, and I have a wonderful professional and personal relationship with all of the partners and associates of that law firm. I consider myself lucky, notwithstanding that the accounting firm closed on me one week after I had been practicing law on my own.

---

2. I am very fortunate to have had that first meeting with Larry Gold and Ray Ostler. They are top-quality lawyers and friends whom I cherish as mentors. Similarly, I have grown tremendously as an attorney through my friendship with Bob Gomberg, a partner with Larry and Ray. Without the access to an office, and all the necessities to start a law firm provided to me by Gomberg, Sharfman, Gold & Ostler, Lavelle Law Ltd. might not exist.

Chapter 8

Departments in Your Law Office; Law Office Management

Although the notion may seem a little premature, you need to understand that there are certain law office management functions that can and should be departmentalized. This way, you can allocate a certain amount of time per week or per month for handling this work. Some of the functions may need to be addressed weekly or possibly even daily. Nonetheless, view these early on as departments, and as you build support staff and attorneys around you, you will need to allocate this work to trusted coworkers and, ultimately, your partners.

Banking and Bill Paying

Obviously, with accounts payable, you can write checks only to the extent that you have money in the bank. As a result, you will deposit incoming client checks several times per week into your various accounts, as set forth in Chapter 6, and write checks to pay your bills on Friday at the end of each week.

> Every month all of the bank accounts need to be reconciled to make sure errors have not been made, either by you or the bank, and to make sure your balances are true.

Sometimes this function is moved to the weekend if you are busy with client-related matters on Fridays. Remember, clients generally operate their businesses Monday through Friday, so sometimes these nonpracticing-law functions get pushed to the weekends or the evening hours.

Every month all of the bank accounts need to be reconciled to make sure errors have not been made, either by you or the bank, and to make sure your balances are true. There is no exception to this rule of reconciling your bank accounts. Every month reconciliation must be done on *every* account.

With respect to writing and posting your payables, your software program may have a system in place; otherwise, if you need an old-fashioned system, list every bill that comes in, when it comes in, on a ledger. These bills, under acceptable commercial terms (unless otherwise set forth in your agreement with the vendor), are payable in thirty days. If you post the bill coming in on a particular day, you will then pay that bill within thirty days thereafter on your banking day, whether it is a Friday or a Saturday.

With online banking, you can get the exact balance at any moment, have some sense of how many checks you have written that are outstanding, and then make an estimate of the true balance. If you review your banking on the same day of every week, again, such as Friday or Saturday, many of the checks that were paid on the previous Friday would have cleared, and your bank balance should be close to accurate. The exact balance is always made at the end of the month as you reconcile all of your checking accounts.

The banking and bill-paying function is an administrative task, but if and when assigned to a support staff member, it is also giving extensive authority to someone to learn about the cash flow of your business. This authority should not be taken lightly. Moreover, do not, at this very early stage, give anyone check-signing authority in your business. This restriction benefits both you and the person handling your books and records, for doing this takes the concept of fraud, embezzlement, and defalcation out of the equation for the person assigned the task of managing bank accounts. As protection against any fraudulent embezzlement, the banking module from your software system should provide a summary of checks that have been processed out of order or checks that have not cleared or are otherwise missing. This procedure will highlight patterns of problems if checks go uncashed for a long period of time, making your monthly reconciliations difficult.

In addition, eventually you will need to hire an outside accountant to look for inaccuracies, accounting mistakes, and banking inconsistencies. The accountant should not necessarily be charged with the duty of providing a forensic audit on the previous year's work or a full-blown audit on the current year. That would be very expensive and not necessarily the best use of your resources. However, an outside, disinterested accountant will be able to opine as to the systems put into place to avoid banking defalcations. The banking is an ongoing function that has to be managed weekly, preferably on the same day, and reconciled monthly.

Billing and Accounts Receivable

Chapter 9 of this book is dedicated to billing and managing income from the business's standpoint. However, the present chapter is intended to alert you, in essence the law firm and managing partner, that the department of billing and receivables is a separate function that needs to be regularly addressed.

Billing is done monthly, although, as discussed later in the book, timekeeping is done hourly and daily. The actual exercise of printing billing drafts, proofing, and reviewing for accuracy and substance is done monthly. It should be done within three days of the beginning of the following month, and all of your monthly bills should be sent out by the third day of the following month.

The billing time seems incredibly short, but there is no sense delaying your invoices once the previous month has closed. Keep in mind that this is a department that is directly correlated to the revenues of your business. Billing cannot be delayed. Bills cannot go out on the fifteenth or twenty-first of the following month. The credit card companies do not send bills out in that fashion. Utility companies do not send their bills out in that fashion. Your mortgage and rent payments are due within a few days of the monthly rotating schedule, so why not your billing invoices?

On the first day of the month, you should have all your bills printed, on your desk, and reviewed that day. Then, changes, credits, and cleanups need to be put into the system, and the bills need to go out on the second or third day of the new month. Once the bills have been copied or scanned and sent out to the client, the billing function is finished for the month.

> On the first day of the month, you should have all your bills printed, on your desk, and reviewed that day.

As a practical matter, you need to set up a system that creates the easiest possible way for clients to pay you. Of course, sending out bills requiring clients to write a check, stuff their own envelopes, put a stamp on those envelopes, and mail them to you seems pretty fundamental. But please keep in mind that you need to be as user friendly and as client friendly as possible. For this reason, give great consideration to accepting credit cards for payment of your fees. While the credit card process is somewhat costly (it will cost at least 2.5% for the amount of the transaction, in addition to all the other documentation fees, accounting fees, and billing fees, all of which are negotiable by your service provider), it is a necessary evil to practicing law and running a business in this economy. In addition, ask your credit card–processing company to include debit cards as part of the processing authorization. A lot of young people are moving toward using debit cards, and so having the ability to receive payment consistent with the banking trends of young clients is necessary.

Talk to your banker first to see if the bank has a preferred vendor for providing the merchant services for accepting credit cards. Remember to ask the merchant service provider whether you actually need to see the credit card or need a machine to scan the credit card. You will not want to have those kinds of arrangements. The vast majority of your credit card payments will come from people filling out a blank credit card form either preprogrammed into the bottom of your invoice or sent by way of a separate sheet of paper to fill out the credit card information and sign authorizing the credit card payment.

Explain that you will need to have the client choose between (1) making a one-time payment for your fees, (2) preauthorizing a payment of your fees every month when the bill goes out, (3) paying the retainer by credit card, or (4) making a monthly fixed payment by credit card. Then, you will need the amount of the charge authorized, the card number, the expiration date and card security code, the name as it appears on the card, the cardholder's billing address, and a signature of the client or an electronic e-mail authorization from the client.

An example of a credit card authorization can be found on the following page:

PAYMENT INFORMATION/AUTHORIZATION

For your convenience, John Smith Lawyers is now accepting payments by credit card. If you choose to submit a payment using this option, please complete the following information, place your signature below, and either mail or fax us this authorization form.

CHARGE AUTHORIZATION FORM

By placing my signature on this form, I hereby AUTHORIZE A CREDIT CARD CHARGE to be placed against my credit card account for the AMOUNT and FREQUENCY indicated by John Smith Lawyers. I HAVE READ THIS ENTIRE AGREEMENT AND UNDERSTAND THAT I WILL BE HELD FULLY RESPONSIBLE FOR ITS TERMS AND CHARGES.

✓　**CHECK ALL APPROPRIATE BOXES**

☐　I choose to make a *ONE-TIME* payment towards my monthly fees and charges by credit card.

☐　I choose to pay *EVERY BILLING PERIOD* towards my monthly fees and charges by credit card. I choose to pay my Retainer by credit card.

☐　I choose to pay my Retainer by credit card.

☐　I choose to make monthly payments of $ _____ on my credit card.
　　AMOUNT AUTHORIZED: $ _____

Please charge my (✓ one box) ☐ VISA ☐ Mastercard

Card No.: _____　Expiration Date: _____

CSC: (3 DIGIT CODE ON BACK OF CARD) _____

NAME on Card (exactly as it appears): _____

CARDHOLDER'S *BILLING* ADDRESS: _____

SIGNATURE: _____ (CLIENT MUST SIGN HERE)

PLEASE FAX SIGNED FORM TO: [FAX NUMBER]

If sending payment by mail, please send to: John Smith Lawyers
　　　　　　　　　　　　　　　　　　123 Elm Street
　　　　　　　　　　　　　　　　　　Anywhere, USA 12345

Once you gather this information authorized by the client, you can run it through your merchant's service provider, and you will receive the money shortly thereafter. Beware that you will need a minimum of two of these accounts with the credit card processor: one that directs the flow of funds to your operating account (for currently due monies) and the second one that directs payment into your IOLTA account for retainers. (See Chapter 6 for more details on bank accounts.)

Last, carefully analyze some of the Internet-friendly payment systems such as PayPal. These are very expensive and costly, however, and may not provide anything better than a credit card payment.

As your practice grows, you may be looking for user-friendly ways for clients to pay their bill through your website or some other Internet-based system. There is no doubt that the legal profession will be moving in that direction, and you should be aware of the opportunities that are out there for this type of client-friendly payment system. Above all else, make sure clients cannot gain access to information in your system that is confidential to other clients and that you accept only inbound payment information from clients and do not allow clients to extract information from your system.

> You, as the managing partner of your own sole proprietorship, need to be aware that the receivables cannot continue to grow.

Next, through your software system or a manually generated report, accounts receivable needs to be managed throughout the month. You, as the managing partner of your own sole proprietorship, need to be aware that the receivables cannot continue to grow. This is an obvious statement as to managing any business and, as the sole proprietor, you are trying to set forth this edict. The accounts receivable report should be in front of you every day as you engage in additional client work or have the strength to disengage from the work for clients who are not paying.

As the practice grows, the billing and accounts receivable function becomes critical and must be managed by a person (who could be an attorney) dedicated to this function.

Payroll

As a function of the banking and bill paying of the law office, you need to understand the federal tax obligations for payroll. Bring this subject up immediately with your accountant, but understand that as the sole owner of an entity, you will have an obligation to be a W-2 employee of the business. Being the owner does not exempt you from payroll tax obligations.

If you choose to operate as a sole proprietor, your income and expenses will be summarized on the Schedule C of your personal F-1040, and as part of that calculation, you will pay self-employment tax (the corporate equivalent of FICA tax) on page 1 of your F-1040.

If you choose to incorporate, you will be a W-2 wage earner of the corporation. As you receive payroll checks, you will need to withhold income taxes and also pay appropriately for your FICA tax obligations. All this information is summarized in IRS publication 15 (Circular E), which is the *Employer's Tax Guide*. In addition, you will have state-specific requirements for your jurisdiction's department of revenue and will be required to make unemployment compensation contributions to the agency that administers your jurisdiction's unemployment claims.

All in all, the foregoing is a complicated set of rules and regulations to follow, both with respect to withholding payment requirements for both the state department of revenue and the IRS, but also for the quarterly filings required by the state department of revenue, the IRS, and the state's unemployment administration office.

The good news is that payroll services, such as Paychex Payroll Services and ADP, perform all of these services for a reasonable fee. I strongly suggest you contact a payroll services company in the first three months of operating your law office to get quotes regarding what it will cost to have the company handle your payroll, even though it may just be your single check, for the law firm. It is incredibly inexpensive; using one of these companies takes the burden of all the Circular E calculations and filings off your shoulders.

Human Resources

It may seem illogical to be concerned with human resource issues at this stage in the life cycle of your firm. If you are a sole proprietorship or a small partnership, however, human resources are critical to manage. These are issues that you need to be aware of, so as you talk to other practitioners, go to seminars, or read articles on human resources, you are thinking about not only the present of your law office but also its future. Questions to consider include these:

- Do I need workers' compensation insurance?
- How do I go about getting health insurance?
- What is the most inexpensive and efficient way to post ads for help?
- How do other sole proprietors hire part-time assistants?
- What are the right questions I can ask when interviewing a new employee?
- How do I terminate an employee?
- What benefits do I give employees at a small law firm?
- What do employees expect, and what does the market dictate?

- At what times of the day do I need an administrative assistant the most?
- Can I afford to hire one part-time administrative assistant for banking and billing functions and a second for secretarial work?
- What is the market rate for salaries for administrative assistants in an urban setting? In a suburban setting? In a rural area?

Eventually, as the practice grows, you will have ongoing issues that are more than just about hiring initial administrative support and, you hope soon, attorneys.

You will be in an ongoing management mode. Initially, your staff will probably be paid by the hour, dictated by what the market will bear, but eventually you will migrate some employees into salaried positions. These decisions need to be made on a human resource level and are ongoing.

Support staff, administrative assistants, and attorneys are all human beings and have different needs in their life outside of work; as a result, unique and individualized issues come up regularly that need to be managed. You will come to be realistic, flexible, and understanding with an eye toward the bigger goal of running a law office that competes and prevails in its market.

Managing the people who work with you has legal, personal, and business implications. These folks will be an extension of your law office and have the ability to get clients and additional work for the office.

Marketing

Chapters 12, 13, and 26 of this book are dedicated to the various levels for marketing your law practice and their complexities. Your marketing plan will include identifying clients, generating leads among that population of potential clients, and converting those leads into clients. The person in charge of marketing has to balance between general branding of your law office versus potential clients calling to hire you for your services. Obviously the latter is preferred, but both are essential.

> Your marketing plan will include identifying clients, generating leads among that population of potential clients, and converting those leads into clients.

There is an enormous amount of work to perform and manage for the marketing manager, as well as for every professional working with you and for you. The marketing manager will need to review marketing efforts at least monthly. Those marketing efforts include writing articles, participation in chamber of commerce events, meeting with other attorneys and referral sources for lunch, setting goals for the following month, public speaking, civic involvement, and more. In addition, the marketing manager must manage the website, social media, blogs, and tweets. There is no short supply of work for the marketing manager. If done properly, the marketing manager's job may be the most time consuming of any job performed by any person in the office.

Technology

The legal profession's core function has to do with producing pleadings, agreements, and other deliverables in the form of paper at a time when the process for production and delivering services relies on technology more than ever. Everything from communications to document production is based on the functionality of technology. You need to be smart enough to know that there is an enormous amount of information that you do not know.

As a result, you are best suited to have an outside person come in and manage your technology information systems and to keep those systems current. However, you might be the technology expert in your law office and may be for a long time. Be cautioned that over an extended period of time, your billable hours may become compromised as you get bogged down in technology issues at the law office. You will become the Mr. Fix-it for everyone's computer if you allow that to happen. Eventually, and it might not be for years, you will need someone to head up your technology department.

The technology department includes the phone system and how it is integrated into your computer, the computers in everyone's office, laptops, tablets, and mobile devices that you will use on a regular basis, the server and the network system for your office, all the hardwiring and WiFi for the same, and then the integration of all of those systems with smartphones. As you can see, the technology in your office is somewhat overwhelming just to describe. But when functioning properly, it allows attorneys to work seamlessly on client matters at almost any location, almost instantly find documents that would otherwise take hours to find, and ultimately, through that technology, better serve clients. With that in mind, remember that as you grow your law office, that skill set needs to be developed or acquired with or by someone in your office as your business grows. Within time, all your attorneys will spend their entire day practicing law, your assistants will spend the entire day supporting those attorneys, and your IT person, whether part-time or consulting, will support your IT infrastructure.

Office Manager

The office manager does not really manage the attorneys and the attorneys' work product. Instead, the office manager's primary job is managing the administrative assistants and support staff. In a newly emerging law office, the office manager may also manage the bookkeeping, banking, and billing functions; in the very early stage of your law office, however, you would like an accounting professional to handle those financial functions.

The benefit of having a strong office manager is that attorneys, particularly you, the founding partner, can focus less on the management of the law office and more on generating clients, providing client services, generating revenue, and managing the administrative tasks of running the business function of the law office. The office manager manages a variety of nonlegal tasks involved in making sure supplies are adequate, coffee and soft drinks are available to employees and clients, and the day-to-day functioning of the office moves forward in an uninterrupted fashion.

> The office manager's primary job is managing the administrative assistants and support staff.

The office manager orders supplies and makes contact with the IT professionals for problems with computers. The office manager will also relieve you of time commitments, once that role can be delegated, from meeting with various vendors about online legal research, improvements to the telephone system, and office furniture, for example, to managing the administrative assistants.

Managing Legal Work

Managing the legal work of the attorney or attorneys working in the office can be done only by an attorney. At first, with you being on your own, you will handle this function. As the firm grows and additional attorneys are hired, you, as the senior attorney, will still manage that function. As you will see in Section 2 of this book, it is generally understood that a managing partner could manage about four or five attorneys, at the maximum. With a managing partner overseeing more than four or five attorneys, however, that partner would be operating at a superficial level in the cases and not understanding the nuances of the cases where discretionary judgment would be of value. As such, this function needs to be managed by an attorney—preferably you. The ratio of partners to associates needs to stay lower than 1:4 or 1:5, but not greater. (There is a far more in-depth discussion on managing legal work from a partner's perspective in Section 2 of the book.)

Chapter 9

Billing

A new, potential client walks into your office to discuss his or her legal problem with you. You have scheduled a time; the new client arrives, and the meeting begins. Usually, either before the meeting or at the beginning of the meeting, have new clients fill out a simple client intake form that asks for the client's name, address, telephone number, and e-mail address, the nature of the problem, and the referral source (or, "how did you hear about us"). Following is a sample of that form.

CLIENT INTAKE FORM

(Hand Directly to Attorney—Confidential Information)

Name: _____

Home Address: _____

Home Phone No. _____ Work Phone No. _____

Cell No. _____

Email: _____

Business Name: _____

Business Address: _____

Business Phone No. _____

How did you hear about John Smith Law? Were you referred to us?

_____

_____

_____

_____

_____

Brief description of your legal issue. (This will be kept strictly confidential.)

_____

_____

_____

_____

_____

Preferred method of contact: ☐   Email

☐   Phone (Cell/Work/Home)

☐   Letter

During the meeting, you should listen intently, take copious notes, provide preliminary thoughts on the case, and after making a determination that you could add value to the case and represent the client, engage in a conversation about being hired by the client.

Whether or not the client brings up the billing and legal fees issue, it is incumbent upon you to raise that issue and have a thorough discussion with the client regarding your billing practices. There are several fee arrangements attorneys use when being hired by clients. The first, the direct hourly billing method, is the most common. The second involves a flat fee whereby the attorney charges a fixed amount to handle the matter for the client. The third is the contingency arrangement. In a fourth fee arrangement, some business clients prefer a fixed monthly retainer amount. A fifth arrangement is "value" billing. There is also sometimes a hybrid for two or more of these methods. There are advantages and disadvantages to all of these types of billing methods.

Hourly Billing

If you and your client understand that you will be taking a case on an hourly basis, you will have the client sign a contract for legal services or a retainer agreement, and you will require a deposit from the client of a retainer amount of money.

Retainer deposits mean different things to many different lawyers. Traditionally, a retainer is a prepayment made by the client to assure the client that you are available for the client on an as-needed basis and that the client has an attorney, and the attorney a client. This amount would not necessarily be refundable, nor would it be applied to future legal services. It is earned when paid.

In some cases, a retainer acts as a security deposit on the client's account whereby the retainer would be deposited in a trust account, most likely the IOLTA account, and the law office would bill the client monthly. The client would pay the fees every month, knowing that the retainer (i.e., the security deposit) remained in the account in case the client were to default.

The third use of a retainer and the most common is a prepayment of legal fees that will be applied to legal services monthly until the amount is depleted, and then a notice would be sent by the law office to the client asking the client to replenish the retainer account. In this instance, since the retainer amount is still the client's money, it must be deposited in the IOLTA account.

Whichever of the aforementioned three methods used by you for your retainer deposits, make sure your contract for legal services clearly specifies whether the retainer deposit is earned by you, the attorney, when paid by the client or whether it is going to be held in the IOLTA for the benefit of the client.

Since this client coming in to meet with you will be hiring you on an hourly basis, either during the first meeting with the client or immediately after the meeting, send the client a contract for legal services for execution and request a retainer deposit. You should have a form to bring to all initial client meetings that has a space for the amount of the retainer (the amount of the retainer may vary depending on the type of case) and be prepared to secure the client in the very first meeting.

The elements of the contract for legal services should include the following:

- Clear identification of the client. You want individuals as your clients (even if the client has a business for which you are performing the work) because you do not want the business that may not have any assets to be the primary obligor under the bill. Require the owners of the business to be the primary obligors for the bill.
- Make sure the client understands that he or she will pay you by the hour and that the hourly rate may change from time to time, most likely annually, and that he or she will be bound by the terms of the agreement. Depending on your jurisdiction, courts will approve the changes in hourly rates so long as they are not abusive under the agreement. Don't hide your hourly rate from your client. Put it in writing if requested.
- Make clear the amount of the retainer and how it will be paid to you. Have a clear understanding that the retainer payment does not make this a "flat fee" case and that there could be fees due and owing after the retainer balance is depleted.
- Make it clear that disbursements, which are your out-of-pocket costs, are in addition to your legal fees and need to be paid by the client.
- Make the payment terms very clear under the contract. Your contract should ask for payment within ten days, which is reasonable, given the business that you are in.
- Bind yourself to diligence and hard work in furtherance of the client's needs. You cannot guarantee the end result in any matter for your client.

Following is an example of a contract you can use for legal services.

CONTRACT FOR LEGAL SERVICES

Name: _____   ("You") Home Phone: _____

Address: _____   Fax Phone: _____

Work Phone: _____   Cell Phone: _____

Referral Source: _____   E-mail: _____

Type of Matter: _____   Social Security No.: _____

This is to confirm our understanding concerning our representation of You with respect to the above matter. We, John Smith Law ("We"), shall be pleased to represent You in this matter at our hourly rates plus costs. Our hourly fees depend on the experience and position of the attorney or paralegal involved. If You continue to use our services beyond the above "Matter," You agree to be bound by the terms of this Agreement with our hourly rates as they may change from time to time.

We acknowledge receipt of a $ retainer ("Retainer") paid to us in connection with this matter. You understand and agree that until a Retainer check in the amount of $ _____ is delivered to our office at the above address, We have not agreed to represent You. You agree to deliver such Retainer to our office no later than _____. You understand that this Agreement is not a "cap" on legal fees, but is instead an Agreement for our office to perform our work on an hourly basis. You further agree to replenish your Retainer to its original balance on depletion or as requested by our office. The Retainer will be held in a trust account for the benefit of You, and then, monthly, the earned portion of the Retainer will be transferred to our operating account when earned.

Disbursements, which are out-of-pocket costs other than legal services (including but not limited to court filing fees, sheriff or special process server fees, express mail, long-distance telephone calls, fax and copy expenses, credit reports, etc.), which are made by us on your behalf are charged separately from legal fees and are distinctly separate in regard to billing.

Legal fees, charges, and out-of-pocket expenses will be billed to You monthly. You further agree to pay in full the amount of each such bill within ten (10) days of the billing date. If no comment or inquiry is received within thirty (30) days of the billing statement date, We shall assume that You have reviewed the bill and found it acceptable. If such payment is not made in a timely fashion, You agree to pay all the costs associated with the collection of this fee, including, but not limited to, attorneys' fees for the collection of the aforementioned fee. You agree to pay interest on any balance that remains unpaid after ten (10) days of the billing date at the rate of 1.5% per month. If You have been referred to our office by another attorney and, by our request, We require that attorney to spend time on your case relating to the above Matter. We will be responsible for the payment of the legal fees of the referring attorney, who will also be responsible to You for the performance of his or her services.

CONTRACT FOR LEGAL SERVICES (continued)

We agree to provide conscientious and diligent services and at all times will seek to achieve solutions that are just and reasonable for You. However, because of the uncertainty of legal and administrative proceedings, the interpretation and changes in the law, and many unknown factors, attorneys cannot, and do not, warrant, predict, or guarantee results or the final outcome of any case.

Signature _____ JOHN SMITH LAW

Print Name _____

Date _____ By: _____

Clearly, the foregoing example is a short, concise version of a contract for legal services. A written arrangement between an attorney and a client should not be longer than one page. You will see retainer agreements for large firms for specialized issues and retainer agreements that are five to six pages long. You do not want to put your client in the initial position of feeling that he or she has to hire an attorney to hire you. Make the agreement simple, with no legal jargon, and the service agreement should basically state that we, as attorneys, are going to work hard on your behalf, and you will pay us for our services.

> A written arrangement between an attorney and a client should not be longer than one page.

Make it clear that you will not start work until you receive:

1. A signed copy of the contract for legal services; and
2. The retainer deposit.

This is the first step to assuring that you will have a clear understanding with your client on legal fees. You need to be paid in advance and without delay. Without a signed contract and a deposit, you are not obligated to start work for the client (based on the terms of your contract for legal services), and you should *not* start work for them.

Keeping Track of Your Time

As indicated above, a software system for tracking your time is an important investment of resources for a law office. Invest in such software. Probably early on you will be balancing your time between several client matters, if not more. As you work on your cases, your billing clock begins when you start work on the case, and it turns off as you put that case away and move onto another matter. You are not expected to have a photographic memory, and so reacquainting yourself with the file may be necessary, especially on old cases. Engaging in client telephone conversations, giving clients advice, doing research, and drafting are all fair hours to track on your time and billing system.

Do not edit your time during the working day. Be truthful and accurate regarding the time you put in on a case.

You will see young attorneys, for example, work four hours on a research project and want to bill only two hours. Their efforts to conserve client money are admirable, but during the month is no time to edit down your efforts. If those inputs are to be reduced or edited down, it is at the end of the month when sample bills are being reviewed by you, and only then, such adjustments should be made.

There is a certain mentality that needs to be understood.

During the day your efforts should be in tracking your time, not billing your clients. All time keeping should be done contemporaneously with the work, not at the end of the day or at the end of the week. As such, if you have a day during which there are no marketing meetings, new client interviews, or other nonbillable work, you should track eight to ten hours (depending on the length of the work day) for client work. Avoid gaps between projects, and track all your time. Learn early on that this is an absolutely necessary skill for a successful law firm. If you do not track your time accurately from the beginning, you will not understand the leakage of time that occurs between projects, before and after lunch, as you settle in at the beginning of the day, as you wind down at the end of the day, and during various casual conversations with the people in your office. This leakage will have a devastating adverse financial effect on your business. Leakage of one hour per day, with about 250 billable working days in the year means 250 missed billable hours per year. At a billing rate of $150 per hour, you can lose up to $37,500 per year. At $200 per hour, you will lose up to $50,000 per year. See the importance of avoiding the leakage?

What does it take to track time accurately? Discipline.

Do not run out to take a lunch break until you have justified every hour of your morning in the office. If a certain portion of that time is dedicated to marketing or nonbillable telephone conversations with referral sources or cold calls from potential clients, track it and be aware of where your hours are going. If you do not have a billing system, use the grid provided on the following page; it is a simple form on which you can track the date of your entry, the client number, the matter number (if your client has separate matters going on that you want to bill separately), the client name, the time, and the description of the work. The form is pretty rudimentary, but it gets the job done. Nonetheless, this information still needs to be put into a format for billing purposes.

BILLING SYSTEM

Date:	Client No.	Matter No.	Client Name	Time	Description of Work

Name: _____

Hourly Rates

There is an enormous amount of discussion that goes into the definitive analysis of what an attorney's hourly rate should be. After all the analyses boil down, the beginning rate of between $100 and $150 per hour for an attorney right out of law school is a fair rate. The rate should increase annually until the attorney, being ten years out of law school, rates approximately $275 to $300 per hour. In keeping with that progression, a rate between $375 and $400 per hour is appropriate for an attorney approximately twenty years out of law school.

Let the debate begin.

These are parameters to use as guidelines. Instead of my preparing an entire treatise on the components that go into an hourly rate, it is best to provide you with guidelines and allow you as the partner in charge of your practice to determine what the appropriate hourly rate should be in your law practice. Consider any specialized study, practical real-world experiences, working with people outside of the law profession, and legal drafting or research experience.

In rural areas, the hourly rate is less and the increase in the hourly rate over time will progress at a slower pace. In large metropolitan areas, the hourly rate far exceeds the parameter set forth above, and justifiably so.

Hourly rates are sometimes difficult for the attorney and the client to accept. You must understand the background and history of your client as you are meeting with him or her. Remember, your clients may be people making $20 per hour or less at a job, and the reality of paying $150 per hour might initially sound quite astonishing to them. But do not be naïve. These clients may have friends who have hired attorneys, may know neighbors who are attorneys, or may have other interactions with attorneys and may be very well aware of what a reasonable billing rate is for a qualified attorney. Be honest, and up front in explaining your billing rate and the value that you provide. It is a marketing and sales moment.

If you are a new attorney and your billable rate is between $100 and $150 per hour, do not be ashamed to tell your potential clients that the rate is probably below the market average. Your rate is below the market average because you are building a business and want to make sure that the billing rate is not an impediment to getting hired. In addition, you may need to explain the components of your hourly rate, which include elements other than experience. The hourly rate includes your cost of running the business: your rent, your administrative assistant, your license costs, continuing education classes, all your insurance expenses, and other expenses that make the hourly rate of an attorney costly. Explain your rate, be proud of it, and be aggressive with your marketing pitch to the client. You, the attorney, need to be comfortable and confident when talking about your billing rate.

The next adjustment that you will have is when your billing rates pass through certain thresholds, which may become uncomfortable for you. You will reach this new, uncomfortable stage once your billing rate passes $200 per hour, $300 per hour, and $400 per hour. Again, do not be naïve. Do not discuss your billing rate with a lack of confidence. Your billing rate increases because you are a better attorney and presumably, when you are a $200-per-hour attorney, you should be able to do work almost twice as fast as a $100-per-hour attorney because of the experience a $200-per-hour attorney has compared to the younger attorney.

As your hourly rate goes up, your selling proposition to the client changes and matures. Also, and you may find this shocking, some clients feel a sense of comfort and additional confidence if they hire a more expensive attorney. Please do not take that view to be ridiculous or extreme. As your rate increases, your value increases too. Ten years from now, when you have a team of associates working with you on cases and your billable rate is over $300 per hour, you will be supervising

> You, the attorney, need to be comfortable and confident when talking about your billing rate.

cases with the work being done by a far lower-paid associate. In that case, the client will be getting the value of a lower hourly rate attorney (being supervised by you) to do the first round of drafting, gathering information from the client and opposing counsel, and doing work that otherwise does not require a $300- or $400-per-hour attorney.

Flat Fee Cases

Clients love flat fee cases. They are quoted by you as a fee amount that, once paid, completes the client's obligation to pay, and the transmission of the deliverables (or service) concludes the matter.

Take flat fee cases only when you are in control of all the parameters of the case or because the market dictates.

A perfect example of a flat fee case is the incorporation or setting up of business entities. When you meet with the client, have him or her fill out your "new business start-up" form, which provides you with all the necessary information. You then incorporate the client, set up the limited liability corporation, and obtain all the tax ID numbers. When the work is completed, the client is happy. Shareholder agreements and operating agreements are not included in the flat fee quote because the negotiation of those documents is outside your control and fees can escalate. Once that client completes the questionnaire of issues that you cover in your shareholder agreement or operating agreement, it is a good practice to quote a flat fee for the production of the first draft of that agreement, without the subsequent negotiations. As you can see, a flat fee quote by you gives the client comfort in his or her legal fee exposure and usually goes a long way to building a client relationship.

Be careful quoting flat fees for litigation cases, business negotiations, and most other matters where you are not in control of all the variables. You do not know what path that matter may take, and you will lose all the goodwill you have built up with the client on a previous deal if you quote a flat fee of, say, $2,000, and then need to go back to the client after the fact to ask for additional fees. Do not. Take the loss and learn your lesson. Client relationships are very important, and you can lose your creditability by quoting a flat fee for a client on a matter and then changing your mind.

You may also quote flat fees on residential real estate closings because the market dictates such a fee arrangement. Compared to the hourly time it takes to perform a residential real estate closing in your jurisdiction, you may take an enormous loss on legal fees. Usually these kinds of offerings are an accommodation for your clients so that they continue to hire you for all their legal needs and not just larger issues.

A note on the future of legal billing: clients love flat fee billing. So you need to keep an open mind to accommodate clients' needs and wants. As a result, on some occasions consider billing certain ongoing litigation matters and business transactions using a flat-fee-by-stage approach. In other words, even though you may not know how many motions to dismiss you may receive as a plaintiff in a commercial litigation matter, you would bill a flat fee through the pleading stage once an answer is filed by the defendant. You would then quote another series of flat fees during the discovery (i.e., each deposition), issuance and analysis of any interrogatories, and requests to produce, to name a few thresholds. A certain degree of legal work is moving in this direction, and creative fee accommodations for clients will always remain in the forefront of your practice management.

Contingency Fee

A contingency fee is a fee arrangement whereby you, as plaintiff's counsel, will receive a percentage of the success award of the case. Contingency fee arrangements work when you represent the plaintiff; you can easily ascertain the liability and the risk associated with representing the plaintiff, and there is a pool of money from which to collect. Simply stated, contingency fee arrangements are usually done for injured plaintiffs where a collection pool of money is coming from an insurance company.

Contingency fee arrangements work best for personal injury cases such as auto accidents, slip-and-fall cases, and medical malpractice. This arrangement also works for workers' compensation cases, torts, and other cases where an insurance company is financially behind the defendant.

You will also see contingency fee cases from collection attorneys who represent businesses on the collection of outstanding receivables, credit cards, and other simple business debts.

A problematic contingency fee case is one in which the client asks you to take the case based on how much money you can save him or her. For example, if your client is a defendant in an economic lawsuit or the government is trying to collect money from him or her, the client asks, "How much can you save me?" Be forewarned against accepting such cases on a contingency because the pool of money from which you will be paid is usually nonexistent. The client would need to deposit money with you up front for you to be assured that he or she has the funds with which to pay you at the end of the case. For example, if the government was trying to collect $1,000,000 from your client and you negotiated the liability down to $400,000 (thus saving the client $600,000) but took the case on a one-third contingency, does the client have $200,000 to write you a check? Be careful going forward with contingency cases when you represent the defendant.

With respect to the contingency fee contract, the elements that you need to set forth in the contract include a clear understanding of the contingency fee arrangement, the amount and percentage of your fees, clear language that the client is responsible for all out-of-pocket costs (and whether they need to pay those on a regular or monthly basis or you will reimburse yourself through the judgment award), and when your obligations end (usually through trial). Some contingency fee arrangements are set forth in stages whereby a certain percentage is set forth for your fee through trial (usually 33%) and an additional percentage will be added if the case is appealed (usually an additional 7%).

> Contingency fee arrangements work best for personal injury cases such as auto accidents, slip-and-fall cases, and medical malpractice.

Remember, the client makes the ultimate call as to accepting or rejecting any settlement proposals that you bring him or her. Therefore, if the client is being completely unreasonable and will not accept a settlement proposal that you believe is in the best interest of the client, you have made a wise contingency arrangement if the agreement has clear language stating that you have the ability to withdraw from the case, and the client will still owe you for your time put into the case. This arrangement becomes very problematic, however, when you have to share the contingency fee award with another attorney who substitutes for you; but please make sure you have the ability to terminate the agreement and stop representing the client when the client is being absolutely unreasonable.

The Monthly Retainer

Some business clients like the certainty and budgeting ability of a fixed monthly retainer paid to their law office. The advantage for the client, of course, is certainty and predictability, as well as the ability to have access to the attorney throughout the month without the hesitation to call about somewhat simple or mundane matters for fear of getting billed for every minute. The downside for the client, of course, is that he or she may not need your services much for a few months, yet he or she still gets a bill from the law office for the agreed-on retainer amount. Business clients are not naïve. They usually figure out a way to leverage the agreement so that they obtain the full value of their monthly retainer check.

This is a good thing.

For one, it certainly makes the client comfortable with calling you, and you become an integral part of their business, offering advice and sharing in their success. Also, a retainer invites the client to use your services to update customer contracts, bills of sale, purchasing orders, equipment leases, and employment agreements with key employees, all with the furtherance of being a business with a rock solid legal foundation and backbone.

The obvious downside for the attorney is that the client may abuse the arrangement and overwhelm you with legal work when the agreed-on fee is far lower than the economic hourly billing equivalent for the time you put in on the client work. Nonetheless, as with flat fee cases, mentioned earlier, you need to honor your agreement. Accept the monthly flat fee retainer and do outstanding legal work for all of your client matters.

The obvious takeaway from this discussion is that the amount of the monthly retainer fee needs to be well thought through between you and the client. A good basis for this type of arrangement is with a client you have been servicing for more than a year. In such case, you take the average monthly bill for the previous year and use that as a basis for the following year. Is the previous year's billing unusually low? Is it unusually high because of a large transaction or litigation matter in which you represented the client during the previous year? Those things need to be analyzed and incorporated in the agreement going forward.

What are the exceptions to the agreement? Traditionally, in corporate retainer billing work, the exceptions are litigation issues. Litigation issues are not in the ordinary course of business; therefore, litigation service is not included in the corporate retainer. However, if your client has regular ongoing litigation—either collection work, title disputes that a title company may have, foreclosure work that a bank or a lender may have, or replevin work that a personal property–based lender may have—it might need to be factored into the monthly retainer because litigation is the nature of the client's business. Nonetheless, a monthly retainer arrangement with a business client is a solid way to endear yourself to the client, become part of the client's management team, and begin a lifetime relationship between your law office and, you hope, a successful business.

The Hybrid Billing Methods

If you creatively took into consideration all the billing methods set forth above, you can see how some hybrid methods come about. There are some cases that you might initially take on an hourly basis but find that the client simply starts to run out of money to continue to fund the litigation; if you believe very strongly in the plaintiff's case, you may not want to withdraw from or dismiss the case. In some of those cases, you will continue to represent the client, thereafter with some negotiated contingency fee award for you upon the success of the case.

In some cases you may want a client to pay a monthly fee of $1,000 or $1,500 per month, in addition to 20%–25% of the judgment award at the end of the case. This way, your overhead for managing the case is somewhat covered by the monthly payment and then, in addition, you will receive a portion of the judgment award, though not the full one-third, which is a traditional recovery for an attorney representing a plaintiff.

In corporate business retainer work, all of your corporate compliance work and contract documentation and negotiation is covered under the corporate retainer monthly payment, but litigation is an exception; as such, litigation is paid for on an hourly basis. In those cases, you and the client must have an honest discussion in which you explain to the client that litigation is a great unknown for both the client and the attorney. Litigation is not part of the ordinary course of business, and as a result such cases need be dealt with on an hourly billing rate basis. Please keep in mind, you should never take the business risks of your client. You have your own business risks, and you cannot possibly absorb all of the risks associated with clients running their business.

Value Billing

You will see the term "value billing" come up in law office management books. Value billing is a way of saying that a client should pay based on the value of your services, as opposed to the hourly billing system that tracks the time you worked on the client's case.

Value billing discussions tend to come up in estate-planning cases, where you purchase or develop a form set of wills and trusts that when applied and modified properly and integrated into a high-net-worth client's estate planning add a tremendous amount of value. Such value includes tax savings and minimized postmortem litigation, which many attorneys bill based on the value of their services, as opposed to the hours put into the document preparation.

In some ways, contingency work can be put into this category. It is traditionally understood that a personal injury lawyer might take a case on a one-third contingency, thus establishing that the value of the lawyer's services equals approximately one-third of the total recovery for the client. As such, the attorney gets paid purportedly on the value he or she adds to the case. Without getting into a confusing value-added discussion on legal fee billing, note that it is a legitimate and ethical way to bill so long as the client understands the rationale and billing system at the beginning of the engagement. In most cases, value billing of estate planning is done on a flat fee basis whereby the attorney sets the value of his or her services at the beginning of the engagement with the client. If the client agrees with the fee arrangement and the attorney honors that fee arrangement, there is nothing unethical about that billing method.

However, as stated early on in this book, and time and time again thereafter, this is a business book. You must in your own case determine whether value billing is a legitimate method for staying competitive in the marketplace and, in fact, overtaking your competition. On behalf of the client and the legal profession, you need to work very hard to try to lower legal fees for clients and try to find ways to bring high-quality legal services to clients at a reduced fee. For example, find ways to produce high-quality estate-planning documents for clients that are based on an hourly fee billing method, delivering the highest-quality documents and services to clients. If that hourly bill is well below the market rate for the total deliverable, over time that fee difference in the marketplace manifests itself, and as a result your estate-planning volume will continue to grow. That is just one example of how you should view growing your business, providing the highest-quality work for your clients, and always keeping in mind that you need to find ways to reduce your legal fees without compromising your work product.

> You must in your own case determine whether value billing is a legitimate method for staying competitive in the marketplace and, in fact, overtaking your competition.

Remember, your law practice is a business, and you need to treat it like a business. In his seminal book on the workings of the Walmart world,[1] William Marquard talks about Walmart's circle of industry pressure that the company puts on suppliers and providers of service to bring costs down to Walmart, resulting in cost savings that Walmart then shares with its customers. As the volume of those lower-priced products increases, Walmart exerts additional pressure on its suppliers (and on itself) to reduce costs and pass through another turn of the cycle to then provide additional retail price reductions to its customers. Sounds like a pretty good business plan, right? Do not confuse this example, the sale of household items at Walmart, with the practice of law, however. The takeaway here is

---

1. WILLIAM H. MARQUARD, WAL-SMART: WHAT IT REALLY TAKES TO PROFIT IN A WAL-MART WORLD (McGraw-Hill 2007).

that big businesses constantly push for market share. The way to increasing the market share of your business is by providing better documents, better service, and at lower fees.

If you intend to capture the market in your area, you must fight and work to drive legal fees down to serve your clients. Recall how Ford Motor transformed the way of life for fifteen million families with the affordable Model T, known then as the "people's car."[2] They did it in large part by reducing prices for the Model T by 58% from 1908 to 1916.[3] Conventional wisdom was, at the time, that Ford had more orders than it could fill and could have *raised* prices.[4] In fact, shareholders filed suit against Henry Ford for his practice of lowering prices. In addition, in the same year, he raised worker salaries at roughly twice the industry standard at that time. In his book *Ford*,[5] Robert Lacey documents that the *Wall Street Journal* even accused Henry Ford of "economic blunders if not crimes which would soon return to plague him and the industry he represents as well as an organized society."[6]

Comparative companies such as General Motors did not fare as well during that time but stayed true to their chief Alfred Peace's corporate architecture and eventually built a successful corporation.[7]

The legal field is not that different. The only way the legal profession is different is that some clients do willingly pay a premium for high quality, and certain clients are willing to pay significantly more for very serious and significant matters, which may require the best attorneys at the largest law firms, at the highest hourly rates.

Again, it is important for you to synthesize the reality of the business exchange. Clients are very smart. Many clients understand that documenting their estate plan is not the same as documenting a Fortune 100 merger. Once you pass the qualification test (and many of your colleagues and competitors will pass the qualification test), then the clients still do some price shopping with respect to lawyers.

The last point on this issue is that you might as well be the attorney who upsets the marketplace by beating your competition. Someday someone else will, and then you will suffer a decline in business as a result of a young, smart, aggressive attorney in your area that wants to build a large, aggressive, successful law firm. Right now, that should be you.

---

2. JAMES C. COLLINS & JERRY I. PORRAS, BUILT TO LAST: SUCCESSFUL HABITS OF VISIONARY COMPANIES 53 (Harper Business 1994).

3. *Id.*

4. *Id.*

5. ROBERT LACEY, FORD: THE MAN AND THE MACHINE 179 (Valentine Books 1986).

6. *See id.*; JAMES C. COLLINS & JERRY I. PORRAS, BUILT TO LAST: SUCCESSFUL HABITS OF VISIONARY COMPANIES 53 (Harper Business 1994).

7. JAMES C. COLLINS & JERRY I. PORRAS, BUILT TO LAST: SUCCESSFUL HABITS OF VISIONARY COMPANIES 54 (Harper Business 1994).

Miscellaneous Notes on Billing

If you as an attorney do not bill, you do not get paid. Billing is an inevitable and real function of operating a business. The act of sending out bills takes discipline, and asking or expecting clients to pay them when due is not pleasant. You need to accept this reality if you intend on operating a successful business. Invoicing should go out, as set forth above, immediately at the end of the month; receivables should be tracked carefully; and client contact needs to be made thirty days after the bill has been sent but remains unpaid. Billing, especially hourly billing, needs to be made with the utmost honesty and integrity by you and every single attorney working in your office. Very early in my career, I caught a young attorney billing time for work that was not done. Overstating the hours an attorney works on a matter is a terminable offense. Once I established conclusively that this young attorney was overbilling (by a matter of hours), the attorney was terminated and asked to leave the office immediately. There is no way the integrity of your law office should be questioned on an issue of such importance as the veracity of your billing system.

> Billing, especially hourly billing, needs to be made with the utmost honesty and integrity by you and every single attorney working in your office.

Honest mistakes happen. Intentional acts of fraud cannot exist under your watch. Is truthfulness and integrity a virtue for an attorney and his or her billing practices? It is more than a virtue—it is a prerequisite. You should not even be in this business if truthfulness and integrity are not embedded in your DNA. Attorneys who lose their way give all honest, hardworking, ethical attorneys a bad name and an image that the legal profession constantly needs to redeem. It is interesting to note that the integrity issue comes up most with attorneys when it comes to handling money and billing. That is why this discussion is important in the billing chapter of this book. Integrity will help you build a career of truthful client relationships. The lack of integrity will damage your business and damage our profession as a whole.

Chapter 10

Collections

If there is any one chapter in this book that could create the "secret sauce" to solve all of your practice problems, it would be this chapter on collecting receivables or, better yet, avoiding having any receivables at all in your law office. This chapter will probably not provide that magical potion, but it will provide a great disciplined approach to execution. As long as you learn the correct way to avoid accounts receivable that can put you out of business early in your career, and you execute this system in a disciplined manner, you will have no problems eliminating accounts receivable.

Every month, no matter what billing method you use, you need to send out bills to clients and need to get paid on time, the exception being the contingency fee arrangement. This process is very difficult, especially for young practitioners who do not have well-established clients with legal fee budgets. This results in the young attorney primarily doing work for individuals and start-up businesses. Truthfully, even if an established business has an understanding of the cost of legal services, does the business really have legal fees built into its budget? Probably not, and as a result, bills from the business's attorneys do not nec-

> What is the best way to get paid on your accounts receivable? Do not have any.

essarily get paid on a regular interval like bills from the utility companies, mortgage debt, lease payments, and payroll. Legal fees are generally outside the ordinary course of business for most businesses, whether they admit it or not.

What is the best way to get paid on your accounts receivable? Do not have any. This is a utopian type of existence that rarely happens, but the concept of not having receivables forces you to work backward through the entire process of sending out bills to maximize your ability to get paid immediately. There are several rules in the billing process that you need to adopt to maximize the positive cash flow for the business.

Create Detailed Specific Bills

When you are keeping track of your time and describing the work you have done for the time interval in which you bill, be detailed and descriptive. Avoid "reviewing contract," "telephone conversation with client," "drafting agreement," and similar short descriptions. These are little summary snippets of what you have done. A better approach is to describe your half hour as "working on the indemnity clause in the distribution agreement between client and ABC Steel," "redraft the hold harmless language," or "telephone call with client regarding request to admit and discussion on the scope of client's liability insurance."

See how the two differ? Obviously the client needs to see the scope of the work as it compares to the amount of time put in. Clients are very unhappy about paying for work that they believe takes only ten minutes and receiving a bill for the true half hour, for example, that it took you to do the project. They need to see in the description the detail of time that then leads them to the obvious conclusion that you spent all the time on that particular nuance of an agreement, or lawsuit, for which you billed them. Detail on your bills is imperative.

Some law firms just put a summary bill together stating how many hours the law firm worked on a case and send out a bill with no detail broken out subhourly.

You will never hear a client say that you put too much detail on the bill. Clients will certainly complain, however, if you do not put enough detail on the bill.

Clients want and deserve the details of your efforts on the bills. If you think that giving them too much detail provides them with information with which to contest your bill, you are largely wrong. Certainly, every now and again a client may call up and say, "I did not talk to you for fifteen minutes on that day, why did you bill me for 0.25 hours?" Certainly you need to have an answer ready for those types of calls, and the answer may just be that the client is wrong. Nonetheless, detailed billing is mandatory, not just good practice.

Further, sometimes when you want to build goodwill with the client or you simply spent too much time on a matter getting up to speed on some new issues on the law that affect your client's case, you might enter "NO CHARGE TO CLIENT" on your timesheet and still provide all of the great details of what you have done, thereby simply not charging the client for that time. Remember, as set forth in the previous chapter, you make your "NO CHARGE TO CLIENT" adjustments at the end of the month when you are reviewing sample bills, not when you are entering time into your daily ledger. "No charge" entries build up an enormous amount of goodwill with the client, and you should log these entries when appropriate.

Keep in mind not to give away an enormous amount of time for your legal services; in reality, however, not charging is fair if you spent time researching or refreshing your knowledge on a pretty basic issue of law that you should have known. You need to provide those free investments into your client's business or personal life.

Also, determine whether you will bill in increments of 0.1 of an hour (six-minute intervals), 0.25 of an hour (fifteen-minute increments), or some mixture of the same. Also find out what the local rules are in your jurisdiction in court for getting court approval for your fees in certain practice areas such as divorce and bankruptcy. Chief judges may require detailed hourly billing. In either case, as set forth above, truthfulness is mandatory, and if you do bill in quarter-hour increments but do not reach fifteen minutes of work, you simply "no charge" the client for what you did during that time. Or over the course of the day, if several short phone calls or brief e-mails aggregate to 0.25 of an hour, thoroughly describe that in the description section of your bill and aggregate that work into 0.25 of an hour. Obviously, never charge the client for a minute more than you have actually worked on his or her case.

Have the Client Sign a Contract and Deposit a Retainer Check

Abraham Lincoln taught the legal profession the rule of having the client sign a contract and making a prepayment retainer deposit with you at the initiation of all legal services so that "the client knows he or she has an attorney, and the attorney knows that he or she has a client."[1] This is an important first step in developing an understanding with a client that (1) he or she is bound by a written agreement and (2) the legal fees need to be paid up front so that you will not finance any litigation or business transaction for the client.

These terms are not as harsh as they seem.

Clients do understand and expect that this is a real relationship being developed, and a simple contract as set forth in the previous chapter gets the point across; furthermore, the prepayment of legal fees also demonstrates your professionalism. This is the simplest and easiest way to separate true clients from "pretenders." With you being the only person in charge to make an exception to this rule—the client cannot do so—make sure all new client matters start with a signed contract and the retainer check deposited with your office.

Make sure to reassure clients that the retainer check will be deposited in your IOLTA account, which remains client money until you earn it. Therefore, if they have a change of heart and decide not to pursue the matter of litigation or they decide to fire you, they will always be able to receive a refund of the unearned portion of the retainer check.

Further, if a client simply cannot afford to pay you, you either have to make a determination not to take the case and refer the client to a legal clinic in the area, possibly at a local law school, or ask the client if he or she knows of any family members or friends who would guarantee the legal fees. If others guarantee payment, a different type of

---

1. Lauren A. Calloway & David J. Bilinsky, *Financing a Law Practice* (GPSOLO Jul./Aug. 2011), *available at* http://www.americanbar.org/publications/gp_solo/2011/july_august/financing_law_practice.html.

retainer agreement needs to be executed between the parties whereby the guarantor will still not be privy to attorney-client privileged information but will guarantee the legal fees.

Focus on the Thirty-Day Delinquency List

In a perfect world, clients pay the required retainer, and throughout the month you work down that retainer balance; at the end of the month, you send out a bill demonstrating to the client the amount of the retainer that was earned by you; then, as part of the banking transaction connected to that bill, you transfer money that you earned on the client matter out of the IOLTA and into your operating account. Once that client has little or no money in his or her retainer account at your law office, you need to ask for an additional retainer deposit to replenish the retainer account. And if life moves in a perfect cycle, every month as you bill, you transfer money from the IOLTA account to your operating account, and you never have any accounts receivable.

> The biggest mistake attorneys make is not addressing accounts receivable problems until they start running short of cash.

Accounts receivable, as defined by accountants, are accounts under which you have earned your fees and are waiting to be paid. If the bill is not paid within thirty days, it is considered a thirty-day past due receivable; a bill not paid within sixty days is considered a sixty-day past due receivable; and so on. Track receivables for 120 days, and at the end of the 120-day period decide whether to sue the client for fees or write the balance off as bad debt. If you have too many receivables that reach the 120-day cycle, you are simply putting your livelihood at risk and the law practice in jeopardy of closing. You cannot possibly pay your rent, supply costs, utilities, payroll, and telephone bills on an ongoing monthly cycle and allow clients to pay you 120 days late. Even if they pay you 120 days late, they had used your money for 120 days and probably will pay no interest on that money, notwithstanding the fact that your billing software program allows you to add interest to past due balances.

Moreover, accumulating large amounts in accounts receivable will put you out of business. You cannot pay your employees with accounts receivable, you cannot pay your home mortgage with accounts receivable, and you cannot pay for gasoline for your car to go to and from work with accounts receivable. All of those debts are paid with cash, and if your clients do not pay you in cash, you cannot survive.

The biggest mistake attorneys make is not addressing accounts receivable problems until they start running short of cash. That is a very unbusinesslike way to run this function of your business. Do not operate on needs, operate on behaviors. The behavior and discipline you need to instill here is to take action and to stay on top of the thirty-day receivables notwithstanding the bank balance in your account. The longer clients do not pay, the higher your accounts receivable balance increases. For obvious reasons, cash paid to your office is better than the growing accounts receivable.

Whether you are a sole practitioner, beginning to institute the strategic foundations for a successful business, or in a small law practice, remember that *all* attorneys working on matters at your law office are responsible for managing the receivables and getting paid by clients. This concept cannot be stated clearer than that. No one attorney should be the collection attorney on everyone else's matters. If you assign an attorney to be the project manager on a particular file, and that project manager–attorney fails to manage the accounts receivable, such failure should be reflected in the year-end review and bonus of the attorney. You cannot possibly pay an attorney a bonus when the attorney's failure to manage the accounts receivable has cost you money.

There are a few things that everyone needs to understand regarding your company policy on accounts receivable and the obvious truisms for running a business that does not collect on receivables:

- You will pay all your bills (including your paychecks to support staff and attorneys) to operate your business on time, and your payment cycle for paying bills is every two weeks to thirty days. If clients do not pay in sixty or ninety days, the firm will run out of cash and not be able to meet its expenses.
- Your retainer contract indicates that all clients must pay in ten days of a billing invoice. After thirty days, when you need to call the client on a past due account balance, you have already given them a twenty-day grace period for payment. Remind them of this.
- Always circulate a thirty-day, sixty-day, ninety-day and litigation imminent list, but really believe that your emphasis should be on the thirty- and sixty-day lists. Sometimes after 90 and 120 days, people have trained you to accept late payments. You need to retrain your attorneys and your clients. The more aged an unpaid balance becomes, the more unlikely it becomes that you will be able to collect the balance.
- If billing occurs as a relaxed, nonaggressive, nonimportant matter, clients will accept that this is your policy and that you view payments nonchalantly and nonaggressively. That perception needs to change immediately and never be fostered.
- The exceptions to these rules are to be made by you, not the associates.
- When you review the collection report or circulate the collection lists among the attorneys to find out information regarding the receivables, the attorneys, not you, need to call clients immediately to find out about payment. An e-mail is good in some instances, but a telephone call is mandatory.
- Ask for monthly credit card charge authorization.

The following is a list of answers to questions or comments that will come from clients:

Q: Is that all you people worry about, money? I wish you would worry about my case the way you worry about money.

A: We do care about your case deeply. We have done everything we promised we would do, aggressively representing you. But the reality is, we cannot work for free, and we cannot pay our bills on accounts receivable. Just imagine if all clients paid late, we would never be able to pay our employees, and I would not get paid. Your bill needs to be paid in full within a week, or we will have to withdraw our representation.

Q: I am sorry, but I have no money; can you continue to represent me? Or, what am I supposed to do?

A: I appreciate your honesty, but when we started this case, you indicated to me that you could pay our fees. Even though the fees have exceeded both of our expectations, this was somewhat unexpected because of [_____]. You need to pay us. If you cannot afford our law firm, I would be happy to work with you on trying to find a legal clinic at a law school that could take over your case. However, your being transferred to a legal clinic does not release you of your obligation to pay us.

Q: What do you mean I owe you money? I never received any bills!

A: That is odd, but let me check the address on the bills. [Once you confirm that the address on the bills is accurate, call the client back immediately.] I confirmed that the address on the bills is accurate. If you had not received any bills within the last few weeks [or months], why didn't you call me? I will e-mail you the bills now, and we need to be paid within a week. You understand, correct?

Q: The check is in the mail.

A: When did you send it out? How much was it made out for? When should I expect to receive it? If I do not receive it on that day, I will call you again and tell you that I did not receive it because that would indicate that the check is lost in the mail, and you should stop payment on it.

Q: Would you let me pay my past due balance over time?

A: We have allowed you to pay over time by sending you your monthly bills. We are concerned about your balance and need to make sure it does not increase further by our continuing to bill time.

Q: There are mistakes on the bills.

A: Send us a payment for the charges that are correct. For the remaining portion of the bill, fax or e-mail me a copy of the bill with the portion claimed to be wrong highlighted. I will then review and, if necessary, make the proper corrections.

Q: I do not have any money.

A: Can you borrow money or use a credit card? Can a family member pay us? Guarantee our fees? We cannot work for free, and I know you understand that.

In the seminal book *The Three Laws of Performance: Rewriting the Future of Your Organization and Your Life* by Steve Zaffron and Dave Logan,[2] you learn that humans react to new concepts and new roles based on how the world has "occurred" to them and, more important, as the "event" has occurred to them in the context of their life. This is a very important insight into attorney billing and collecting on receivables.

If the client has never hired an attorney in the past, it will take a few billing cycles for the client to understand your expectation of payment for your services. If the client has dealt with attorneys in the past, the billing and collection of the legal fees has already "occurred to them" in another context, and they will understand and be somewhat predisposed to accept how the billing and payment cycle goes with attorneys.

You need to educate new clients so that it "occurs to them" that your law office works in a disciplined, emphatic fashion and that your legal fees contract may say ten days, but they will receive a telephone call and an e-mail in thirty days requesting payment. If you are not training them, they are training you to accept late payments.

Remember this: if it is not important to you to receive payment on your legal fees, it will not be important to the client to pay. Although you may shout, "It is important to me!" your actions speak more authoritatively than your internal voice that sits behind your desk and wonders why the client is not paying. For all the reasons set forth, then, your expectation of payment needs to "occur to the client" very early in the relationship in a consistent, disciplined fashion for you to maximize the ability to reduce your receivables.

Finally, as set forth in Chapter 15 on best practices, for some unexplained reason clients love paper. Inundate them with information, preferably with paper. E-mails are good, but letters are better. Make sure that you send copies of all drafts of agreements to clients because they will be billed for the work you do for them and, therefore, they need to understand what you are doing to justify that bill. Make sure, again as set forth in Chapter 15 of this book, that they get copies of every court order, summary letters at the end of every month on their case, and even, if necessary, internal memoranda summarizing research that has been performed for them, summarizing meetings held with opposing counsel or witness interviews. Clients need to see the work product, and when they do, they will pay their bills. How could they not?

There is no question that this is a very difficult process, but keep in mind that clients pay a significant fee for good legal services (experienced attorneys' hourly fees are very high), and they deserve top-quality service and transparency of the work that you provide for them.

---

2. STEVE ZAFFRON & DAVE LOGAN, THE THREE LAWS OF PERFORMANCE: REWRITING THE FUTURE OF YOUR ORGANIZATION AND YOUR LIFE (Wiley & Sons 2011).

Payment Plans

Once you have done everything you can to provide top-quality legal services for your client, and the client is struggling to make payments, the question comes up as to whether or not you should accept a payment plan in lieu of the full payment every month.

A payment plan during an ongoing matter does not really make much sense unless you are willing to completely nullify the fee arrangement with the client and go on a monthly retainer or employ some hybrid method whereby the client agrees to pay a monthly amount regardless of the amount of work done until the full amount of the balance due and owing to your office is paid in full. These types of arrangements are oddities that seldom, if ever, work.

For example, clients usually come up with these ideas after they owe you $5,000 or $10,000 and suggest paying you $500 a month if you keep working on their case. Well, if you keep working on their case, it is highly likely that you will have months where you will exceed $500 of work on their case, and thus the balance just keeps getting larger, which is completely contrary to your goal of eliminating accounts receivable.

> If you decide to change the billing arrangement with a client, make sure you do so in writing, thoroughly discussing it with the client, and have the client sign off on the amended billing arrangement.

You will eventually talk at length with clients about hybrid billing methods that you might be willing to convert to in the middle of an engagement to demonstrate to the client that you can be flexible on fee issues, but really the original billing arrangement (i.e., paying on a monthly basis) has failed, and it seems unlikely that any conversion regarding an alternative payment plan, such as fixed monthly payments, will really work out in the long run.

If you decide to change the billing arrangement with a client, make sure you do so in writing, thoroughly discussing it with the client, and have the client sign off on the amended billing arrangement. This documentation is important because if you later need to sue the client for fees, you will have to demonstrate that there has been an amendment to the billing arrangement and that on the particular day the client executed the amendment, the client was pleased with your services, acknowledged the amount of the debt, and agreed to be bound by the debt and the further accrued obligation going forward.

In some cases, after the case is over a large receivable is pending and you are faced with having to collect this large debt. In these cases, a reasonable payment plan seems to make sense as an alternative to suing the client for fees and taking the attendant risks that go along with bringing a lawsuit against the client. You should develop a payment plan that is acceptable to you and make it a policy available in your office so that clients do not feel the necessity to negotiate your proposal. For example, 20% down? 30% down? And the balance paid in equal monthly installments over the next ten months? Or should the balance be paid over the next twelve months? No matter what your payment plan policy, it should not be a negotiable issue with a client.

Unfortunately, clients put themselves in this situation either by being a plaintiff or defendant or a party to some commercial transaction in which they elected to be involved, and now the client's legal fees are due and owing. A $100-per-month payment plan on a $10,000 bill is virtually worthless. The present value of that payment plan is probably not even worth $500 because the client will inevitably default every few months. Remember, the client has already received all of the services needed from you, and now this is a debt hanging over his or her head. The likelihood of a continued payment stream is almost nil.

If you are confronted with a payment plan arrangement, make sure the client signs a promissory note or make another arrangement that could be subject to a summary proceeding in court if the client defaults. Make it very clear that the client must sign a document stating that if he or she defaults on the payment plan, the full amount becomes due and owing immediately, and make sure the client acknowledges that the balance is due and owing.

In summary, a payment plan arranged while work is ongoing is usually a bad idea. Think carefully before entering into some sort of an arrangement whereby the client is basically acknowledging that he or she cannot afford your legal services as you work on the case. Payment plans at the end of the engagement are certainly better than filing a lawsuit against the client for fees, but the amortization of the payment plan needs to be reasonable. Payment plans extending beyond one year have a high default rate; therefore, be careful with those negligible monthly payments.

Handling Client Complaints About Bills

Unfortunately, but inevitably, clients will call to complain about their bills. These complaints will come in one of three categories.

The first is when there is a prima facie mistake such as "telephone conversation with Internal Revenue Service regarding payment plan" on a bill for a client on which you are preparing an estate plan. This type of obvious mistake is unequivocally an error.

The second category involves errors you determine as such. For example, you spend an excessive amount of time on a particular matter or item that should not have been passed through to the client.

The third category of complaints is straightforward. For example, a bill has been prepared absolutely correctly, but the client just does not want to pay.

With respect to the first category, the prima facie mistake on the bill, you need to apologize profusely to the client for that mistake, immediately issue a corrected bill crediting the client or taking the wrong entry off the bill, as appropriate, and sending it to the client. It was your mistake, own the mistake, apologize for it, and make the correction. In fact, in some instances, actually thank the client for pointing out the error because correcting your errors helps make you a better law firm. In addition to being a little embarrassed by the mistake, make the client feel appreciated for the time he or she took to point out the mistake and for you to correct your mistake. Remember, the client invested his or her time to correct your mistake, so acknowledge it as such.

The second complaint category, the mistake of allowing excessive research time or drafting time to post to the client's bill, is problematic. Mistakes happen, and this kind of mistake may happen—but it should not. This is a major problem for your law office if this type of mistake regularly happens and goes on unchecked. What you will be inviting the client to do is to check your bills regularly and fight about the amount of time you put in on projects. This is a tragic mistake because as noted earlier, clients will only learn how to talk about bills with you as that conversation "occurs" to them the first time they challenge a bill. In other words, if they challenge you on six hours of billing time on a particular document, and you acknowledge the mistake and reduce the bill to three hours (which might be the more appropriate charge), you have taught them that if they are unhappy with the bills, they should come back and challenge you, and then you will reduce certain entries by 50%. This is a terrible practice to be caught in with your clients. Notwithstanding the foregoing, you must still do what is right to make the appropriate adjustment on the bills.

> Once a bill is approved by you to get sent out to the client, you must be steadfast in your belief that the bill is accurate, and you should be paid for the entire bill.

This type of billing error should not occur because you need to proof every one of your draft bills or sample bills before they are converted to final bills and sent out to the client. Watch carefully for this exact entry mistake. Once a bill is approved by you to get sent out to the client, you must be steadfast in your belief that the bill is accurate, and you should be paid for the entire bill. If you proofread in haste or are sloppy in your proofing of the bill, these errors will occur, and the integrity of your billing system will be called into play with such clients for the rest of the relationship. You do not want to create a give-and-take relationship with the client about your bills. You do not want to create a suggestion that bills are negotiable and that you overinflate bills to see who will pay them, expecting to negotiate the bills after you have sent them. This is no way to run a business and no way to maintain your integrity in the billing process and in the practice of law with your clients and referral sources. Reviewing sample bills before sending out the final bills to clients is critically important for the betterment of the firm and the betterment of the client relationship. Once the bill is absolutely accurate and correct, send it out to the client. If the client complains about a proper bill, then those complaints fall into the third category of client complaints.

Sometimes the clients just complain about bills because legal fees can be expensive and the clients needs a place to vent about them. Respond to this type of complaint by following a very strict set of rules, or take these calls and cajole the clients to make them comfortable paying those bills. Remember, if you compromise the bills that are correct, you are inviting a monthly conversation with these clients to renegotiate their bills.

If you get a call from a client to complain about a bill that is absolutely accurate, understand that the client may have very little experience in dealing with lawyers and understanding the expense involved in legal services (although you should have made good estimates to the client in your initial consultation), or the client really cannot afford your law office. Remember, for individuals, more so than businesses, the expense of hiring a law firm is not ordinarily included in their monthly budget; as a result, the bills they receive from your law office are over and above their regular monthly expenses. Therefore, it is difficult for them to come up with the money to pay those bills as they come due. Unlike personal monthly budgets, many businesses, especially medium- and large-sized companies, have budgets for paying legal fees; they have paid legal fees in the past, and they understand the cost of legal services. Often, small businesses are shocked at the cost of legal services.

If you choose to hear out the clients and let them vent to you about their bills, be empathetic and explain to them that you understand that legal services are expensive; try to transition the anger and hostility away from your law firm to the cost of legal fees in general. If you can transition the target of the client complaint, you can get on a client's side and basically say, "I know it is very expensive, but legal services are expensive, and we are trying to perform the service for you as inexpensively as possible, and I do not think any law office in the area is less expensive than we are." Subtly remind clients that they have chosen the right law office, that you are working very hard at keeping legal fees down, and that you still want to be on their side to advocate for them. Do not compromise the bill if the bill is correct.

The more direct route to take with client complaints about bills that are absolutely accurate is to tell the client, "The bill is accurate. In fact, because our office is working on this, it is far less costly than the market demands for this work, and I would appreciate your paying the bill within the next ten days." The delivery of legal services is different than the delivery of necessary living expenses such as rent and utility bills, but from your standpoint, you cannot spend the time talking about accurate bills with clients who have the money to pay but do not want to pay. Use the "three strikes and you're out" approach to client complaints on bills that are accurate. The first time, state that you are not going to discuss bills and the client should pay them pursuant to your contract. The second time the client calls to complain about a bill that is absolutely accurate, remind him or her of what you said the first time, and do not engage in any further conversation about the bill. You may also suggest to clients that maybe they are just calling to complain about the bill because they cannot afford a lawyer or your law firm and that you would be very pleased to work with them to transition the case to another lawyer or a law clinic in the area at a local law school. Remember, you want to sincerely help your clients, and if the clients cannot afford your law office, they may be better off at a clinic at a law school. At the suggestion of referring them to a law clinic, they may concede that they cannot afford you as a lawyer, and it may be a good professional approach to part ways. On the other hand, a client may also step up and say, "No, no, no, I can afford you, and I do not want a law student working on my case. I want you working on my case." This is a reaffirmation that the client understands that you are doing a good job and are working hard on his or her behalf. If this conversation occurs a second time the client complains about a meritorious bill, you are sending the signal that you are not happy about these conversations and you are not interested in having these conversations any further. Again, be honest with clients and be sincere about trying to help them. If they cannot pay you, then you do not need to continue to represent them. Remember this is not about pro bono. The legal profession wants all attorneys to engage in *voluntary* pro bono work, not involuntary pro bono work. Wish the client well and try to do what is right by the client.

The third time clients call to complain about a bill that is absolutely accurate should be the last time. At that point in time withdraw from the case, explain to them that you cannot talk about bills constantly with your clients and that you need to part ways with them. Again, you want to wish them well, take the high road and transition them to another lawyer, and make the transition as seamless and as beneficial as possible for the client.

You are in it to practice law and to help clients. It is doubtful that the clients call the mortgage company every month, or the electric company, or the gas company to complain about the amount they have to pay and, therefore, you need to simply concentrate on doing the best, high-quality legal work for clients that you possibly can without taking the time to talk through accurate bills. The bill is what it is. You have reviewed it and feel confident that there are no errors on the bills and that the client should pay the bill. Certainly, you need to be sensitive to the client's concerns. Remember, a client's reaction to your bills may be a result of the client's dealing with other attorneys in the past and how the client learned to deal with attorneys on billing issues. Some unscrupulous attorneys overcharge with the expectation that the client will complain about bills and then the bill will be compromised and reduced by the attorney based on the level of the complaint by the client. You are not like that, and you should not run your business along those lines. If their experience with attorneys has occurred in that fashion, the client does not know better and will take that knowledge and treat you the way he or she has learned to treat other attorneys, which is to complain about the bill. Set the table honestly; be forthright that that is not the way your law office operates and that unless there is an obvious mistake that you have missed proofreading the bill, the bills, stand for what they are.

Should We Sue a Former Client for Fees?

Once the receivables are carried beyond 90 days and 120 days, it is safe to say that the client probably cannot or will not pay you. Certainly, some exceptions exist. For example, the client might be waiting for a closing to occur whereby he or she will receive proceeds from the closing and expects to pay you at that time. Be careful of those "I'll pay you at the end" scenarios. Many times, for reasons totally out of your control, the deal does not close. You probably put in a great amount of time trying to get the deal to close, and a large bill is due and owing to you from the client. These are sometimes referred to as involuntary contingency fee arrangements. It is unwarranted because you are working to get paid contingent on the deal closing, with no increased upside. In other words, unlike a personal injury case, if you, through your skilled advocacy, could beat and exceed client expectation, your fees would go up because you are charging one-third of the recovery for legal fees. Here, in the "I'll pay you at the closing" scenario, you are just getting paid your hourly rate, and it's still contingent on the closing. This is a bad scenario. Be careful of these involuntary contingency type arrangements.

Some telltale signs of a client being unable to pay you any further for your work are a client who stops returning your phone calls or does not respond to bills or correspondence. The two actions of a growing bill to your office, combined with a client "going dark" is a clear indication that the client has no intention of paying you. At that time, you need to make a determination whether or not to sue the client for the legal fees.

It is a difficult decision, but as a matter of policy you may sue clients who do not pay you. Your malpractice carrier will not like you suing clients for fees. It is a concern that clients will file unwarranted malpractice claims against you and/or professional conduct grievances against you with your jurisdiction's Attorney Registration & Disciplinary Commission if you sue them for fees.

However, there are certain factors you should consider in deciding whether you should sue a client for fees. The following questions will guide you:

- Did you do a great job for the client and get a good result?
- Is there anything in the process of your representation of the client that you did less than great?
- What's the sum total of the fees that the client has already paid you?

- What is the relationship between the amount you are trying to collect from the client and the sum total of the fees that the client has already paid? Is it significant?
- Were there any ethical slip-ups or potential causes for a grievance filed against you at the Attorney Registration & Disciplinary Commission?
- Do you feel this client used you or took advantage of you?
- Was the growing accounts receivable balance of this client partially your fault? Objectively speaking, is the amount you are trying to collect, in part, for hours put in on the client matter, somewhat excessive, which is why the client is refusing to pay?
- Is obtaining a judgment against this client worth anything? Would it be collectible?
- Does the client have money and is just being obstinate and does not want to pay you?

These are some of the factors that you need to consider before you file a lawsuit against the client. As you can see, trying to do what is right by your law firm and balancing the often unpredictable and unethical nature of some clients is often a tenuous procedure. When accounts receivable are managed properly, however, this issue should not come up often. In reality, of course, it will come up on occasion with every law office.

In litigation matters, you also need to seek court approval to withdraw from the case before you file a lawsuit against a client for fees. While this may not be the law in your jurisdiction, it is a practical view on representing a client in one matter and suing a client for fees. Ask experienced attorneys in your jurisdiction whether judges will let you out of a case at certain times in the progress of a case. Usually once a judge sets a trial date, you are stuck in the case and a judge will not grant your motion to withdraw even if the client *has stopped* paying you. You may add language and allegations in your motion to withdraw that you and your client are having philosophical differences on the representation of the case, that the client is no longer taking your advice, or that the client is no longer cooperating with you, but the judge simply may not allow you to withdraw from the case if the case has been set for trial. Judges want to keep their docket moving and may not necessarily allow the case to be set back another six months. Be aware of your obligations to the court and to the tribunal you are in front of when you want to withdraw from a particular case. This is true whether or not you want to eventually sue the client for fees.

Obviously, these are complicated issues, and suing the client for fees *is a last resort*. It is nothing you want to do, nothing you enjoy doing, and it is absolutely the final termination of a client relationship. Unfortunately, sometimes you will take a very principled stance and sue clients because of a wonderful job you have done and a client has the money to pay but has simply not paid, and for no good reason! Do not take these matters personally, and do not sue a client to make a point. Be wise and think through your decision as though you were giving advice to another attorney on the same matter. Balance the potential retaliatory action of the client by filing a malpractice claim or a grievance with your disciplinary commission versus the real value that you'll receive back from the lawsuit, if any, and your time invested in the collection of that suit.

Remember, stay on top of the thirty-day delinquency list.

Chapter 11

Specialist versus Generalist

A great deal of thoughtful energy may go into the question of whether, as you open your new law office, you will be a generalist, taking on all types of legal matters, or a specialist, concentrating on practice with only one, two, or perhaps three related practice areas. Starting in law school, plan on specializing and becoming an expert in a narrow area of the law.

That is right: you should initially plan on specializing in one narrow area of the law. Do you need other skills and general skill sets to survive in your own practice? Absolutely yes. In fact, the further you analyze this issue, and the more experience you have at practicing law, you will see that clients rarely come to you with issues in the law that narrowly address only one practice or substantive area of the law.

Most times, client issues and problems touch on multiple legal disciplines. For example, clients visit you regarding estate planning and would like to put properties into a trust for their adult children and want you to analyze the benefits of their suggested plan of action. You certainly need to understand estate planning and trust law, potentially provide the clients with other suggestions on titling the property, which requires a certain level of real estate background; on the potential for a gift tax issue, which requires a federal estate and gift tax background; and on potentially a family law issue with respect to converting the clients' property into their children's marital property. As you can see, almost four separate disciplines of law are needed in one hypothetical client issue.

> A deep understanding of one or a few areas of the law is fantastic and very necessary with which to build your practice.

A general understanding of many areas of the law is good and necessary. A deep understanding of one or a few areas of the law is fantastic and very necessary with which to build your practice.

With respect to advertising one's specialty, please review the Model Rules of Professional Conduct, in particular rule 7.4, which provides that only patent attorneys and attorneys of "admiralty" are allowed to use such specializations in communications with clients.

Simply stated, "[A] lawyer shall not state or imply that a lawyer is certified as a specialist in any particular field of law unless the specialty is approved by the state authority, and accredited by the ABA, and the name of the certifying organization is clearly identified in the communication."[1]

For that reason, lawyers cannot hold themselves out as specializing in any particular substantive area of the law; therefore lawyers sometimes indicate that they concentrate or limit their practice to particular areas of the law.

Even without advertising as such, lawyers can promote that they perform legal services only in one or two areas of the law, thus conveying to clients, potential clients, and referral sources that they, in fact, limit their practice to that select area of the law, and thus, by conclusion and implication, clients and potential referral sources believe the lawyers are experts in only one area of the law.

This is a *fantastic* way to market your services to other lawyers. You need to understand that once you become very proficient, knowledgeable, and efficient in a particular practice area of the law, you can go out to market your services to every other lawyer in the community and the outlying area who does not practice in your specialty and ask for referrals.

This is very similar to the business model for physicians. The specialists participate in industry gatherings to network and to connect with other generalists and specialists in other fields, to obtain referrals from their colleagues. Similarly, you will do the same at bar association meetings, "judges' nights," with ballrooms full of lawyers, and even other networking events that are widely attended by attorneys. If your specialty is not represented by the other attorneys in the room, you must make contact with the other attorneys in those rooms and stay in front of them for the rest of your career. Sounds aggressive? It is solely the biggest reason to specialize your practice in the narrow area. If you work the specialization practice properly, and you can and will for five to ten years out of law school, build a wonderful network of complimentary attorneys around you with whom you will share business and referrals.

As you grow the practice, you will grow with an eye toward broadening the breadth of services you provide. That is, as you add attorneys, you will look to bring in other attorneys, either with or without experience, to concentrate the practice in additional areas of the law. As a practical matter, your practice will become more diversified as you grow. In fact, as will be discussed later in Section 2, as you grow your practice, you will also grow your practice areas. Most likely, the additional attorneys will come in and perform in the same or similar practice area in which you perform at first, but overall and over time, the firm will start to offer more services as it grows.

I know you are wondering, "What about me personally—will I be a specialist forever?" Probably not.

---

1. MODEL RULES OF PROF'L CONDUCT R. 7.4.

A natural progression in law as you start in one practice area is to begin picking up related practice areas near that concentration. As set forth in the example above, an estate-planning lawyer does have a certain amount of work that flows over into general real estate as well as estate and gift tax (estate and gift tax is a critically important area of the law to understand if you work in the estate planning area). You tend to start with one practice area and begin to understand and learn practice areas related to that one main practice area—for example, some litigation lawyers begin to specialize in appeals work if they have an exposure to appeals work at a law firm that handled appeals regularly.

Some family law lawyers who fight about marital property every day may start appearing in court representing clients with general litigation issues and potential guardianships, adoptions, and other similar family law matters. As you diversify your own knowledge, it is fair to market those services to your existing clients and other referral sources as it seems to fit and make the most sense. However, to your colleagues, the lawyers who have been referring business to you because of the concentration of your practice, you still want to keep the image of a tightly concentrated law office in just one or two practice areas. Remember, however, it is important that you continue to learn more and more practice areas to protect yourself against any changes in the law that may significantly curtail or eliminate your original area of concentration. However, it is a very important marketing advantage to narrowly define your concentration.

> As you grow the practice, you will grow with an eye toward broadening the breadth of services you provide.

I was once at a marketing seminar for lawyers where this exact topic came up and questions were raised to the presenting marketing guru. The presenter told an interesting story.

If you hurt your elbow playing tennis, and you know you need to see a doctor, you may call your general practitioner doctor to discuss the matter or you may look in the Yellow Pages for a doctor. After a certain point in time, you realize that you really need to find an orthopedic doctor, (i.e., doctor who treats disorders of the bones, joints, ligaments, and muscles). So you start looking in the Yellow Pages or in your health care plan for an orthopedic doctor. Then, you realize some orthopedic doctors actually specialize in knees and ankles—doctors of no use to you. You do not want a doctor practicing on your elbow; you want a doctor who just treats elbow pain.

Next, you look for orthopedic doctors who specialize in arm injuries. After sorting through shoulder injuries and wrist injuries, you actually find a doctor who specializes in elbow injuries resulting from playing tennis. That is your guy, and that is the doctor you want to see to take care of your injury. Why? Because just by the narrow scope of his practice, his concentration, he will not be practicing on you; rather, he will have the vast experiences of looking at just one type of joint and be able to diagnose and treat you as quickly as possible.

Does it make sense that the same applies to lawyers? Of course. Time and time again, clients wants to hire an attorney who has worked on the exact problem that they have. That, simply stated, is the value of marketing your specialty, conveying to the next potential client that you speak to that you have experience in exactly the subject matter of the client's problem.

Does marketing as a specialist eliminate a lot of telephone calls from individuals looking for a generalist? Maybe, just as it does for the generalist doctor who receives many telephone calls in the area from patients he may be unable to treat because of the difficulty of the specialized joint, organ, or problem that requires a specialist. However, the telephone calls that the specialist does get are usually high-quality leads. They are clients who have done the research, understand their problem, and in short order come to understand that your concentration will solve their problem.

Having a deep and thorough understanding of the law in a narrow subject area and the ability to market that concentration among other lawyers are two good reasons that concentrating your initial practice is a good idea. First is attorney-to-attorney marketing, which will greatly enhance your ability to get referrals from your peer group. Second, when it comes time to be hired by a client, the client does not want to hire a lawyer who will practice on him or her. Clients want to hire someone who has handled a similar type problem time and time again. That is the reputation you will build up in a short period of time by concentrating your practice.

How will it feel when you turn away a client because the issue is not in your specialty? First of all, it will be difficult for you as a young attorney to turn away any work if you need money and you feel you can really add value and take care of the client.

This situation may occur if, for example, you concentrate your practice in personal injury and a client comes to you with a business dispute over a shareholder agreement. You certainly do not have the experience litigating shareholder disputes, but you may find that the dispute seems to turn on a narrow set of facts, and as you are very comfortable in the courtroom, you decide to take on the case, telling the client that you are making an exception from your ordinary area of concentration to help him or her. In this case, you certainly do not need to turn the client away if you feel you can do a great job and add value. Also, many of the other principles you would utilize with respect to representing clients in personal injury matters will translate and apply, such as your courtroom demeanor, preparedness, research abilities, and overall courtroom savvy to assist the client in the shareholder dispute.

Certainly, more complicated cases may come up that you will have to pass on, but you would refer those to the colleagues who you met through your networking and provide the client with the best possible legal experience that you can.

Pick Your Concentration Cautiously

While I truly believe that you should follow your passion and heart with respect to your area of concentration, be advised that certain levels of concentration, or your "specialty," command different hourly rates in the marketplace. For example, many lawyers coming right out of school without much experience and without a good mentor base tend to gravitate toward civil matters such as representing clients in traffic court, tax return preparation, or residential real estate transactions. While these are all important levels of concentration and a great level of expertise is built up in serving these clients, be advised that since these are the practice areas that most new attorneys gravitate to, there is a great deal of competition (and sometimes not highly qualified competition); as a result, the fees are low, making the practice area less profitable than other practice areas. This is only a cautionary warning if you build your law practice around these practice groups. There is no doubt that there are some very successful law firms built around these practice areas.

It is more likely that you will use these practice areas as a training ground to gain a greater level of expertise in more complicated practice areas. For example, an attorney representing clients in traffic court will eventually grow into handling misdemeanor crimes and ultimately felonies. An attorney who starts representing clients in residential real estate transactions will eventually start to handle more commercial buildings, strip mall shopping centers, and other larger development areas and market himself or herself as a commercial real estate attorney.

> While the breadth of your experience and practice groups will change over the years, your principles will not.

Generally speaking, our profession receives a lot of criticism for stereotypes about lawyers. The one issue that is never written about lawyers is that attorneys do better than most professional service providers because attorneys really do care about clients and making sure clients are in the right hands with the right attorney. After years of experience, you will have passed on many cases when you believed another attorney could do a better job for the client than you could because of your limited practice area experience. While the breadth of your experience and practice groups will change over the years, your principles will not. If you believe you can refer the client to an attorney who is more experienced in a particular practice area, do so instantly. There is value in those types of referrals, and you want to make sure that the client's interests come first. Lawyers do a great job at this, and our profession needs to continue to put the client's interests first by making high-quality referrals.

The bottom line is that every attorney should have one or two areas of law that he or she is deeply knowledgeable about and well versed in, in representing clients. Three practice areas would be the most beneficial. Any more than three related areas and you are just a generalist, and it is difficult to get out of that perception with third parties. It is not enough to be good, you need to be great. As a result, seek a deep and thorough understanding of the area of law that you wish to practice in, and as you develop your path through this book, you will find ways to market and manage that concentration of the law.

Chapter 12

Social Media Networking

Social media—Facebook, Twitter, LinkedIn, Instagram, Pinterest, and others—is the portal to the outside world for millions of people. These tools have become the source of information and news, the means to interact with family and friends, and the way to find job opportunities, shop for goods and services, and connect with their networks at every level. Therefore, the first thing to understand and accept regarding social media is that it is broadly defined, and it is the way people now connect . . . *for everything*.

It may be fair to assume that many people still seek legal services in more traditional ways, but that is changing, and changing quickly. For example, as you need employees and seek to hire additional support staff, and ultimately even attorneys, you should now be posting your ads online rather than in print publications (or at least in addition to). Further, as you grow your business, you need a strong presence in the digital media or, using the broadest definition, in social media.

> Your branding and marketing efforts need to include a comprehensive digital component.

A recent study by BI Intelligence sets forth, with great detail, the shopping habits of younger demographic consumers.[1] The study looks at the influence of sites such as Facebook, Twitter, Pinterest, Tumblr, and other e-commerce. It depicts how various sites are used for shopping ideas, fashion tips, and wish lists. What the sites have in common is the adherence to the fundamental rule of e-commerce championed by the likes of Amazon—consumers will click to buy when it is a relatively effortless process.

There is no shortage of purported experts who regularly write articles describing the secrets to generating leads and sales from social media. What does all this mean to a lawyer building a law practice?

---

1. Josh Luger, *The Rise of Social Commerce: How Tweets, Pins and Likes Can Turn into Sales*, Business Insider (Apr. 17, 2014), http://www.businessinsider.com/the-rise-of-social-commerce-2013-5.

It means that your branding and marketing efforts need to include a comprehensive digital component. You need to be where your potential clients are shopping, conversing, researching, and communicating with each other.

To begin, commit to one or two social media platforms rather than trying to manage too many. Facebook, Twitter, and LinkedIn offer the broadest reach for you to start. Begin building contacts and as extensive a network as you can. However, don't just pursue a large number of friends, likes, or contacts. As you build your network on each platform, be an active participant. Share information, join conversations, and contribute in ways that allow others to learn about you. Not all your activity should be selling and marketing. Social media sites are digital meeting places, so treat the experience as you would a social event where everyone is meeting in person. Be social, discuss ideas, and when appropriate promote your law firm.

How to Get the Message Out

You need to write short informational messages for your platform at least twice per week. This is a matter of strategy and requires a fine balance between staying in front of your network and pestering your network. Communicate no less than once per week and, conversely, not more than three times per week.

The types of messages that should be sent by you are reminders of the law, so include a hyperlink to an article on your website, reminders for clients to take certain actions on scheduled events such as tax deadlines, and commentary on legal issues in the news. As you noticed, these are all value-driven informational tweets. The intent is to constantly give value to your network with respect to legal issues. With luck, in your network you are the only lawyer practicing in your particular specialty, and your network is filled with people who are not lawyers. As such, it is important that you constantly provide content and information to your network.

Should your messages look like advertisements?

No, not too often. Maybe once per month, including a call to action to your network to call you for a particular service is not unreasonable, but only about once per month. You do not want to look as if you are inundating your network with advertisements and direct requests for others to call you. Remember, the name of the game here is adding value.

Keep in mind that sites like LinkedIn are connected to Twitter, so with a certain adjustment on your postings, you can send your short message out simultaneously to both LinkedIn and Twitter. You may find it uncomfortable to ask your network to join you in different social networks, therefore, dedicate your time staying on top of one platform.

Where else can you add value?

What about starting a group on LinkedIn or a fan page on Facebook? This is, again, an extension of your charge to add value to your networks and build other networks within your concentrated practice area. Keep the information fresh, highly topical, and content driven. Commenting on celebrity legal issues is always a client favorite because if the issue is covered in *People Magazine*, for example, it is probably of general interest to the public. Putting a legal spin and analysis on celebrity legal issues is a wonderful way to convey that you are a regular person and that you look at even sensationalistic news with an eye toward the legal issues, thus gaining respect in your network of colleagues and potential referral sources.

Currently, many of the social networking platforms invite endorsements or allow an individual to ask for endorsements from individuals in a network. This is fair game. Do not hesitate to ask for an honest, unbiased opinion and recommendations. There are other attorney rating and review sites that likewise, based on your peer review and client review, provide a ranking for the attorney. Obviously, you would seek endorsements only from friends, family, and referral sources that have had a great experience with you or from clients who really appreciate your work.

Is this approach biased?

It certainly seems to be, but it is also truthful and accurate. Do not hesitate to ask for endorsements to build up your digital profile. Remember, this is where potential clients go to vet their legal needs before making purchasing decisions. You would be compared against a lineup of other attorneys who may or may not be engaging in the same serious digital marketing plan in which you engage. As in all things set forth in this book, be the best at every nuance in the practice of law, including owning the best digital footprint in your market.

E-mail Blasts

If you use Microsoft Outlook and your contacts sync with other devices, you will always have your contact information with you. Most important, since a majority of your correspondence with clients and referral sources is done through e-mail, you will build up an enormous number of e-mail addresses saved in your contacts folder. As part of the Outlook system, you can, and must, create distribution lists categorizing your e-mail addresses by careers, interests, clubs, and marketing needs. For example, you have distribution lists of accountants, bankers, local business people in your community, and other segmented industries and organizations.

When you write an article or have commentary on the news of the day that affects one of these groups, send out a blind carbon copy e-mail blast attaching an article and commenting on the article or the news of the day to that segmented group via an e-mail blast. The e-mail is short, informative, and as always, content driven. It does not have any mandate in it for someone to do anything other than read it. Send some of those e-mail blasts with a tagline that reads, "If you have any other questions on this matter, do not hesitate to e-mail me at . . . for further information." Since it is an e-mail, your e-mail address comes up as a hyperlink, which makes it very easy for the reader to send you a follow-up e-mail.

Do not be in a predictable cycle on your e-mail blast, but do one or two a month depending on the news of the day. These e-mail blasts and tweets all fall into the category of producing information for your clients, referral sources, and other more broad networks. Imagine staying in front of your network with timely, informative content and having the network members regularly see and read that information alongside your logo. How can they ever think of calling any lawyer other than you for any legal problem, when you have communicated with them in such a professional manner? They will not. This e-mail blast is an important digital marketing method, one that is virtually free except for your time.

> Imagine staying in front of your network with timely, informative content and having the network members regularly see and read that information alongside your logo.

Your ability to consistently send a pulse out to your networking group shows that you are on the cutting edge of the law, synthesizing information for their benefit so that they do not need to do the same. In addition, they will think of your legal services on a regular basis.

At what point do you start to pester people with your message?

Your message needs to be balanced delicately with your information, but keep in mind that tweets of once or twice a week and additional content-filled e-mail blasts are not offensive. If the headlines are written in a creative fashion to grab the attention of the reader, recipients will be able to review the e-mail, unintrusively, to determine to delete it or read it as they deem fit. One final thought on tweets and e-mails blasts—do not become part of the digital noise that we are all inundated with daily. Create informational headlines that are noticeable and provide value and content for your readers, any of who may be clients or referral sources.

Notes on Legal Advertising

Throughout this chapter and other chapters on your marketing efforts, please be aware of the Model Rules of Professional Conduct, specifically the rules under information about legal services, rules 7.1–7.6. At present, there is no distinctive authority that prohibits the exchange of information over social media, especially since presumably your contacts have affirmatively elected to be part of your network and, as a result, presumably acquiesce to accept your information. You need to monitor this issue going forward to determine whether any specific disclaimers and/or notes on advertising need to be included in your tweets and informational material. It is always advisable, depending on the depth of the article, to put a disclaimer at the end that indicates that your articles should not be taken as legal advice, for due to the changes in the laws, jurisdictional rules, and interpretation of the laws, as well as client facts, the article should not be relied on or interpreted by clients as applicable to their legal needs.

Website

A website, per se, is not identified as social media but is part of the digital world, and it becomes the digital world's portal into your practice. Therefore, it needs to be discussed along with digital marketing.

As indicated in Chapter 6, a website is a mandatory part of marketing and branding your law office. Keep in mind the things discussed in Chapter 6, such as design elements and programming the ability to expand and update the website with little effort.

> Your digital footprint will be reviewed and must therefore send a consistent, clear message to your potential clients and your referral sources.

On the website, it is important for marketing purposes to constantly upload additional articles and add new, fresh content that will, over time, develop as a search facility on its own for potential clients. As a result, it will potentially be the go-to site for people in your municipality trying to find legal answers. This is a grandiose undertaking, but there is no smoke-and-mirrors approach to a quality website.

Your website is an entire digital portal of your firm's work and, ultimately, your attorneys' professional work. You should have links to other valuable sites and extensive bios of you and your work. Include all articles, tweets, newspaper interviews, and anything about you that could be found in a digital format with a Google search, all neatly organized and searchable on your website.

Obviously, your practice areas need to be listed, and explanations for the headings and subheadings in each practice area need to be set forth as well, but that is the same requirement for every website for every service business in the world. Yours will be unique to you; you will provide your information and your content on your website.

All articles and content that you prepare for various publications will be repurposed as much as possible; you will use your work not only for its original publication purpose but also for e-mail blasts, social media postings, and ultimately your website content. This is a matter of efficiency. Take your article, or the subject matter of your article, and make it as available as you can on multiple platforms as you get the message out to your digital network. Then, always, save that content and post it on your website to create a content-driven website for your clients, potential clients, and referral sources.

General Notes on Your Digital Footprint

It is important to note that much of your digital work will not necessarily make the telephone ring. However, make no mistake that clients will thoroughly research you before they walk in the front door of your office to meet with you. As such, your digital footprint, whether it be on Facebook, Twitter, LinkedIn, or your website, will be reviewed and must therefore send a consistent, clear message to your potential clients and your referral sources, showing who you are, what you stand for, and your ability to practice law. This imaging resonates with clients and will either enhance your ability to get hired by the client or thwart your ability to have people come to your office to meet with you.

It is still true that the client's first and very important impression of you will be from the referral source that gave the client your name, but the client's research of you does not end with the referral source. A client will do independent research on you, and the most logical place to find you is on the social media platforms and your website.

Will use of your website be somewhat self-serving? Sure it will, but remember that based on the presentation and the professionalism of your digital messaging, the client will gain great comfort in knowing that he or she is meeting with the right person and the correct firm that is aligned with his or her thinking.

Chapter 13

Traditional Networking

Later in the book, following the discussions on networking, advertising, public relations, and branding, there is a detailed discussion about how you will position your law firm in the marketplace. However, coming right out of school or starting the practice after gaining some experience at another firm, you need to understand the necessity of traditional networking. There are many avenues to cultivate clients for your law firm. Those avenues might include direct mail, Yellow Pages advertising, printed advertising, website hits, seminars and speaking engagements, large-scale media advertising, client referrals, and the like. But one of the largest categories of marketing will always be traditional attorney networking. The networking that an attorney does may ultimately yield clients from referral sources such as accountants, other attorneys, and financial advisors. Ultimately, for tracking purposes you may break down those client referral sources separately, but there is no doubt that going out to chamber of commerce events, trade shows, golf outings, sitting on boards, and other similar types of externalities of practicing law will yield clients. All of these externalities are considered attorney networking.

> The networking that an attorney does may ultimately yield clients from referral sources such as accountants, other attorneys, and financial advisors.

Get Connected with People

In order to start your networking push, you really do need to get involved with some level of civic involvement. It is absolutely imperative that you contact some not-for-profit organizations in your area to see if they need volunteer work on a regular basis. Get involved in your children's activities, even with the local parent-teacher organizations or school districts. Certainly join the local bar association and actively participate in one or two committees. Get involved in your children's youth sports either administratively or as a coach or advisor. If you can't seem to make the commitment because of time constraints, volunteer on game days or for fundraisers or other projects. You need to be involved, and you need to be committed. During all of these types of events and at planning meetings, you will have an opportunity to meet new people.

Most places of worship have various committees, ministries, and church subgroups in which you can be involved. Again, it is not until you are well established and well-known and respected that people ever think of contacting your law office for legal work.

If people do not contact your office for legal work, so what; you have made a positive impact in your community. Remember, as a lawyer, you need to be a community leader. It does not matter if you lead a bar association committee or lead a coat drive, your standing in the community rises as you take a leadership role. Passive involvement is no involvement at all. Go to all the meetings you want, sit in the last row of the meeting room, take notes—nothing will happen, and you will not be noticed nor will you be contributing to the advancement of the organization of which you are purportedly a part. Stand up and lead, and people will take notice.

You have heard the old saying, "You only get out as much as you put into it." That is absolutely true. You get a lot more out of a committee, association, not-for-profit corporation, or chamber of commerce if you take an advanced leadership role.

"How do I take a leadership role if they do not give me a title?"

All of these organizations are looking for people to stand up and volunteer to take control or chair a fundraiser, a food drive, a coat drive, a campout with the Boy Scouts, a rules committee for a sporting association, or the PTA. When something needs to happen in these organizations, raise your hand and say, "I'll volunteer to take that over." It might be a solo role where you are operating on your own, or you may be able to enlist other committee members to join you so long as you lead. In either event, the person who takes an active role will always be noticed and respected.

The Marketing Mindset

Whether you are an experienced attorney or a young attorney just getting out of law school, you must accept the fact that for you to be successful in the law business, your job will need to be more than just being an exceptional and outstanding practitioner of the law. While all that is necessary, as you recall from the discussion on the five-tool attorney, attorney networking and marketing are mandatory.

Does this mean you have to be a salesperson?

You need to be ready to sell the benefits you bring to a relationship. You are in the business of trying to help individuals any way you can. As you meet people, you need to think, "How can I help them?"[1] As you go through your professional career, you will come in contact with hundreds, if not thousands, of people. If during those meetings you ask yourself, and more overtly ask them, "How can I help you?" you will start off at the correct marketing mindset necessary to be successful. The name of the game here is connecting with people and keeping a true eye on their needs. You do this by listening carefully and closely and by truly trying to find ways you can help them, even if their concern *has nothing* to do with you providing legal services to their business. You and your colleagues or your other networking resources may be able to assist the client in nonlegal ways. For example, can you introduce this individual who has had banking or loan problems to a banker? Or to a real estate broker to assist him in selling his house?

Remember, many of the people you will meet in the networking circuit, such as chamber of commerce events and other professional organization events, may want to be selling their services to you. Do not be surprised by this. Just deal with this situation on a very honest and open level. While you cannot promise to buy the person's services on a regular basis, you may want to get quotes from her on occasion or have her bid on certain work for you. Be careful going down this road because eventually the relationship could be frustrating for all involved. For example, if a printer in your chamber of commerce is asked to bid on three or four printing projects for you and is never hired, he will grow somewhat anxious and unhappy with your process. There may need to be an occasion where you may have to hire him and perhaps pay a little premium to keep him as a genuine referral source.

> You need to be ready to sell the benefits you bring to a relationship.

The scope of this book is not to teach you how to negotiate with vendors, but in those kinds of cases, very simply talk to that vendor and say, "You are about $50 more expensive than the lowest quote, but if you think you can match that price or come close to it, I would love to give you the business." In those cases, the vendor sometimes appreciates the last look, and you will not need to pay a premium to give that person some of your business.

Law offices use third-party vendors quite a bit for printing matters, telecommunications, IT support, computer equipment, furniture, and other items required on a regular basis. Sometimes it is good to spread those purchases out among several vendors.

---

1. Mark M. Maraia, Rainmaking Made Simple: What Every Professional Must Know 8 (Professional Services Publishing 2003).

The Elevator Speech

Develop an elevator speech. An elevator speech is a description about your law office that is as long as it takes to go from the first floor to the tenth floor of a building, where you have only a very short period of time to speak to someone about your law office, about fifteen seconds. What makes your law office unique, what is your unique selling proposition (see Chapter 26), and why are you different? These are some points to cover.

Your elevator speech will be given hundreds or thousands of times throughout your career. The elevator speech that you give to people you meet along the way when you are a solo practitioner will not be the same as when you are running a law office with five to ten attorneys or twenty to fifty attorneys. It will develop and grow as your law office does.

Put your speech in writing and rework it, redraft it, read it to your spouse or significant other, and get feedback. Get it to a point that seems very natural to say, and practice saying it on multiple occasions without notes.

Then, when you are in social situations and you meet people and tell them that you are a lawyer, they will inevitably ask, "What kind of law do you practice?" That is the invitation to go into your elevator speech. Do not be concerned with dominating a conversation for fifteen seconds. A well-rehearsed and well-meaning fifteen-second elevator speech about your firm is a reasonably short answer, and if your elevator speech is better than the next attorney's, it will give your new acquaintance a positive impression. As a solo practitioner, you will make your law office elevator speech and your own personal elevator speech identical. But as you grow, your subsequent associates and partners should integrate the concept of the law office as part of their elevator speech, adding to it their own personal practice area and why your law office performs so well in a particular practice group.

Keep in mind that many attorneys simply say, for example, "I'm a divorce lawyer." That does not set that attorney apart from the many other divorce lawyers in the municipality or large city. You will develop an excellent elevator speech once you thoroughly do the analysis on your unique selling proposition (see Section 2).

The First Meeting

Generally, during the first meeting in a social situation with every potential client or referral source, you will take the lead in a very forward manner by just putting your hand out to shake the potential client's hand and introduce yourself: "Hello, I'm John Smith, and I'm pleased to meet you," simultaneously handing him or her your business card. This way the potential client is holding your business card and can always look at it if he or she did not clearly hear you introduce yourself and your name. When you hand out a business card, you should always ask, "Do you have a card on you?" In this scenario, the exchange of business cards happens up front and at least you have something to talk about as you both look at each other's business names and logos; the exchange is usually a conversation starter based on a common business interest.

Conversely, sometimes folks meet, and the conversation starts flowing after lighthearted introductions. This is also a great way to start speaking to people in a big room. Initially you begin talking to them about what you immediately have in common, such as the keynote speaker, the not-for-profit organization that brought you together at the fundraiser, a common person who introduced you, the big game on television the previous evening, or any other topic that is immediately recognizable as being a common theme between the two of you.

Many times as you meet other lawyers, there is an easy way to start a conversation. You usually talk about the law, about common friends in the law profession, common-law firms, or their particular practice group. With other lawyers, it's easy.

During an exchange in conversation with a person you have just met, eventually a transition in the conversation needs to be made. A usual transition is to say, "So tell me, what do you do for a living?" or something of that nature. Because eventually you need to talk about business. Before the person you are speaking with gets too far into the conversation, simply say, "That is very interesting. Do you have a business card in case I ever need to contact you on that topic?" This is an easy icebreaker. No one will ever turn down giving you a business card. As part of that exchange, and without a word being spoken, go into your pocket or wallet, pull out your business card, and exchange the business cards simultaneously. Remember, you would like to leave the contact something from you to remember about you, and that business card exchange will go seamlessly and flawlessly.

> The exchange of business cards happens up front and at least you have something to talk about as you both look at each other's business names and logos.

Mission accomplished. You have had a general, lighthearted conversation with a new contact, you have talked business with the new contact, and you have exchanged business cards. If you are in a room full of potential new contacts, do *not* spend the entire evening with just one person. A good time frame for small talk with a new contact is between ten and fifteen minutes, maximum. Once you reach that limit, you need to excuse yourself politely, saying, for example, "It was great talking to you but I need to refill my drink," or "I don't want to tie you up all night. It was great talking to you," or "I see somebody I need to make contact with today. It was great talking to you." Remember to shake your contact's hand before you walk away. None of these conversation enders is offensive or problematic in the social setting. But you are at the social setting to make contacts, and as long as you had a genuine conversation on personal issues, social issues, or business and exchanged business cards, you have accomplished a lot.

Also, during the first meeting, it is imperative that you are a great listener and let the other person do as much talking as possible. Nothing is more boring than listening to an attorney tell you how great he or she is and how he or she can handle sophisticated deals and then start to go into the nuances of the latest big deal he or she closed.

Do not be that attorney.

Have the other person speak and tell you everything about himself or herself personally and professionally; where possible, interject to make a connection that you understand about the business or family issues mentioned. If the person mentions children, ask the next follow-up questions: "How many children do you have and what are their ages? Do they go to school?" When the person talks about his or her job, ask, "How many years have you been there? Are they good people to work for? Do you see yourself there for your whole career?" If the person has a business and talks about it, ask the obvious follow-up questions to learn more about the business so that you understand what is going well and what is becoming problematic. Remember, you want to help this potential client in any way you can, and being a good listener is the first step to being able to help solve any potential client problems.

> Remember, you want to help this potential client in any way you can, and being a good listener is the first step to being able to help solve any potential client problems.

Listening is learning not only about this particular individual or business but also about the market. You may be hearing just one person's view on the industry, but that view is still important. Listening to others' views is a key component to understanding the values of individuals and their business. Further, you *must* do your research. While social "lunches" or "coffees" are always beneficial for expanding your friendship network, in the business scenario, it makes little sense to go to a subsequent lunch or coffee meeting with no plan of action, no further knowledge about the potential client or referral source's background, connectivity, and social circles. Have a plan and execute it.

I met a very mature, young financial advisor recently, and I told him how impressed I was with his networking abilities as a young person. We talked at length about the things that he does, and when I asked him about networking with his peers, he said very honestly that a young person's idea of networking is going out to happy hours at the local bars after work and socializing. He said nothing serious gets done at those events, but some camaraderie and friendships are developed. The end result of those social events is not necessarily all bad, but the events are simply not focused and directed with an end result in mind. Very little research gets done prior to those meetings, which are basically fun settings to get to know other people outside the workplace. I am not against such social events, but in the long run a lot more can be accomplished with focused, well-prepared meetings and understanding the client's needs.

The Follow-Up

At the end of every conversation you have with new potential clients or referral sources, you need to walk away with some sort of tangible contact information from them, such as a business card. The next day, prepare a handwritten note to your new contacts and in just a few short sentences tell them it was a delight to meet them (if that is sincere) and that you wish them well in business. Mention that you'd like to keep in touch with them and that either they should call you in a week or you will call them in a week or two to schedule a meeting over lunch or coffee. This next step, sometimes referred to as a follow-up or an advance,[2] is very important in making a sincere effort to start developing a business relationship.

Under no circumstance should you expect that a person you meet at a social event will remember you six months after the event and refer you business or hire you without any further contact. Unfortunately, many young attorneys fail at attorney networking opportunities because they expect too much, too fast. Networking is about developing lifetime business relationships, and those things take a long period of time. You are not so important that people want to send you business immediately. The first thing you need to do is develop trust and internalize a sincere belief that you want to help another person. The help may, coincidentally, be legal services, but not necessarily. The person you met may in fact become a lifetime connection and may end up wielding a great deal of power to send you business or hire your law firm over time.

Do not prejudge anyone. Although the person may be much older than you, much younger than you, or have a few initial personality ticks that may not impress you or may even slightly offend you, viewing all new contacts with an open mind and giving people a chance even if they have seemed offensive is a good social rule and certainly good business. After the thank-you letter has been sent, wait a week or two, and then call the person to set up a lunch or a meeting in a local coffee shop. The luncheon does not have to be extravagant, but it is an opportunity for you to sit down and start talking about the business and personal needs of this contact and, in addition, about the contact's network. If your contact is a CPA, many of that person's clients may need a lawyer. Talk through those issues, talk through your network of contacts to see if you can introduce your new contact to some of your close friends, business associates, or other value-added individuals

---

2. *See id.* 93.

in your network. Sometimes businesses refer to these folks as your circle of influence. These are people who have made an impact in your business, and the people you have influenced in their business. Building your professional network takes time and patience. Young attorneys usually do not invest the necessary time, and they are sorely lacking in patience. The old rule that "a potential client needs to see your name seven times before he buys" is understated. Sometimes it takes someone twenty times to see your name before that person will call you for your legal services, and sometimes it will take seven years of networking with a particular individual before he or she will ever send you some business. It does not matter initially because the immediate goal is not deriving business from these social contacts; the goal is building your network in a trustworthy, honest way. Business will absolutely come in time. The immediate goal is to listen intently to what people say and to try to add value to their needs whether or not they are legal needs.

As an alternative to the path outlined above, you can certainly set up a second meeting during your first social contact with a potential client or referral source. During a chamber of commerce meeting, for example, perhaps you meet someone and start talking to that person about either personal or business matters but need to end the conversation to listen to a presentation or some other conversation breaker; if you wish to continue the conversation, simply suggest, "Hey, let's get together soon for lunch or coffee because I'd like to get to hear more about your business—should I call you, or will you call me?" Do not hesitate. Has anyone ever said, "No, let's not meet?" In every case your suggestion would be a perfect way to then segue into the next meeting with this potential contact. After the initial social meeting, schedule a subsequent meeting to talk about business. Once that is done, you have accomplished a lot.

Do Your Research

Before the next lunch or coffee meeting, thoroughly research the person you are meeting and his or her business. Check out the person's website, Google the names of the individual as well as the business, and go into trade journals, if available, and do your online research. This may include, for example, *Dun & Bradstreet Reports*, to find out as much about the business as you can. In addition to that, you may need to find out about the customers of the business. Sometimes the customers of a business are the best reflection of the business. Going into a lunch or a breakfast meeting with just more social conversation is worthless when it comes to developing a business relationship.

Know what services the business provides, know what parts the business manufactures, know where your potential client went to school, and check the person out on any of the social networking sites to see if you have common connections. The common touch between people is the easiest way to get people to trust your character and your personality.

Please always remember that people will do business with you if they like you, trust you, and think you can help them. It is the commonality of contacts and friends that will get them to like you and, to some degree, trust you. If you do not have that commonality, the liking you and trusting you portion of this phase of the relationship building may take longer. It may take years; but if the person is worth it, invest your time.

The third idea—the belief that you can help the person—must be either subtly or overtly sold by you. And remember, just getting the contact to refer cases to you or to hire you directly is not always helping that contact. Sometimes, whether you are talking to a high-level banker, a CPA, or another financial professional, for example, helping that person may mean more than just providing a good service to that person's business. That is helping that person's *business*. If you want to help the *person*, you need to understand what stress he or she has over this issue and how you can relieve that stress from him or her.[3] For example, an accountant may perceive a conflict of interest in a case where a client may have a potential lawsuit pending or may have a cause of action against another client of the accountant, who may perform tax or accounting services for that other party. The accountant may have been trying to mediate a resolution in the matter, but it is now at a point where a resolution may not be had. The accountant may not want to hand the case over to an attorney for fear of looking bad and facing an exchange of finger-pointing or heartless allegations. Knowing this, you can reassure the accountant that you will be an aggressive advocate for the client and will proceed without any superfluous name-calling and accountant bashing throughout the process. Assure the accountant that you will get permission from the client to hire the accountant under a confidentiality work product agreement whereby to preserve the attorney-client privilege and still remain involved in the case, the accountant will be working for your law firm.

> The follow-up to any introductory meeting is critical.

As stated before, it is very important to listen carefully to the conversations you are having with these contacts so that you will understand what is really concerning them. There is usually a secondary agenda at play, and you need to ascertain that agenda, bring it out into open conversation, and try to solve all of the problems.

In summary, the follow-up to any introductory meeting is critical. No matter if the contact is a high-flying financial wizard or a blue-collar tradesperson, these folks will eventually need legal services or have friends who will need legal services, and they will have their own ad hoc networks of people they are in contact with regularly to discuss many matters, including their own legal needs.

---

3. *See id.*

Finally, remember that it takes years, not months, to develop a good network of contacts. After twenty-five years of practicing law, you will still be trying to expand your network. Continue to go to chamber of commerce events, golf outings, and events for not-for-profit organizations and participate in your bar association activities, primarily because it is the right thing to do and demonstrates that you want to be a leader in your community. You also continue to do these things because you want to broaden your law firm's network to try to benefit as many individuals and businesses as possible.

The Subsequent Follow-Through

You made the connection, you enjoyed your first meeting with the potential client or referral source, you proceeded to the advanced stage by meeting the contact the second time and presenting yourself professionally, and now you have a newfound friendship with your new contact.

What do you do from here?

First of all, all that data from the client should go into your mailing database, your electronic database, or your e-mail distribution lists for e-mail blasts. Also make sure your contact is connected to you via your social networking platform. Further, depending on the contact's business or profession, you need to add the contact to your distribution list of similar, like-minded individuals on your e-mailing system. This way, as you find information, news articles, recent changes in the law, or any other news that would interest this contact, you can forward that news to let the contact know you are thinking about him or her and are attempting to add value to the relationship.

Once all the contact's information is in your systems, follow through two to three times per year with a telephone call and at least a meeting once or twice a year. Perhaps you will see the same contact at social events and so a formalized meeting may not be necessary, but you certainly need to stay in front of the contact.

Make no mistake about it, the single best way to endear this contact to you for a long period of time is to refer a customer or a client to the contact. If you can refer a customer or client to this contact, you will probably have a friend and business acquaintance for a long period of time. If you do refer clients, maximum twice, but never see any reciprocal attempt at sending you a client, that contact does not understand the networking and connectivity you are trying to build. It is difficult for people to sell their own services on a regular basis and also sell the services of their connections in networking groups. But remember, your mindset is to try to help any new connections as well as your existing connections. If you believe your contacts can truly be a help to your connections, by all means make that referral and follow through to make sure that connection has been made.

Sometimes You Need to Ask for the Sale

In the sales world, one of the paradigms often studied is the balance between adding value, networking, relationship building, and personal branding with your clients. This chapter sets forth, in somewhat great detail, the necessity for you to build relationships and add value to those relationships whether or not the value is law related. No doubt you could spend your career trying to help people and yet wonder why over a long period of time you have not received referrals from your network of people.

If this pattern begins to develop, you may be perceived as a genuine do-gooder who does not really want referrals of legal work. It is an odd perception, but depending on the people in your network, there could be this genuine disconnect between the things you are doing to try to help people and their ability to see you as a lawyer trying to grow your practice.

This perception does not mean there are ill-intentioned people in your networking groups, nor does it mean they do not necessarily have any connections to people who need legal work. Over a long period of time, everybody knows somebody who is purchasing a house, needs a will or a trust, or was hurt in an automobile accident and so needs representation. The question is, of course, "Why are they not calling me?"

After a year or two pass and you have developed a genuine personal and business relationship with certain people, have connected them with other people in your network for their benefit, and find that they still have not sent you any work, you can simply ask them, "Hey, do you know of anybody in your network of friends or family who will be starting a business soon, buying a home, or need a will or trust and who may need a lawyer?" Then say, "I would love to help them. Can you give them my name?" If, when talking to one of these individuals in your network, that person starts to tell you about his or her business and you can identify a need for an employment agreement, consulting agreement, or some other legal documentation to help fortify the relationship, do not hesitate to suggest, "Hey, those consulting agreements are important because there are termination date pitfalls [or fill in some other potential pitfalls in the agreement]. Do you think I should take a look at your agreement before you sign it?"

Injecting yourself and your legal services into the conversation is somewhat of a departure from what was recommended earlier, but at some point you *do* need to ask for the sale. Asking for the sale is not new in the world of marketing. However, although there are conflicting statistics on this matter, approximately 85% of all interactions between sales people and potential customers end without the salesperson ever asking for the sale.[4]

---

4. Bob Janet, *It's OK to Ask for the Sale . . . Really It's OK!*, National Association of Sales Professionals (Apr. 8, 2014), *available at* http://www.nasp.com/article/DA02C4CB-C52C/it-s-ok-to-ask-for-the-sale-really-it-s-ok.html (quoting Richard Fenton & Andrea Waltz, Go for No! Yes Is the Destination, No Is How You Get There [2007]); Sam Manfer, *The Most Powerful, yet Least Used, Sales Question*, SalesHQ (Apr. 17, 2014),

So that means 15% actually ask for the sale, which sounds about right in the world of professional marketing. Do not go out aggressively to ask for the sale every time you meet someone new. Doing so is not appropriate, nor is it professional.

However, sometimes a potential prospect or referral source needs to be nudged into being reminded about what you do for a living and how you help people. There is nothing wrong with eventually asking for the legal work. You may possibly not get the work on the day you ask for it, or on that particular project, but you will send a clear signal to your referral source that you are in business to serve clients and that you would appreciate being first and foremost on their mind when it comes to referring clients or hiring an attorney for legal work. Remember, a general reminder of this fact, even if it does not get you the work when you ask, will put you in second place to the existing lawyer of the client, and second place is the next best place to be, as you will see in Chapter 14.

Chapter 14

Clients

As a new, young attorney or as a practicing attorney, as you begin to embrace the idea of opening a law office, your thoughts usually focus on the functionality of the law office, the specialty of the attorney (or attorneys) involved, and the location and support staff that will exist.

This is an egocentric view.

Lawyers tend to think about building the business based on who they are, what they do, and what value each individual attorney presents to the marketplace. Probably, in addition to reading this book, you have read some materials or books on marketing, and you will try to analyze your unique selling proposition (USP) to the market and how you will differentiate yourself from your competitors.

Certainly analyzing who you are and why you exist is of critical importance (fully examined in the subsequent chapters of the book), but you will go nowhere without thoroughly understanding the client.

The 1980s introduced the concepts of management guru Peter Drucker and his analysis of businesses. Drucker assembled numerous materials and a book on the "self-assessment process," which states that the most important aspect of the self-assessment tool is the questions it poses.[1] Answers are important; you need answers because you need action. But the most important thing to ask are these questions:[2] The first question, "What is our mission?"[3] will be thoroughly analyzed in Section 2 of the book. However, question number 2, "Who is our client?"[4] needs to be asked, and asked again, and then constantly revisited for you to understand who your target client is.

As you understand, the combination of your specialty, coupled with the analysis of "Who is our client?" forms the basis for the pairing between you and your future clients.

---

1. Peter F. Drucker with Jim Collins, Philip Kotler, James Kouzes, Judith Rodin, V. Kasturi Rangan & Frances Hesselbein, The Five Most Important Questions You Will Ever Ask About Your Organization 1 (Jossey-Bass 2008).
2. *Id.* at 2.
3. *Id.* at 9.
4. *Id.* at 21.

As you are starting your business, you will inevitably take the position that "I will do work for anyone who will hire me!" That may be true, but it is impossible to build a marketing plan and ultimately a business around that approach.

Identify who your clients can be, where they are located, and what common demographics they have.

Print lists of supporting clients, such as volunteers, trade group members, partners, referral sources, employees, and other vendors, who may all be inside or outside the organization to be served and satisfied. What value do you have to the client and all of the client's attendant projects? Do your strengths, competencies, and resources match the needs of these clients? What other clients match your strengths and resources? What other outer circle of clients, or secondary contracts of those clients, or customers of those clients, should you be approaching?

> Identify who your clients can be, where they are located, and what common demographics they have.

The next question, "What does your client value?"[5] is a reiteration of a concept recently discussed in this book about listening carefully to the new contacts, potential clients, and referral sources and trying to find out what they need to make their life easier. "What do they *really* value?" How can you provide satisfaction to your client and the people who run the organization (if the client is an entity)? What benefits will you provide to the client, and does the client value those benefits? Providing inexpensive annual minutes to your business clients is a great marketing tool, but if the client does not see the value in inexpensive minutes, what good does it do? That is one example of providing a great service that the client might not value. Does your client have short-term needs to be satisfied? Or is your client a long-term thinker and you need to adapt to match your value proposition with ideas that your client values?

If you were to completely understand your potential client universe and the things potential clients value and the things they need, are you ready to deliver on those needs through services, training, education, innovation, and marketing?

The Drucker analysis is intended to move the reader away from the self-centered planning process to analyzing the client. If you as the leader of your firm can analyze where the client exists both physically and emotionally, what the client needs and wants, and what the client values, you have a very good opportunity to determine whether or not there is a match between the client and your set of skills and values. In Chapter 13, there is an emphasis on listening to potential clients to ascertain their needs. Without listening, you will just become the attorney no one wants to talk to at a social event.

Listening is learning.

---

5. *Id.* at 37.

How Do I Add Value?

Adding value is an important concept. In fact, "How can I add value to the client?" should be the litmus test question that is asked *before* any new client engagement. If you cannot add value to a matter for which a client hires you, you cannot take the engagement. This is true in every single attorney-client relationship.

For example, a client comes into your office to explain the dispute he or she is having with another business owner, neighbor, or other adversary. After you listen to the facts and make some preliminary analysis on the application of the facts to the law in your jurisdiction, you believe the client has a valid case. But will you add value? If the claimant's dispute is over $5,000, and you win the case in its entirety, but you charge the client $6,000 for your time, have you added value? You probably have not added any value at all but, in fact, you cost the client an additional $1,000. Understandably, other issues come into play with this oversimplified analysis, such as the litigant's reputation, community status, or fighting for what is right, but the value-added requirement needs to be vetted between the attorney and the client.

You know the story about the client who comes in the office over a small matter and says, "It's not about the money, it's about the principle." That is what the client believes at the moment, but the case will absolutely eventually be about the money. So you need to be stronger than the client at that point in time. Remind him that you take cases only where you can add value, and then decline the case.

This scenario plays out in myriad scripts and under different sets of facts. The most common are small-value cases where clients are very emotional about the case and want satisfaction quickly. Be careful taking those cases. It seems to follow, then, that cases where larger monetary values are at stake are cases where it is somewhat easier to add value. That may be true, but because the stakes are higher, the client's emotional and monetary investment in pursuing justice may be much higher also.

In business transactions, certainly some clients believe that any lawyer could get the matter closed. But in order to add value in business transactions, you need to push the transactions forward, covering the scope of risk and liability for the clients, minimizing their risk and maximizing their satisfaction at the closing table. Doing that many times boils down to unequivocal preparedness and organization to make sure every potential risk and liability has been eliminated or, with thorough transparency to the clients, minimized all to the benefit of the clients.

Adding value to clients is not just an economic equation.

Whether it is a young couple buying their first house or a banker preparing to close a big loan with a borrower, adding value always entails reducing the stress of your client and conveying to the client repeatedly by actions and words that you are ahead of the transaction, thinking about the next legal issue, dealing with documentation issues, filing motions, and responding to motions and other document exchanges.

Often, clients try to paint attorneys into a corner by asking them a litany of hypothetical questions that start with "What if they do this . . . ?" or "And if you receive that motion . . . ," "What will you do if they say . . . ?" or "What should I do if they don't counter my offer?" Now you will need to play out a few of these hypotheticals with your clients, but at some point always remember to let your clients know that as the case or transaction develops, other factors and information come into play, so everyone will best be served by waiting until those hypothetical questions are no longer hypothetical and you can answer them collectively with better information.

Be sensitive and kind to clients who ask ongoing hypothetical questions. Remember, you may have twenty or thirty cases or transactions going on at one time in your office. Your client has only one. Clients spend all their waking moments concerned with their transaction or litigation matter and, as a result, play through ten, if not a hundred, scenarios in their head about how a transaction or a case can progress. Be sensitive to this mindset and be willing to listen to and answer reasonable questions on these issues. Remember, your core anchor in all this is to ask yourself, "Am I adding value?"

> Be sensitive and kind to clients who ask ongoing hypothetical questions.

Answering unlimited hypothetical questions may be adding no value whatsoever to the client's matter. Answering a few of those questions to calm the stress of the client is a good idea and does add value. Draw the line and do not continue down that path to the extreme.

Whether the matter be a speeding ticket, a more serious criminal matter, a car accident, starting a new business, or a dispute with a neighbor, start with that core question to yourself, "Can I add value?" Then, throughout the transaction, as it progresses, you need to continuously be adding value as you work on the client matter.

In any case that has, for example, $50,000 at issue, you need to calculate the net victory for your client after paying your legal fees (if no fee shifting, contractual provisions, or statutes are applicable). Speak directly to that issue with the client in your initial meeting. Tell him or her that a $50,000 lawsuit may require $25,000 to $30,000 in legal fees and will net them only $15,000 to $25,000—and that amount only if you win on every count and the judge awards the plaintiff 100% of his or her prayer for damages. Let your clients know up front what the value add will be in the equation.

The clients may forget that conversation, so document it in a letter or e-mail. In addition, you need to conduct yourself under the constant mantra, "Am I adding value?"

Second Place Is the Next Best Place to Be

When young attorneys are marketing, their expectation for immediate results may be somewhat unrealistic. It takes a long time to develop friendships, trusted business relationships, and business contacts to the point where someone will actually hire you to be their lawyer. If you were to hang out your shingle today, the first thing that you might notice is that everyone already seems to have an attorney.

Starting with that premise, which is false, you need to be able to find people who are unhappy with their existing attorney or whose existing attorney relationship may be ending; put yourself in second place so that when something unfavorable in the potential client's relationship with the existing attorney occurs, you are next in line. Sometimes nothing bad happens with that relationship at all. Sometimes the existing attorney retires or stops practicing law altogether. The reason doesn't matter. Although you want to be hired by clients immediately, remember that sometimes putting yourself in second place is the next best place to be.

Indeed, as many experienced attorneys will attest, many of our best clients will take years to develop, and you will become very close friends with them before they ever hire you or your law office. Generally, it is so because they already have attorneys they liked. You should always support the notion of loyalty and always appreciate their loyalty to their existing attorneys. It is good hearing when clients are loyal to their attorneys because eventually, when you have an opportunity to do work for those clients, they will be loyal to you, too (and you should be absolutely loyal to your clients).

These are good relationships to have. Generally, take the position that you will never speak negatively about another lawyer to a client. The exception to that rule is, of course, if you know that the lawyer conducts himself in ways that are bad for our profession and that they may ultimately hurt a friend or a friend's business. The legal profession has a hard enough time rehabilitating itself every time a negative story hits the press about attorneys, and you would never want a friend involved with an unscrupulous attorney.

Nonetheless, it is always best to show a high level of professionalism and encourage loyalty between clients and their attorneys, as well as enforce with these potential clients the good things you have heard about their existing attorneys. Such affirmations really go a long way to speak to your professionalism. Moreover, stay with these potential clients, listen to their stories about their attorneys, and, when appropriate, support an attorney's advice. Or, if necessary, give an alternative path or second opinion, but always encourage loyalty between a client and an attorney while that relationship is ongoing—and be sure that you are in second place. Further, within time, a potential client may begin to recognize his or her existing attorney's strengths, specialties, and weaknesses. You may be asked to look into matters that might be closer to your strengths and start working with the client on a limited basis.

If you are not in second place, you will not get that opportunity.

The same goes for referral sources. A predominant banker in the area may have a favorite lawyer to whom he refers cases. That is fine, especially if that lawyer is a high-quality, professional, ethical individual. Get into second place with that referral source. It is important that a referral source sees you regularly and understands what you do and, as mentioned earlier in the networking chapter, that you continue to try to add value to that referral source.

The strategy set forth in this section—making sure you are in second place—takes a while to develop and years to come to fruition. If you are committed to the practice of law and intend on making a career and building a law office second to none in your community, you will, over time, retain many clients by positioning yourself second behind the existing attorney.

Respect Your Clients

As your law practice develops and your contacts and networks expand, the one truism that will develop over time, if not immediately, is that clients are smart, oftentimes smarter than you. Except for matters of law, clients will very often surprise you with certain nuances of their intelligence. Many of your clients may not have gone to college but are successful business people. The tendency for attorneys who are well educated, who probably overperformed in undergrad and then went on to law school and ultimately passed the bar, is to assume that because of their credentials they are smarter than their clients. Honestly, for young attorneys, the assumption should be that the client is smarter than the attorney in almost all ways except for the analysis of the law. The quicker you learn this, the quicker you will learn that clients like to be respected, and then you could have a mature business and legal discussion on their issues.

Eventually, you will be impressed by your clients' understanding and grasp of the nuances of a sophisticated legal issue. Our firm once worked on a case for a client involving sections of the federal tax code relating to alternative minimum tax (AMT). After we discussed certain components of the AMT at length and in great detail, the client asked for some additional time to think through the strategies that we discussed. Weeks later the client called and asked follow-up questions, basically regurgitating in great detail the nuances that we talked about weeks earlier. I was flabbergasted and impressed. This is an exceptionally bright client, but keep in mind that your business clients are generally very skilled mathematically and can calculate profit-and-loss figures and the cause and effect of certain business costs and expenses in their head far quicker than you can calculate them on a calculator (at least to an incredible close degree of estimation).

The point of this section is not only to warn you not to speak down to and patronize clients but also to forewarn you that they are probably great readers of dialogue and body language; they intuitively perceive strengths and weaknesses, reading the attorney's level of confidence, and are high evaluators of human nature. Said another way, you cannot fake your way through a meeting with a client or potential client.

Being an honest, forthright individual is the best rule of thumb for client relationships. Sometimes when a client matter does not go as planned, if you are remotely to blame for the end result, you need to look the client square in the eye and say, "We could have done a few things better," if that is, in fact, true. Do not fall on the sword just to take the blame for something that you did not do wrong. Many times there are discretionary decisions that have to be made in a litigated matter, documentation drafting, and business transactions that have more than one option. If the wrong option was chosen and you were part of that decision-making process, you should own it, analyze all the secondary routes with which to proceed, and meet with the client to have an honest discussion about the fallout.

As you will see in your career, attorneys are infamous for blaming other people, blaming outside circumstances, or blaming the client, sometimes right to the client's face. If it is appropriate to allocate blame to someone other than yourself, certainly stand up for yourself and your law office and, in a professional manner, discuss the problem and the problems that exist and how to solve them. However, although lawyers are constantly concerned with being sued for malpractice,

> Many times there are discretionary decisions that have to be made in a litigated matter, documentation drafting, and business transactions that have more than one option.

somewhat subconsciously, they are taught never to admit a mistake or in any way admit that some discretionary decision went wrong.

Similarly, in ordinary nonlegal dialogue with clients, you need to apologize to clients if you show up to a meeting late. Sometimes that happens in the legal profession because of an extended court hearing, meeting, or telephone call. Moreover, some lighthearted "sorry about that" is insufficient. A sincere handshake with a direct look in the client's eye and apologizing for being late to a meeting is a step in the right direction and then move right on into the meeting. At the end of the meeting, saying one final time, "I do not want to belabor this point, but I am really sorry for being late to our meeting" is a good way to end the meeting. You will never experience a client to be anything less than forgiving once you have apologized at the beginning of the meeting and the end of the meeting when the meeting went well.

Clients are as important as you are, and their schedule is equally important. It is impolite and unprofessional to make them wait; moreover, to make them wait without a sincere apology is unacceptable.

Last, you need to know that although this type of honest dialogue with clients may make you feel uncomfortable, it helps reduce malpractice claims against your office. As you will see in the next section of this chapter, clients who pursue malpractice suits usually cite a lack of communication, respect, and empathy as the reasons why they pursue actions against their attorneys. It is well documented that the most malpractice claims against doctors are filed against the specialist (i.e., the surgeon). Medical malpractice claims against the family doctor or the attending physician are far more rare, even if the attending physician treated the patient and was a member of the diagnosis team. In other words, people do not want to sue people (attorneys and physicians) with whom they feel a human connection. If the human side of practicing law is not enough, the fear of malpractice actions should be.

The Things That Clients Hate

As you review countless sections of this book, including Chapter 15, on best practices in this book, one common theme you will see is the importance of communication with the client. You cannot underestimate the importance of this to attorneys and administrative support staff in your office. While good communication is an affirmative requirement that sounds like just good business advice or good client management, conversely the lack of client communication will thwart any possibility for the growth of your business and be the precursor for the failure of your firm.

Clear, timely communication with clients is essential, and the failure to take this recommendation in client relations will anger clients, give clients an opportunity and invitation to seek a new attorney, and in the worst case, sue you for malpractice. Many times you will not even realize how offending your lack of communication is to the client, and you will be phased out of working for that client without really knowing about it. The ABA has, on multiple occasions, issued studies and client surveys on clients' commentary about their attorneys.

In September 2006, the *ABA Journal* reported on in-house counsel and their review of law firms and cited a study that was nothing short of an eye-opening masterpiece on what clients want most from their lawyers. The ABA E-report article was based on the results of an extensive survey conducted by a private consulting company, the BTI

Consulting Group of Wellesley, Massachusetts.[6] BTI surveyed general counsels of large corporations regarding what these general counsels expect from their attorneys and why, when it became necessary, they fired attorneys.[7] The bottom line, as you can imagine, is "ineffective lawyer-client communication." BTI's 2005 research revealed that seven out of ten general counsels do not recommend their primary law firm to others for legal work.[8]

The survey results reported by BTI indicate that *neither* case outcome *nor* cost of services were the most frequently mentioned cause of dissatisfaction.[9] Imagine that neither the outcome of the case nor the fees you charge were mentioned as the most frequently used reasons for client dissatisfaction. Instead, when asked, "What is the one thing that your outside counsel does that just drives you crazy?" more than half of the general counsels gave answers that can be summarily categorized as "poor communication":[10]

21%—Failure to keep clients adequately informed
15%—Lack of client focus (i.e., failure to listen, nonresponsiveness, arrogance)
10%—Making decisions without clear authorization of awareness
 7%—Failure to give clear, direct advice
53%—TOTAL

How clear does the communication need to be? The top general counsels in Fortune 500 companies indicated that end results in a case were not the most important decision when firing their attorneys.[11]

A July 2012 publication of the International Bar Association reported data from Western Europe that is consistent with the 2005 study of American law firms by BTI citing a survey of 219 senior corporate counsels by Martin-Dale Hubble that indicated "poor communication was one of the top reasons for ceasing to retain a law firm."[12]

For years sociologists have weighed in on the matter. Tom Tyler, a leading researcher in this area, made the following bold statement in *American Social Psychologist*: "Clients care most about the process—having their problems or disputes settled in a way that they view as fair, second most important is achieving a fair settlement, the least important factor is the number of assets they may end up winning."[13]

---

6. Clark D. Cunningham, *What Do Clients Want from Their Lawyers?* 3 THE JOURNAL OF DISPUTE RESOLUTION (forthcoming); Mary Heaney, *Communications Breakdown*, IN-HOUSE PERSPECTIVE: THE MAGAZINE OF THE IBA CORPORATE COUNSEL FORUM no. 3, 13 (July 2012).
7. *See id.*
8. *Id.*
9. *See id.*
10. *Id.*
11. *Id.*
12. *Id.*
13. Clark D. Cunningham, *What Do Clients Want from Their Lawyers?* 3 THE JOURNAL OF DISPUTE RESOLUTION (forthcoming); Tom Tyler, *Client Perceptions of Litigation—What Counts: Process or Results?* TRIAL 40 (July 1998).

The data is incredibly clear.

Australia's largest indemnity insurer for lawyers, LawCover, commissioned a risk management project to study a representative sample from over two thousand professional liability claims.[14] The researchers in most cases also interviewed the lawyer retained by LawCover to defend the claim. The results were disturbing. Lawyers did not seem to understand the dynamics of the claims against them. The researchers concluded that most lawyers "need to see the patterns to understand how they should act differently in the future to reduce their inherent exposure."[15] By far the most significant cause of professional negligence claims was not dissatisfaction of the outcome but instead related to the handling of the client relationship: the most frequent problems were failure to listen to the client, failure to ask appropriate questions, and failure to explain relevant aspects of the matter.[16]

The evaluators concluded that

> consideration should be given by the profession to introducing additional training to redress identified performance deficits in the related areas of interpersonal skills and client management techniques. This training should be client focused, rather than transaction focused: it should train practitioners to recognize that client needs are not confined to obtaining objective outcomes; and it should help lawyers listen to clients more attentively, diagnose their various levels of needs and demonstrate empathy.[17]

The empirical evidence is undeniable. If you want to keep clients, keep them absolutely informed and communicate with them. If you want to avoid getting sued for malpractice, be available to take your clients' calls, communicate with them, and update them on their legal issues constantly.

If you do the things often enough that clients hate, you will be sued for malpractice. Examine an analogy to medical malpractice from the stunning analysis in Malcolm Gladwell's bestseller *Blink: The Power of Thinking Without Thinking*.[18] In it, Gladwell discusses thin-slicing subtle human attributes and finding characteristics of physicians that get sued for malpractice, as well as the characteristics of physicians that do not get sued for malpractice.

---

14. *Id.* at 4.
15. *Id.*; Ronwin North & Peter North, *Managing Client Expectation and Professional Risk: A Unique Insight Into Professional Negligence Exposure in the Australian Legal Profession*, at ix (Streeton Consulting, 1994), *available at* http://clarkcunningham.org/PR/North&North.htm.
16. *See id.*
17. *Id.*
18. Malcolm Gladwell, Blink: The Power of Thinking Without Thinking (Little, Brown 2005).

At first, one would think it is obvious that physicians who make mistakes would get sued, and the smartest, brightest, and best physicians do not make those mistakes, and as such do not get sued. Gladwell's study indicates that physicians getting sued has very little to do with how many mistakes the doctor makes.[19] The analysis of malpractice lawsuit shows that there are physicians who make lots of mistakes and never get sued.[20] Moreover, an overwhelming number of patients who are harmed by physician malpractice never sue any physician at all.[21] In other words, patients, at least in the medical malpractice scenario, do not file lawsuits because they have been harmed with poor medical care; they file lawsuits for other reasons.[22]

Gladwell quotes Alice Burkin, a leading medical malpractice lawyer, and says that

> people just don't sue doctors they like. . . . In all the years I've been in this business, I've never had a potential client walk in and say "I really like this doctor and I feel terrible about doing it, but I want to sue him." We've had people come in saying they want to sue some specialist, and we'll say "We don't think that doctor was negligent. We think it's your primary care doctor who was at fault." And the client will say, "I don't care what she did. I love her, and I'm not suing her."[23]

The stories are clear that if a patient likes and connects with the physician, the patient will not sue that physician for medical malpractice.

How do you get to that position?

Gladwell cites medical researcher Wendy Levinson's study between a group of physicians who get sued and a group of physicians who do not get sued. She concludes that surgeons who have never been sued spend more than three minutes longer with each patient than do those who have been sued.[24] Doctors who did not get sued made more "orienting comments such as 'First I'll examine you, and then we will talk the problem over' or 'After the examination, I will leave time for your questions.'"[25] Levinson further stated that such physicians were *more likely* to engage in the act of listening, saying such things as "Go on, tell me more about that," and they were far more likely to laugh and be funny during the visit.[26] There was no difference between the doctors who have been sued and the doctors who have not been sued with respect to the details about the medications or

---

19. *Id.* at 40.
20. *Id.*
21. *Id.*
22. *Id.*
23. *Id.* at 41.
24. *Id.*
25. *Id.* at 42.
26. *Id.*

the patient's condition that they conveyed to the patient. The difference was *entirely* on how they talked to their patients.[27]

Gladwell's research went on to cite other studies about filtering conversations between patients and their physicians. After content filtering the conversations, Gladwell's research showed that all that was left was an emphasis on the intonations, pitch, and rhythm of the conversations. As Gladwell would say, these are thin-slicing qualities. By analyzing attributes other than content—the person's voice for warmth, hostility, dominance, and anxiousness— psychologists could determine which surgeons got sued and which did not. Incredibly, not even knowing what the doctors were saying to the patients, the psychologists were able to pinpoint which doctors would get sued based on *how* they talked to the patients. If the voice sounded less dominant and more concerned, the surgeon tended to be in the nonsued group.[28]

What is the upshot lesson? Consistent with the tone of the best practices theme in this book, Gladwell reinforces that it all comes down to a matter of respect, and the simplest way that respect is communicated is through your tone of voice. How does a client feel when you talk to him or her?

By design, this very necessary information is in this section relating to things that clients hate, as opposed to the affirmative drill about how to satisfy clients with good service. You need to know clearly what clients expect and how they feel when you talk to them. While this may sound like a difficult set of expectations to meet, it should actually be viewed in a very upbeat and positive manner. Clear, empathetic client communication, evident in your tone and how you listen, means more to the client than the actual results of his or her case and the legal fees associated with your work on the client matter. If that is not a good enough reason to maintain active communication with your client, keeping happy clients and growing your practice is an additional bonus.

Finally, without overemphasizing the obvious here, communication is so easy with e-mails and texts. While a phone conversation is, by far, the best way to communicate with clients, that may lead to nonlegal discussions and social conversation. When you are looking at the pile of papers on your desk and anxious to get off the phone with a client to get to other matters, simple e-mails keep the client informed and happy between phone calls.

Please read and double check the section in this book on best practices and create a best practices booklet and policy for you and your firm. At every stage of the way, real and sincere client communication is a best practice.

---

27. *Id.*
28. *Id.* at 43.

Clients on Which to Take a Pass

Notwithstanding all your efforts to make the phone ring, meet with new clients, and meet with new referral sources, you may need to pass on the case of a client who comes into your office at a time when you need work.

Remember, you are open for business and networking for every opportunity to perform legal services for clients, but that does *not* mean that you must take every case that walks in the door. You can evaluate the case and/or the client on its merits to determine whether to take a pass on the case, or based on a character and ethical read of the client himself or herself. As a result, be forewarned on the following cases:

1. *The client has gone through too many attorneys on the same case.* As you inquire about a case with a client, and presumably not the beginning of the case, the client indicates that he or she wants to switch attorneys because the former attorney is incompetent, has a personality conflict with the client, or "messed up my case." Whatever the reason, be suspect of being the second attorney on such a case. However, sometimes after thorough research and diligence, you may come to the conclusion that the client has an accurate read on the attorney or that the attorney really is out over his or her skill limits or is perhaps just overworked and not putting enough time in on this case; then

   > Avoid cases of clients who habitually change lawyers.

   you might agree to substitute on the case. Generally speaking, do not substitute if you find out that you are to be the proposed third attorney on a single case. Unfortunately, some lawyers are overworked and do not give the right amount of attention to cases that such cases deserve. However, more times than not, such attorneys are working hard on all of their cases and are competent and do want to do the best possible job for their client. Avoid cases of clients who habitually change lawyers. Another thing to consider is whether you had a relationship with the client in the past. That may have some bearing on the history of the case and your trust level with this particular client. Also, see how much is available in the published record, such as the court file, to make your own evaluation of the attorney's competence. These are all things that should come into play if you know you are not the first attorney contacted on a particular case. Similarly, also inquire about the client's previous attorney on other matters. Why hasn't the client called the previous lawyer? These are all fair questions to ask based on the understanding that you are not the only attorney the client knows and are trying to find out how the client came into your office. Also evaluate the referral source. Call up the referral source to ask if he or she knows that client well, what this client's history is with respect to being litigious, and whether the client seems to be a rational businessperson.

2. *Avoid overly emotionally charged clients.* Avoid cases where the client's expectations cannot be reasonably managed. Many times clients (with no legal background whatsoever) believe that they have a slam-dunk case and that you should be dying to take the case to somehow benefit you. Often in those cases, the clients do not have the budget to foresee a litigation matter through to trial. Many times the clients who have unmanageable expectations also are so personally invested that their judgment about a case is overtaken by their emotion. Sometimes these are divorce cases where there is a high degree of emotional stress on the client, bankruptcy cases where clients may be losing their home, or other neighborhood disputes where one client does not want to be pushed around by another neighbor. Again, the guiding force should be whether you can add value. Moreover, will the client see the value you are adding? Needless to say, in all of these cases the client must be willing to deposit a retainer check with you to start the case. The client's deposit of a retainer check is a result of his or her emotional state; if you have evaluated the client correctly, however, eventually the payment for your legal services will evaporate as the client gains control of his or her emotions. What brings these emotions in check, more times than not, are monthly bills from your office as you fight to vindicate your client's rights. Within time, the client's emotion against the other party will diminish, and the client will start to become angry with you for sending them monthly bills as you fight for his or her rights. In these cases, it is very difficult to get the client to appreciate your efforts in the long run.

3. *Avoid the "easy cases" or where the client promises to give you a large contingency fee, and sometimes all the recovery.* First of all, be very concerned in civil litigation where the client wants you to take the case on a contingency fee basis. Contingency fee cases are usually reserved for class-action suits and personal injury matters where you, as the attorney, know that there will be a pool of money from which to collect (i.e., money from the insurance company) once you prevail justifying your assessment of liability early on in the case. If there is no such pool of money from which to collect, taking a case on a contingency, even if the client promises to give you 100% of what you recover, is a bad idea. These are cases from which to run away. If you are working on a purely contingent basis for a client in a civil case or a commercial transaction based on your receiving money at the closing, there is a high probability that the client will not cooperate with you throughout the proceeding and in the end you will have no case to put on and no cooperation with which to close the deal. Again, these cases fall closely in line with emotionally charged cases: if the client is not willing to invest his or her own money in the case, and in the end if the client is not telling you all of the facts of the case, you may wind up with a far

worse result than you ever thought. If it is a great case, factually, the client should pay you on an hourly basis to represent his or her interest.

4. *Cases with bad facts and bad law.* Sometimes potential clients come in asking if they have any rights in a dispute. Such a question is a legitimate reason for a client to call your office to schedule an appointment and for you to provide the individual with a free initial consultation. But that does *not* mean you must take the case. After a full vetting of the facts of the case, as presented to you in a probably somewhat biased fashion from the client, and finding that the applicable law does not help your client's position, take a pass on the case. It is sometimes difficult to break the news to the client that you will pass on the case because that sounds like a critical judgment of the client's conduct, but you can also encourage the client to get a second opinion. Indeed, potentially referring the individual to one of your colleagues for a second opinion might be good for you, the client, and your colleague. Nonetheless, you have had an opportunity to have an honest discussion with the client. If during that process you have tried to encourage the client or give some legal advice on how to conduct himself or herself if a similar situation happens in the future, then the client will have gotten value out of the meeting with you and will probably appreciate that and call you the next time another matter comes up. Also, during those initial client interviews, no matter how uncomfortable the meeting is, the person should have filled out a new client intake sheet so that you can capture the individual's contact information, which allows you to add the potential client to your master lists for mailing, e-mailing, and other social media platforms.

Notwithstanding all the cases set forth above with respect to client matters on which you will pass, do not forget to send a disengagement letter to the client, very briefly documenting the general facts of the case and your inability to represent the client. Also make the client aware that a statute of limitations may be pending on the case and that he or she should seek other counsel immediately. Following is an example of this type of nonengagement letter that you may use.

NONENGAGEMENT LETTER

JOHN SMITH LAW OFFICE, LTD.

SENT VIA U.S. CERTIFIED MAIL
RETURN RECEIPT REQUESTED

_____

_____

_____

Dear _____:

You recently contacted our firm and requested that we represent you in connection with
_____. Unfortunately, after a review of the facts, our firm has decided
not to represent you in this matter.

In declining to accept your matter, our firm is not expressing an opinion as to its merits. You should be aware that failure to proceed promptly may result in your legal matter being barred by a time limit. Therefore, I recommend that you contact another attorney or take appropriate action on your own regarding this matter immediately.

Thank you for contacting John Smith Law Office, Ltd.

Sincerely,
JOHN SMITH LAW OFFICE, LTD.

John Smith

Although your words in turning down the case sound unambiguous to you, the client may, in fact, walk out of your office thinking that you are still considering taking the case, about to take the case, or in fact have agreed to represent him or her in the matter. Send the client a letter making it clear that you are not taking the case.

Chapter 15

Best Practices

The intent of this chapter is to speak directly to individuals starting a law firm who have never worked in a law firm, preferably a top-quality law firm, in the past. It is difficult, absent experience working as a clerk, an attorney, or other professional in a law office, to know the right way to do everything. In fact, without the right training, it is impossible. Therefore, this chapter is intended to create a blueprint, through the examples given, for building a best practices manual for your firm so that all your employees are trained the way you want them trained and so that every client receives the same exceptional client experience. This chapter does not purport to set forth an exhaustive list of all you will need to do. Instead, it recommends that you document the right way to do things, because doing so is necessary for the successful future of your operation.

As your firm grows, you need to develop a series of best practices that will maximize the quality of your services, create efficiency, and minimize any potential for errors and mismanagement of client files. Your best practices initiative should be an ongoing working document you regularly revisit, but not less often than annually, to remind yourself of the procedures that you and every employee working with you need to follow in order to make your law office the best law firm in its market by providing excellent service.

> As your firm grows, you need to develop a series of best practices that will maximize the quality of your services, create efficiency, and minimize any potential for errors and mismanagement of client files.

These best practices need to be institutionalized into your firm's DNA so that everyone understands. Doing this will maximize the continuity of service your law office brings to a client.

New Clients and Initial Meetings

The goal of a telephone call to your office is to schedule an appointment with the clients so that they can meet in your office to discuss their matter with an attorney. Each one of the initial meetings is unique and has to be handled accordingly, but with experience a pattern has emerged that is the best format for an initial client consultation.

- Engage in Introductions.
  - Be prompt. Shake hands with every person in the room—potential clients, family members, business partners—while handing out business cards and firm brochures. Thank the clients for taking time to come to your office. Smile and welcome them as if they are guests in your home.
  - Offer coffee or water.
  - Be prepared. Bring your retainer contract, your business card, and any other documents that may be needed.
  - If the new clients have not filled out a client intake form, obtain preliminary information, including their name, address, and telephone number, and ask, "How did you hear about us?" Make sure you understand the answer clearly.
  - If a new client arrives early, your assistant or receptionist should give the client the client intake form and ask the client to fill it out before the meeting.
- Begin with Fact-Finding Questions.
  - It is usually best to stick with a chronological order. The potential client's memory of the facts and circumstances is oftentimes jumbled, and if the client's recitation moves out of chronological order, keep bringing the client back to a timeline. This way you understand the sequence of events, and your notes are also very clear. Interviews vary from practice group to practice group but tend to work well using chronological order when dealing with business litigation, criminal matters, business disputes, and evictions, as well as other dispute resolution issues.
  - Certain practice groups favor question-and-answer (Q&A) checklists that need to be followed precisely with you, the attorney, controlling the interview. Checklist interviews are included in estate planning, business organizations, bankruptcy, and noncontested estate administration cases.
  - Some controversies are usually handled on a year-by-year basis, enabling you to get a thorough, full understanding of each year's events, and sometimes the interview involves more of a checklist type of analysis.
  - Take thorough notes. Keep your head down and keep writing. Clients will be impressed. Look the client in the eye with questions, but take copious notes.
- Show Empathy and Make the Human Connection.

- Explain to the potential client, especially in dispute and problematic cases, that you understand the situation he or she is in. Give examples of similar conversations that you have had with other clients (not using names, of course) regarding the emotional aspect of what the client is going through.
- Try to make a personal connection with potential clients. Empathize with them and let them know that you are emotionally on their side of the case. It is very important that you make a sincere human connection with the clients if possible. If they feel you understand them and are truly concerned, this will increase the chance of being hired.
- Focus on earning their trust and confidence. This is a very important intangible consideration of any potential client's willingness to hire you. If the clients feel that they can trust you, and you have earned their confidence that their livelihood is in good care, there is a higher probability they will retain your office.
- Be a good listener.
- Make a Preliminary Legal Analysis.
  - New clients want a legal opinion of their case. It is very difficult to tell them after a forty-five-minute interview that they are going to win a case that may involve two or three years of litigation. The initial client consultation should be of a high professional level in order to gather facts, and only qualified, preliminary opinions should be given if at all. Clients will value you based on your aggressiveness as well as your empathy to their situation. You also need to advise them as to the strengths and weaknesses of their case or the complexities of the legal transactions. Whether the matter is a litigation matter or transactional work, clients need to understand that issues come up that are not foreseen in the very first client meeting, but that the clients will be kept informed of all of these matters. Emphasize all the positive points to the case that you feel very good about and that will help the clients with the results they are seeking. Warn clients of the pitfalls of their case and how you will prepare for those problems and other problems that will inevitably come up that have not been discussed during the first meeting. This may be an appropriate time in the meeting to explain the resources that are available to you and how and why the client would be best served by hiring your office.
  - When faced with a difficult question, do not hesitate to say that you will be able to answer the question only after careful research and analysis.
  - Explain that the law does not always address every fact pattern and that, in those situations, prior court decisions must be analyzed in order to obtain a better picture of how a court may handle the client's issue.
- Explain Your Services.
  - Explain how you bill (whether hourly or flat fee); explain your monthly billing practice and urge the client to review the bill and call with any questions.

- Advise the client that he or she will be copied on letters and emphasize how you make certain that clients are kept well informed of their case throughout the entire matter.
- Highlight that your office has a strict policy of promptly returning client phone calls (many attorneys often have a poor reputation of not returning calls).
- If more than one attorney is in your firm, explain how the firm is structured such that the attorney working on the issue has focused his or her practice on that specific area of the law and will, therefore, be efficient. The client will not have a generalist learning on the client's dime.
- Discuss how the fee will be determined, and emphasize that the retainer is not a cap on fees.
- Explain that you understand the desire to minimize fees and will assign the simple, more routine aspects of the case to younger attorneys or clerks (if they exist in your office) with lower hourly rates than those of more experienced attorneys, but stress that at all times you will remain in charge of the matter.
- Explain that there are many variables that could affect the fee amount, that these are variables that you cannot control, such as the opposition, how organized the client is in providing information and documents, and rulings by judges or governmental agencies.

> When faced with a difficult question, do not hesitate to say that you will be able to answer the question only after careful research and analysis.

- Close the Interview.
  - Have a retainer contract ready (see Chapter 9) and ask the new clients if you have answered all of their questions. Explain the need for a retainer check, and ask them when you can expect a signed copy of the retainer contract and check.
  - Remind clients that you have given them your business card, and invite them to contact you with any follow-up questions.
  - Shake hands and walk clients to the door as you would guests in your home.
- Additional Considerations.
  - Initial meetings should be held, when possible, at your office. Considering that the initial client consultations are probably free of charge, a client should invest the time to come to your office for the initial meeting. Deviations to this general rule should be for marketing or referral purposes.
  - At the outset of the meeting, the potential client should be informed that the discussions during such meetings will be held confidential and that you, as an attorney, are prohibited from disclosing the conversation without the client's consent.

- Experienced attorneys should have a new, less experienced attorney (if there is one in your office) sit in on an initial client meeting for that attorney to gain experience. New attorneys (i.e., anyone with less than three years of experience) must have a more experienced attorney sit in with them during initial client consultations.
- An attorney sitting in the first meeting should prepare an extensive memo detailing all information given to you by the client (in documents and words), highlighting critical deadlines, impressions of the client, the client's expectations, and the advice or opinions, if any, rendered by you as lawyers. It is important to include in that memorandum the fact that you explained the weaknesses of the case or the unique complexities of the transaction. The memo should conclude by identifying the final action items, the expected action of the client, and the client's expected action of you. All clients should understand that you cannot take any action on their case until you received the signed retainer agreement and a retainer check.
- Sometimes an abbreviated version of the memorandum of the first meeting should be converted to a client letter, and a client should receive a letter from your office summarizing the first meeting. This letter does not need to be as detailed as the internal memorandum.
- A "thank you for retaining us" letter to the client, reaffirming the billing procedures at your office, must be mailed to the client (flat fee cases and cases taken on a contingency basis will have their own unique thank-you letter). This letter should reaffirm that other attorneys may be working on the matter. On the following page is an example of a sample letter. You will see that this letter also helps to minimize accounts receivables and gets clients to pay.
- Remember to send letters of nonengagement to clients who have come into your office but have not hired you after thirty days (see Chapter 14). Those potential clients who drop off documents but do not retain you should also be sent a nonengagement letter after a reasonable time period has elapsed. Be sure to return any copies of documents to the client along with that letter.
- Run the client name, his or her business name, and the known opposing party through your conflict-of-interest system as described in Chapter 18.

THANK-YOU LETTER

JOHN SMITH LAW OFFICE, LTD.

THANK YOU FOR CHOOSING
John Smith Law Office, Ltd.

Dear _____:

We are pleased you have chosen John Smith Law Office, Ltd. to assist you in your matter. I wanted to take a moment to briefly reemphasize our billing procedure to you. Under separate cover, you should expect to receive a bill from our office detailing any work performed for the past month (and every month thereafter) in addition to any applicable charges and/or costs for work performed, if any.

Please recall that in accordance to the terms of your legal services contract with us, you have agreed to pay your account in full within ten (10) days from the date of your billing statement to avoid any interest charge from accruing, and to enable us to continue providing you with legal assistance. Timely payment of your billing statement is crucial in that it is the strict policy of our firm that any balance that remains unpaid for a period of sixty (60) days or more is basis for either discontinuing work on your case or our immediate withdrawal from your case altogether.

As a reminder to you, the retainer deposit you furnished to us is not a cap on legal fees and will be held in our trust account, separately from our operating account. You will be billed on an hourly basis—not a flat fee. The fees and costs portion of your monthly statement will reflect any time expended on your behalf along with a description of the work performed and the attorney who performed the work. Although I will be performing the bulk of the work on your case, other attorneys may be involved in your case as well and perform a limited amount of work to support my efforts.

We ask that you take a moment to carefully review your billing statements sent to you by our office each month. If you should ever have any questions concerning the work performed or legal fees and/or costs billed to you, please contact our office immediately so we can address your concern. Otherwise, we will assume that the billing statements are satisfactory to you. Lastly, should you ever have a change of mailing address or other contact information, please provide our office with your new information.

THANK-YOU LETTER (continued)

Please note that at any time during our handling of your case should you receive any notices, correspondence, or any other contact from the opposing party, please be sure to contact our office immediately and be sure to forward us a copy of the aforementioned, as it may be time-sensitive for you (that is, our office) to provide a response.

That being said, we appreciate your business. If you have any questions concerning this letter, please do not hesitate to contact my office.

> Sincerely,
> JOHN SMITH LAW OFFICE, LTD.
>
>
> John Smith

Client Communication and File Documentation

Keep good, organized files. One of the most important components of the client file is all of your client communication. As such, commit to the following:

- Clients should be kept informed of their cases at all times. All e-mails to and from clients and any third party should be printed and kept in the client file in the same way that you maintain copies of all traditional letters and correspondence.
- When possible, material conversations with the opposing side or the client, whether in litigation or a business transaction, should be documented in a letter or memo to the file and sent to the client.
- Correspondence and e-mails among the lawyers in your office about a client matter should be prepared in a way that is completely transparent, and the client should be copied on the matter. The client needs to know that you consult among each other to provide the best and lowest-cost services to the client. The attorney replying to an e-mail should always do so with the awareness that he or she is writing something that the client will see. The writing standards applied to traditional correspondence (in terms of spelling and grammar) should also be applied to any e-mail.
- Keep the client absolutely informed of everything you do because then, when the client receives the bill, he or she can appreciate the extent of the work you have done for him or her and is less likely to raise issues regarding the bill. Use the "no charge" entry (hereafter a No Charge) to document time spent but not charged to a client. It is better, even on the most minimal action that you would not bill for, to put said action on the bill as a No Charge.
- Use certified mail on all correspondence going to a government agency and follow up with the green card. A green card alone might be sufficient if the right person did not receive the documents.
- On matters that move slowly, such as federal tax cases or clients who drag out estate planning, remember to send a letter to a client approximately every thirty days to give the client an update as to what is happening on the matter. If nothing has happened, please let them know this as well. If a client is taking an extended period of time to return signed documents or otherwise respond, send the client a letter reminding him or her that the project is awaiting their response. This ensures that the file is properly documented if the client causes deadlines to be missed.
- If you promise that you will call the client back by a certain time, such as the end of the day, make sure to do so or e-mail them to let the client know what happened; if nothing happened, call or e-mail the client to let him or her know. Inform your support staff that you have promised a return call, and ask them to follow up to be sure

you do so. Clients become livid when they are promised a phone call that they do not receive from their attorney.

- Before sending any critical (something other than a transmittal letter) correspondence to the opposing side, always send it to the client first to review and approve with a date to respond. Clients appreciate the input, and it keeps them engaged in the process.

- During the last week of every month, go through the files in your office; if you find that contact with the client has not been made in the last two weeks, dictate a quick letter to the client, billing appropriately, to let him or her know that you are still working the case, that it is on your mind, and that you will contact him or her with any substantive follow-up as soon as you have information to convey. Summarize what happened in the last thirty days, and set forth the critical dates coming up in the next thirty days. Doing this could help your month-end billing as well as improve the client's confidence in you and your efforts on this case.

- Have a second attorney (or another qualified assistant, if one exists in your office) review substantive correspondence.

- All assignments to other attorneys in your office requesting research should be prepared in memo form. It is not necessary to send this to the client.

Correspondence and e-mails among the lawyers in your office about a client matter should be prepared in a way that is completely transparent, and the client should be copied on the matter.

- When sending faxes, be mindful that the client's fax machine may be shared with others. Be sure the client has given permission to send a fax to him or her. Otherwise, you may inadvertently disclose confidential information to third parties.

- When sending e-mails, be sure not to recklessly "Reply to All" unless you are clear on who is on the recipient list. Many times a client will send an e-mail and copy an opposing party. If you respond, do not "Reply to All" unless you intend that all see your response.

- Always get the client's permission before you authorize a service from another company on a client's behalf (e.g., appraiser, inspector, private investigator, process server), and send a certified letter or an e-mail to the client explaining whom you have hired, the fee structure discussed, and the terms of payment; also note that the client will be billed directly for the services.

- All letters and e-mails should be saved and stored in the client's electronic file.

Client Files

- Determine your terminology for client files. Every client should have a working file that has the current information in it and documentation for the most recent case on which you are working. In addition, the client matter should also have an electronic file on your server where all documents are saved.

- Determine the numbering system you will use for your client files. You may use an alpha system based on the last name of the client or the name of the corporation, or a numeric system, perhaps just based on chronology. For a numeric system, create a decimal format in which the client identifier is to the left of the decimal. To the right, you can extend the numeric system to identify different matters for the same client. As an example, your first three clients might be set up as 1001.001, 1002.001, and 1003.001. When that first client comes to you for a second project, that new file will be set up as 1001.002.

- Every file needs to have some consistent filing arrangement. The first thing in a client file is the client intake form, which gives all the basic client information in terms of phone numbers, e-mail addresses, postal addresses, referral sources, and other contact information. Once that information is scanned in or placed up front in the client file, there should be another insert for correspondence, then notes and memoranda, powers of attorney, and client papers, and then a miscellaneous run of inserts for specific documentation, pleadings, and other relevant documents. In order to retrieve litigation matters quickly, for example, you will need a separate insert for just the pleadings, discovery, and other court-related filings. As the client files get larger, you may need to expand all the inserts with more specificity.

- Everything in the paper working file must be included in the electronic file. Letters and other documentation need to be saved electronically. Letters in particular need to be scanned in after they are signed and sent. Keeping an unsigned copy of a letter is worthless.

- Keep files organized. If you are opening the office on your own, you will know how you like to organize the file, and you will be able to navigate around an ad hoc disorganized file system because you may be the *only one* touching those files. However, in order to create the right discipline in your system that will lend itself to growth in your law firm, keep the client files organized, and demand that everybody who works with you and around you keep client files organized in the same manner.

- Once a client matter is completed, keep the file in your office or storage room for about six months. There may be follow-up questions after the closing, and you will want to have the paper file handy. Once the six-month seasoning period is completed, you or your support staff should do one more confirmation that every sheet of paper in the client file has been scanned into your electronic file system before the paper file is destroyed.

- Destroy client files either internally by shredding them or through a confidential shredding service. Remember, privileged information is in the client file, and as such the file cannot be discarded in the common trash.
- Develop a company policy for original documentation. With the broad availability for scanning and electronic documentation, you will move away from keeping any original documents in your files. Even after the closings of commercial transactions, you will eventually gather all those original documents and send them back to the client. You do not want the liability of keeping original documents any longer, and as the industry moves (ever so slowly) to truly being paperless, you do not want to keep original documents.
- Have your electronic file system mirror, to the best degree possible, your paper filing system. Once you go into a client number on your server, make sure there is a client intake sheet scanned in, a correspondence file, a notes and memo file, a powers of attorney file, a client papers file, and other specific client information files on your electronic file. This way, finding documents will immediately be easier. It will save you an unbelievable amount of time in retrieving old documents if your files are in order and electronically organized.
- It is important to keep files organized so that important documents can be located efficiently when necessary. This is also important in the event another attorney needs to step in on a case and become familiar with the matter. Also, when multiple attorneys are working on a matter and each has his or her own working file, these working files should be combined and organized upon completion of the matter.
- Avoid storing inactive files in attorneys' offices. Files that have not been active in ninety days and are not due to become active in the next ninety days should be reshelved in your file room (or scanned in, if you have adopted scanning procedures) to avoid the need to search for files. There are certain exceptions for clients with constant ongoing work, but these files should be the exception and not the rule.

Litigation

- Explain to the clients up front that you have no idea whether the opposing party will pursue or ignore or delay litigation and that it is therefore absolutely impossible to predict with any degree of certainty the amount of the legal cost on any litigation case. It is imperative that you inform the client that litigation is time-consuming and expensive. There will be multiple court hearings, documents to review, legal research, fact investigation, and drafting and preparation of necessary filings with the court that will require many hours of attorney work. However, stress to the client that you will always try to keep legal fees to a minimum by trying to schedule other court hearings on the same days as theirs and utilizing skilled attorneys at lower hourly rates whenever possible. If you have an associate or associates, you view the utilization of your young associate attorneys as a way to save clients money, not cost them more money. Make this clear to the client—that he or she is hiring a team of legal experts. The client will also have the opportunity to review and approve every court filing. Always empathize with your client's plight. This will be a stressful experience for the client, who will think about it when waking up every morning and when trying to go to sleep every night. Let your clients know you are here for them, and they have an advocate in you.

- Talk openly and honestly about the estimated costs of litigating the matter with a client and how difficult it is to predict the amount of legal fees in a particular case. Whether through raising the initial retainer or getting a guarantor on the legal fees, this financial matter must be thoroughly flushed out with the client at the initial meeting. If you can tell that costs are going to escalate due to some unanticipated filing or occurrence, advise the clients immediately and explain why the costs are necessary and how you will try to accomplish your objective in a cost-efficient manner.

- Investigate the facts. Ask many questions of your client throughout the litigation process. One of the biggest keys to success in litigation is identifying key witnesses and documents early. If there are key witnesses out there, work with the client to gain access to these witnesses and interview them regarding the facts of the case. If possible, try to obtain written statements from witnesses signed by them and witnessed by someone other

> If you have an associate or associates, you view the utilization of your young associate attorneys as a way to save clients money, not cost them more money.

than yourself. Your opponent will try to do the same thing, so this analysis should occur right after you are retained and should continue throughout the litigation process. Early in the case, create a timeline and a witness list that you can amend and expand upon as the litigation progresses.

- At the beginning of every case, envision what you would like to argue in closing argument at trial and work backward from there. What do you want to say? How do you want to say it? Then work backward and determine what evidence you will need in order to present the closing argument you envision.

- Know the Code of Civil Procedure. This comes with experience, but every first-year attorney needs to read and understand the Code of Civil Procedure and the Supreme Court Rules. The fact that you just took the bar should make it that much easier. The best lawyers know how to utilize the Code and the Rules to their client's advantage.

- Gain experience. Sit in on oral arguments, arbitrations, and trials performed by partners and senior associates. While waiting for your case to be called, watch how each judge conducts his or her call, and always get a copy of the judge's standing order or local courtroom rules at the initial status hearing call so that you know the rules of the particular judge.

- Clients must get a written report and a copy of the court order every single time you go into court on the matter. Telephone calls are insufficient. As noted earlier, if this written update is via e-mail, that e-mail should be printed and placed in the file.

- Clients should review every complaint, answer, significant motion, and discovery document prepared by you prior to filing. Oftentimes the clients appreciate overzealous advocacy of their position and can, notwithstanding the court's ruling, appreciate that you are advocating for their position. Also, it helps that they have the ability to correct any factual errors in any motions.

- Send correspondence to clients monthly, reporting and summarizing what happened in the previous month and identifying the relevant dates coming up and the filings that are necessary in the following month.

- Some of the highest compliments clients give about other attorneys' work are when clients report that the attorney told them in advance about the range of potential outcomes for certain motions and strategies. For that reason, through correspondence, you should provide clients with the range of probabilities that may occur in every step of the litigation process.

- Always monitor and manage the client's expectations.

- Make sure clients always feel welcome to come to court, and encourage their attendance at important court hearings, such as motion to dismiss, motion for summary judgment, motion for temporary restraining orders, and motion for preliminary injunctions and any deposition of any witness. Obviously, clients will be required to be present for their own depositions and trials.

- Prepare clients for depositions. When presenting your client for deposition, spend time the day before to prepare him or her for all of the questions that may be asked by opposing counsel. Tell the client the three rules of depositions. First, tell the truth: This is obviously the most important rule but must be stressed to the client. If clients are caught in a half-truth or lie, it will only ruin their creditability and diminish all the otherwise truthful testimony they gave. Second, be nice: Clients need to understand that in most cases, their deposition is opposing counsel's first chance to evaluate them, their demeanor, their creditability, and what kind of witness they will make. Your client needs to remain in control. Third, listen to the question, pause and think before answering, and do not guess: Listening and thinking before answering will enable clients to give better answers and will give you the chance to object to the question if necessary. Nobody wants testimony based on a guess or speculation. It has to be about facts. If clients do not know the answer, tell them that responding "I don't know" is a perfectly acceptable answer in many instances. Also, less is more. Tell them not to give narratives when yes or no will suffice. It is up to opposing counsel to ask the right questions. In addition, you will have the opportunity if necessary to ask questions of your client in order to rehabilitate harmful or confusing testimony. You should take copious notes throughout the deposition and then go back to troublesome areas once opposing counsel is finished. Learn proper objections.

- Know how to take depositions. For your deposition, create an outline of the topics you need to cover. Do not create a word-for-word script, but plan your examination in detail in advance. Listen to the answer your witness gives and ask follow-up questions. Find out the names and areas of knowledge of all other witnesses. Go in chronological order whenever possible. Be courteous and professional at all times. Do not allow yourself to be bullied. You are in charge of the deposition. If confronted with an aggressive or problematic witness, remind the witness that he or she is the one under oath and the one required to answer questions, not the other way around. Learn how to certify questions if the witness refuses to answer.

Transactional and Commercial Real Estate

- Explain to the clients up front that you have no idea how the opposing party will negotiate any contract and that it is therefore absolutely impossible to predict the amount of the legal fees on any transactional case.

> Avoid having a client create a first draft of any agreement.

- Have clients review and approve drafts of asset-purchase agreements and sale agreements before submitting them to the other side.

- Save all drafts, notes, and e-mails relating to document drafts and contracts to be able to revisit the negotiating process electronically years later if necessary. It is best to keep these records in the file in chronological order of their creation so that the development process of the document can be recalled at a later date.

- Even though the client may have made a cursory review of the document, make sure the documents are sent "subject to our client's review and approval" to opposing parties because of subsequent changes that the opposing parties may make.

- When preparing large documents for asset purchases, commercial real estate documents, and loan documents, whenever possible always have a second attorney review the agreements for content, grammar, and form.

- It is always best for one attorney to negotiate a contract from drafting through execution. That attorney will have the most knowledge about the history of the provisions that are negotiated and the final conclusions on each of those issues. After a contract is executed, the time is appropriate to get a second attorney involved, beyond the review noted earlier, in preparing the related documents required to close the transaction.

- Avoid telling clients that your law office has a document library (discussed later in this book) to provide legal documents to clients at the most reasonable possible cost. If you say this to clients, they will expect a "fill in the blanks" agreement at "fill in the blanks" fees. As you know, even though you use documents from your document library, each document still needs to be reviewed line by line, which takes time and causes legal fees. Sophisticated clients know that you do not start every document from scratch.
- Use a consistent form when drafting agreements.
- On closing a major transaction, create a closing book that holds all of the material documents and provide a set to a client.
- On major closings, ask clients if they would like to have a press release.
- Avoid having a client create a first draft of any agreement. Although a client may believe writing a draft will save on legal fees, that typically is not the case. The document the client produces is usually difficult to work with, and the attorney will often spend more time modifying the client's draft document than if the attorney alone drafted the document.
- When possible, as the attorney you, not opposing counsel, should attempt to prepare the first draft of any document. This would give you the advantage in negotiating the terms of the contract.

Estate Planning and Estate Administration
- Be sensitive to what caused the client to come in to see you on the particular matter. Even somewhat benign estate planning may have been triggered by a family tragedy.
- Estate-planning clients are notoriously slow to turn around documents and finish the project. Emphasize in the initial client meeting that you will have a set of documents sent out to them in two weeks—but really try to get the documents out within ten days—and that you would want to have the documents signed within a month of your initial meeting. Set the expectations early that you would like to work with these clients to get the matter concluded within a month.
- Start to introduce, at the will signing or as early as possible, the postexecution work that you can do for your clients on their estate plan—for example, retitling assets; recommending financial advisors and insurance professionals; taking a closer look at their real estate holdings, retirement accounts, and company pension plans. In counties where land records are available online, do not wait for the client to provide a copy of his or her deed to get property transferred into the trust. Obtain a copy of the deed in advance of the will signing and have the appropriate conveyance documents prepared to be signed at that time.

- It is a great idea to create a system to send reminder update letters as early as two years after estate plans are documented. The letter may trigger some thought regarding personal changes in the lives of clients, changes in their retirement situation, or a reminder that their assets should be reviewed again to make sure they were properly titled in the name of their trusts.

- A letter should be sent to all residential real estate clients one year after closing to invite them to your office for a free estate-planning consultation.

- The complete set of executed estate-planning documents should be scanned and saved to the client file on the server. This helps in situations where clients need signed copies of their documents, but their paper file is in storage and cannot be accessed immediately.

- When any original documents are returned to the client, they should be sent by certified mail and marked confidential.

- Advise clients when they are transferring real estate into trust that they will need to contact their title insurance company to have the policy assigned to the trust.

- If the client has sensitive family issues—for example, wanting to disinherit a child, grandchild, or other family member—prepare a memo to the file documenting the reasons for the client's decision. You should have appropriate documentation in the file should there end up being a will or trust contest in the future.

- Follow up every estate-planning marketing call by sending by mail or e-mail a copy of your estate-planning questionnaire.

Family Law and Divorce Matters

- This is a highly problematic area of nonpayment. Talk openly and honestly about the estimated costs of litigating the divorce matter with a client. Whether through raising the initial retainer or getting a guarantor on the legal fees, this matter must be thoroughly flushed out with the client at the initial meeting.

- You understand how emotionally charged divorce clients are, but keep them informed through written correspondence as much as possible. Some attorney, preferably the attorney who has the most knowledge about a client's case, must be available for the client's phone calls and/or return phone calls within the next half day.

- All court orders should be sent to the client with a summary of what happened in court. All of the general litigation rules apply here also.

- Introduce divorce clients (via letter) to real estate or business lawyers with whom to consult on other issues.

- You should work to get all financial discovery documents from clients as soon as possible after receiving the retainer and signed client agreement.

- You should send letters to the client with ample time before each court date, informing the client of the date, time, and location of the court appearance and whether the client's attendance is necessary. Always let the client make the decision to attend or not attend court calls where attendance is not required.

Tax Controversies

- Be well advised that you are competing against an enormous number of tax professionals, among them some very unscrupulous "professionals" trying to solicit potential clients to solve their federal tax problems. As an attorney, take the high road and focus on your approach, not theirs.
- With all initial meetings, you should explain to the client alternative solutions and a potential best possible solution. The client must be counseled on the benefits and burdens of all potential paths, and as these cases tend to move slowly, clients should have summary letters sent to them every month summarizing what has happened in the past and what to expect from future contact with the Internal Revenue Service. In such correspondence, remind clients that they need to contact you or send the IRS documents to you every time they receive something from the Internal Revenue Service.
- Differentiate yourself from an "enrolled agent" by explaining that you are local, that you do not create unreasonable client expectations without a full analysis of the facts and the client's financial situation, and that you are accessible. Many of the enrolled agents are *not* attorneys. Only attorneys are permitted to appear on behalf of a client in U.S. Tax Court.
- Be sure to request an appropriate retainer based on the anticipated immediate amount of work involved in a client's tax case. Do not underestimate a client's ability to pay the requested retainer. Attorneys are often led to believe that a client cannot afford to pay a retainer. Perhaps the client cannot afford your services; in such case, you should suggest that the client seek assistance from pro bono legal sources such as low-income taxpayer clinics maintained at area law schools or, perhaps, the local bar association.
- Make sure each new client executes a contract for legal services and a power of attorney before making contact with the government agency.
- Send every tax client a welcome letter to thank clients for retaining your law firm to represent them before the government agency. This will emphasize and summarize your billing procedures.
- Send the client a summary letter of the initial consultation and the tax strategies discussed and agreed on.
- Mark deadlines that may be applicable to the tax client. Often, there are thirty-day, sixty-day, and other statutory time periods in which to respond and/or preserve a taxpayer's right to challenge the government.
- Unless there are special circumstances that warrant otherwise, contact should be made with the IRS officer, agent, or taxing authority within twenty-four hours of being

retained by the client. A fully executed power of attorney should also be sent to the taxing agency to advise agents of your tax representation of the client.

- When an Offer in Compromise is submitted, the attorney should send to the client an Offer in Compromise procedure letter that outlines the offer process, states the requirements for a successful offer, and identifies the substantiation that should be maintained while pending.

- With Offer in Compromise cases, remind the client to make monthly payments to you to build up the retainer for when the case becomes active and also to provide documentation to the IRS that monthly legal fees are incurred and paid by the taxpayer.

- Powers of attorney documents should be scanned and saved on the server.

- All conversations with the IRS officer, such as those about holds on accounts or extensions of due dates, should be documented in writing.

Chapter 16

Checklists and Document Library

As you begin to think larger and more efficiently for the long run, all your work needs to start being processed and documented in a fashion to improve the firm's future. As I train young people, whether it is for attorney positions or support staff positions, I always remind them never to make the same mistake twice. This fundamental adage about growth really comes into play in the legal field. If you believe that you will go through your whole legal career without ever being surprised at a closing when asked to produce a document that you did not even know existed, or you missed a technical pleading requirement in court, or you discussed the legal issue using some common-law cases with an opposing party, but the opposing counsel then demonstrated to you that there is a local statute that resolves the issue, you might be planning on practicing law in fantasyland.

The growth curve for a young attorney is the same today as it was years ago; you need to roll up your sleeves, work extraordinarily hard with determination, and handle client matters as diligently as possible. The law is so complex and all-encompassing that inevitably issues (only very minor ones, you hope) may be missed, and you will be a better lawyer for it the next time.

> To enhance your growth and the growth of every attorney and support staff and administrative assistant who follows in your law firm, systems need to be put in place to ensure that comprehensive and thorough checklists are executed and followed.

For this reason, in order to enhance your growth and the growth of every attorney and support staff and administrative assistant who follows in your law firm, systems need to be put in place to ensure that comprehensive and thorough checklists are executed and followed.

In addition, in order to effectively bring down the costs of legal services, you need a searchable document library on your computer system, one you can go to at every opportunity. Start with the same excellent and thorough form documents you use for the preparation of client deliverables. Think through the opportunities for checklists and the benefits of them. Everything from substantial legal analysis to practical reminder charts, to human resource issues, could be made more efficient through the use of checklists. The only things that ever hold the practitioner back from creating the greatest checklists are time and discipline.

Included as an appendix to this book are sample checklists and myriad forms that should become the basis for your checklist library. You will find

- Initial probate client meeting checklist;
- Estate-opening checklist;
- Business acquisition: due diligence checklist;
- Checklist for real estate closing;
- New company checklist;
- Estate-planning checklist; and
- Dissolution of marriage checklist.

After you have developed a comprehensive set of checklists for every practice group and administrative function and reviewed them no less than annually, they should become part of your culture, and all your firm's attorneys and administrative assistants need to follow the checklists that you set forth to support the best practices of your firm.

Document Library

Next, create a system where you do not need to start a new document from the beginning more than once.

You need to create a library that is in a searchable database for you to find documents easily. This could be done with a simple system using Microsoft Word or some other shelf document management system. At first, you may populate your document library with form documents that are sold along with books on CD-ROM discs. Once you start to use these documents and feel comfortable that the set you have purchased works for you, input the documents into your document library. If you customize the documents in some fashion, save the customized version also, but annotate it in a way that reminds you how you customized that document.

Attorneys today are preparing and personalizing more of their own documents instead of purchasing set forms, and so consider starting off with good form documents customized by you and your firm to provide the highest-quality documents for your clients at the lowest possible investment and legal fees. Later in this chapter is a grid into which you input your documents for organizational and accessibility purposes. Your electronic document library could simply be a separate document library folder, sitting in your server, that opens up into myriad insert folders under the different practice groups of your firm such as these:

- Family Law
- Commercial Real Estate
- Residential Real Estate
- Estate Planning
- Employment Law
- Health Care Law
- Evictions
- Collection Cases
- Immigration
- Bankruptcy
- Corporate Dissolution
- Litigation
- Personal Injury
- Criminal Law
- Estate and Trust Administration
- Business Start-Ups
- Mechanic's Liens and Construction Law
- Tax Controversies

Using these folders as a starting point, you can fit all relevant documents within these folders and then add others that you need. Then you might need subfolders within the main folders; for example in the estate-planning folder, you could set up subfolders for wills, trusts, health care directives, and life insurance trusts.

As you can see, organization is the first key and discipline the second.

Once the organizational system is set up for your document library, you need to make sure that you or your administrative assistant, in a disciplined fashion and on a regular basis, converts your used documents to sanitized versions (i.e., takes out all client names, addresses, contact information, and deal-specific information) and saves them as blanks so that they are easily reusable for similar deals or matters. Examine the following chart to determine how you can start depositing your own documents into this grid: [1]

---

1. The grid can be created in any fashion that is usable, teachable, searchable, and functional. The formatting of this document library has worked for our firm.

Document Directory

Categories/Folder

- Banking
- Bankruptcy
- Client Management Letters
- Collection
- Commercial Real Estate—Leases
- Commercial Real Estate—Sales
- Condominium
- Conflict of Interest
- Construction and Mechanics Liens
- Employment Law
- Estate Planning
- Family Law
- Foreclosure
- General Business
- Health Care
- How-to Guides
- Immigration
- Litigation
- Loan Documents
- Miscellaneous and Office
- New Client Documents
- Probate
- Residential Real Estate
- Social Media
- Tax
- Traffic

CATEGORY: BANKING

Document Name	Key Words & Document Description	Added by	Reference Client or Number
Commercial Real Estate Documents			
Miscellaneous Documents & Bank Policy			
Syndicated Loan Documents			
Commercial Loan Documents			
Foreclosure			
Workouts			
Loan Documents			

CATEGORY: BANKRUPTCY

Document Name	Key Words & Document Description	Added by	Reference Client or Number
Cover Letters			
Motions			
Adversary Claims			
Claims			

CATEGORY: CLIENT MANAGEMENT LETTERS

Document Name	Key Words & Document Description	Added by	Reference Client or Number
Welcome Letters			

CATEGORY: COLLECTION

Document Name	Key Words & Document Description	Added by	Reference Client or Number
Demand Letters & 30-, 60-, and 90-Day Letters			
County-Specific Documents			
Miscellaneous			
Complaints, Affidavits, Motions			
Proceedings			

CATEGORY: COMMERCIAL REAL ESTATE—LEASES

Document Name	Key Words & Document Description	Added by	Reference Client or Number
Correspondence			
Leases			
Memoranda & Assignment of Lease			
Eviction & Notices of Default Documents			
Lease Option, Termination, Extension Documents			

CATEGORY: COMMERCIAL REAL ESTATE—SALES

Document Name	Key Words & Document Description	Added by	Reference Client or Number
Correspondence			
Contracts for Sale of Property			
Closing Documents			
General Documents			
Due Diligence Items			

CATEGORY: CONDOMINIUM

Document Name	Key Words & Document Description	Added by	Reference Client or Number

CATEGORY: CONFLICT OF INTEREST

Document Name	Key Words & Document Description	Added by	Reference Client or Number
Letters			
Miscellaneous			

CATEGORY: CONSTRUCTION LAW

Document Name	Key Words & Document Description	Added by	Reference Client or Number
AIA Documents			
Mechanic's Lien Documents			
Foreclosure Lawsuit Documents			
Subcontractor Documents			

CATEGORY: EMPLOYMENT LAW

Document Library	Key Words & Document Description	Added by	Reference Client or Number
Cover Letters			
Employment & Hiring Agreements			
Separation, Termination, Severance Agreements			
Employment Litigation			
Department of Labor			
Employer Handbooks & Policies			

CATEGORY: ESTATE PLANNING

Document Name	Key Words & Document Description	Added by	Reference Client or Number
Cover Letters			
Powers of Attorney			
Wills			
Trusts			
ILITs			
Family Limited Partnerships & LLCs			
GRATs			
Miscellaneous			

CATEGORY: FAMILY LAW

Document Name	Key Words & Document Description	Added by	Reference Client or Number
Cover Letters & Correspondence			
Motions & Other Petitions			
Visitation Documents			
Discovery Documents			
Child Support Forms			
Parenting Agreements			
Paternity Agreements			
Prenuptial Agreements			
Petitions for Dissolution			
Adoption			
Adoption—Miscellaneous			
Settlement & Mediation Agreements			
Subpoenas			
Court Forms			
Questionnaires			
Miscellaneous			

CATEGORY: FORECLOSURE

Document Name	Key Words & Document Description	Added by	Reference Client or Number

CATEGORY: GENERAL BUSINESS

Document Name	Description	Added by	Reference Client or Number
Correspondence & Cover Letters			
Equity & Stock Option Documents			
Franchise Agreements			
Escrow Agreements			
Asset Purchase Agreements & Documents			
Nondisclosure, Noncompete, & Confidentiality Agreements			
Consulting & Independent Contractor Agreements			
Equipment Leases			
Intellectual Property Agreements			
Stock & Membership Transfer			
By-Laws, Operating Agreements, Shareholder Agreements			
Authorizations & Resolutions			
Business Start-Up Documents			

Document Name	Description	Added by	Reference Client or Number
Corporate Dissolution			
Miscellaneous			

CATEGORY: HEALTH CARE

Document Name	Key Words & Document Description	Added by	Reference Client or Number
Employment Agreements			
Service Contracts			
Purchase Documents—Corporation			
Compliance			
Regulations & Applications			
Letters			

CATEGORY: HOW-TO GUIDES

Document Name	Key Words & Document Description	Added by	Reference Client or Number

CATEGORY: IMMIGRATION

Document Name	Key Words & Document Description	Added by	Reference Client or Number
Correspondence & Cover Letters			
USCIS Forms			
Family Visa Documents			
Travel Documents			
Labor Certifications			
H1Bs			
Deportation Documents			

CATEGORY: LITIGATION

Document Name	Key Words & Document Description	Added by	Reference Client or Number
Pleadings & Complaints			
Subpoenas & Riders			
Depositions			
Motions			
Court Forms			
Miscellaneous			

CATEGORY: LOAN DOCUMENTS

Document Name	Key Words & Document Description	Added by	Reference Client or Number
Basic Loans			
Bank Loan Documents			
Personal Loan Documents			
UCC Forms			
Mortgages			
Loan Default Notices & Demand Letters			
Miscellaneous			

CATEGORY: MISCELLANEOUS AND OFFICE

Document Name	Key Words & Document Description	Added by	Reference Client or Number
Client Payments, Forms, Correspondence			

CATEGORY: NEW CLIENTS

Document Name	Key Words & Document Description	Added by	Reference Client or Number

CATEGORY: PROBATE

Document Name	Key Words & Document Description	Added by	Reference Client or Number
General Documents			
County-Specific-Documents			
Guardianship—Minor Child			
Guardianship—Disabled Adult			

CATEGORY: RESIDENTIAL REAL ESTATE

Document Name	Key Words & Document Description	Added by	Reference Client or Number
Contracts			
Seller Documents			
Closing Day Documents			
Buyer Documents			
Real Estate Documents			

CATEGORY: SOCIAL MEDIA

Document Name	Key Words & Document Description	Added by	Reference Client or Number

CATEGORY: TAX

Document Name	Key Words & Document Description	Added by	Reference Client or Number
Cover Letters			
IRS Forms			
Installment Agreements			
Offer in Compromise			
U.S. Tax Court Petition			
Trust Fund Recovery Penalty & Abatement Documents			
Private Letter Ruling			

CATEGORY: TRAFFIC

Document Name	Key Words & Document Description	Added by	Reference Client or Number
County Supervision Documents			
Miscellaneous			

Chapter 17

Perils of Being a Solo Practitioner

There seems to be a dichotomy in the sizes of groups of attorneys. You know all about the large firms that populate the large metropolitan areas in our country, and far separate from those large firms are the small groups of attorneys and solo practitioners who practice in outlying areas, suburbs, and rural communities across the country. Attorneys in this latter group may be enjoying a comfortable lifestyle and, one hopes, contributing to their communities. It should be noted, however, that without using principles found in this book, it is very difficult to get over certain thresholds when starting and growing a law practice. In fact, much the same can be said for the accounting field, which is similarly situated between the large accounting firms involved in tax and audit matters in the large metropolitan areas and the smaller, local groups of accountants in some metropolitan areas, suburbs, and rural communities.

The first threshold issue that you as a sole practitioner need to consider for growth is hiring assistants and, ultimately, hiring your first attorney.

Accountants are more adept than attorneys at crossing this threshold. Accountants, when busy, can hire different layers of assistants to work below them in the line of production before ever hiring another CPA. One accountant can leverage his contacts and his expertise with possibly five to ten different lower-level accountants, not necessarily CPAs, to produce monthly financial statements, general ledgers, and tax returns during tax season.

An attorney, on the other hand, can go only so far with top-quality administrative assistants and paralegals. An accountant can teach another skilled financial person how to put together a general ledger; whereas it is impossible for an attorney to teach someone who is not an attorney how to draft a lease or prepare a motion for summary judgment. As a result, at the beginning it is only you, one attorney, doing the legal work.

Section 2 of this book, about growing the law practice, gets into more detail on hiring. But for now, consider the goal of the sole practitioner, you, which is built around hiring your first attorney. It is critically important and intimidating.

You need to have the confidence that the attorney you hire will more than pay for himself or herself even if it means delegating all your work to the new attorney and you put yourself in a "reviewing attorney" mode to check the attorney's work and manage the client contact. Often, attorneys who are at the cusp of being very busy and know intellectually that having the assistance of another attorney would be greatly beneficial are afraid to hire the next lawyer because they do not see the benefits of the growth, the change in time commitment between working *in* the business and working *on* the business, and the potential for financial profit from having another professional in the office. Instead, the attorney, who is overworked and busy, sees only another expense in the salary of the second attorney and cannot get over the hurdle to make a hiring decision to grow the business. The fear of hiring a person because of the added cost associated with that additional attorney freezes out many attorneys from taking the first big step to growth.

In addition, more so than because of a lack of clients, many sole practitioners barely survive because they lack the proactive discipline required to collect legal fees. An entire chapter (Chapter 10) is dedicated in this book to the importance of this discipline, for unless that discipline becomes a priority, your business will fail or you will resign yourself to a life of struggling between billing your time and waiting for payment. This is no way to grow your firm. It requires constant surveying of all aspects of the business, including the timeliness of billing and collections, to run a business that happens to be a law firm.

> The fear of hiring a person because of the added cost associated with that additional attorney freezes out many attorneys from taking the first big step to growth.

Another reason some small law offices barely survive is because they are proud of the fact that they do not do any advertising or marketing but get all of their clients by word of mouth. Obtaining clients by word of mouth is no game plan at all. It is not a system, and it is nothing to be proud of. Yet attorneys often brag that all of their clients are found this way.

Certainly a large portion of your clients will come from referrals either from existing clients, referral sources, or your network of people, but you still need to actively lay the seeds that will eventually grow into paying clients. You need to create your own plan for increasing new client sign-ups, *your* networking plan—that is, your plan to get your name and your brand talked about in your community and within your network. Those referrals that are purportedly word of mouth are really strategically cultivated by you with your marketing plan. How you generate your leads is no accident. When you reach the conclusion of this book, you will have far better tracking devices, systems, and methodologies built into your growth plan that are far more measurable than word of mouth.

Clients who come to you by happenstance or pure serendipity are the result of luck, not a business plan. Sure, you can get some clients just by hanging out your shingle, but is that really a business plan? Absolutely not. You need a sophisticated plan for lead generation and converting those leads to clients, and you need to have your own marketing plan to bring in clients.

Another reason some small law firms stay small is because the founding partner simply cannot let go of the client contact. Referral sources, contacts, and other people in their network send cases to a particular lawyer, usually the founding partner, and the founding partner is absolutely insistent on handling the case himself or herself, including all of the nuances, administrative telephone calls, and until completion on a particular case. This approach is an absolutely wrong way to grow your practice. Some lawyers believe that if they get another lawyer involved in a client matter and give that other lawyer client contact, eventually the client will become comfortable with the associate lawyer and the associate lawyer will be able to steal the client and leave the law firm. Although this could be true, it will not be true if you are building a great law firm as set forth in this book, particularly and especially in Section 2. You cannot go on to meet the next potential client, referral source, or contact if you possessively demand that you, and only you, have the client contact and perform the client work. You must understand that clients need to know the other attorneys in your law office, as well as the administrative assistants, so that they feel comfortable seeking information from others in the office besides you. You will, of course, advise legal assistants not to give legal advice, but it is critical that you delegate work to other associates so that you are able to continue to network and work *on* the business.

> Once you have hired an associate, or even more than one associate, every meeting with clients in your office should include at least one associate to sit in on the meeting and take notes.

You will see as this book unfolds that the idea of working *on* the business is a reoccurring important theme; it is an idea to adopt if you intend on building a large, successful law practice. You cannot limit the growth of your firm by being possessive of client contact. Once you have hired an associate, or even more than one associate, every meeting with clients in your office should include at least one associate to sit in on the meeting and take notes. This way, the client will begin to understand that you operate as a firm and not as a solo practitioner.

Finally, some small law firms struggle and sometimes fail because of their reliance on one major client. This business fault really lies typically in the five- to eight-person law firm. Those firms grow to that size by relying on a major client, often a large business concern, that provides an enormous amount of work in different practice areas that pay the salaries of several attorneys in the office. The small firm may, for example, have one or two transactional lawyers working on client matters, a few litigation attorneys, and possibly some other individual work for the owners of the business. In those types of cases, heavy reliance on one client, while it is good when the cash is flowing in, puts the law firm in a precarious and vulnerable position, sometimes limiting its growth, and sometimes making the law firm's systems for lead generation and lead conversion lazy and inarticulate, all resulting in a fragile firm that will go out of business when something detrimental happens to the client. Solutions to these vulnerable firms are set forth in Section 3 in a chapter designed to fix the ailing mature law practice.

All in all, these failures are the result of treating your law firm as something other than a business and pushing on all business disciplines seven days a week. Unfortunately, I did not say it will be easy, but it will be rewarding.

Chapter 18

Ethical Rules and Avoiding Disciplinary Action

It is necessary to address, to some degree, the ethical rules and canons under which law-yers conduct their daily lives. Ethical canons are not rules that you leave behind when you leave the office to go home. They follow us every day, everywhere, and throughout the weekends. They need to be adopted by you, held in sanctity, and used as a fundamental foundation on which you build your practice.

The intent of this chapter is not to reiterate the class you took in law school on profes-sional responsibility. It is intended to highlight areas in the Model Code of Professional Conduct, rules on which many experienced practitioners must take the high road and be leaders in their profession. This brief summary of the model rules is intended to be a conversation from practitioner to practitioner on how they view the rules. It is not a sub-stitute for keeping up with your continuing legal education on professional and ethical rules, nor is it a substitute for reading through the rules thoroughly once per year. Further, it is not a substitute for calling your professional conduct liaison at the state bar associa-tion if you have questions under these rules.

This chapter is intended as a high-level summary of good advice, honest business candor, and years of experience dealing with these rules and mentoring new attorneys.

The Lawyer-Client Relationship

At the beginning of any attorney-client relationship, all new cases start with a contract and, unless it requires a very unusual fee arrangement, a retainer check. This establishes the most important business element of the relationship: the client has a lawyer, and the lawyer has a client. It is mutual, and there are responsibilities that flow from that relation-ship on the day the contract is signed and the check is accepted by the lawyer.

Obviously because of the privilege involved in the information provided by the client, the attorney's relationship with clients has been likened to that between a priest and penitents. The privilege is something a client can assert in court. The duty of confidentiality is never relaxed.

From a purely business standpoint, the best thing you could do to grow your business is to not talk about the client's business or mention the client's name to anyone, ever. That may seem obvious to you because the rules provide that you may not talk about the client's matters, but when you are at a party and your friends are talking about "Joe's house closing" or say, "Did you hear about Mary's parents' estate and the family fight?" it will be harder than you think to remain absolutely silent on those topics when *you* are the attorney representing Joe or Mary or another family member in those matters. Under the rules, certainly, you are not allowed to talk about those matters; but equally important, as a business-building mechanism, later on when Mary or Joe tells friends that you were the representing attorney, your friends will be incredibly surprised and impressed with the premium you put on confidentiality because they will remember that you were present during that conversation but never leaked a word about it to them. They will inevitably hire you in the future.

> At the beginning of any attorney-client relationship, all new cases start with a contract and, unless it requires a very unusual fee arrangement, a retainer check.

Nobody likes their dirty laundry aired out among their friends. Once people can trust that you do not talk about legal matters with anybody, even your spouse, you have taken a huge step forward in understanding that if you do, you are putting your law license at risk. Now you understand that business-building aspect of keeping confidential matters confidential.

You will always need to reread the conflict-of-interest rules and the gray areas of conflicts when you do a conflict search. Make sure your law office has a system in place for doing conflict searches. There is a high probability that your billing software has a way to scan for names and entities that provides a basis for an electronic conflict search system. If there is any doubt as to whether a conflict exists, check with the local liaison at the state bar association for an opinion or do your own research. If you are still unsure whether a conflict exists, ask for a waiver from the opposing parties or decline the representation.

Sometimes a simple transaction deals with family members, and the family members on both sides of the transaction may just want to hire you to "document the deal." This situation will come up on a periodic basis. Be disciplined enough to explain to them your conflict rules and agree that you will represent just one of the parties to the deal and will do all the documents for the deal. Send appropriate letters to both sides stating that you are representing only one party and will encourage the other party to get independent counsel.

Counselor, Advisor

Clients deserve and pay for honest advice. The idea of sugarcoating a problem and misleading a client by stating that you can get a result that seems doubtful in an initial client conversation is unethical. However, over time, you will see again and again, an attorney trying to give clients false hope so that that client will hire that attorney and the attorney will be able to make money off the client. An attorney may do this notwithstanding the day in the future when the attorney's luck runs out, and the attorney is faced with the inevitable job of telling the client that he or she will not prevail in the case or has compromised negotiating leverage due to a document and, as a consequence, an unfavorable result is forthcoming.

Always remember that clients appreciate and admire attorneys who seem able to lay out, in advance, the probable courses of action of the other attorneys, the courts, and the transactional process. You do not have a crystal ball to predict the future, but as you gain more experience, you will explain to clients in advance the probable and possible outcomes of certain motions, certain demands, and documents. Remember, you need to be correct in one of several potential outcomes that you have laid out to the client—for that is why you as an attorney need to work hard, do legal research, and understand the judge that you are before, so that you have a reasonable degree of predictability in terms of the outcome of certain conduct. Given adequate research, you are in the business of understanding the law and applying clients' facts to the law and predicting a probable outcome. You are not expected to be held perfectly accountable for the outcome, but if you understand the law and ask all of the hard questions relating to the facts, you should have a high percentage of probability relating to the results.

If the client provides you with bad information, with facts that prove to be untrue, the probability of your anticipated result will be very low. Nonetheless, before you can evaluate the probability of the result, the burden is on you to understand the law and ascertain the facts by asking the client all of the hard questions. In an initial client consultation, however, you may be unable to do that because you may need to research the law and you may need to review documents that the client failed to bring to make that determination. Nonetheless, at the beginning of the attorney-client relationship, and every step thereafter, the client deserves a candid and honest assessment of his or her case and the legal matters going forward.

An Advocate

Respect for judges and opposing counsel is mandatory for the type of business you want to build. Bullying other attorneys only goes so far and brutally damages the perception of lawyers in general. Civility among lawyers is at an all-time low. Nonetheless, you are an officer of the court, and your showing respect and following the decorum of the court is not just good business, it is mandatory.

As part of good business, and again based on a foundation of the model code, you must be honest. Lying for a client will put your license at risk and ultimately put you out of business. There is no client for whom you should put your license at risk. That client will be long gone and out of your life at the conclusion of the case, but the tribunal and adversary attorneys will always be there. A client who asks you to lie on his or her behalf will show no loyalty to you in the long run. For the work you do before government agencies, your credibility in front of such government agencies is of paramount importance. If you were to lie on a regular basis, you would, in the long run, lose your credibility with the government agencies (yes, you will see these people over and over again). Building a successful law practice with honesty and integrity is far more important than losing all the goodwill you have built up with opposing counsel, judges, and government agencies. Trying to further the interest of one client who expects you to lie for him or her isn't worth it. That client is not a lifetime client on which you can build your business.

Advertising

Please read the section on advertising, specifically in your jurisdiction. Lawyer advertising is prevalent in this day and age, and it is addressed in great detail in Section 2 of this book. However, follow the rules closely. The general rule is that you do not mislead your client or offer false promises. You cannot make false or misleading communications about your services. Communication is considered false or misleading if it contains a material representation of facts or law or omits certain things that would mislead a potential client.

Why do it?

Much of your print advertising will be for purposes of branding and getting your name out to the public. It will be connected to positive events in the community and in industry trade groups in order to connect your law firm with something good in the eyes of potential clients. Obviously, you cannot pay others to recommend you because as an attorney you may not share fees with individuals who are not lawyers.[1] Fee-sharing arrangements with lawyers need to be done strictly in conformity with the rules. Review the rules in your jurisdiction carefully.

For the record, avoid fee sharing as much as possible. Ask yourself if it is good for the practice groups in which you operate. Fee sharing in personal injury cases is standard, and clients understand that; it helps protect clients in those complicated cases by being

---

1. MODEL CODE OF PROF'L CONDUCT R. 7.2.

handled only by trial lawyers in those areas. The best type of reciprocal arrangement that you can make with your network of attorneys is on mutually respectful referrals to each other, putting the client in the best position with the best attorney you know in his or her particular field of concentration. And why not? The client is better off, and you are building a referral network among highly qualified attorneys who view service to clients the same way you do; as a result, referrals will be mutually beneficial to all of those involved.

Money

Violations of many of the things mentioned in the preceding sections will put your license at risk, potentially get you sanctioned or suspended from the practice of law, and upon repeated offenses, disbarred.

Stealing clients' money, or as defense counsel usually says, "borrowing" clients' money, will get you disbarred. There is no more tragic form of conduct than that of an attorney using client monies to fund his or her own personal business, lifestyle, or in the worst case, addictions. It is important that you treat the client trust account for what it is: *not* your money. The client has put the money in your hands to hold in trust, and if you use it, or "borrow it," which you may not do, the sanctions from the attorney disciplinary commissions will be extreme—disbarment.

Miscellaneous

Following the Model Code of Professional Conduct is critical because doing so allows attorneys to self-regulate the profession and set standards that attorneys or their representatives promulgate, by which all attorneys agree to abide. Attorneys should be happy to support their peers by creating the Model Code of Professional Conduct and abiding by those rules.

Why challenge the rules?

Remember, bank robbers are always successful until they get caught. The last robbery is the one in which they get caught. The potential for misconduct set forth earlier, if continued until you get caught, and you will inevitably get caught, will result in the demise of your law practice.

You cannot possibly expect to build a long-term successful business by cheating the system. Moreover, a common theme in this book is your contribution to the profession, and such conduct is an absolute detriment.

Lastly, remind yourself of your role in a growing law firm. Remember to engage in the externalities of practicing law, all of which require civic involvement, among them bar association activities and leadership roles in community organizations. How can you do both—cheat the system, degrade the legal profession, and yet be involved as a leader in your community and furthering the interests of your profession? These ends are mutually exclusive and cannot be balanced.

Section 2

Growing a Law Practice

Chapter 19

General Concepts in Growing a Law Practice

Having established, in Section 1 of the book the basic needs, mindset, and disciplines needed to start your law practice, Section 2 of the book focuses on growing your law practice.

It may be obvious, but you cannot think about growing a law practice until you have been successful at obtaining clients, billing your time efficiently, sending out bills in a timely manner, and collecting on those bills. Further, your networking skills must be honed and developed, and your contact groups and people network must be growing exponentially as you become involved in your community, social groups, and your local bar association. You may or may not have an administrative assistant helping you with some of this work, but assuming that you do not, you are looking for the upward trajectory of your growing law firm.

Section 2 of the book is built around people, systems, and culture. There is a need to emphasize these three themes in this section of the book.

First, as a law office, you are in the labor business. Do not make any mistake about it. You will obtain projects from clients, which are often segregated projects, not annuity work, and you will allocate labor to the project—until now it has only been you who completes work—and work the project through to a successful conclusion.

When the next project comes along, you will assign labor to the project; then, the project will come to a successful conclusion and you will move on. As a result, the business model of a law office is all about putting the best people on the right project and managing them. The highest expense in a law office is payroll. So, therefore, the people you invite into your firm must be of the caliber that either share your values, both business values and moral values, or are able to adopt and internalize your values. The constant pursuit of the finest employees is an ongoing reality of your business. Interestingly enough, although it is absolutely core to your business, finding the best people is an imperfect science that some professionals are better at than most, but you, as the managing partner of your one-person law office, need to become as good as possible at finding the right employees.

This section of this book talks at length about identifying the necessary attributes of great employees and about training existing employees to cultivate the necessary attributes to buy into your values and culture.

What an individual might call values, an organization calls culture. Culture could be an unspoken way of operating around the office, and it can be pronounced in a well-publicized mission statement. Be careful if your mission statement starts to look like that of every other firm's mission statement. If you were to poll twenty-five key employees in a big corporation as to what to include in your mission statement, you would probably capture all the good things that people aspire to be, in both their personal life and their work life. If a leader in an organization wants to appease all those employees, he or she will include all their ideas in the company's mission statement and have a mission statement that reads along the lines of

- Providing high-quality service;
- Providing outstanding legal thinking and strategy;
- Being dedicated to high degrees of integrity and honesty;
- Being dedicated to unparalleled customer satisfaction;
- Treating employees with respect and dignity; and
- Creating a work environment where employees are energized to come to work and overperform.

> The business model of a law office is all about putting the best people on the right project and managing them.

All of these goals relate to the good things that we want to be. The goals are words, not really a culture. Your firm culture is twofold. First, it is the reason you exist—what drives you to practice law, your purpose. Second, it comprises the pillars or values that you hold in an uncompromised fashion that you use to pursue your purpose. You, as the founding member of the organization, must lead by example and provide a core purpose and core ideals and values that will never sway and change despite changes in society, the economy, laws, and ideals. Once that core purpose is embedded into the culture of your company, the selection process for employees, the retention of employees, and the training of employees will have focus.

Last, during the growth of a law firm, systems must be developed, fine-tuned, and regularly reviewed. The checklists developed when you are a sole practitioner are the precursor to the corporate systems that you will develop. Checklists give birth to systems as the second, third, fourth, and every employee thereafter, is hired.

Showing a new employee how things are to be done and handing him or her a systems manual on how you do it is the formula for consistent patterning of all phases of your law practice. Sound boring? A little bit. Does it sound like the plan for building the best law practice you can? You bet.

Lawyers are bright, often brilliant people but they are not artists. They should not be left to ad lib projects to get the end result that the client requires. Although your systems will not be mechanical, they will be structured to make sure mistakes do not happen, that all issues are covered, and that everyone's efforts are efficiently maximized to get the best end result possible for the client, at the lowest possible legal fees.

Systems do not include just checklists that minimize mistakes in a particular practice group project. Systems also include marketing, how to handle telephone calls that come into your office, how to greet people at the front door, how to conduct yourself at client meetings, how to follow up with clients on a regular basis, how to follow up with former clients you have not spoken to since the conclusion of their case, how to stay in front of your network and referral sources, and also how to handle the financial aspects of the business such as bill paying, process-ing incoming checks, sending out bills, and collecting receivables.

All of these processes need to be exam-ined, created, developed, and fine-tuned as the firm grows. If they are not, consistency of your work product will fail, putting your business at risk.

> The checklists developed when you are a sole practitioner are the precursor to the corporate systems that you will develop.

In summary, people, culture, and systems are the three elements that need to be developed during the growth cycle of your business. Developing these elements will lay the foundation for growing the firm without limita-tion. This juncture is an exciting time, and the acceptance and absorption of these three foundational principles will skyrocket you to success.

Chapter 20

Hiring Support Staff

There is only so much time in a day. It is sometimes difficult for you to evaluate the best use of your time when money is tight. You will find that you will try to handle all of the problems and projects around the office yourself, and in time your anxiety and stress level will increase and the practice of law (and your life) will become unbearable.

We each need to objectively identify our own limitations. Maybe your limitation is typing. If it is, you will know that once you can afford your first employee, it will be as your secretary or administrative assistant.

Now, with the risk of running afoul of political correctness, an old-fashioned secretary does secretarial work such as typing and putting papers away in files. However, assistants currently have far broader skill sets than that, and as a result, you will rely on them to do much more around the office. In fact, recall that our profession generally separates employees into two groups in a law office: the attorneys and the support staff. The support staff consists of bookkeeping clerks, assistants performing secretarial roles, paralegals, general administrative assistants, law clerks, and file clerks, who are often students who assist with file management, scanning, and other file work. All of these folks support the attorneys to make the attorneys as efficient as possible, enabling them to maximize their hours during the day working on billable client work and thus making the law office successful and profitable. Remember, if an attorney is not billing during the day or working on client development, you are wasting his or her time.

Attorneys are generally the only employees in the law office who generate revenue. This situation differs from that of an accounting office, where lower-end accounting professionals (i.e., employees who are probably not CPAs) can put together financial statements, work on general ledgers, and balance checkbooks and where the accounting firm can bill clients for their work. In a law office, well over 95% of revenue-generating work is done by attorneys. The only exception to that is in some large law offices where some paralegal time is billed to the clients. You will keep an open mind to that possibility, but in small- and medium-sized law offices, cash is generated by billing solely attorney time.

Therefore, your first hire will be someone to make you more efficient at billing your time. Look at yourself objectively. Is there a need for someone to come into your law office to assist you with a trainable task that will make you more efficient? Again, the task might simply be typing. Currently, attorneys coming out of law school happen to be tremendously fast and proficient at typing and often do most of their own typing. This is a bad idea, but sometimes it is hard to teach a new dog new tricks. These young attorneys cannot get away from doing a lot of their own typing because they claim they think better as the document is laid out before them while they are producing it on a computer screen. They further believe that their organizational skills on the document are enhanced when they are working on it by themselves.

You may truly believe that. But make no mistake about it, you can dictate into a hand-held dictation machine or dictate on a voice recognition system much faster than any person can type. It is understood that a young attorney would claim that he or she cannot organize the document as well as possible by dictating and therefore prefers to do his or her own typing. Also keep in mind that sometimes a document that is dictated needs significant edits before it can go out the door to a client or to opposing counsel, so the young attorney might claim, "I might as well just do it myself. That way, when it's done, it is perfect, and I can send it out the door." It is hard to argue with that, but again, if you as an attorney are doing secretarial work, you have to ask yourself whether doing that is the most efficient use of your time. Moreover, it is not ethical for you to charge the client for an attorney doing secretarial work.

> Your first hire will be someone to make you more efficient at billing your time.

Remember, the attorneys are generally the only source for generating revenue for the firm, and any distraction to an attorney's ability to generate billable work costs the firm money.

How much?

In the business world, we all use the expression "Time is money!" In the legal profession, time is clearly translated to money by virtue of the billable hour. Therefore, if you spend three hours a week at IT troubleshooting, and your billable rate is $150 an hour, you just lost $450 for your IT work; the question then becomes, can an IT professional solve the same problem for less than $450? This is a fundamental math equation you need to ask yourself for every nonbillable project. Because attorneys' billable rates are high compared to those of other professionals, it is cheaper for you to be dedicating yourself to billable legal work than doing any other task in the office.

There is one caveat. You will supervise and oversee many nonbillable tasks in the office. However, you should not get down into the day-to-day work in the law office that does not generate money for the firm.

You have probably already done that for a year or even years as a sole practitioner and have worked lengthy hours to handle the tasks, listed in Chapter 2, that have nothing to do with billing your time. During the time you were a sole practitioner, you built a foundation of different departments in your law office (all of which you managed and worked by yourself) and allocated time, probably before eight o'clock in the morning and after six o'clock at night and all of your weekend hours, to perform those nonbillable tasks. Now, as you grow your law office, you will seek to put people, the right people, in slots that they will succeed in and that will relieve you of nonbillable work. Do not get confused about the goal of hiring support staff: it is to free up your time to work on billable client matters.

Your First Administrative Assistant

Do you need your first administrative assistant twenty hours a week? or forty hours a week? or somewhere in between? Consider expanding your law office cautiously, and so hire a part-time person initially.

There are online services you can use to solicit resumes; in the ads you post, make it clear where your law office is located, the number of hours you will need, the approximate starting salary, and the skills required.

Make the ad or announcement as brief as possible. Name the town, part of the city, or some identifiable location of your office in the ad. You want to hire someone who lives close to your office. At the starting salary you are willing to pay, probably at the $10–$15-per-hour range, that person will not travel far or stay with you very long if he or she is not conveniently located to your office. When résumés do start coming in, summarily eliminate people who would have to drive over forty-five minutes in order to come to work for this particular administrative assistant position. If you can add a short description of your firm's culture, include that too.

Next, you should include an hourly salary range commensurate with experience or skills because you will eliminate the lifetime law office secretaries who expect rates above what you can pay. If they are looking to make more, they may already have experience in a large firm culture, and that would be not be a good fit for your business. Such a person would not be a long-term employee, notwithstanding how great of a worker the person is or how established the person's skills.

Last, vet potential employees' skill sets. They will need to know how to use your word-processing software, most likely Microsoft Word. Inevitably, every applicant who comes into your office for an interview will say he or she is proficient at using Microsoft Word. In actuality, though, few of them are. Microsoft Word is a dynamic and robust software program that does things that very few people understand and know how to operate. Certainly, traditional typing of letters and documents can easily be mastered with Microsoft Word, but that is using only a small part of the functionality of that software program. If you want to humble a candidate quickly, ask him or her about preparing tables of contents, creating mail merges, setting different styles of footnotes, or using other lesser-known functions of the software. Rarely do candidates understand how to do these things. As the firm expands and as culture and values are established in your firm, you will interview and select candidates more closely aligned with the criteria set forth in Chapters 22 and 29.

Do not focus on objective typing criteria such as a high number of words per minute. That means nothing. I would rather have an administrative assistant able to type forty words per minute and be efficient in all things between the typing projects. Somebody who can type ninety words per minute but is lazy and inefficient in completing all the other tasks you require that he or she do for you between actual typing projects has no value.

Transcription experience is a skill your assistant will need if you plan on doing a lot of dictation, as you should. This is a skill that can be learned with extensive practice, and it is a fair to ask any new candidate if he or she has this skill.

When looking for support staff, post job listings at local colleges, especially junior colleges and secretarial colleges. While you know that a college student may not be a long-term employee, keep in mind that because college students are trying to get an advanced education, they may offer strong skills, and in the case of junior colleges, they usually live in the area.

Keep in mind that colleges all have placement offices whose counselors are delighted to talk with you about placing part-time workers. When hiring a person from a college, you are usually getting a high-quality, upwardly mobile young person who really works hard, tries hard, and will probably have computer skills better than those of somebody twenty years senior.

But you need to take the good with the bad. When hiring a college student, remember that he or she is probably not going to be a long-term employee, so you need to be creating manuals so that when a particular college student cycles out, the retraining of the next college student becomes easier.

With respect to full-time administrative assistants, it is very fortunate and somewhat easy in the practice of law to be able to find high-quality assistants who want to work in a law office. Generally, consider hiring college graduates for administrative assistant positions. You may want to look at people coming out of paralegal programs. The starting salaries for these individuals are higher, but when hiring a full-time employee, you are expecting a person to stay with you for a long period of time. Your investment and training will have a far better return for you in hiring a full-time rather than a part-time, somewhat transient, employee.

In general, the skill sets of young people who come out of college is rather incredible. Many of those young people are "A players," and you will be very lucky to find them.

Once you find those types of administrative assistant to help you and subsequent attorneys with the generation of legal work, you will be far more efficient, you will bill more of your daily hours to clients, and your work will become more fun. You doing what you do best and your assistant doing what he or she does best allows you to provide your core services (i.e., practicing law) through a very efficient process. Remember, training, which is discussed later, is critical to the growth of your new employee.

Hiring Help for the Accounting Department

Hiring somebody to work in the billing and bookkeeping department of a law office is very important and will save you an enormous amount of time and, primarily, reduce your anxiety as work starts to pick up and you become busier at practicing law.

Using the same basic system for finding a qualified administrative assistant to find your first bookkeeping employee, you can advertise online and in college campuses looking for talent. This person does not necessarily need to have a legal background but should certainly have knowledge and experience in basic banking and bill-paying functions.

> Make your first hire with an eye toward building systems, drafting an operating procedures manual, and creating other documentation and checklists to run that department efficiently.

If you place your ads with local colleges, schools, churches, and online services specifically delineating a tight geographic proximity, you may get a young mom who has an accounting background who wants to resume her career. You may potentially find a newly retired person who has an extensive financial background and just wants to stay active. These would be wonderful employees to help you out at this stage of your practice. In fact, they would probably add a lot of value to your accounting department, which would elevate the firm in that regard.

Make your first hire with an eye toward building systems, drafting an operating procedures manual, and creating other documentation and checklists to run that department efficiently. Remember, this new hire may or may not be the person to grow with you for the next twenty or thirty years, but you can learn from that person, and he or she will learn the way you like things done. Combine their financial background with your business background, and that will yield management reports and systems that will be in place going forward for all subsequent hires for that position.

Keep in mind that bookkeeping is a unique and complicated position that you are filling. In the early stage of your practice, it might seem that all you need is an accounting professional who will help you with your banking and billing systems. But as you look to the future, you need to ask yourself, "How will this department develop?" The answer is that it will develop into something more than just an accounting department. A major office administrator in a medium-sized law firm handles more than just financial statements. That is certainly one important area of the practice, but the individual you are hiring to handle the banking and the accounting department will also begin to take on other tasks, those listed in Chapter 2, that you have been doing on your own up to this point. For example, he or she will manage ordering supplies, deal with some software issues, handle human resource issues, handle payroll and billing, resolve law library issues, make bank deposits, and reconcile bank accounts. So this position is a hybrid position to manage and be responsible for all nonlegal work in the law office. Everything this person handles should be with a goal for you and the other attorneys to be more efficient at producing billable client work.

Also, if cash flow is good, this accounting professional may perhaps free you up on weekends. As much of the accounting work that you may have been handling on your own has been done on the weekends and late evenings, this particular employee will start bringing some balance and reasonableness to your life. Remember, you have brought in this individual to handle day-to-day work for these particular functions, but he or she still needs to report to you on all issues (initially, even on purchasing paper clips) so that all pertinent information flows upstream to you at all times. It will not always be like this, and as trust is developed between the accounting department and you and certain skill sets grow, there are certain responsibilities you will delegate solely to your office manager.

However, as a matter of forewarning, do not delegate check-signing authority for many, many years.

Do not let the professional relationship evolve in a relaxed, unbusinesslike fashion. If you cannot afford a CPA to do a thorough audit on your company (which you cannot), then putting that level of trust in an accounting manager makes no sense. The only level of oversight and audit that you have in your small law office is you. Therefore, the safest way to make sure that money is not dispersed out of your account without your knowledge and without your authority is to have *you* sign all the checks. As a note of further forewarning, there are plenty of other ways that an accounting department can steal from you even if you are a check signer, but at least you are controlling the checks and also retaining the authority to wire money, which functions minimize many of those risks. One of the methods of stealing includes setting up a fake vendor, such as an office supply company, owned by the accounting manager or a family member. The fake company then sends an invoice, and the accounting manager prepares the check for you to sign. Unless you personally count the paper clips and Post-it notes, your money just paid a bogus invoice. In another method, if you do not use a payroll service (which you should), you could find yourself in a situation like others we have seen where the office manager fails to make tax deposits to the federal and state governments, even though you signed the checks, and finds other ways to withdraw for his or her own benefit the money that would have otherwise gone to the government. When the government starts to send delinquency notices, the office manager intercepts them and never discloses them to you.

Your keeping the responsibility of signing checks could actually be viewed as a relief to an honest accounting professional. This way, he or she knows that any appearance of impropriety is minimized for his or her sake if the books and records of the company seem askew. The accounting professional will probably understand it and appreciate that without a problem.

On the other hand, if your office manager becomes insistent on being able to sign checks, that may give rise to suspicion that may be warranted. Make your own judgment, but retaining the right to sign checks is a good practice. Over time, there will be instances when it is inconvenient, such as when you are out of the office and a check needs to be signed; overall, though, vendors can usually wait a day to get their checks, and this way you will be able to properly vet who is getting paid and the amount of the payment.

Many times your personal administrative assistant grows into this bookkeeping role. It happens in very many law firms, but that does not make it a good idea. Please keep in mind that there are different skill sets required of the bookkeeping department and your administrative assistant. The reason the administrative assistant of the founding partner usually moves into the bookkeeping role is because it appears to be a promotion for the administrative assistant whereby the title for that person is elevated to that of the office manager. And then the office manager handles

> The only level of oversight and audit that you have in your small law office is you.

all the bill paying, banking, and bill generating every month, along with being the ad hoc human resource director and "birthday coordinator." This is a typical progression in a small law office. Keep in mind that your personal administrative assistant may be handling some of the banking work while you are at court or out at meetings and that he or she just progresses into the role of handling more than just your typing and filing. I caution you on how you separate the work between your personal administrative assistant and the accounting department or office manager. It is better to have several part-time administrative assistants dedicated to certain office functions than one who purports to be a jack-of-all-trades.

Your budget may dictate whom you can afford to hire, but you need to consider all of these issues when hiring a personal assistant or someone for your bookkeeping and accounting department.

Clerks

As you continue to grow, it is only good business to segment workloads and work responsibilities that match the sophistication of the work with a commensurately paid worker to manage it. Said another way, do not have an $18-an-hour person doing $9-an-hour work.

As you continue to grow, you will be able to find high school or college students who can be hired as file clerks. File clerks run various errands, file documents, and scan documents into your electronic file system for document retention. It is tedious, time-consuming work to scan documents and move them into the proper electronic client file and then appropriately shred or discard client documents. With that in mind, there are administrative tasks around a law office that can be handled by an $8.50–$10.00-an-hour person with the oversight of an administrative assistant.

When you have a file clerk in the office, everyone wins. The file clerk wins because he or she is getting valuable lessons in life by working with professionals and adults and learning how to conduct himself or herself in an office environment. The administrative assistants win because now he or she is not tied down to the mundane tasks of filing and scanning documents and, in some cases, stuffing envelopes that can be done by a file clerk. The accounting and bookkeeping department is also appreciative of the law clerk because the law clerk can run errands, copy bills, and perform other administrative tasks that can save the department time.

> The administrative assistants should be working on their own manuals describing what they do on a daily, weekly, or monthly basis and explaining how they do it.

Overall, the more you pay your support staff, the more you need them to assume responsibility, solve problems, and do higher-level work. The better training you give to all of these people and the better documentation you do in preparing manuals and how-to checklists as discussed in more detail in Chapter 25, the more fluid the turnaround is for these positions and the more seamlessly your office will work as people turn over.

It is a cliché to say that "we can all do better at this" when running a law office, but now is the time to create the foundation to organize and systematize the roles as they develop in your law office.

Do *you* need to prepare all of these manuals? No, absolutely not. But the administrative assistants should be working on their own manuals describing what they do on a daily, weekly, or monthly basis and explaining how they do it. As the manuals are developed, they will be placed in binders, saved on your electronic server, and reviewed annually to make sure they are accurate as your practice changes and grows. The role of firm management, discussed in Chapter 25 provides greater detail about the needs for manuals in the law office.

It truly does enhance the energy and morale around the office to have individuals at different levels responsibly performing the appropriate task for their level.

Incentives and Bonuses for Support Staff

Under the Model Rule of Professional Conduct, rule 1.5, you cannot share legal fees with individuals who are not lawyers. This rule is largely intended to prohibit lawyers from creating incentives for people who are not lawyers to get paid based on referring cases to a law firm. It is, of course, an excellent rule for the profession. However, that does not mean that the profits of a law firm cannot be shared with support staff, even though the profits of a law firm are derived from legal fees. You cannot bonus support staff and incentivize them as you can an attorney under the Code of Professional Conduct, but it is entirely appropriate to provide year-end bonuses to support staff and your accounting department for a job exceptionally well done, such as the integration of new technology that makes everyone's job more efficient, or for work that was done above the realistic expectations of you, the supervising attorney. This applies to all administrative assistants, accounting clerks, and clerks. They are there to assist attorneys, the revenue-generating employees of a law firm, so therefore their extra effort and the successful outcomes that add unexpected value should be recognized monetarily.

Keep in mind that bonuses are just that, bonuses that are there for the added value that such an employee brings to the law firm. Sometimes it is a good idea to have a company policy identifying what qualifies for these bonuses, but be advised that a bonus should be treated as something extra, not as an annual distribution of money that employees comes to expect and rely on as part of the firm's culture. Once that happens, the incentive for employees to provide that extra value is diminished, and the year-end payment that was intended to be a bonus ends up being just an extension of an employee's expected salary.

Chapter 21

Hiring Attorneys

One of the earliest failures of a small professional service business is the failure to take controlled, measured risk and to hire the first income-producing employee. In the law office environment, that employee is an attorney.

Imagine, you are busy working hard, with one or two staff working to support you to be more efficient in billing hours, closing deals, and otherwise focusing on revenue-generating work, and yet you still have very little free time in the evenings and on weekends.

Those are good problems to have.

If you feel comfortable that your personal administrative assistant is turning over work efficiently and producing high-quality work and your accounting and office manager role is filled by an honest, ethical, hard-working individual, yet you are still bogged down in the day-to-day grind of practicing law, you must consider hiring your first attorney.

You will probably embrace the idea of having a new attorney replicate your skill sets and basically do the work that you do, but do it behind the scenes. This will allow you more freedom to network, write more articles, and overall work *on* your business and not necessarily *in* your business.

When analyzing the skill sets needed to hire your first attorney, the general default rule is to hire somebody with a similar skill set to your own. The associate attorney's primary job will be to relieve you of some of your day-to-day work of practicing law. Do not give a new attorney direct client contact immediately; he or she will be working behind the scenes to draft pleadings, write briefs, prepare documents, appearing at routine court hearings, and doing other work—billable work—that you have typically been doing that takes up an enormous amount of time. Remember, the work the associate attorney is doing should be billable work, and your support staff should be there to support the attorney so he or she can be as efficient as possible.

As you interview potential candidates, it is unlikely that you will hire somebody far your senior in experience, but that is not out of the question. There may be certain things that happened in that particular attorney's career or life that causes him or her to work for a mobile and aggressive entrepreneurial attorney like you. However, more likely than not, you will be hiring somebody out of law school whom you will be able to train and bill at a low hourly rate.

Reach out to some ex–law school professors and place ads in various law school placement offices looking for résumés to review. Get a recommendation from a professor, and you should feel comfortable that the candidate has done independent research with the law school professor and is a high-quality candidate. Remember, hiring somebody right out of law school to be an attorney will require your providing that person with extensive training, which will be time consuming, though in the long run it will yield great results and benefits for your firm.

Do not ever get caught up in the "I am too busy to train someone" mindset by stating, "It is faster if I just do it myself instead of training someone how to do it." Accept the fact that you need to make an investment into training your new attorney so that the new attorney will yield economic benefits to you in the future. Investment is an absolutely appropriate term for your work with this young attorney. All of the hours that you invest in training a young attorney will come back and yield economic benefits to you for years to come.

Don't be concerned that if you invest in this training, the attorney will take that experience and leave the office and you will have to start over again. As you build a high-energy culture around your office and pay employees fairly, there is not a presumption that they will leave once they are trained. In fact, based on the principles set forth in this book, they will want to stay with you and continue to be part of your upwardly mobile team and recognize their opportunity for what it is—an opportunity to get in on the ground floor of a growing law office. What an opportunity!

> Do not give a new attorney direct client contact immediately.

Do an analysis of the numbers. If you are a new attorney, billing at a rate of $150 an hour for about fifteen hundred hours a year (about 75% of the day), you should bill revenue at approximately $225,000 a year. Even if only 80% of that billed revenue is collected, that is still $180,000 of revenue brought into the firm. Based on our compensation discussion following this section, this attorney, if the work is present in the office, will form the basis of growing the firm.

The paradigm changes slightly when analyzing the hiring of a lateral attorney—in other words, hiring a lawyer who has experience practicing law, potentially more experience in a particular practice area than you have.

Ask yourself if that is what is most needed for the firm at this time. You may be getting a lot of telephone calls and referrals for a certain type of work (such as immigration work or divorce work) that you cannot handle but that you would like to capitalize on for your growth. If that is the case, note that you will not be able to train or guide the new attorney and that he or she must be somewhat self-sufficient. These situations are rarely successful. Unless you have a client base that you believe you can help feed this attorney work and have the staying power to invest in this new practice group over a long period of time, do not hire a lateral early on in the growth of the firm. Eventually that will happen, but not with the first few hires.

For those of you thinking about the difference between transactional lawyers and litigation lawyers and the need to hire a lawyer who brings a different skill set to your skill package, be advised that when you are a transactional lawyer, hiring a litigation attorney—or vice versa—may sound like a good idea. However, the blending of those different skill sets usually works in a partnership context where the two partners have similar years of experience.

Here, it is far more common to hire your first, and then a few subsequent lawyers, with a similar skill set as yours to build up your specialty practice and allow you to train the attorney properly and manage the attorney's work. Keep in mind that with this type of growth into a narrow set of practice areas, you will be enhancing your selling proposition to the market of your unique skill sets; also, internally, you will already have access to all of the practice books and other research materials needed for your existing practice groups.

Do not worry about the apparently limited nature of your practice.

Over time, although attorneys will be brought in with skills closely resembling yours, each will find a new niche in which to enjoy practicing that is apart from the skills that you have taught each, and slowly but surely the breadth of your practice groups will expand. Not until you have approximately four or five attorneys in your office will you take a risk on expanding to a completely unrelated area of the law about which you have little knowledge and in which you have no practice experience. At that point in time, you will expand to these new areas of the law because of increased telephone inquiries in these areas or other connections that you will have to generate the work.

Base Salary

Attorneys need to be paid a competitive base salary. In your new and growing law office, make sure that your offer to new attorneys out of law school is commensurate or slightly above the amount the government pays attorneys for work in the state's attorney's office, the public defender's office, and federal agencies such as the U.S. Attorney's Office, the Internal Revenue Service, and/or the Immigration and Naturalization Service. As long as you offer slightly above the starting salaries of those government agencies, you will hire talented people.

Currently, the job market is so bad for law school students that it is a buyer's market for law firms, and so very talented people are readily available for positions. Certainly, to oversimplify the matter, the market should dictate the starting salary for attorneys. The problem with that market analysis is that it varies so greatly between the large firms that are able to overpay students coming out of law school. These young attorneys are not at all prepared to practice law, but the large firms place them on projects for clients that can (over)pay for their services when they are managed by a talented partner in a large law firm.

In your business model, you cannot compete with those large law firms; as a result, you are faced with the economic reality of paying for production from new hires in their first year out of law school. Therefore, again, using a salary slightly above what the government will pay, take that amount to see if it has a logical relationship to the new attorney's billing rate.

A fair salary for an associate attorney should be approximately between 25% and 33% of the economic value the attorney brings to the law firm. Therefore, if the attorney's billing rate is $150 an hour and the law firm bills and collects for fifteen hundred hours of the attorney's work, the total revenue for the law firm would be about $225,000, and 25% of that amount is about $56,000 and 33% of that amount is about $75,000. Therefore, the logical relationship between $150-an-hour attorney is a base salary of between $56,000 and $75,000 per year. Again, that is *if* the attorney is billing and collecting on approximately fifteen hundred hours a year. The 25%-to-33% rule for an attorney's base salary is a good rule of thumb if you can honestly and accurately calculate the revenues coming in from the attorney's work.

> A fair salary for an associate attorney should be approximately between 25% and 33% of the economic value the attorney brings to the law firm.

The point of the compensation discussion set forth herein is to try to draw your attention to the relationship between the base salary and the revenues brought in by the new attorney. If you determine that paying the new attorney for 45% of what he or she can generate in revenue, you will obviously be paying a premium for top talent that may work out great in the long run. Next, give serious thought to incentivizing the new attorney to do the two things that you need to have the attorney do: bill hours and bring in new clients. As long as your incentive plan and your base salary programs are fair and provide a financial incentive to do the things you need to have done, you and your attorneys will be pulling on the same side of the rope as you as you grow your practice.

Compensation Incentives

Very smart business advisors, in discussing business acquisitions totally unrelated to law offices, always talk about incentivizing management under compensation agreements to get managers to do the things that are important to the owners of the business. If the economic incentives are rich enough and reasonable, and if the managers meet their incentive goals, everyone wins. For example, if the incentive package in a manufacturing company is very well designed whereby the employee or manager is compensated based on orders; revenue such as earnings before interest, taxes, depreciation, and amortization (EBITDA) or gross profit; or in any other manner that is 100% objective and calculable, and if that management person hit those numbers or greatly exceeded those numbers, the business owner should be thrilled to pay those bonuses. If that is true, then the business probably has a good bonus program in place.

Sometimes business owners want to give the manager an incentive to be successful but then, *wrongfully*, want to limit the executive's potential bonus compensation, claiming that enough is enough, that if the executive hits these numbers, he or she will make plenty of money and the business owner should make 100% of the balance. This type of thinking is completely wrong and shortsighted. A good incentive program for revenue-generating employees needs to be such that there is no limitation to the bonus so that the employee can make substantial amounts of money. You could be the employee's greatest cheerleader for making that money, and your company benefits commensurately.

> A good incentive program for revenue-generating employees needs to be such that there is no limitation to the bonus so that the employee can make substantial amounts of money.

Translate that discussion into the law office environment.

There are two things that you need from your newly hired attorney that are within the attorney's control: (1) to bill a significant number of hours, assuming the work is there for the attorney to address, and (2) to bring in additional good clients. If the new attorney succeeds in both, shouldn't he or she reap the rewards of that success? Why put a cap on the new attorney's success? Why not see to it that there is no cap and that if the new attorney is successful, he or she should be financially rewarded for achieving the things that you put a premium on achieving. The law firm will be greatly benefited without limitation as to his or her success.

Here are the specifics.

First, address billable hours. If the industry standard is for lawyers to work two thousand hours per year (that is basically eight hours a day for fifty weeks a year), why not pay the attorney 15%, 25%, or 33% of a bonus for every revenue dollar the attorney brings in above that threshold? Maybe that threshold is too high. Is it really achievable and realizable?

What about a billing threshold of 1,750 hours per year? What about sixteen hundred hours per year, or fifteen hundred? Remember, the higher and more out of reach your billing threshold is, the less incentive you might be providing to the new attorney because the goal may simply be unachievable. It must be achievable for it to make a difference and provide the incentive you want to provide.

Before you settle in as to what your incentive program will be, just keep in mind that you need to calculate the number based on the attorney knocking the cover off the ball and far exceeding your expectations. So what? If you are paying the attorney 25% of the revenue derived after exceeding the incentive threshold, you are still keeping 75% of those dollars for the firm. Be delighted to pay the attorney on that type of basis. Do you want him or her to work harder and bill more hours? Then pay the attorney more than 25%.

Next, with respect to incentivizing the new attorney to bring in additional clients based on the same networking advice covered in the first section of the book, you need to pay the attorney based on the revenues received by the law firm on the clients he or she brought into the firm.

The first litmus test in determining whether the attorney brought in the client is a simple "but for" test. With every new client, ask yourself, "But for the contacts of the new attorney, would we have this client?" If the answer is solely yes, then the attorney should receive the bonus for bringing in the client.

If the new client is a referral from an existing client on whose account the new attorney was working, then the new attorney did not qualify under the "but for" test because he or she was not the sole procuring cause that brought in the client—it was really because of the good work being performed for the existing client by the firm. Even if the new attorney was doing the work for the existing client, the attorney was being paid a base salary to perform that work and should get no additional credit just for doing his or her job. Referrals from existing clients never qualify for an attorney bonus because that new referral is a result of the great work your firm is doing for the existing client, and everyone is getting a base salary to provide those exceptional services. However, if the new client came in because of the networking efforts of the new attorney from a new referral source or a new social group or networking group, then certainly the new attorney should be paid for bringing in that business.

How much should the new attorney be paid? Well, that is up to you, but determine whether your business model can afford to pay 20%, 25%, or 33%. Remember, the higher you go, the more incentive you provide the new attorney to bring in new work. Is that not what you want to do? Keep in mind that to bring in more new clients, it will cost you money and time. Why not pay that money to your own revenue-producing attorney? Even if your payment is 33% of the fees generated from the new client, you get to keep 67% for the firm, a large portion of which will go to your overhead costs (which really do not increase immediately but will increase in the future), and the rest goes to the bottom-line profit of the law firm. Remember, the goal here is to provide economic incentive for the new attorney to do the two things that you need him or her to do: perform on billable-hour goals and bring in clients.

There is an adjustment that you need to consider on these bonus programs.

If the attorney runs up billable hours on clients who ultimately do not pay, the year-end bonus, which is the bonus based on accumulated hours for the year, must be adjusted to take into account the false billables, those on the clients who do not pay. Remember, this is a business, and as a business, sometimes the attorneys have to face the grim realities of economics. You cannot pay the attorney on monies that you did not receive from the client. It seems pretty fundamental, but attorneys may expect to be paid on work they did for clients who did not pay. That is not a logical business model. The attorneys need to be trained to watch accounts receivables, and then they will have an eye-opening revelation when their bonuses are reduced because they spent time doing work for clients who are not paying. That makes them responsible for keeping an eye on the accounts receivable balance for the client and calling the client every month on the thirty-day notice for the client to pay. That way, the attorney is given an incentive to get the client to pay or withdraw from the case. You are the managing partner of the firm, and whether the firm has only one other attorney or fifty other attorneys, it should not be your job to be the collection attorney for your firm. All of the attorneys share the responsibility of doing the work for clients who pay.

> If you hire a third-year law student, plan on investing at least one year of intense training for that associate.

Hiring out of Law School versus Laterals

When hiring your first, second, third, or tenth attorney, you will be confronted with deciding whether to hire a graduating third-year law student or making a lateral hire who has been working in a law firm presumably between two and six years.

There are some obvious truisms here that will help in the decision-making process.

First, a new hire right out of law school will probably be less expensive for you but require much training and oversight. Conversely, a lateral hire, depending on the individual's level of experience, will most likely require a higher salary (so he or she is compensated for the years of experience after law school) and need less training—presumably. Further, depending on the experience of the lateral, one would think that more is better, but also remember the old adage that "you can't teach an old dog new tricks." Some laterals are set in their ways and interested in practicing law the way they have learned at their former law firm. Despite the fact that they were unhappy enough to leave, it is possible that they will not adopt a new culture to adjust their daily rituals.

The opposite is true with third-year law students getting their first job with you out of law school. In those cases, they have no preconceived notion of what it is like to be an associate at a law office. Notwithstanding the fact that they may have clerked at another law firm, they just saw how other associates operated, but they did not live that experience and, therefore, would be very open to learning the job as an associate with you. However, be advised that new first-year associates are background attorneys and every letter, document, pleading, or any other deliverable they produce needs to be reviewed by you or a senior associate or partner, all for the purposes of training the new associate into the system in which your firm operates. If you do not take the time to train the new associate, it is unfair to the new associate because then he or she will never meet your expectations, it is unfair to the firm because you are making an investment in the new associate by paying the person's salary and yet not accelerating the person's growth to the point where he or she will be financially beneficial to the firm, and it is unfair to the client because the client is getting second-tier legal services.

If you hire a third-year law student, plan on investing at least one year of intense training for that associate. There is still more training after the first year, but it is less intensive.

As noted, laterals come at a higher cost but will be absolutely necessary if you want to move into a practice area in which you have no experience. If your law office is situated in a geographic area that needs immigration lawyers and you are a business lawyer, eventually you will need to serve the community with immigration counsel. The same goes for a personal injury lawyer moving into a town with business needs or other specific needs you do not fulfill.

Eventually, if the phone keeps ringing and clients are repeatedly asking for the same services, you will make a very simple business decision that it is necessary for you to add a practice group and that the only way you will be able to do it is by hiring someone with expertise in this area of the law. This hire will have to be a lateral hire because if you hire someone out of law school for a completely new area of the law, you will not have the substantive expertise to help train that new attorney.

With respect to laterals, do not be naïve as to the relationships between you, the founder of the firm, and somebody who has far more experience in a particular area of the law than you and might be five or ten years older than you. That human dynamic may not work out as perfectly as you might think. That would require an honest and long conversation, as well as an extended vetting process with the lateral hire as to how comfortable that lateral hire is with that relationship. Examine the lateral's background, history with law firms, and other reasons why the lateral hire feels that your firm is his or her best fit. These are all issues that you must consider when making a significant commitment to a lateral hire.

So what is the best solution?

As you become busier with your time and work, a sound idea is to hire a second- or third-year law student as a law clerk to help with some of the background attorney work. This would be 100% supervised and reviewed by you and will go out under your name.

How many other business models do you know of where you can literally interview your candidate a few days a week for nine months? The law firm model of being able to hire inexpensive law clerks to come in and help you with your work so that you can get an extended period of time to evaluate their work product, work ethic, commitment to excellence, drive for success, and other valuable and relevant work criteria is fantastic. Take advantage of it. In fact, as your business is moving forward and growing, you should always consider having a law clerk on your payroll. If you can bill his or her time out at $50 an hour (for truly billable work), the clients benefit, the law clerk benefits, and you benefit over the long run. This is a way to ease in additional hours of work for client services, and through the whole process, the third-year law student is gaining an understanding of the systems and culture in your law office, and the transition then comes almost seamlessly between the individual's law clerk role and, once he or she passes the bar exam, his or her role as an attorney in the law office.

Chapter 22

Hiring the Right People

It is very difficult to prioritize the three elements of growing your business: people, culture, and systems. Logic dictates that if you knew the direction your firm was going and had a direct vision as to where the company was heading, you would hire the right people with the necessary skill sets to get you to the promised land.

In the bestseller *Good to Great* by Jim Collins, Collins dedicates a chapter to the subject "First Who . . . Then What" and has done definitive research that shows that top-level "good to great companies" first find the right people to get on the bus, get them in the right seats, and then figure out the best path to greatness.[1]

> The executives who ignited the transformations from good to great did not first figure out where to drive the bus and then get people to take it there. No, they *first* got the right people on the bus (and the wrong people off the bus) and *then* figured out where to drive it. They said, in essence, "Look, I don't really know where we should take this bus. But I know this much: if we get the right people on the bus, the right people in the right seats, and the wrong people off the bus, then we'll figure out how to take it someplace great."[2]

Collins emphasizes that the companies that exceeded good and became great understood that you first had to get in your organization the right people who can take you to where you want to go in an ever-changing world and marketplace.

Nothing stays static. With the right people in your organization and with the understanding that while your goals may be crystal clear, the path is somewhat dynamic. Having the right people who will adopt that philosophy will successfully take your firm on an upward trajectory.

---

1. Jim Collins, Good to Great: Why Some Companies Make the Leap . . . and Others Don't 47 (Harper Business 2001).
2. *Id.* at 41.

Collins, through empirical research, highlights the case of Wells Fargo Bank when it began its fifteen-year run of overperformance in 1983. Before to that date, CEO Dick Cooley began building what was labeled by Warren Buffet as the "most talented management team in the industry."[3] Cooley foresaw that the banking industry would eventually undergo enormous change but did not pretend to know what form that change would take or how to react to the change. He focused on people and on injecting the company with the top talent in the entire industry. He was quoted as stating, "That's how you build the future. If I'm not smart enough to see the changes that are coming, they will. And they'll be flexible enough to deal with them."[4] As a follow-up to the Wells Fargo success in the 1980s and 1990s, Collins indicates that many of the former management team working for Cooley went on to become CEOs of major companies such as Household Finance, U.S. Bancorp, Bankers Trust, Bank of America, and Westpac Banking.[5]

Sound simple?

It sounds very simple, almost fundamental, and everyone who hires employees believes that is exactly what the hiring process is about—to hire the best available people.

> A person who is highly skilled but has no interest in adopting your core values and your firm's culture is an easy, identifiable person to be offloaded and terminated.

The second point that is often ignored, overlooked, or simply missed is the degree of *pure rigor* needed to select people who will take the company from good to great.[6] Collins highlighted the work of Fannie Mae CEO David Maxwell, who held off on developing a success strategy for Fannie Mae while the company was losing $1 million every single business day, with $56 billion of loans under water. His conduct was under the microscope, but he did not relent, and he "made it absolutely clear that there would only be seats for A players who were going to put forth A+ effort, and if you were not up for it, you had better get off the bus, and get off *now*."[7]

One final thought on getting the right people on the bus and getting them into the right seats. Depending on your hiring style, and the attorneys' maturity and experience, be somewhat patient and allow people to grow and progress. As people make the same mistake multiple times though you have moved them into different roles in the office, they need to be offloaded in a professional manner if those mistakes continue. However, each person should be treated individually, and his or her work product needs to be reviewed

---

3. *Id.* at 42.
4. *Id.*
5. *Id.* at 43.
6. *Id.* at 44.
7. *Id.* at 45.

on a regular basis with a fresh approach. People change and should be allowed to grow to a certain point. The key here is to watch for the individual's growth and progress in the job and in his or her role in the law firm before you make a final judgment. Many times it takes a while for a person who has very little experience working in a law office to adopt the culture and values of your organization. It is easier to teach skills to an administrative assistant or support staff than it is to teach an attorney to adopt your core values and the firm's culture. A person who is highly skilled but has no interest in adopting your core values and your firm's culture is an easy, identifiable person to be offloaded and terminated. That person will cause more harm to the firm than add value through his or her skill sets. He or she will be petty, disruptive, and often through debilitating and counter-constructive conversations with coworkers detrimental to the firm. However, an employee who does adopt the firm's culture and has a core belief and value system aligned with the firm's core purpose and values should be tolerated for a particular time as his or her skill set grows and he or she avoids repeatedly making the same mistakes.

As indicated earlier, the management of a law office is placing people on projects to solve client issues and problems. This sounds cliché, but the legal profession is a people business. Having said that, in your career you will see many different, interesting personalities, or the lack thereof, of so many attorneys. Some are successful, it seems, despite themselves. The legal profession is in the people business, and you will succeed when you adopt the understanding that you need to have dynamic, personable, and confident individuals on your bus. Every connection that your people make with clients, referral sources, and outlying networks is a reflection of your law office, and all those impressions need to be good and the message delivered must be consistent. You need *team players* who adopt your culture, buy in to it, own it, and convey it.

Recognition

Understand, early in the growth of your organization, the value of recognition and how important it is in an organization.

Do not be slow to this realization. Many people believe, incorrectly, that the only thing that incentivizes employees is money. With your incentive package and year-end reviews, you may falsely believe that a pat on the back or "atta boy" has little value. Such forms of recognition should never be a substitute for the proper economic bonuses and economic incentives you provide to your support staff and attorneys. However, *added* to the economic incentives you set forth in your practice, they are very meaningful. In *The Advantage*, Patrick Lencioni succinctly states, "As important as compensation or rewards are, they aren't the most effective or important means of motivating people in a healthy organization."[8] Lencioni believes that when leaders fail to tell employees that they are doing a great job, they might as well be taking money out of their pockets and throwing it into a fire because they are wasting an opportunity to give people the recognition they crave more than anything else. Direct, personal feedback really is the simplest and most effective form of motivation.[9] Remember, there are many leaders who believe that employees believe that giving praise to an employee would be interpreted as a cheap replacement for a financial reward. Here is the fact, and it is dead-on accurate:

> What leaders need to understand is that the vast majority of employees, at all levels of an organization, see financial rewards as a satisfier, not a driver. That means they want to receive enough compensation to make them feel good about their job, but additional money doesn't yield proportionate increases in their job satisfaction. And while they're not going to turn down an offer of more money, that is not what they're really looking for. In fact, gratitude, recognition, increased responsibilities, and other forms of genuine appreciation are drivers. That means an employee can never really get enough of those and will always welcome more.[10]

> Do not wait for the end of the year for recognition awards.

The foregoing comments should be a game changer in your thought process. You have read through the first few chapters in Section 2 of the book and now understand the economic incentives for the attorneys. These are incentives to provide the attorney economic benefit to do the things that are most important for the firm and for you to grow the business; they are important, and they help satisfy employees. Recognition, increased responsibilities, gratitude, other acknowledgments of appreciation, and words of thanks are drivers. So, in summary, if your economic package is right, the employee will be highly satisfied. With acts of appreciation and gratitude, you will drive your attorneys to be more successful and work harder.

One last point on recognition: It is always best made as close to the happening of a positive event as possible. Do not wait for the end of the year for recognition awards. The end of the year might be the right time for bonuses and other monetary rewards, but recognition, gratitude, and thanks need to be ongoing contemporaneously to the employee's successful act as possible. That is the way to drive your team to success.

---

8. PATRICK LENCIONI, THE ADVANTAGE: WHY ORGANIZATIONAL HEALTH TRUMPS EVERYTHING ELSE IN BUSINESS 166 (Jossey-Bass 2012).
   9. *Id.* at 167.
   10. *Id.* at 168.

Managing the Process

Everyone hopes that there is a system and a series of questions to ask applicants to ascertain how they align with your values and culture, as well as to ascertain their skill sets and work ethic. It is not easy.

The whole process of recruiting and hiring people seems so fundamental that it is a misleading directive. Your goal is to hire the right people and put them in the right position for success, but the reality is that not many law offices are good at doing so for a variety of reasons.[11] Basically, many law offices fail because they have not defined what they are looking for in people; they have not identified behavioral values and ethical values, ascertained skill sets, and determined the experience that will help in the process. Hiring without clear and strict criteria for a cultural fit greatly hampers the potential for success of any organization.[12]

Lencioni, in *The Advantage*, indicated how most small business leaders believe they have the gut feeling to identify A players and look back at their careers and point out all of the successful people they hired while conveniently forgetting many unsuccessful hires they have made.[13] Most small business owners absolutely believe that they can go about the hiring process based on gut feeling without much structure. Even those who believe that they have a screening, interviewing, and evaluation process are often kidding themselves, and the process is not followed at all.[14] Lencioni provides these comments:

> It is truly stupefying to think that the most important decision a leader can make—who to invite to become part of the organization—is often handled in such a cavalier way. One of the reasons this persists, I think, has to do with the considerable time lag between when a bad hiring decision is made and when everyone realizes the problem.[15]

Cause and effect and the lag time to discover and admit you made a bad hire stunts the ability to go back to reevaluate the process when a bad hire was made and to correct the process.

Here is the good news.

The other extreme does not work much better at all. Lencioni reiterates that when organizations add layers of bureaucratic forms and approvals and analysis, they often diminish the role that judgment must play in the selection of good people.[16] It is more

---

11. *Id.* at 156.
12. *Id.*
13. *Id.* at 157.
14. *Id.*
15. *Id.*
16. *Id.*

common in larger organizations and must be understood in any small organization so as not to fail or be paralyzed with overanalysis.

So what is the answer?

> The best approach to hiring is to put just enough structure in place to ensure a measure of consistency and adherence to core values—and no more. That's right. When it comes to the continuum of hiring, ironically, I find that it is better to be somewhere closer to having a little less structure than more. I believe this because too much structure almost always interferes with a person's ability to use their common sense, and because it is far easier to add a little structure later to a fairly bare system than it is to deconstruct an already overcomplicated process.[17]

So what is the endgame? In your process of hiring, and once you understand thoroughly and create your own set of core values and your core purpose, you will be able to start to ask job candidates (both attorneys and support staff) specific questions and measure their reaction to affirmative statements about your core purpose and core value; also, before talking about your core values and core purpose, ask the candidates about their values and what they are looking for in a job. Obviously, a lot of the answers will be "interview-prepared script," but it is important to evaluate all this information when trying to find the right people to bring into your law firm.

With respect to the selection process, the actual vetting process and interviewing, you need to sell the vision of the company and its core values. Many books have been written exclusively on the subject of hiring, but there are few truisms that you need to stick to and understand.

First, the hiring process is a numbers game, and so you need to obtain as many résumés as you possibly can through as many resources as possible. The hiring process is far less reliant on ads in newspapers than it once was. Secretarial schools (for administrative assistants), the law schools in your area, ex-professors from law school, and placement offices of the local colleges and junior colleges (for support staff) are all good places to start. You will need to continue to have lines of communication with all of these sources for potential candidates. To fill one position you may need, at a minimum, one hundred resumés from which you will reduce the number to ten potential qualified candidates you will reach out to and invite in for their first interview. Out of those ten, just six or seven will actually come for the first interview; out of the two or three candidates that you may like, one or two may already have a job by the time you are ready to offer the position.

With respect to support staff, you need to go out to as many resources as possible to get a diversified group of résumés.

---

17. *Id.* at 158.

Reaching out to all of the local law schools is about diversified as you will get for an attorney search. You will probably not be in a position to travel far to start interviewing attorneys from neighboring states and various law schools located more than 100 to 150 miles from your place of business.

Design your ad in a way that succinctly states the minimum skill set, like mastery of a particular word-processing software, and spend more of the space in your ad on capturing the culture, core purpose, and core values of the firm. Make it unusual, and make it stand out to attract attention. State your unique selling proposition if that helps to convey your firm's culture. Understand that anyone in need of a job may still send you a résumé and have no interest in aligning himself or herself with your core values, but your ad will generate a diverse set of responses from unique individuals.

When interviewing potential candidates, it is best to have more than one person interview the candidate to be able to share impressions and evaluate the candidate's responses to certain questions. Many employee experts suggest outsourcing the testing process to determine, with some objectivity, the alignment between the candidate and your core purpose.[18] The costs are between $500 and $1,000 per candidate and could become expensive. Be cautious. As you adopt the concepts set forth in these chapters, you will be the best judge of the personality you need to hire, and you will be able to find that person with a higher probability of success through an outside service. As you will quickly find out, quality support staff candidates do not stay unemployed very long, and you need to make quick decisions.

> When interviewing potential candidates, it is best to have more than one person interview the candidate to be able to share impressions and evaluate the candidate's responses to certain questions.

The most important thing you are trying to discern in the selection process is the candidate's fit with your culture.[19]

All in all, when hiring support staff, the best approach, as stated earlier, is a balanced approach between objectivity and subjectivity, testing the candidate's alignments with your core values. Also, as previously discussed, the greatest interviewing technique for attorneys is simply hiring the potential attorney as a law clerk during the third year of law school and testing his or her adherence to your systems and cultural values, or, more realistically, to the person's adoption of your culture and core values during his or her law clerk experience with your law office.

---

18. VERNE HARNISH, MASTERING THE ROCKEFELLER HABITS: WHAT YOU MUST DO TO INCREASE THE VALUE OF YOUR GROWING FIRM 20 (Gazelles 2002).

19. *Id.* at 21.

Collins summarizes three practical disciplines for being a rigorous, not ruthless, leader in human resources:

1. When in doubt, don't hire—keep looking. (*Corollary*: a firm should limit its growth based on its ability to attract enough of the right people.)
2. When you know you need to make a people change, act. (*Corollary*: first be sure you don't have someone in the wrong seat.)
3. Put your best people on your biggest opportunities, not your biggest problems. (*Corollary*: if you sell off your problems, don't sell off your best people.)[20]

Obviously, the takeaway for the law firm is that people matter and so you cannot compromise finding and hiring the right people. They are so important that hiring the right people (or not hiring the right people) is the ultimate litmus test for growth. Once the right people are in place, you need to put your A players on the biggest projects. Do not waste your top talent on matters of least economic benefit.

Keep an Open Mind

Take note that the layers of limitations you put on hiring the right person may cause you to not hire the right person. There is a certain amount of work that can be done by attorneys working out of their home and by support staff job sharing.

With respect to attorneys, you will find quality people who add value to your office while only working part-time. The types of tasks and jobs for a part-time attorney are unique and need to be managed carefully. The work of a part-time attorney might be limited to brief writing, estate planning, or other finite manageable legal work with assignments that are clearly understandable and ascertainable. The main question is whether a part-time lawyer can work in your office environment. Ascertain whether this part-time accommodation is for a short time or a permanent arrangement. If it works for you and the attorney can continue to add value under those circumstances, there is no reason not to engage in that arrangement.

Similarly, with support staff, part-time workers are very good so long as there is a process and a system in place where all part-time workers pull from an ongoing typing pool and everybody works in good faith to do the best job possible. If two assistants job share and work in good faith to always complete the tasks at hand, this arrangement will also be successful. Usually, the breakdown on part-time support staff and job sharing comes

---

20. Jim Collins, Good to Great: Why Some Companies Make the Leap . . . and Others Don't 63 (Harper Business 2001).

from one or two people accusing the others of leaving the difficult projects, or the mundane projects, for the next person; the dissatisfaction will increase. As such cases persist, you either have the wrong people working in part-time positions and job sharing or the program needs to be dismantled and you need to move into full-time workers who are dedicated to completing their own projects and tasks on their own.

Year-End Reviews

Depending on your preference, you should meet with all employees annually to review their progress and the value they have added to the firm in the last twelve months. The cycle that you choose is up to you, but in a law practice, year-end review is done most often in the month of December, with bonus calculations made for attorneys on a cycle beginning December 1 and ending on November 30. This way the bonus calculations based on any objective criteria can be tallied at the end of November and bonuses distributed in December.

With respect to support staff, an honest and open dialogue should be encouraged whereby you solicit commentary from the employees to learn about positive issues with respect to the office and challenges that can be addressed in the new year. Again, the annual review should be about the value that the administrative assistant, accounting clerk, and other support staff members added to the firm. For example:

- Are they faster typists?
- Have they mastered more of your word-processing software?
- Are they more skilled at transcription?
- Have they taken on some paralegal roles?
- Have they assisted you in practice management issues?
- Have they furthered their education in a junior college, college program, or paralegal program?
- Have they begun assisting other attorneys?

These are just a few of the criteria you can use when determining whether your support staff deserve a pay increase or a year-end bonus.

With respect to attorneys, you can simply go to the five-tool attorney chapter (Chapter 4) to see how your associates are doing on the progress of becoming a five-tool attorney. As part of that, focus on productivity and billing, the quality of the work, and the employee's commitment to marketing. Also, during the year-end interview of senior associates, discuss their commitment to training younger attorneys and helping run the business.

Again, as for support staff, the purpose of the year-end review is to create a dialogue to express your views of the individual's progress in the past year and his or her expectations for the coming year, and also to solicit direct feedback on improving the individual's place in the law firm and the law firm in general.

Chapter 23

Leadership

Your success begins with leadership, and the role it plays with employees and clients cannot be understated. The discussion in this chapter is primarily on your leadership role in the law office. Later in the book, we will talk about the management team and the leadership requirements of the management team as you take on partners.

For now, as you lead the company, empirical evidence shows that you cannot and will not ultimately succeed by trying to single-handedly push your team to greatness. No; instead, you need to build a management team through true leadership, to position your firm to make the transition after you are no longer there to lead the team. This is quite an optimistic goal, but it needs to be stated early on in the growth of your firm. You accomplish nothing other than having a rewarding career and a great job if you do not concentrate on building a management and leadership team to run the firm after you retire. To work your entire career and build what you consider a great firm and then to see it all dissipate upon your retirement from the practice of law is tragic.

Starting with the end in mind, we are seeking the level 5 leader,[1] someone who goes beyond the typical leader that we often see in small and growing law firms. Often, small law firms, as referenced earlier, are driven by a dynamic leader with a relentless work ethic, a commitment to and a vigorous pursuit of a clear and compelling vision, and able to stimulate high performance standards from all those around him. That sounds pretty good, does it not?

It is not really good enough because the level 5 leader exceeds that previously described effective leader. The top level 5 leaders "channel their ego needs away from themselves and into the larger goal of building a great company. It's not that Level 5 leaders have no ego or self-interest. Indeed, they are incredibly ambitious—*but their ambition is first and foremost for the institution, not themselves.*"[2] As a leader, you must remember that the ongoing mantra must be that the firm comes first. Indeed, the firm must always come

---

1. JIM COLLINS, GOOD TO GREAT: WHY SOME COMPANIES MAKE THE LEAP . . . AND OTHERS DON'T 20 (Harper Business 2001).
2. *Id.* at 21.

first, not your ego or personality, nor pocketbook. In order to build the company that will exceed all expectations and set the gold standard, decisions must be based on taking actions that are best for the firm.

There is no sense analyzing what you need to take out of the company before you build this highly recognizable and sought-after law firm. Our goal is building the clock, not telling the time.[3]

> Having a great idea or being a charismatic visionary leader is "time telling"; building a [law firm] that can prosper far beyond the presence of any single leader and through multiple [. . .] life cycles is "clock building." . . . [Visionary leaders] concentrate primarily on building an organization—building a ticking clock—rather than on hitting a market just right with a visionary product idea and riding the growth curve of an attractive product life cycle.[4]

In order to build the company that will exceed all expectations and set the gold standard, decisions must be based on taking actions that are best for the firm.

Collins and Porras have compelling, empirical research that indicates that leaders of great organizations take an architectural approach and concentrate on building the organization's traits, which are like those of other visionary successful companies. The primary output of the level 5 visionary leader is not the tangible implementation of a great idea, the expression of a charismatic personality, the gratification of ego, or the accumulation of personal wealth. The greatest creation is *the company itself and what it stands for*.[5] This is powerful concept, and it needs to be understood early on in your decision-making processes as you hire people, create a firm culture, and implement systems to be the best.

It is, indeed, *your responsibility* to the firm to create the greatest firm possible.

True, the level 5 leader has a paradoxical blend of personal humility and professional will. He or she must be a driven leader infected with an incurable need to produce firm-level results. The discussion on level 5 leadership in *Good to Great* is an interestingly humbling experience. It indicates, after thorough research, that level 5 leaders display workmanlike diligence and likens them more to a plow horse than a show horse.[6] When things go poorly, level 5 leaders look in the mirror and blame themselves, and yet when

---

3. *Id.* at 22.
4. *Id.* at 23.
5. *Id.*
6. *Id.* at 33.

things go well they look out the window to credit success to the team.[7] All level 5 leaders need to lead by words and actions.

So now that you know the personality, what are the disciplines?

Embrace the *E-Myth Mastery*[8] disciplines for successful companies, and when applying those required for a law firm, the first discipline is concentration.

During your practice of law, ideas, research, deadlines, billing goals, software problems, and telephone calls will all tend to scatter your concentration. However, your role in the firm is one of a leader vested with leadership responsibilities. Leadership responsibilities do have gravity to them.[9] A great part of your role is sorting through the noise and focusing and prioritizing on those issues that demand the highest thought level that you can give. You need to focus your attention. That is why earlier, in Section 1 of the book, it clearly states that sometime during the day, whether it be 9:00 a.m. to 5:00 p.m., Monday through Friday, certain set-aside time must be dedicated to serving clients. You may find a different schedule to work for you and, based on your client needs, that might be flexible, but there may be other times during the course of the week where you concentrate on your bookkeeping, financial management of the firm, human resource issues, and other growth matters. Remember, practicing law will be a majority of your concentration during the week. But do not ever dismiss the level of concentration you need to work *on* your firm as opposed to working as an attorney *in* your firm.

The second discipline is discrimination.[10] If concentration is the skill of how to focus one's attention, discrimination is the skill of *where* to focus one's attention.[11] If you can never learn to focus your attention and concentrate, you will never learn how to determine what issues become the most important issues of the day, the week, the month, and the year, and ultimately, for the five- and ten-year plan.

Every management guru for the office worker suggests making a list of things you need to do every day. The best time to make the list for the day is before you go home from work on the prior day. Therefore, if you plan on leaving the office at 6:00 p.m., at 5:45 p.m. pull out a yellow pad of paper and make a list of things you need to do the next day. Jot down random thoughts, without much discrimination. You may need to do some legal research, draft a letter, prepare a brief, or look into some new software, chase down some clients who are past due on bills, call the bank on a bounced check, or other tasks that need to be completed. Write all those tasks down. Then, the last thing you do before you leave the office is to grade all tasks for the next day either as A, B, or C, with A being the most important and C being the least important. Your yellow pad should have

---

7. *Id.* at 35.
8. Michael E. Gerber, E-Myth Mastery: The Seven Essential Disciplines for Building a World Class Company 75 (HarperCollins 2005).
9. *See id* at 75.
10. *Id.* at 76.
11. *Id.*

a list of these items that need to be accomplished that will greet you when you arrive to work the next day.

Subject to the time when you arrive in the office in the morning, and the availability of third parties you need to contact, start ticking off the A projects from the beginning to the end. Remember, the A projects are the most important priorities in your life for that day, and you need to get those done. Some of the A projects may come later because you will need to make certain phone calls where the other party will not be in until a later time. Nonetheless, do not move to any of the B projects until the A projects are completed or, at least, started.

It will be incredible how much you can get done when working off a list, maintaining concentration, and using the ABC system for discrimination.

In a more macro sense with respect to organization and discrimination, you need to lead the firm in focusing its attention when there is a certain finite set of problems and issues to correct. You know the adage, "The organization with too many priorities has no priorities."[12] Regularly, but no less than annually, after taking a survey of all employees in the company and giving great weight to high-level associates and your office manager, you need to create a task list of the things that need to be addressed in the business. Included on this list are your ideas for required initiatives to better the practice. You manage these issues with your first discipline of concentration, but it is really about prioritizing the list that is the exercise of *discrimination* that blocks out the organizational noise to focus on the items that really need to be addressed. Harnish[13] states that you should undertake five of the greatest-need items and address those in the greatest-need priority. The greatest need goes first, then the second, and so on. Whether you determine that five greatest-need items per year are sufficient, or three, do not take on the top fifteen initiatives for the law office for one year. Again, if everything is a priority, nothing is a priority.

> The best time to make the list for the day is before you go home from work on the prior day.

These top five items have to be of core importance to improving the systems in the law office. In fact, once you begin to build your business plan and start setting one-, five- and ten-year plans, and you will need to start working on your pay-to-play requirements. The pay-to-play requirements articulated in Chapter 24 are the items that need to exist in order to reach your one-, five- and ten-year goals. They are not goals in themselves; they are requirements of the firm. During your first exercise of the discrimination process and determining what your five objectives are, pay-to-play requirements need to exist, and all

---

12. VERNE HARNISH, MASTERING THE ROCKEFELLER HABITS: WHAT YOU MUST DO TO INCREASE THE VALUE OF YOUR GROWING FIRM 53 (Gazelles 2002).

13. *Id.* at 54.

effort needs to go into meeting those requirements in order to ultimately grow the firm and meet your one-, five- and ten-year goals.

As you prioritize the various top five initiatives annually, at first your top two or three priorities may be of such critical importance that without conquering the shortfalls, the firm will fail and dissolve. Therefore, it is very likely that in the early years of this process, several of the top five priorities are life-and-death priorities for the firm. All in all, as the years move forward and the pay-to-play requirements are set in stone, your top five priorities will start to move toward growth and innovation type priorities.

The third essential leadership skill is organization.[14] Organization is a pretty simple skill to understand. What I describe as concentration and discrimination are both organization-building skills. But really, the organization we are talking about here is the organizational leadership for the law firm, not necessarily your daily activity. The organization defines the functional components of a whole and the relationship between the parts. You need to foster the right organization in your law firm. You need to set standards, consistent in both your words and your actions, regarding how your bookkeeping department interfaces with your administrative assistants, who interface with the attorneys.

> As the support staff must grow in skill and understanding of the particular attorney's practice area, so they can take on more responsibility and add more value, which sustains their personal growth and the firm's growth.

Since all businesses are revenue driven, the money starts with the attorney's billable time, and everything else supports that activity. As such, the relationships that are developed to support the attorneys' billing time need to be established in a cohesive, organizational structure.

You need to understand and acculturate members of your organization to understand that the attorneys do 99% of the fee-generating work in our office, so the support staff (i.e., the administrative assistants and the accounting department) are there to *support* the attorneys so that they can produce more billable work. Everyone must interact with each other respectfully, with professionalism, and with a great understanding that attorneys can be great only with the right support staff. As the support staff must grow in skill and understanding of the particular attorney's practice area, so they can take on more responsibility and add more value, which sustains their personal growth and the firm's growth. This relationship is an area of mutual respect; but most importantly, it improves and enhances the functionality of the firm. Bottom line, your organization needs organization.

---

14. Michael E. Gerber, E-Myth Mastery: The Seven Essential Disciplines for Building a World Class Company 78 (HarperCollins 2005).

The fourth essential skill of leadership is innovation.[15] This is fun. This is when the leader of the organization is working *on* the firm, not *in* the firm. What is the new software that can make us more efficient? What is the new practice group that we need to get into? Are we looking for ways to get the best résumés from available resources? Do we understand our client? What is important to our client? How can we market for new clients in a better, more efficient manner? What is our unique selling proposition? Is there a quicker way to retrieve documents and build a better document library?

These are just a sampling of innovative questions that you constantly need to revisit to make sure your management team is always staying current and innovative relative to other law offices. You are always looking for the next great idea. While some of these ideas are not true innovations in the world of technology and business, they are a new way of doing things for a law office, generally an old-world profession. It is the leader's responsibility to continue to try to reinvent the law office so that it grabs attention in the marketplace and fires up employee morale.

The fifth and last leadership skill is communication.[16] Communication is certainly an important part of leadership in your law office.

Remember the old adage that "your actions speak louder than words." Well, although this lengthy discussion on leadership indicates that actions certainly do speak loud and clear, your words have an equal effect on your organization. Your oral and written messages to the organization are critical; they *are* the message.

Many times level 4 leaders use an authoritative management style, and simply by their force of personality will issue edicts and set the rules that need to be followed. Again, this approach might be a way for their minions to follow the lead and get the job done, but it is no way to build a world-class firm.

Strong-handed memos styled as edicts with bold letters, underlined emphasis, and exclamation points are not necessarily an effective way to communicate to the organization. The effective manager leads by actions and reinforces by words. Words need to be honest, truthful, sustainable, and spoken directly to the organization. In order for the organization to get an unfiltered, clear message from the leader, the message should be set forth in company meetings where everyone hears the message in the same, unedited fashion. The leader must inspire, must educate, must be seen rolling up his or her sleeves, implementing change, applying his or her written or spoken principles, and always looking to improve the organization.[17]

The leader is there to inspire and bring out the best in his or her people. If the leader has taken the steps necessary to surround himself with only the best people, he or she will further inspire those employees who are in the position to help make the best decision for

---

15. *Id.* at 79.
16. *Id.* at 81.
17. *Id.*

the organization. After it is all said and done, and all the analysis is factored in, the number 1 requirement of the leader of the firm is always to reinforce that the firm comes first.

Chapter 24

Building the Business Plan

The concept of preparing a business plan sounds like a budgeting exercise with pro forma guesstimates of the money flowing in and out of a business or project done solely to impress some banker to lend money to a new small business. Some cynics believe that the exercise of preparing a business plan is a complete and utter waste of time and that if you just roll up your sleeves and work hard, you will be moving in the correct direction.

Keep in mind the old sayings such as "Failing to plan is planning to fail" and "Planning is bringing the future into the present so that you can do something about it now." Further, the old adage that "if you do not know where you are going, any road will get you there" is absolutely true. The business plan that you prepare is a plan that speaks directly to where you are going and maps out in great detail, with all the disciplines necessary, a route to get you to your ultimate destination—the top law firm in your municipality, state, and possibly the country.

As such, you need to incorporate the following eight items into your comprehensive business plan:

1. Your goals for the next one, five, and ten years. As a part of goal setting, you need to create a list of assumptions that will have to be met in order for you to meet your goals (see Chapter 24).
2. Your leadership function and the role that you will play in the law office. Largely, this is set forth in the previous chapter, but as you develop your leadership paradigm and disciplines, you will incorporate those into your business plan (see Chapter 23).
3. The management structure of the firm. Depending on where you are on the growth curve, you need to assign and delegate the various disciplines of running the firm to other people, with your oversight (see Chapter 25).
4. Employee policies. The foundation of your firm will be based on the quality and success of the people who work with you. The values that you adopted from previous chapters of the book need to be input into your business plan and outline how

you will handle employees in order to meet your one-, five- and ten-year plan and goals (see Chapters 20, 21, and 22).

5. Marketing and lead generation. It is critical when you are a solo practitioner to always be actively networking, setting the right foundation by doing the fundamental acts to generate leads. Including marketing plans in the business plan is an important process to segregate and understand how you will generate clients for the law firm (see Chapters 12, 13, and 26).

6. Lead conversion. You need to specifically have a plan to convert telephone calls, introductions, and enquiries into clients (see Chapter 27).

7. Client fulfillment and satisfaction. Again, dealt with earlier in multiple areas of Section 1, your business plan needs to include the firm's internal mechanisms to satisfy every client so that when you have an opportunity to perform legal services for someone for the first time, you will set the foundation to have a client for life (see Chapter 28).

8. Commit to writing the firm's culture and core values. Subsequent chapters in Section 2 give you the process in which to identify and adopt your firm's culture and core values. As you work through those chapters to develop your culture and core values, you will ultimately distill those down into your business plan (see Chapter 29 and 30).

> As you develop your firm goals for the one-, five-, and ten-year plans, you need to think realistically, and boldly, regarding the direction in which your firm will grow.

Setting the One-, Five-, and Ten-Year Plans

Writing a business plan is an important starting point for the firm, probably the first opportunity you will ever have to create the destination for your law firm and committing those goals to writing.

People who set goals and write them down have a higher probability of succeeding. Keep in mind this magnificent quotation: "The greater danger for most of us lies not in setting our aim too high and falling short; but in setting our aim too low, and achieving our mark."[1]

As you develop your firm goals for the one-, five-, and ten-year plans, you need to think realistically, and boldly, regarding the direction in which your firm will grow. As you set

---

1. Michelangelo cited in KEN ROBINSON, THE ELEMENT: HOW FINDING YOUR PASSION CHANGES EVERYTHING 260 (Penguin Books 2009).

the one-, five-, and ten-year plans, keep in mind that it is a rolling plan that will be readjusted annually. Therefore, at the end of the year, you will review how you have done on accomplishing your goals under the one-year plan. Hopefully, you will have met all of your goals, and you will redraft a new one-year plan for the subsequent year. Also, you will look at your previously drafted five- and ten-year plans to see if you have set the right foundation in place to accomplish them. At the end of year 1, you may need to readjust the five- and ten-year plans, which is perfectly fine. Always keep previous drafts of these documents at hand so that at the end of year 5, you will be able to go back to the very first draft of your five-year plan to see how much you have accomplished.

The One-Year Plan

Depending on where you are in the growth of your firm will have a bearing on what your one-year goals are. Here are some suggestions for you to consider for your one-year plan:

- Hire an administrative assistant;
- Hire an accounting professional on a part-time basis;
- Open five new files (i.e., clients) per month for the entire year;
- Cross-sell additional legal services to at least 20% of your existing clients—for example, an estate plan to your business clients;
- Bill thirty or thirty-five hours per week for client matters on average every week of the year;
- Collect on 95% of all billable hours from clients;
- Find and move into new renovated office space;
- Systematize a document scanning and storage program;
- Stop working for clients when their retainer balance goes to $0—effectively eliminating receivables and collecting on 100% of all client billable work;
- Create operations manuals for each phase and segment of the law office;
- Create good human resource employee files;
- Document all employee meetings with memos that go into their human resource folder;
- Move into one new practice area in the new year;
- Dedicate the year to exhaustively learning about and mastering one social networking platform such as LinkedIn or Facebook;
- Improve the accounting areas in the office to determine which practice area generates the most revenue;
- Create management reports where the accounting department gives you a monthly report on items such as total billing, new clients, incoming telephone calls, sources of incoming telephone calls, and any other measurables relevant to your practice area;

- Institutionalize client satisfaction measurables such as returning phone calls in two or four hours, month-end summary letters on the status of cases, and other measurables that you deem critical to your firm's success;
- Prepare a best-practices manual for your law office;
- Go to three on-campus interview days to meet some third-year law students who may ultimately work for you in the future;
- Start to develop skills and processes to identify the type of people who would adopt your culture;
- Adopt a pro bono policy for your law office;
- Commit that client bills are to be sent out on the second day of the following month every month;
- Completely overhaul your existing website; and
- Implement new branding initiatives.

The Five-Year Plan

Here are some suggestions for you to consider for your five-year plan:

- Have five new attorneys at your law office;
- Add five hundred new clients;
- Move your practice into at least two new practice areas, either through your own migration into a new area or by hiring a new associate with some experience in a completely new practice area;
- Allocate some management roles to other attorneys;
- Reevaluate existing office space and sign a five-year lease;
- Take a socially important case—one followed by the media—on a pro bono basis;
- Meet at least five new referral sources per year, ones that actually refer you cases where you can document twenty-five new clients from twenty-five different referral sources in the next five years (that is approximately one new referral source every two months);
- Become the chairperson of a bar association committee;
- Serve on a board for at least three years on a local not-for-profit organization;
- Continue to evolve your management reports to include more microstatistics such as revenue generated from new clients, revenue generated from a specific referral source, or revenue identified from a particular marketing campaign such as radio, billboard, and print ads; and
- Add diversification to the office by hiring bilingual attorneys or support staff.

The Ten-Year Plan

Here are some suggestions for you to consider for your ten-year plan:

- Promote at least one attorney to partner status;
- Make a thoughtful estimate as to the number of new clients you will have through the tenth year. Remember, if one attorney should bring in a certain number of clients per month, relate that growth to the attorney growth in your firm. Do not be timid, be aggressive;
- Eliminate employees quitting by offering them a great work environment, fair salaries, proper incentives, and real-time recognition;
- Develop a system for potentially merging with existing small firms or aging practices;
- Open a second office in another location (maybe in another state);
- Have a well-defined and complimentary practice of transactional lawyers and litigators; and
- Create a specialization culture in your firm to migrate away from generalists to having your attorneys do repetitive work in one to three complementary practice areas.

Audacious Goals

> Think big, act big, and shamelessly talk about big accomplishments, big goals, and, perhaps, an opportunity to change the world. Someone has to do it—why not you?

In addition to very real important goals set for the one-, five- and ten-year time horizon, you need to adopt the Collins and Porras concept of "big hairy audacious goals."[2] Most people do not think big. They do not think big because they are fearful of having tremendous goals and falling short, and then feeling like a failure. That mentality should not exist within the culture of your firm. Think big, act big, and shamelessly talk about big accomplishments, big goals, and, perhaps, an opportunity to change the world. Someone has to do it—why not you?

Big conversation-stopping goals energize workers, energize the support staff, and give you a clear path on which you are headed. Remember, it was John F. Kennedy who stated he wanted to send a man to the moon by the end of the 1960s. A lofty goal, correct? Big hairy audacious goals stimulate thought and stimulate progress in the firm. Sometimes, when you have the wrong people in your firm, these goals seem like another thing hanging over their head that they cannot get to while they are actively involved in the grind of the business day. However, with the right people, it energizes them to help create a winning team. Remember, back in the 1960s President Kennedy could have set a goal of "let's beef

---

2. JAMES C. COLLINS & JERRY I. PORRAS, BUILT TO LAST: SUCCESSFUL HABITS OF VISIONARY COMPANIES 91 (Harper Business 1994).

up our space program"[3] or something else as vague. On May 25, 1961, President Kennedy proclaimed "that this nation should commit itself to achieving the goal, before this decade is out, of landing a man on the moon and returning him safely to earth."[4] The statement was at the time outrageous. But along with the charismatic leadership of the president, it helped to vigorously move the country forward. And, it is important to note that President Kennedy's goal was accomplished after his untimely assassination. Big hairy audacious goals are sometimes part salesmanship and part goal setting. Some people in the organization will call such goals unreasonable. Those are the people who need to be reviewed for their commitment to the organization. What are your big hairy audacious goals?

Here are some suggestions for you to consider:

- Have your firm grow to one hundred lawyers;
- Have one of your attorneys be appointed to judge or win a political election;
- Promote yourself or one of your attorneys to win an election for state or federal government;
- Argue a case in the state or federal supreme court;
- Take a pro bono case and win it to improve the lives of the underprivileged;
- File a class-action lawsuit and fight for the rights of consumers;
- Represent every small business on the main street in your town or community;
- Organize a grassroots fundraiser and raise $1 million to save a church in your community; or
- Open a law office and be licensed in every state that surrounds the state in which you operate.

Big hairy audacious goals are critical to the long-term success of a firm. Make no mistake about it—these goals are just not put on a poster that people can see as they walk by. They are actual goals that people are working toward. It is the commitment from the employees that makes the outrageous goal worthwhile. In fact, it should be talked about freely inside the law office. If the big hairy audacious goal looks crazy and unachievable to outsiders and yet inside employees see it as a real objective of the operation of the entity, you have achieved what you set out to achieve. You have the right people in place when they simply cannot conceive *not achieving* the big hairy audacious goal.

How do you do it? You do it by making your one-year, five-year, and ten-year plans public within the firm and achieving them. As you readjust your plans every year and meet or exceed your previous year's goals (or most of them), you will gain credibility with the employees, and with credibility, you will gain buy-in.

---

3. *Id.* at 94.
4. *Id.*

The big hairy audacious goal may not be achieved during their term with the law firm, and here is what is important, it may not be achieved *during your lifetime*. It is okay if the big hairy audacious goal is to be achieved after you are long retired. That is how big it could be.

Pay-to-Play Requirements

To achieve your one-year, five-year, ten-year big hairy audacious goals, you have to have some assumptions that are really pay-to-play requirements. In other words, there is really no discussion as to the assumptions because without the assumptions being followed, finalized, and institutionalized, goals simply cannot be met. You will develop your own set of assumptions that are requirements even to get in the door of your law firm. Consider some of these:

- The firm meets or exceeds billing goals;
- The firm collects on 95% (or 85%) of all billable work;
- Attorneys and support staff carry out your core purpose and culture on a daily basis but are called out and corrected during times of complacency;
- Attorneys and support staff diligently work to produce exemplary work product;
- The responsibility of marketing is institutionalized, accepted, and implemented by all attorneys as a requirement of employment;
- Leadership emerges by words and actions by you first, then attorneys, then support staff;
- The firm obtains and retains the highest-quality people as attorneys and support staff;
- The firm provides a salary structure to fairly compensate employees and provide incentives and rewards to individuals that overperform on expectations and goals; and
- Attorneys stop work when clients fall behind on payments.

> The annual meeting, usually done in the first quarter of the year, not only is a good review of the previous year but also helps you gain critically important information from the employees of the firm to help set the top three or five priorities for the new year.

These are just some ways in which to create your goals that are the starting point of your business plan. Ultimately, your business plan will be distributed and adopted by all the attorneys and support staff in the office. There should be no secrets, and everyone needs to adopt these goals as part of the firm's culture.

Annual Firm Meeting

Section 3 of the book has an extensive discussion on meetings and the management team's need for meetings and the integration of those meetings with attorneys. However, for purposes of a discussion on goal setting, it is a good idea to have a firmwide meeting for everyone, including all support staff and the accounting department, to discuss the needs of the law firm. The support staff will truly appreciate being involved in this annual meeting to talk about office efficiencies, and their input is highly valuable.

At this annual meeting, you will take everyone's input as you craft your one-, five-, and ten-year plan. In addition, as part of that meeting, it is a great idea to pull out the previous year's one-year plan and talk about how the firm has done in accomplishing those one-year goals. Certainly, if you have accomplished most of them, the firm will be energized, and all employees will feel that they were part of the goal setting in the previous year and helped the firm grow and accomplish those goals. If many of the goals were not met, an open dialogue as to the challenges that the firm faced that prevented it from meeting its goals is appropriate. The other attorneys in the firm, as well as the support staff, do not necessarily expect you to solve all of the problems of the firm, although many times you think that they do. They will participate and offer suggestions to try to support you, the founding partner, in goal setting and accomplishing those goals. There is nothing to hide, and having all of the employees as part of the goal setting and goal reviewing heightens buy-in from the employees that is so necessary for a successful law firm.

The annual meeting, usually done in the first quarter of the year, not only is a good review of the previous year but also helps you gain critically important information from the employees of the firm to help set the top three or five priorities for the new year. After all things are considered and handled correctly, it is a very positive event.

Chapter 25

Firm Management

Firm management is not to be confused with leadership and the mantra that the firm comes first. As part of the business plan building process, you need to think through and commit to writing the management structures and philosophies of the firm. In addition, as part of that process, you may need to review Chapter 8 on departments in your law office. Your business model will be broken into the disciplines, and many of the items listed in Chapters 2 and 8 will be incorporated to build your business plan.

Now, at first, it will be obvious that you will handle virtually all of the management aspects of the firm, but as head of a small growing firm, you need to solicit assistance from all of those around you, including administrative assistants and your accounting department. Either you or a subsequent leader of a particular function of the office will need to start creating manuals for critically important systems. This will allow people to become interchangeable in their daily activities. So, for starters, what are the things you want to measure?

For the things you want to measure, you need reports to review on a regular basis. At this juncture, nothing is too big, too small, or too insignificant to measure. In *Mastering the Rockefeller Habits*,[1] Harnish relates that the data available for your firm have to be analyzed and reviewed regularly—in some businesses, daily.

In order to know if you're acting consistent with your priorities you need feedback in terms of real time data. There are key metrics within a [firm] that you want to measure over an extended period of time called Smart Numbers; and there are metrics that provide a short term laser focus on an aspect of the business or someone's job called Critical Numbers. It's the balance between short term and long term.[2]

---

1. VERNE HARNISH, MASTERING THE ROCKEFELLER HABITS: WHAT YOU MUST DO TO INCREASE THE VALUE OF YOUR GROWING FIRM (Gazelles 2002).

2. *Id.* at xxi.

So as part of the management discipline of the law office, you need to gather data and continually review the reported data (on a daily, weekly, or monthly basis?) and adjust expectations and goals as the firm develops.

The best data will probably come from the accounting or bookkeeping department. Members of this department are involved in the numbers every day, and they should be instructed to provide the data to you in synthesized, simple-to-understand reports as part of their daily and weekly ritual.

What are examples of management reports that you would like to see?

- Number of new clients monthly and annually;
- Gross billing monthly;
- Actual collection revenue;
- Profit-and-loss statement for the month;
- Year-to-year growth charts (in actual billing and collecting, expressed as a percentage);
- Year-to-year changes in cash flow and profits;
- Bank account balances weekly;
- Number of appointments for new, potential clients weekly or monthly;
- Grid showing the sources of potential clients, how they heard about your firm;
- Incoming telephone calls from potential clients;
- Client sign-ups or conversions from marketing efforts;
- Actual fees generated from your marketing efforts specifically linked to a particular marketing effort;
- Repeat work from existing clients;
- Cross-selling from one practice group to another practice group of existing clients;
- Referrals from existing clients;
- New clients generated from traditional marketing (i.e., network marketing, set forth in Chapter 13);
- Documented appointment of relationship managers for all clients;
- Personnel files and internal record keeping:
  - Vacation days
  - Absenteeism
  - Personal and emergency days
  - Payroll information
  - Overtime pay to employees

> At first, you will handle virtually all of the management aspects of the firm, but as head of a small growing firm, you need to solicit assistance from all of those around you.

- Bonuses paid out to attorneys for client origination
- Pro bono hours;
- Client complaints:
  - Billing inaccuracies
  - Not returning phone calls.

What other measurables are you interested in keeping track of in your law office? The generation of these reports is not a task in which you should engage personally, but these management reports need to be prepared at a minimum monthly and provided to you with accurate data for you to track the measurables of your growing firm. You need data, and in many cases, you need to share the data with people in your firm. Remember, that data will ultimately determine if many of the goals that you set forth in the one-year, five-year and ten-year plans were met.

How Will We Become What We Are Not?

This book has layered foundational values for you to build a winning law firm. It is rather idealistic, and the system works presupposing the incredible level of discipline that it requires. However, you may already have a small law firm, be a partner in a small law firm, or be transitioning your sole proprietor firm into a larger business. In any case, you should ask yourself, "Where do I need to improve?" and "How can I fix the things that are not right in our law office?" and "Overall, how can I help the firm become what it is not?"

> Remember, the visionary leader's second discipline—discrimination—is where you should focus your attention.

In your business plan, you need to have this difficult planning moment and have your imperfections and shortcomings distilled so that you are not floundering in uncertainty as to where to focus your attention. Remember, the visionary leader's second discipline—discrimination—is where you should focus your attention.

First, keep the best of what you do. There are some things that you do well, and you know that, and you can probably identify them. Those items might simply be client fulfillment, or networking, or having a good process for identifying top people, or just being a great technician (i.e., attorney). No matter what your strengths are, identify them and embrace them because they will help create the identity of who you are and what your firm is all about.

Next, eliminate the factors that inhibit further success and growth of the firm. Harnish reminds us that there are three barriers to growth to all growing firms:

1. The need for the [management] team to grow as leaders and their abilities to delegate;
2. The need for systems and structures to handle the complexity that comes with growth; and
3. The need to navigate increasingly tricky market dynamics that mark arrival in a larger marketplace.[3]

You and your future management team need to continue to grow in your management abilities. That part is a function of delegating work and managing work. Anybody can delegate a project and then when it falls flat or becomes a disaster claim that the person to whom you delegated the job is incompetent. That is not management. Remember, it is not what you *expect* from the person to whom you delegate work, it is what you *inspect*.[4] You need to review your subordinates' work *multiple times* before they can be trusted to perform any project in a manner satisfactory to you. Simply stated, that is called training.

It seems obvious—correct?

You will never have a first-year associate prepare a motion for summary judgment and then you not review it and just file it. As an attorney, you are far better wired to manage a younger attorney's work than you will be to review the accounting department's work or your administrative staff's work. But nonetheless, unless you can delegate work, review it, and inspect it—and have the work come back excellent—you will cause your own growth to be hindered.

The second barrier to growth, the need for systems and structures to handle the complexities that come with growth, is a fundamental topic in this section of the book. As stated early in this section, the growth of the firm is built upon people, systems, and culture. If systems are not put in place and reviewed and regularly improved as the firm grows, you will constantly be playing a game of catch-up to figure out why things keep going wrong. Remember the following forever: Running a three-attorney firm is different than operating a seven-attorney firm; running a seven-attorney firm is very different than running a twelve-attorney firm; running a twelve-attorney firm is different than operating a seventeen-attorney firm, and so on. In other words, with growth, there become different problems and different barriers that you need to conquer. The small problems you face in a two- or three-attorney firm are just not scalable when the firm hits seventeen or twenty attorneys. The problems are different.

---

3. *Id.* at 1.
4. This quotation that will forever ring in my head is from my friend, mentor, and client John Kotara. He knew my father well and attributes these words to my dad. I find myself using this phrase and the concept of this expression over and over again as I delegate work, both legal work and practice management work, to other attorneys and support staff. In summary, it is all about proper training. People want to do well, and you need to guide them as to what you expect, and if you do so in a positive, constructive manner, your employees will respond favorably.

Harnish's third barrier to growth is the need to navigate the increasingly tricky market dynamics in which your firm operates. As an example, before 2007 the law profession's marketplace dynamics did not change very often. However, the recession that began in 2008 was a game changer, if not a life changer, for many attorneys. The market changed, and the demand for legal services shifted dramatically and, in some cases, dried up entirely. Your management team, led by you, needs to be dynamic enough and nimble enough to navigate through these changes.

In addition, the market is changing, ever so slowly, such that more of our legal systems are being competitively bid on the Internet and through do-it-yourself software purportedly there to replace attorney work. It will not, but nonetheless, it is another competitive force in the legal landscape. As a result, as you race to become what you are not, be aware that you need to eliminate the factors that further prohibit success and growth.

Not included in the foregoing list is the firm's lack of highly qualified assistants and people. Remember, a bad hire for an attorney position not only will limit your growth but will set you back. Giving an inexperienced attorney work on cases and client contact could cause a disaster if that attorney does a bad job, for that could hurt the client relationship or, worst, terminate it forever.

How else will you become what you are not? Continue to focus on your vision of the future. Pull out the one-year plan monthly and check your progress. What are your impediments to growth? Are you innovative? Are there software solutions that can help improve results with your deliverables? Consider creating a list in your business plan that addresses the most important functions of your law office that will allow it to continue to grow. After you get this plan through this book, your list may include these activities:

- Return phone calls immediately;
- Take good clients;
- Reject problematic clients and cases;
- Maintain great relationships with referral sources;
- Cultivate additional work from existing clients;
- Know how to identify potential clients;
- Follow up properly with referrals and leads for work;
- Have a high degree or specialization and expertise in one or a few areas of the law;
- Enhance, improve, and perfect the client service experience;
- Continue to provide excellent legal services;
- Improve your marketing and lead generation systems (even if they are good, improve them);
- Utilize social media;
- Recruit A+ employees;
- Hit billing goals;

- Manage or eliminate receivables;
- Ensure proper branding of your law office;
- Make contributions to the community; and
- Make contributions to the legal community.

You will see within time that the foregoing checklist showing the most important functions required for the law office to continue to grow will need to be reviewed regularly.

Organizational Charts

Another stepchild of the big corporate world is the organizational chart created to understand where everyone fits in. Without taking too much time and overemphasizing structure in your organization, you should, as your business grows, commit to writing the reporting system at the office. If there are only three workers in your office—you, an accounting person, and an administrative assistant, with the latter two not necessarily even being full time—yours may not be a very complicated organizational chart, since everybody reports to you. But as you continue to grow and other attorneys start working in your office taking on some management responsibility, the hierarchy may get a little bit more complicated. But the reporting chart is not necessarily the only one in the law firm. You may want to create a flowchart for your process for scanning, document retention, file building, brief writing, agreement preparation, and other internal law office—specific tasks that need to be systematized.

Creating a High-Performance Environment[5]

The management team needs to constantly fine-tune, work on, and polish the environment in the firm to create one of high performance.

What makes a business a high-performance organization is its dedication to its purpose, its ability to consciously create a structure uniquely designed for that purpose, and its commitment to giving its people the tools they need to get the results expected. *Vision*, *structure*, and *tools*, in a nutshell.[6]

---

5. MICHAEL E. GERBER, E-MYTH MASTERY: THE SEVEN ESSENTIAL DISCIPLINES FOR BUILDING A WORLD CLASS COMPANY 250 (Collins 2005).
6. *Id.* at 250.

As you can see, a critically important part of a high-performance environment for your law office is vision. Without the one-year plan, five-year plan, and ten-year plans and big hairy audacious goals, there will be no vision, and there will be no future. You need to see the future today. All of these long-term goals create alignment and have your colleagues and coworkers pursuing the same set of goals. Certainly, part of your high-performance environment will be your commitment to the truth of your culture and core values, but most importantly, it is built on the firm's vision, the structure and reporting requirements of the firm, and whether you have given the attorneys and support staff the right resources (e.g., software, computers, work environment, administrative assistance support, and clerks) to energize the firm.

Specifically, in a law office, the necessary resources are:

- Support staff (i.e., administrative assistants);
- Resources and supplies;
- Technology;
- Physical space;
- Continuing education;
- Law clerks; and
- File clerks.

If the tools and resources are in place, you need to execute daily and revisit your management reports to quantify and evaluate the performance of your law office.

> You need to create position-specific content, such as operating manuals for administrative assistants, the accounting department, attorney work policies, and overall partner responsibilities and expectations.

Operating Manuals

The main operating manual of the entire firm is the business plan, the topic of this chapter. To encompass all of the elements set forth in Chapter 24, the plan must be under constant revision.

You also need to create position-specific content, such as operating manuals for administrative assistants, the accounting department, attorney work policies, and overall partner responsibilities and expectations.

What other institutionalized manuals and systems do you need to create for your high-performance work environment? The ideas with which to improve your firm could be almost limitless, but as noted in previous chapters of the book, please consider manuals for the following tasks:

- Hourly billing rules and standards;
- Management of client payments and accounts receivable;
- Bill reviews, standards, and rules;
- Accounting department standards, protocol;
- A document library;
- Marketing and networking systems;
- Public relations and community development manuals;
- Conflict-of-interest management;
- Best practices written policy;
- Attorney-client meeting protocol;
- Website management review;
- Continuing education and skills development among attorneys and administrative assistants;
- Seminars and public speaking protocol and systems; and
- Practice area–specific administration assistant protocol.

As you can see, the management team responsibilities set forth in this chapter are critically important. At first, the management team may be only you. But it is important to institutionalize and understand the barriers the firm will run into as it continues to grow. One of your duties is to continue to work *on* your business with an eye toward building a management team that embraces these concepts and will accept the nonbillable work that it takes to run the law firm. Those individuals who plan on making partner need to be ready to make an investment in adopting your management philosophies, being committed to working on the systems manuals, flowcharts, management reports, and marketing systems that are required to help you avoid the barriers to your growth. Moreover, your future management team members need to embrace your vision and add their input to the vision so that they may participate in the successful growth of the firm.

Chapter 26

Marketing and Lead Generation System

Management guru Peter Drucker has asked the initial questions, "Who is your [client] ?"[1], and "What does your [client] value?"[2] It is through Drucker and his colleagues' analysis that the entire marketing program is built. Depending on your practice areas and your expertise, the answers to "Who is your client?" and "What does your client value?" are identified in different ways.

For example, a family-law lawyer might identify his or her clients differently than a transactional-law lawyer looking for work in the mergers and acquisitions field might look at his or her own clients. Estate-planning lawyers try to find their clients differently than a personal-injury lawyer does. Criminal lawyers certainly try to market to potential clients differently than do residential real estate lawyers.

The whole notion of identifying your potential client and then trying to find your potential client seems fundamentally easy in light of the comparative questions asked rhetorically: "Who is your potential client if you are a criminal lawyer?" or "Who is your potential client who needs estate planning services?"

However, sorting through the process to identify these potential clients and the lead generation process necessary to identify them is a combination of art and science. Clients in any practice group, whether it be construction law, mechanic's liens, bankruptcy, immigration, banking law, eviction cases, general business, or employment law, are found in different ways, and you need to identify who your client is and the process through which that client will buy legal services.

Would it surprise you to know, for example, that many women initiate the conversation in their home relating to estate planning? To make the matter more complicated, that role changes as a married couple gets older. In my experience, young mothers more so than

---

1. Throughout this discussion, when referencing the Peter F. Drucker principles, I have substituted the word *client* for the word *customer*, making the quotation more directly related to the legal profession. Peter F. Drucker with Jim Collins, Philip Kotler, James Kouzes, Judith Rodin, V. Kasturi Rangan & Frances Hesselbein, The Five Most Important Questions You Will Ever Ask about Your Organization 25 (Jossey-Bass 2008).

2. *Id.* at 39.

young fathers tend to be concerned and more driven to solve any ambiguity with respect to guardianship provisions for their children. The roles might reverse depending on the career path of the husband and wife. You may find some patterns emerging at certain levels as to who the instigator for legal services is among the couple.

As couples get older and family wealth increases, depending on the source of the asset accumulation and the sophistication of the career path of both spouses, you may find that more male clients are the instigators of seeking legal services, in particular to minimize tax exposure; some also see the estate-planning process as one function in the overall family financial plan.

That role reversal is a good example of what lawyers need to keep in mind when trying to identify the purchaser of legal services for estate planning and how that purchaser might change over time. It is only one example of how estate-planning purchasing decisions change in a market. Markets may be very different across the country, and the market certainly changes as you move from rural America into large municipal areas. Nonetheless, the point is made just to highlight that you need to know your market and your practice area to know who your potential client is. Analyze who your potential client is if you are working in a different practice area. For example, finding business clients needing start-ups, incorporations, and contract review is very different than finding clients who are buying businesses, making venture capital investments in other businesses, and reviewing and renewing million-dollar lines of credit. Whereas, on one hand, we can acknowledge that those individuals are all basically business clients, the actual finding of those clients and the purchasers of the different legal services require a very different strategy in each case.

Keep in mind that in the discussion on the externalities of practicing law, there is an emphasis on every single attorney being involved in at least one trade organization; remember, be part of all three of the classes that make up the externalities of practicing law: a bar association committee, a community not-for-profit group, and a trade association or chamber of commerce.

It is digging deep into the trade association where you will learn more about who your potential clients are, how they make buying decisions for legal services, and how they test the water with attorney services. Find out the status level of all of the members in a particular trade association (i.e., who are the biggest clients, the medium-sized clients, and the smaller clients). Once you find out, you may focus on some of the smaller clients who are emerging and are successful—those who will ultimately be large players in the future in a particular industry.

Second, remember this simple rule: it is always easiest to develop a relationship in groups (with traditional networking, as outlined in Chapter 13) with somebody near to your own age. This sounds fundamentally simple, as well as potentially limiting, but it is reality.

Certainly, if you are in your thirties, do not hesitate to try to build trust and relationships with someone in his or her fifties or sixties. But do not ignore reality. Successful men and women in the business field in their fifties and sixties probably have many years of established relationships with lawyers. That does not make it impossible to develop a beneficial relationship with somebody considerably outside your age bracket, but it is more difficult.

When marketing to a person who is a generation older than you, keep in mind that although the person's attorneys have potentially been with that person for over thirty years, those attorneys can also be getting near the point of retirement; recall, as noted earlier in this book, that being in second place might be the next best place to be. Even if you do not get work instantly from a businessperson who is considerably older than you, continue to try to add value to that person's business and its needs. Also, remember that honesty is the only place to start with any business relationship. Do not be afraid to talk to the person and say, "Tell me a little bit about your business. How has it changed over the years?" or "Tell me about your existing attorney. How many years have you been working with him, and what do you like about him?" In most cases, an elderly states-man or stateswoman at any trade association, chamber of commerce, or Rotary meeting would be delighted to impart wisdom to a young attorney.

Those types of conversations are critically valuable to any young attorney.

What young attorneys often lack is the business knowledge of certain industries. This lack goes back to the Peter Drucker questions of who is your client and what does that client value.

If you do not know what your clients value, then you are really trying to fight the fight with blinders on. When you meet businesspeople in an industry you may be serving, ask those direct questions—"What do you value in legal services?" or "How have other attorneys disappointed you?" or "When have you seen an attorney recently 'knock the cover off the ball'?"

What does the client value?

Remember that it may not just be what benefits the client's business; the client might really value what benefits him or her. When talking to a high-ranking senior vice president of a bank where you would like to get hired for loan workout work, ask yourself how you can make that senior vice president's life easier? It is that senior vice president that you need to please and make his or her life easier, not improve the entire banking system in the country or have a positive effect on the bottom-line earnings report of Bank of America. You need to make that senior vice president's life easier and simpler.

Analyzing what the potential client values takes a different plan in every practice group. It is your job to analyze the practice area in which you will operate to deliver on this very necessary analysis. After you break down every one of your specific practice areas and identify the potential client, you may believe you know what *those* clients value. Let me provide you with a list of items that *all* clients value:

- Finding responsiveness to telephone calls (i.e., return phone calls as quickly as possible);
- Receiving paper. Clients love to be copied on all agreements, letters, e-mails, and any other deliverable or internal work papers that you create on behalf of the client;
- Receiving ongoing status reports. Let it be a telephone call, letter, or e-mail. Since clients like to talk to you, and talking is the best way to develop a relationship with a client beyond the case on which you are working for the client, telephone calls are best;
- Being heard and listened to. Clients want to know that you are absorbing everything they have to say. Listen to what they have to say and respond to what they have to say, not just to what you want to say;
- Being given answers. As part of listening to the client, answer his or her questions. Do not deliver a monologue of hornbook law on their problem. Answer the client's question. If the client asks you the time, tell the time, and do not explain how to build a clock;
- Being advised about the future of the case. For example, when a hearing is scheduled in the future, they would like to know the continuum of possible outcomes and also the outcome that you believe is the most likely.
- Being respected. No matter if your client is a laborer who has been hurt on the job and you are representing the client in a workers' compensation case or your client is the CFO of a publicly traded corporation, people want to be respected. Treat them with dignity and talk to them in a language that is understandable to them and otherwise treat the entire attorney-client interaction with respect. The way you might speak to a potential client on a workers' compensation case or on an immigration case is obviously different than the way a business lawyer might talk to a CFO of a large corporation. Nonetheless, you need to be understandable to the client. Your explanation does not need to be dumbed down. You are a lawyer, and there is still an expectation about your use of words and your level of sophistication. However, treat every client with respect.

Referral Sources

Drucker extends his seminal question, "Who is your client?" to "Who are your 'supporting clients' and individuals?" This distinction is critically important in the legal profession. When you were advised, early in Chapter 13, to identify your network, you needed to make it as large as possible through the use of social media and being connected to the outside world through the externalities of practicing law. As you develop your network, it may directly be converted to clients, but your network may also refer cases to you. Therefore, the ring, or subset, that is inside your network is a ring known as referral sources.[3] Inside the circle of referral sources are prospective clients, and the bull's eye is clients. Certainly the supporting clients are your referral sources and prospective clients. They are not your clients yet and may never be (such as a referral source), but you need to identify who they are and what they value. If you are a personal injury lawyer or a workers' compensation lawyer, union officials may be a good referral source for you. If you are a labor lawyer, people connected to unions may be a referral source for you. If you are a residential real estate lawyer, certainly realtors are a referral source for you. All of these potential referral sources are a subset of your network.

Not all potential referral sources are alike. In order to get a referral source to the tipping point,[4] you need to identify the connectors, mavens, and salespeople who can help influence people to become clients.[5]

First are the connectors, who are individuals who know a wide range of people.[6] When you walk into a chamber of commerce meeting, for example, you will, in very short order, identify the connectors. They are shaking everyone's hand, talking to people from small group to small group, and being constantly interrupted in their conversations by other people wanting to stop by and say hello. They cannot walk through a room full of people without stopping five or ten times to say hello to somebody or shake someone's hand. Those people are the connectors in that particular environment.

Other connectors, in a broader sense, are influencers in trade groups or bar associations. Many times, individuals who are very good in sales (no matter what service or items they are selling) know a lot of people and are classic connectors. Often, commercial bankers know many business owners and are connectors. Insurance salespeople or financial service providers, who are similar to you, constantly going out to meet new people, are classic connectors. Identify those people and the fraternity of individuals they are connected with, and that will give you some insight or inroads into their circle of influence or network of people. Connectors are great to know, and it tends to be true that as a person gets older, his or her connectivity expands and grows. Spend as much time as possible with connectors.

The second group that is of great importance to attorneys are mavens.[7]

Mavens can be obsessive and can be almost an annoyance, but they are well recognized as experts on particular matters.

---

3. Mark M. Maraia, Rainmaking Made Simple: What Every Professional Must Know 142 (Professional Services Publishing 2003).
4. Malcolm Gladwell, The Tipping Point: How Little Things Can Make a Big Difference 30 (Back Bay Books 2002).
5. *Id.*
6. *Id.* at 38.
7. *Id.* at 62.

The critical thing about mavens, though, is that they aren't passive collectors of information. It isn't just that they are obsessed with how to get the best deal on a can of coffee. What sets them apart is that once they figure out how to get that deal, they want to tell you too. "A maven is a person who has information on a lot of different products or prices or places [or legal services]. This person likes to initiate discussions with consumers and respond to requests . . . they like to be helpers in the marketplace."[8]

Now imagine, a person who works in a financial area, whether that person be an accountant, banker, or financial planner, is considered an expert in all things financial. As a result, the higher the person's maven status is in his or her network, the more people will listen to the person's referrals to lawyers. Be careful. Some people come across as mavens when they really do not have the credibility that they believe they have, or at least they are not perceived that way by their network. True mavens are high-level, successful individuals. People seek their advice on many subject matters, including the question of who is the best lawyer in town. Mavens have the information, but they are not persuaders.[9] Mavens want to help and educate people, but they are not salespeople.

Mavens bank data. They provide the message. Connectors are social glue: they spread it.[10]

Last, and possibly the most important, are the salespeople. These are people with the skills to persuade third parties. Salespeople are critical in the connectivity chain as the quickest line of referrals. Keep in mind that not all people are interested in sales. By definition, if you can find a good cluster of connectors, mavens, and salespeople, you are way ahead of your competition in terms of identifying the right referral sources for your law office. Do not misunderstand the labels and the descriptions adopted here from the Gladwell book, *The Tipping Point*. You, as a lawyer, cannot really have a salesperson who goes out to sell your services. These are labels that summarize characteristics of individuals in the marketplace whom you will meet and come to know, individuals who are very good for your business. There are no such titles as professional connector and maven; these are simply roles that people play affirmatively, or sometimes unconsciously, in certain environments. The individuals who play those roles are, to some degree, all influencers and are the people you should seek when trying to find good referral sources.

Similar to the foregoing discussion, every one of the referral sources for various types of legal services may have different needs and wants. You must develop a policy on how your office will handle and treat referral sources and must incorporate the policy into your business plan to make sure you satisfy your referral sources. Included in that policy will be these points:

---

8. *Id.*
9. *Id.* at 69.
10. *Id.* at 70.

- A referral source does not want to receive a phone call from a client complaining about your lack of returning phone calls or your showing indifference to the client's problem;
- The referral source wants to hear that you are a great person and that you connected personally with the client and that the client would refer you to other, similarly situated individuals;
- The referral source, in certain cases, wants to be involved in the process but only to the extent possible with respect to the attorney-client privilege and your duty of confidentiality. The privilege issue needs to be handled very carefully because in a court of law, having a third person present in client meetings can taint the privilege. The duty of confidentiality can be waived by the client, but make sure the client makes an informed decision on that issue. The referral source—for example, an insurance salesperson referring estate-planning work to your office—will want to know how the trust preparation work is going, but he or she can know about it only to the extent that the client allows you to share that information;
- The referral source wants to look good in making a referral to you, so therefore make the referral source look good; and
- The referral source would like a reciprocal referral. If possible, and if the referral source is competent in his or her field of endeavor, try to refer a case or cases to that referral source.

As you can see, an enormous amount of information needs to be synthesized about who is your potential client, who is your supporting network of potential referral sources, and what do each of those value.

What Is Your Franchise?

Calling your law office a franchise may trigger an adverse reaction from the legal community. However, in fact, here calling your law office a franchise is really a way to initiate an analysis and a discussion in how your law practice looks to the outside world, to third parties, to referral sources, and ultimately to clients. What signals do you send out as to what your total franchise is like?

Answer the following questions:

- What is your dress code at outside events?
- What is your dress code in the office?
- How is your office decorated?
- How does your support staff dress and how do they look?
- Does your firm have a brand?

- What is the first thing people think of when they see your name, you or your law office?
- What is your USP (your unique selling proposition)?
- What makes your approach to selling your services different than that of the lawyer down the street or down the hall?
- What do you do well?
- What do you do better than everybody else?
- How do you differentiate yourself from other law firms?
- Do you engage in public relations? Do you manage them?
- Do you have a retailer sensibility?
- How do you promote your experience? credentials? degrees? years of experience?
- What are you known for in your community?
- What community initiatives have you owned?
- What have you done for the legal profession lately?

You need to begin to start putting together your target clients, the clients' wants and needs, what they value, and what you and your franchise offer to the market.

As you begin to identify who your clients are and what they value, you will focus in on your total package (i.e., franchise). You will begin to establish how to make a connection between the potential client and your law office, and that conduct is known as marketing.

> The referral source wants to look good in making a referral to you, so therefore make the referral source look good.

A discussion on traditional networking is set forth in Chapter 13. First and foremost, you will have been engaged in those efforts from the time you began practicing law, and it will not change and be diminished throughout your entire career. That is the most fundamental and most important way to continue your marketing efforts. All traditional attorney networking will always be necessary.

Your business plan, discussed earlier, must have an extensive set of rules and expectations set forth with respect to everyone's conduct for traditional networking and expectations on electronic and social media networking. For example,

- How many e-mail blasts will you send out per month?
- How active will you be on Twitter? How many tweets will be content driven and how many will be truly "goodwill" driven?
- Where will your emphasis be—on Facebook? Twitter? LinkedIn?
- Will you manage a blog?
- Will you solicit electronic questions for free advice?

- How will you generate hits to your website? Will your website be content driven? interactive? or basically an electronic Yellow Pages ad?
- How often will you transmit an e-newsletter?

Similarly, with respect to traditional networking, your business plan should include these points:

- How many lunch meetings with potential clients and referral sources should you have per week?
- Which clients do you want to thank for their services and take out to dinner or for a round of golf?
- How many follow-up advances do you expect of yourself, your partners, and your associates over the course of a month? a year?
- How many chambers of commerce do you expect associates to join?
- How many trade associations should you be involved in?
- How many bar association committees are your associates expected to join?
- How many years do they need to be practicing law before they are expected to chair a committee?
- What are your expectations on community involvement for your attorneys? for the local YMCA? school district? park district? township? local not-for-profit entities?
- How often will you send out a newsletter?

> Your business plan, discussed earlier, must have an extensive set of rules and expectations set forth with respect to everyone's conduct for traditional networking and expectations on electronic and social media networking.

As you can see, with respect to both traditional networking and social media networking, your game plan has to be thought through, well established, and indoctrinated into your business plan. The signals you send out, on a repeated basis, are your franchise. You need to send the signals thoughtfully and consistently.

Your expectations should be lofty but achievable, and if they are, reviewing your business plan every few months will keep you on track, provide a little boost or incentive needed to get you out to follow the path that you set forth, and provide you the incentive to remind and nudge your attorneys into following the expectations of the firm.

Yellow Pages Advertising and Internet Searches

Yellow Pages advertising for attorneys continues to generate an enormous amount of revenues for telephone books, but for many practice areas, it is generally regarded as a dying method of generating new clients for the law firm. Many, but not all.

It is clear that if you have identified your clients as individuals who have probably not purchased legal services in the past, their instincts may be to go to the Yellow Pages to find an attorney. In those practice areas, Yellow Pages advertising still seems to be working. Those practice areas include bankruptcy, personal injury, workers' compensation claims, mortgage foreclosure defense, and divorce.

All you need to do is review the Yellow Pages advertisement in your local Yellow Pages for attorneys, and you will see where the money is being spent. Since money is still being spent in those practice areas, the logical conclusion is, therefore, that it must still be economically beneficial for those attorneys.

Successful businesspeople and others who have hired lawyers in the past simply do not go to the Yellow Pages to find their attorneys. Similarly, individuals who live in more affluent areas and have access to information, neighbors, business partners, business associates, or like-minded and similarly situated people often ask their peers (those who they think have or may have had similar legal issues) for a referral. Of course, that is the reason you want to engage in traditional social networking so that your name will surface as part of the discussion. Stated another way, if you were offering services to an identified client group that is in this category of connectivity, Yellow Pages advertising will not serve you well.

Also note that when somebody needed the services of an attorney twenty years ago and had nowhere else to turn, the Yellow Pages were the natural first step. In fact, it was the natural first step for somebody who needed to have gutters cleaned, the lawn cut, the car fixed, and a leaky faucet fixed.

Today consumers are likely to go to the Internet to search for solutions to their needs. In fact, a recent Fleischman-Hillard study determined that 89% of all consumers turned to Google, Bing, or another search engine to find information on products, services, or businesses before making their purchases.[11] With that information, it is clear that your client is probably going to a commercial search engine to find his or her next attorney which, clearly, punctuates the need for strong search engine optimization for your site. Further, at http://www.brafton.com, Brafton argues that content is the key for search engine optimization, consistent with our message in Section 1 that your website, tweets, posts on LinkedIn and Facebook, all need to be content driven and not necessarily a call to action

---

11. Brafton Editorial, *89 Percent of Consumers Use Search Engines for Purchase Decisions* (2012), *available at* http://www.brafton.com/news/89-percent-of-consumers-use-search-engines-for-purchase-decisions.

for the consumer or business owner to contact your office.[12] Fleischman-Hillard findings, paired with the Brafton position, supports the idea that creating original content aimed at informing and educating business-to-business buyers without aggressive selling language will help businesses appeal to new prospects.[13] The Fleischman-Hillard findings go on to say that pairing content-driven marketing with a social media marketing initiative may help businesses further reach consumers making purchasing decisions.[14]

How often will your client go to the Internet to seek services?

A recent online survey conducted by http://www.searchengineland.com indicated that 16% of consumers indicated that they used the Internet *every week* to find local business.[15] Moreover, only 15% of consumers said they have not used the Internet to find a local business within the last year.[16] All this is directed to one conclusion, namely, that consumers for legal services are increasingly moving toward the Internet to find the right attorney for themselves.

At least 75% of consumers surveyed answered that they at least occasionally read between two and ten reviews, when available, on services and products.[17] This finding directly supports the conclusion that the Internet is now trumping all other sources, including advice from friends and family, on buying decisions for products and services.[18]

For the first time on the survey, Canada reported that the Internet is now more influential overall in purchasing decisions that family and friends.[19] Comparatively, in the United States, the Internet rated about equal in importance (46% versus 47% for family and friends). The Internet's greatest influence was in Asia, where the gap between the influence of the Internet and than of family and friends was 9% in China (79% to 70%) and far greater in India (79% to 60%).[20] As a result, as attorneys you need to be aware that the Internet and search engine optimization is an area of marketing in which you need to invest your time and money to maximize the possibility of attracting potential clients. It is undeniable, then, that your consumers are finding you on the Internet.

You should search your law firm's name or your personal name, along with your municipality, to see where you come up using various Internet search engines. With Google, keep in mind that the top three firms listed are there because they paid for that positioning

---

12. *See id.*

13. *Id.*

14. *Id.*

15. Myles Anderson, Study: *72% of Consumers Trust Online Reviews as Much as Personal Recommendations* (2012), *available at* http://searchengineland.com/study-72-of-consumers-trust-online-reviews-as-much-as-personal-recommendations-114152.

16. *Id.*

17. *Id.*

18. *2012 Digital Influence Index Shows Internet as Leading Influence in Consumer Purchasing Choices* (2012), *available at* http://fleishmanhillard.com/2012/01/news-and-opinions/2012-digital-influence-index-shows-internet-as-leading-influence-in-consumer-purchasing-choices.

19. *Id.*

20. *Id.*

with Google AdWords. Also, the smaller ads running down the right margin are also paid advertising. Then run other searches on your municipality and your practice area to see where you come up on the list of hits for the search. The farther you are from the top, the more time you need to spend on search engine optimization. Whether it be just reviewing the hidden metatags in your website or other conduct you can engage in to increase your exposure in Google searches, you need to incorporate the management of your Internet exposure into your business plan and the things that you will do to increase that exposure. There are many good, available books on search engine optimization. Also, there are consultants who help with this specific discipline.

You should at least investigate Google AdWords. It is expensive and you need to proceed cautiously initially, but in certain markets it may not be cost prohibitive to get your name to the top of the list in Google searches.

In summary, Internet searches and search engine optimization are critically important to your success. However, the Internet will not completely eliminate Yellow Pages advertising for the practice groups that serve clients who do not have regular connections to lawyers. It seems that Yellow Pages advertising is fading out, but it will not be eliminated. Obviously, your standing in general searches on the Internet needs to continue to improve, and all of your marketing efforts must be conducted with that in mind.

Marketing Letters

The Supreme Court ruled in *Shapero v. Kentucky Bar Association*, 108 S. Ct. 1916 (1988), that lawyers can directly advertise, with the use of letters, to people they know are in need of legal services. So long as your advertising pieces are in conformance with the rules of professional conduct, you can send direct marketing letters out to individuals you know are in need of your services. After a quick review of the rules, you will understand that your marketing letters cannot be misleading, false, and must have the words ADVERTISING MATERIAL on the outside of the envelope. Again, knowing who your potential client is, you can, in an effort to match those potential clients with your services, buy mailing lists of people who need your services, and you can send them a direct mailing piece, in conformance with the Model Code of Professional Conduct, to let them know of the services that you provide.

Such mailing lists can be purchased at http://www.infousa.com, your local service provider for Uniform Commercial Code (UCC) filings, and if you ask, the local courthouse usually works with search companies that come in to cull the daily filings for data. You can obtain lists of people who have recently been sued; who have been sued for divorce; who have federal tax liens filed against them, recent criminal charges filed against them, foreclosures filed against them; and who have other recording- and courtroom-specific filings that reveal the nature of a client in need. If that client is identified as *your* potential client, that list will be valuable to you for building your practice.

If you engage in a marketing letter campaign, identify the cost of the campaign (i.e., cost of paper, envelopes, postage, inserts, time for the clerk to stuff the envelopes). Keep excellent tracking records of the amount of revenues brought in on that particular marketing campaign. Although the Supreme Court has approved this method of advertising, be advised that consumers are being inundated with more and more third-class mail and first-class marketing mail and are more and more discriminating about which letters to open and the extent to which they read them. There are many great books out there on direct mail advertising, such as *The Ultimate Sales Letter*[21] and *No B.S. Direct Marketing*,[22] and after you take in all the information—the ploys and the tricks about oddly sized envelopes, color print, and the like—you should not cheapen the practice of law with too much unprofessional creativity.

Remember this: Clients want the best, most affordable attorney who can help them solve their problems. If you have the opportunity to meet them, they will hire you *if they like you, trust you,* and *believe you can help them.* It is just that simple. The direct mail campaign is a campaign to accomplish one goal—to get potential clients to call your law office. So consider, therefore, whether a completely unprofessional letter will assist them in getting them to like you, trust you, and believe you can help them. If the answer is yes, go ahead and do it. But anything more extravagant than a professional letter explaining how you approach cases will come across looking tacky, cheap, and insincere.

> The direct mail campaign is a campaign to accomplish one goal—to get potential clients to call your law office.

In direct marketing campaigns, the letter must introduce your firm to get the recipient to like you. To do this, the letter must be written in a tone that connects with potential clients and allows them to trust you and believe that you can help them. Include professional criteria that will assist in meeting those objectives. Various degrees, professional accreditations, years of experience, and other information to show that you will not be a novice practitioner but, rather, that you have handled other cases similar to their cases.

Direct marketing letters to potential clients are less effective now than they were twenty years ago; nonetheless, if you engage in a direct mail marketing campaign, as an attorney do it professionally and tastefully.

---

21. DAN S. KENNEDY, THE ULTIMATE SALES LETTER, 3RD ED. (Adams Media 2006).
22. DAN KENNEDY, NO B.S. DIRECT MARKETING: THE ULTIMATE NO HOLDS BARRED KICK BUTT TAKE NO PRISONERS DIRECT MARKETING FOR NON-DIRECT MARKETING BUSINESSES (Entrepreneur Media 2006).

Public Relations

Public relations need to be part of your marketing campaign, not the marketing campaign in and of itself. Public relations is the act of sending press releases, answering press inquiries, and passing along information about your firm or the conduct of your firm that is a general interest to individuals, businesses, colleagues, or the community at large. Public relations experts are able to discern information that is critically important in the legal field, that is really not of any interest to the public at large, versus things that may have a lightweight legal effect around the law office and the legal community but may be critically important to the community at large.

Also, a public relations expert can take those two different types of information and direct them to the right market. All in all, a public relations initiative is an important part of the marketing program of a law office because it connects your law office and the work that you do (many times nonlegal work) to the community and the profession.

One important note on public relations: At no time should you speak about a client, seeking a press benefit without the client's full approval. It seems obvious, but it is important to state that the client's confidences come first; under no circumstances should it be compromised.

Nonetheless, there are a lot of things that your law office can be doing that are worthy of community notice. Some examples are running a coat drive or a toy drive, writing a book or an article, seeking and gaining an appointment on the board of a not-for-profit company, hiring of a new associate, and supporting the appointment of one of your employees on a school board or in any other position of authority that would begin to start connecting your law office to some community development activities.

Public Speaking

It would be easy to say never say no to a public speaking opportunity, but in reality public speaking opportunities just do not come out of the woodwork very often. Public speaking is a great way for you to enhance your expertise and further your brand. I highly encourage it.

You need to have an affirmative program in place for public speaking. If you want to get public speaking opportunities, first come up with a short outline of your speech, make sure it can be tailored to fit a time between thirty minutes and two hours, and send it out to appropriate executive directors of venues for an opportunity. For example, you can speak at trade shows and trade conventions regarding workplace safety, or you can give speeches at senior citizen homes and senior centers regarding estate planning. Also, you can speak about small businesses at your local library or junior colleges, and you can speak about tax-planning issues at year-end at almost any venue.

Create a public library circuit, speaking on a similar series of topics at all the public libraries in your county. The first benefit is that it will allow you to become very confident on your feet in giving these presentations, and second, everyone will walk away with a packet of information on you and your firm that includes your name, telephone number, and other contact information about your law office. At first you will not have much to give to potential clients in terms of materials or marketing information, but always have an outline for them to walk away with; the outline should have your contact information. Always have a stack of cards at the back of the room available to the attendees as they leave.

This approach should hold true for the rest of your career. When speaking at CPA societies, accountant groups, or senior citizen centers, always have an outline to give attendees with your contact information on it. Eventually, you will also offer some colorful brochures and other information about your firm. Always give them your contact information at the beginning so that they have it in front of them when you are speaking and they can connect you to the outline they are taking away. Also, build a system at your office to create high-quality, content-driven handouts. There is no fluff in good handouts; you want people to know that the handouts are great value so that they keep them.

> As part of your business plan, there must be a mandate that every attorney participate in a bar association's activities and join at least one or two committees and attend those meetings.

Public speaking requires an ongoing effort, and it needs to be built into your business plan mandating that you and your attorneys get in front of a group to speak on a topic at least several times per year. As you progress in you career, you will do public speaking far more than that, but it is an important part of everyone's evolution. A new, young attorney should be speaking at the local high schools. A more advanced attorney should be speaking at some chamber of commerce events, the Rotary, and other community or trade organizations where people come together to discuss business issues.

Community Development

As part of the externality of practicing law, you need to be visible in your community. As part of your business plan, there must be a mandate that every attorney participate in a bar association's activities and join at least one or two committees and attend those meetings, with the absolute goal of chairing a committee within a few years.

In addition to bar association committees, get involved in high school events, civic organizations, or your local YMCA.

Every single attorney in the office should be a member of a chamber of commerce in the community in which he or she lives, and also one trade association. Keep in mind the difference between bar association activities and those at trade associations. In the bar association, you raise your standing in the legal community and learn a lot of information from attorneys who are more experienced than you. Eventually, young attorneys will be learning from you. With respect to trade associations, you should be viewed as the authoritative figure among potential clients. Both organizations have value, and they must both be pursued on an ongoing basis throughout your career.

Do something fun that people will remember. Sponsor kids' sports teams and buy all of the kids ice cream cones after the last game of the year. Sponsor or run a toy drive, shoe drive, food drive, or coat drive.

The initial pushback on developing a community tie is always "It takes so much time!" It could be viewed that way, but it is also a necessary part of your law office's place in your community (and each attorney's place in the community in which he or she lives). So, therefore, it cannot be dismissed as a time waster. It is a commitment of time that will pay great dividends in the long run following the techniques set forth in Chapter 13 on building relationships, adding value, and third-party referral sources.

Branding

Although there are many marketing books written on the subject of branding, this section of the chapter offers you information on your firm's marketing efforts, wherein a certain portion of your marketing effort must be directed towards branding.

Branding is a process that involves creating a unique look or image for your legal services in the individual and business consumer's mind primarily through community outreach and advertising, both with a consistent theme. Your branding campaign should aim to establish and differentiate your law office in the marketplace so as to attract and retain loyal clients.

Therefore, branding starts with your firm's logo, font, typeset, and repeatable style that will be taken to the market through personal presentations, speeches, billboards, radio advertising, television advertising, print ads, Yellow Pages, event programs, newspapers, e-mail blasts, social networking, website, and every other outreach program that you develop for the law office.

Remember that branding may be only words and image at this stage. But something needs to stand behind that icon before it is branded. That which stands behind you is your USP—your unique selling proposition.

Truth be told, if you are an estate-planning lawyer, all your competition prepares wills and trusts. The same can be held true among a whole host of practice groups, whether you are a divorce lawyer or a lawyer involved in real estate, employment law, business advice, a litigator, or an immigration, personal injury, bankruptcy, or criminal lawyer. All your competition does what you do!

What makes your service, and the delivery thereof, unique that would attract a new client? Are you cheaper than the competition? More expensive—a high-end attorney? Do you return phone calls in one hour or less? Do you turn around documents in one day or less? Are you a member of particular trade groups? Do you specialize in one industry— such as health care or construction? What was your former career? Are you familiar with and comfortable talking with people from certain industries? What makes you unique to your competition that would cause a client to hire you? Your uniqueness and specialized understanding of a particular industry of the law is the message that needs to be conveyed consistently every time your logo is displayed. Then the image of your logo will immediately trigger a viewer's reaction to what you stand for and what your USP is. Once that connection becomes instantaneous and recognizable throughout the community, municipality, and ultimately the region in which you practice, your branding is successful.

> Your branding campaign should aim to establish and differentiate your law office in the marketplace so as to attract and retain loyal clients.

As you can guess, branding could be expensive.

It is best to always direct your marketing dollars to efforts that will get the phone to ring. However, to enhance that opportunity, you must be a recognizable name in a person's mind, home, and business before you increase the chance that the person will call you. You do this through branding and marketing. You need to have your logo out in front of potential clients a multitude of times so that when they are talking to a friend and ask for a referral to a lawyer and that friend provides the names of three lawyers the friend knows of, one of them should be you. For if one of them is your already recognizable name, which already makes a positive impression, the potential clients will call you and may already be presold on hiring your firm.

Branding helps close the deal on the very first mention of your name to a potential client from a referral source. If a referral source gives your name to a potential client and that is the first time the potential client has ever heard your name, your name will quickly be forgotten or, more likely, your name has simply not made a sufficient impression on the client to cause him or her to call you. However, if your name is recognizable to the potential client and is connected to your USP, and if the client is comfortable with that USP, you will immediately get the work from that client.

Again, it may become expensive to buy all of these impressions with potential clients. Branding works hand in hand with public relations. For that reason, dollars must be spent wisely whether they are spent on radio, billboards, television, or any other media to build name or brand recognition. The cost per impression may be low in the mass media purchases such as radio and television advertisements, but remember, you are sending out your message to thousands if not millions of people who may not need your services at all. Spending money to connect directly with a person who needs your service is a high-quality connection for you.

Nonetheless, even though some of those advertising dollars are being spent to get your name in front of people who do not have an immediate need for your services, you are building your brand recognizability with your name and logo for when they will need your services.

Start off slow and in a small geographic area. Remember, it is always better to be the big fish in a small pond than to be a minnow in an ocean. As a result, start with the town in which your office is located or with your neighborhood if you are in a big city. It might be a rural town with a population of five thousand or a suburb of fifty thousand people. It does not matter, but you need to saturate your immediate market over time, though limited by affordability, to the point where residents of that town know your name and logo.

Depending on the size of the municipality, it may take from two to five years to saturate your name within that municipality. Once you do, certainly start going out beyond that municipality and become more involved in community outreach to those other communities that border your municipality. Continue to expand and branch out to the extent that you can within your budget.

Do not ever lose sight of who your potential client is. It is best to do your branding directly to your clients first, potential clients second, and the general public at large last. Therefore, if you can find your customers at trade associations, buy ads in the trade association magazines, write articles in those magazines, and otherwise be available to those members. Once you determine who your clients are, what they value, and where they exist in the market, that is where you should spend your time, effort, and money in terms of building your brand.

If you market to individuals, find out the shared characteristics of those individuals who will buy your services, and then market to those groups and organizations. It is not easy, and it is not inexpensive, but limited to what you can afford, so understand what branding is and get your name, logo, and USP out to your potential clients.

Billboards, TV, and Radio

Inevitably, in any book on law office marketing, you will be confronted with a discussion on and an analysis of purchasing mass media marketing alternatives such as radio, TV, and billboards.

Demographics of certain TV shows are readily available, and an attorney is able to purchase commercial time on TV, potentially on certain stations and during certain television shows, whereby the viewers (i.e., the viewer demographic) match up closely to answer your question, "Who is my potential client?"

Demographic research on television is a science and highly accurate. The same can be said for radio, but with a little less accuracy. Likewise, billboard advertising has very little demographic accuracy but, nonetheless, still reaches a wide and broad market.

In all of these cases, by just simply analyzing the attorneys who do advertise in these mass media, it seems that purchasers of legal services for personal injury, class-action cases relating to chemical or asbestos harm, and bankruptcy are still influenced by mass-media advertising. To a smaller degree, there are still some divorce lawyers advertising on television and billboards.

> The one thing that is certain about purchasing these mass media options is that you need to be committed to the strategy for a minimum of one year and closer to two years.

Following our previous discussion, as to how to go about finding a client and analyzing the client's buying decision for legal services, you can see that is very unlikely that sophisticated business people rely on billboard advertising when purchasing legal services. Again, as in the discussion on Yellow Pages advertising, it seems that people with certain degrees of connectivity in their business circles, community circles, or economic levels have better access to attorney referrals than do others in need of legal services. For that reason, it continues to hold true that many individuals who have never hired a lawyer in the past can be influenced in their buying decision for legal services by television ads, billboards, and radio advertising.

The one thing that is certain about purchasing these mass-media options is that you need to be committed to the strategy for a minimum of one year and closer to two years. So, therefore, as you make that analysis on spending your dollars to generate business, be well aware that it may not economically pay off for longer than twelve months.

As part of your branding strategy, advertising assists you to getting your name and face to be a recognized image by potential clients. Over time, your image, logo, and brand will become embedded with those who will need the legal services that you provide. Again, it takes a long time to develop. These ads should include a call to action. Radio ads, television ads, and billboards should include a request to pick up the phone and call you for immediate assistance.[23]

Expensive mass-media spending is risky. Research has indicated that it does work, over the long run, for the practice groups set forth earlier. However, the unknown question is whether you can sustain the short run as you are bleeding cash buying advertising space and time and not getting in the commensurate work to offset those costs.

Like most of the planning in this book, it is advisable to start in a very small geographic area to saturate the small area in which you live or operate to get your name recognizable with other tactics. Within time, as your name increases in recognizability, you should continue to broaden your advertising grid; eventually, depending on your practice area, you will be able to afford billboards on expressways, commercials on the local broadcast of CNN, and the radio stations in your area.

Building Loyalty

Building loyalty from clients seems as easy as just providing outstanding legal services, at a fair rate, and expecting clients to come back. You hope they will, but, it takes more than that. This discussion on building loyalty straddles the marketing disciplines in this book, found in this Chapter 26, and the culture aspects of the business plan, found in Chapters 29 and 30.

A great book by Simon Sinek, *Start with Why: How Great Leaders Inspire Everyone to Take Action*,[24] is a best seller because of its unique view on building culture, direction, and brand loyalty for your business. Of the three questions that your law office will answer about its business, two of which have been discussed throughout this book, the third, "Why?" is a complex, engaging analysis of you and your business and what will help make clients loyal to you for a lifetime.

The first question is "*What* do you do?" The answer is simple: You practice law. It is not more complicated than that and does not merit any more discussion.

The next question is "*How* do you do it?" The how is your USP.[25] What is unique about how you deliver your legal services? What is your brand? Most companies—and after

---

23. I have not gone into length about the science of telephone numbers and easy-to-remember telephone numbers. There is a certain limitation that your telephone provider will give you when ordering telephone numbers. Everyone in business wants a simple last four digits to his or her business telephone number. Sometimes it is not easy to obtain. Nonetheless, do what you can to get as simple a telephone number as possible, and be certain that the number is transferable to other area codes. If it is not, you will need to be able to buy permanent call forwarding of your very first number to various area codes and call centers that you develop, depending on the specialty area of your practice.

24. SIMON SINEK, START WITH WHY: HOW GREAT LEADERS INSPIRE EVERYONE TO TAKE ACTION (Penguin Group 2009).

25. *Id.* at 39.

the analysis in this chapter, your law firm—must know *how* they practice law. Whether you call your system a differentiating value proposition or a proprietary process or a USP, your "how we do it" is often given to explain *how* your law office is different or better.[26] It is your elevator speech. You need to think through your marketing edge with your business plan list on marketing.

However, those issues do not create loyalty.

What creates loyalty is the third question: "*Why* do you practice law?" In fact, Sinek wants you to "start with the *Why?!*"[27] The *why* question is directed to an entire analysis of *inspiring* people to buy your services versus *manipulating* them to buy your services.

If you ask most people why they hire the lawyer that they do, the answer is usually "Because he is a great lawyer," or "I've known him/her for twenty-five years, and he [or she] is a real shark," or "He [or she] and I have been doing business for a long time and we always get good results."

Sure, if an attorney has done nothing but win cases for the client, the client will be very loyal to the attorney—or will he or she? If you talk to some lawyers, they will tell you that clients have very short memories and that you cannot buy a lot of goodwill with clients by simply winning cases. Many times you are only as good as the last brief you have written. In all cases, it takes more.

> If you talk to some lawyers, they will tell you that clients have very short memories and that you cannot buy a lot of goodwill with clients by simply winning cases.

When analyzing the difference between inspiration and manipulation, the author[28] talks about the manipulative ways that manufactures, retailers, and sellers of service manipulate the customer to increase sales. Certainly, price is a game that many sellers play, but I hope you, as a lawyer, do not. Price your services at the market value, not below and not above. It sounds like a good idea to make sure you never lose any new business by virtue of a $10-an-hour price difference, but you need to build client loyalty, and there are many more important ways to do that than price. Price does not promote loyalty; it is a manipulative way to gain an introduction to a potential client. Similarly, various promotions in businesses have never worked in the long run.[29]

Remember, there is a difference between repeat business and loyalty.

---

26. *Id.* at 78.
27. *Id.*
28. *Id.* at 16.
29. Please note that I understand that certain industries, such as retailing and grocery stores, engage in everyday low-pricing (EDLP) strategies as well as high-then-low pricing to establish excitement with sale plans and sale advertising. While these strategies are manipulative to a certain degree, they are ingrained in the buying decision of everyday homogenous, commodity-type items. Discounting sales in retail is a way to build excitement at the store level.

Repeat business is when people do business with you multiple times. Loyalty is when people are willing to turn down a better product or a better price to continue doing business with you. Loyal customers often don't even bother to research the competition or entertain other options. Loyalty is not easily won. Repeat business, however, is. All it takes is more manipulations.[30]

What lawyers need to do is understand how to build brand loyalty, and you do that by analyzing *why* you practice law. There is a thorough exercise and analysis later in this section of the book on finding out your *why*. But once you analyze your *why* and incorporate it into your culture, which becomes part of the very fabric of your law office, your clients will connect with you and be loyal forever.[31]

Clearly, the discussion is getting vague on the connection between marketing and *why* we practice law, but this may make it clear: Would you not want your brand, your logo, and your business to have clients as loyal as the customers of Harley-Davidson? That which we are seeking helps better explain why people tattoo Harley-Davidson logos on their bodies, many of whom do not even own a Harley-Davidson.[32] Imagine being so fanatical and loyal to a brand as to tattoo the company logo and name on your body.

What does that take?

It takes a connection between what that customer (or potential customer, or hoped-for customer) stands for and what Harley-Davidson stands for. Freedom? Counterculture? Defiance of authority?

As an exercise in the virtues of *why*, go to YouTube, type in "Apple 1984 commercial," and watch the video.

Apple launched its Macintosh computer in its famed 1984 commercial that aired during the Super Bowl. Directed by Ridley Scott, the commercial was a complete cultural change for Apple. Watch the commercial, and the one thing that should strike you is that nowhere in this extended commercial did the makers show a computer or any of its functionality. It conveys an attitude: Nonconformance. Uniqueness. "Think different." But nowhere does it answer the question, "*What* does Apple do?" or "*How* does Apple do it?" It does not discuss the unique selling proposition, nor does it discuss any of its differentiating value propositions or its proprietary process.[33] What it does is match the attitudes and belief system of the potential purchaser to those of Apple. When aligning the value system of

---

30. *Id.* at 28.

31. Your *why* is not necessarily put on your billboards, stated in your TV commercials, or put on your letterhead. Your *why* is so incorporated in your DNA that every client, potential client, referral source, and employee will know it.

32. Simon Sinek, Start with Why: How Great Leaders Inspire Everyone to Take Action 162 (Penguin Group 2009).

33. Believe me, if you followed all the patent litigation of the computer litigation, you can certainly believe that Apple had "proprietary processes" owned through patent filings.

the law office with the potential client, you will build tremendous brand and law office loyalty. That which is important to the law office will be important to certain clients who will be clients for a lifetime.

This type of alignment is not and should not be manufactured. It has to be real, and it has to be an absolute goal and a long-term plan of living true to your *why*.[34]

Law firms are always shouting out what they do and how they do it. Sinek oversimplifies the typical law office pitch, relating to business-to-business sellers of services and states, "Here's our law firm. Our lawyers went to the best schools and we represent the biggest clients. Hire us."[35] It is an unfair simplification, but it gets the point across. Much of law office advertising wants to convey what the firm's lawyers do and how they do it. In the long run, real loyal clients do not buy *what* you do or *how* you do it, they buy *why* you do it.[36] You will find your *why* in Chapter 29.

In order to build loyalty, you need to know *why* you exist and, to the extent possible, convey *why* you exist (not what you do and how you do it) implicitly to your clients. Martin Luther King was an inspiration, no doubt. He certainly did not use any of the manipulative techniques articulated earlier to get people to buy in to his set of values. In 1963, a quarter of a million people showed up to hear his famous speech on the steps of the Lincoln Memorial. Arguably, no one showed up for Dr. King himself. They showed up for themselves.[37] They showed up because of what *they* believed. They went to listen to a man speak on a subject that aligned with their core beliefs. He spoke about what he believed, not the blueprint for changing a nation. The speech is there to reinforce a set of values owned by everyone who attended that event in August 1963. The speech has come to be known as the "I Have a Dream" speech, not the "I Have a Plan" speech, not the "Here Is My Blueprint for Ending Racial Discrimination" speech.

[Dr. King's speech] was a statement of purpose and not a comprehensive twelve-point plan to achieving civil rights in America. Dr. King offered America a place to go, not a plan to follow. The plan had its place, but not on the steps of the Lincoln Memorial. Dr. King's articulation of his belief was something powerful enough to rally those who shared that belief even if they weren't personally affected by the inequalities. Nearly a quarter of the people who came to the rally that day were white. This was a belief not about black America, this was a belief about a shared America. Dr. King was the leader of a cause. A cause for all those who believed what he believed regardless of skin color.[38]

---

34. In the culture building portions of Chapters 30 and 31, we will go into great length about building the firm's core purpose.
35. *Id.* at 40.
36. *Id.* at 41.
37. *Id.* at 128.
38. *Id.* at 129.

Arguably, people followed Dr. King not because of *his* idea of a new America but because of *their* idea of a new America.[39]

Similarly, if your core purpose, your *why*, is strong enough, powerful enough, committed enough, uncompromised enough, true enough, clear enough, a world of clients will stop at your doorstep, align themselves with you, and seek your representation—for a lifetime.

Build a Marketing Culture

Marketing, or lead generating, is a culture that needs to be ingrained into the fabric of the firm. Marketing is *not* something just delegated to partners.

You could explain to every new associate that he or she is not responsible for bringing in any work, that he or she is being hired because you and the other attorneys are over-worked and you need additional hands on deck to get the work out to satisfy clients. It very well could be the truth. It is a good hiring pitch, but it is a rotten business model. As your firm is very small, all new hires must be very comfortable with the fact that your law office is a young, growing firm with plenty of work to do. That may be true, but it does not bode well for the marketing culture that is needed to be ingrained in your firm very early on. Your marketing culture needs to be explained to young attorneys and third-year law students who are interviewing for a job.

> Believe it, live it, and your results will prove it.

Explain to all new hires, as well as existing employees, that you have adopted this aggressive marketing culture in your firm and that your firm will grow exponentially. Tell the potential hires that they will be mentored and will be taught how to most efficiently build their own connectivity by networking with all the attendant follow-through rules to be successful at bringing in business. Believe it, live it, and your results will prove it.

Even doing something as simple as getting business cards for your administrative assistants is a way to send a signal internally that they are emissaries of your office wherever they travel and that they should be willing to introduce your law office to their friends, family members, and associates.

Remember, sometimes people will ask an administrative assistant who works in a law office a legal question about their problem. Your legal assistants will obviously be trained and coached on not giving legal advice, but they should make an honest offer to introduce their family or friend in need of legal services to you or to a lawyer in your office. If

---

39. *Id.*

your administrative assistant follows through on that introduction, he or she will certainly understand the marketing system in your office.

Marketing Additional Services to Existing Clients

It is a fair estimate to say that 25% to 50% of your new clients every year will come from a referral from an existing client. This is something that needs to be tracked. If it is on your low end, it may be because you are doing a bad job at marketing additional services to your existing clients and keeping in front of them after their cases end. Or, in the alternative, you may be doing such a great job at so many other types of marketing methods that the sheer volume of cases you are getting from other marketing methods just shrinks the percentage of the referrals from existing clients. Nonetheless, after you spread out the source of referrals grid, many, many of your clients will come from referrals from existing clients. See the following example of such a tracking device:

CLIENT REFERRALS

2013	JAN	FEB	MAR	APR	MAY	JUN	JUL	AUG	SEP	OCT	NOV	DEC
Realtors*												
Accountant*												
Client Referrals*												
Financial Advisor*												
Attorney*												
Walk In												
Yellow Pages												
Print Advertising												
Website/Internet												
Attorney Networking												
Seminars												
Marketing Letters												
Support Staff												
Radio												
Television												
Billboards												
Total:												

* = Referral sources

How can I make that number greater?

Remember that existing clients are wonderful, fertile ground for new business. You need to constantly stay in front of your existing clients and send them information regularly. As articulated in an earlier chapter on digital social networking, make sure they get regular e-mail blasts and regular tweets on your social media platform. Also, send out a written newsletter (via the U.S. Postal Service) once or twice a year. If they are good clients, thank them for the legal work and take them out to lunch or dinner once or twice a year and possibly to some other event, such as a play or a round of golf, on a regular basis.

As you can see, in the overall marketing plan, many of these ways of connecting with people are to build friendships and to get to know the basic set of values you and your clients have and to ensure that those values are aligned. Once they are, and your clients believe in your set of values and your *why*, you will develop clients, as well as friendships, for a lifetime.

How about docketing certain events in a client's case for one month, six months, or one year from a triggering date? Does it seem like a good idea to send a client a letter six months after a real estate closing on their home to ask if he or she would like to begin the estate-planning process? How about a letter one year after a business closing to ask the business client if he or she would like you to review the employee handbook? employment agreements?

> As your firm grows, always introduce a client who is in your office to another attorney by giving a brief summary of the skill set that is unique to that attorney.

How about a genuine phone call to ask how a client is doing after you settled a big personal injury case for him or her? The clients you contact may not need any additional legal services, but your thoughtful call will mean a lot to them.

A short checklist of ways to encourage existing clients to rehire you or purchase other legal work from your law office will include the following activities:

- Treat clients as though they were your only client;
- Treat them as if they are as important as a Fortune 500 client;
- Regularly make your clients aware of other services that your office provides;
- Regularly make introductions to other attorneys in your firm. As your firm grows, always introduce a client who is in your office to another attorney by giving a brief summary of the skill set that is unique to that attorney;
- Listen carefully; often clients tip information about other issues that they or their neighbors are involved in that may need legal work;

- Call them for no reason. See how they are doing, wish them well for upcoming holidays, or mention events that you know will matter to them;
- When engaging in casual conversation with existing clients, do not be afraid to tell some stories about other client work (without disclosing confidential information, of course) or other cases you are working on that relate to a different practice group whose services your client has used in the past; and
- Speak to them as a friend.

To be perfectly honest, marketing for additional work and referrals from existing or past happy clients is to reach for low-hanging fruit. Make it a point and a commitment to stay in touch with those clients to make sure that they, as well as any of their friends and relatives, do not call another lawyer first.

Tracking the Firm's Marketing Efforts

An attorney or marketing coordinator needs to undertake the obligation to track your marketing efforts. Of course, the results of the marketing efforts need to be tracked in management reports and circulated monthly, but on an ongoing basis, the marketing coordinator—either an administrative assistant educated in marketing or a senior attorney charged with the duty of managing the firm's marketing—must keep track of the firm's total marketing efforts. Therefore, the marketing scorecard needs to be updated regularly to include the efforts made throughout the year, and ultimately results need to be calculated from these efforts.

Whoever agrees to undertake this function will need to be made aware of the amount of time and energy required to manage the marketing efforts of this firm. In fact, use the following grid to track the marketing initiatives (and also the grid set forth here for the individual attorney marketing efforts) for the ongoing marketing work for the firm:

MARKETING

	JAN	FEB	MAR	APR	MAY	JUN	JUL	AUG	SEP	OCT	NOV	DEC
Chamber of Commerce Events												
Facebook/LinkedIn Postings												
E-blasts												
Sponsored Events												
Press Releases												
Mass-Media Advertising												
Local Senior Center												
Website Content Posting												
Super Lawyer Applications												
Podcasts												
Direct Mail Campaign												
Food [clothing, toy, etc.] Drive												
Local Community Race												
Industry Seminar												
Total:												

Further, a broader marketing checklist must be maintained. In keeping with the requirements of traditional networking, all attorneys, including you, the founding partner, need to be held accountable for making contact with your top clients and top referral sources. These requirements will be assigned to the relationship manager for each of those clients and referral sources. Each individual attorney will need to book the client's name, the contact dates, and the description of the contacts they made with the client at least quarterly. In some cases, the contacts might simply be telephone calls or a meeting for coffee or lunch. In any case, the effort needs to be put into tracking contacts with each relationship manager's top clients and top referral sources. In addition, each attorney will also be required to complete a checklist on marketing activities, filling out information on press releases, articles, presentations, newsletter articles, activity in various organizations, and any additional personal contacts made.

Here is a sample of a summary marketing checklist for an individual attorney's efforts relating to the role as relationship manager for clients and top referral sources and the attorney's various other marketing activities:

INDIVIDUAL ATTORNEY MARKETING CHECKLIST

Top Clients

Name/Company	Contact Date	Description

Top Referral Sources

Name/Company	Contact Date	Description

Marketing Activities

Date	Advertising/Press Release	Media	Possible Business	Date	Follow-up Step	Results

Chapter 27

Lead Conversion

You have engaged extensively in marketing, having sent out e-mail blasts or marketing letters, potentially purchased advertising on radio and billboards, attended every chamber of commerce event, and mingled with community leaders in your municipality. Trust me, eventually the phone starts to ring. And when it does, how will that incoming phone call be handled?

Keep in mind that depending on where your office is located and the exposure your office has to the street, the probability of a walk-in is highly unlikely. So, taking the unusual walk-in out of the equation, you will agree that all prospective clients start with a phone call to your law office. Their phone call is a revenue opportunity, and it is a direct result of all the work you have done to get the phone to ring. The phone call has to be handled properly without any flaws.

The first rule around your office should be that you always have an attorney take phone calls from potential clients. Here is an exercise showing how important this is. Go to the Yellow Pages in your municipality, look up attorneys, and start calling law offices. If you call ten, try to figure out how many lawyers out of ten are available to take your call. I would be surprised if the number was more than two or three. Many, depending on the time you call, will be in court or out of the office in meetings or will be holding phone calls because they are working on an important brief or contract, or they may be on another phone call.

This is a lost opportunity if you cannot take that first call coming in.

The first attorney who speaks to a client calling in will have the best opportunity to convert that potential client into a paying client. Do not assume that the potential client is calling in because he or she received a referral to only one attorney and that attorney is you. Do not assume that the potential client is presold on you and hiring only you. Do not assume that the potential client will be patient and wait for you.

With all incoming calls, always assume that the potential client is calling out of the Yellow Pages or off a Google search and will hire the first person who is available. We all know that is not accurate, but it keeps you and your attorneys on their toes and fortifies your strategy that any incoming call must be transferred to an available attorney. Of course, you would like the attorney with the skill set necessary for the client's needs to take the call. If, however, the attorney with the skill set necessary to answer the client's questions is not available, *any attorney* will do. It is important that a potential client speak to an attorney the first time the client calls.

If somebody calls your office and you are the only attorney available, but the inquiry is on a legal matter about which you have no expertise, you will still take the call, ask factual questions about the caller's case, engage the person in a five- or ten-minute telephone call about the case, display true and real empathy for the caller's situation, and politely ask if you can have an attorney with the right level of expertise return the call as soon as possible. Then further say that you will make sure to talk to the attorney who will make the return call, explain the facts to the caller so that attorney is up to speed when he or she returns the call.

Therefore, rule 1 is that all incoming calls must be transferred to an attorney, and the attorney must take the call.

> The first rule around your office should be that you always have an attorney take phone calls from potential clients.

In the event that there is no attorney present in the office, your administrative assistants should be coached to e-mail or text you when a call comes in and that a person needs a call back immediately. Then, whether you are in a car or walking down the halls of a courthouse, you can respond to the client's phone call immediately, stating right up front that you received the message from your office, that the call seemed important, and that you wanted to talk to the client right away. An important tracking grid that you need to set up in your law office is an incoming call log that is filled in by the receptionist and every person in the office who is authorized to answer the phone.

The incoming call log will have several columns, and the person answering the phone should feel comfortable asking potential clients for the following information:

- Their name;
- Their phone number;
- Their type of legal matter;
- How they heard about you;
- Who the receptionist transferred the case to;
- In a follow-up column: Did they come in for a meeting?

Below is a sample grid of an incoming call log:

INCOMING CALL LOG

Date	Client Name	Phone #	Type of Legal Matter	How did they hear about us?	Attorney Transferred to: Did They Come in for a Meeting?

Rule 2 is that the purpose of speaking to any potential client on the phone is to schedule an appointment in the office.

During the initial phone conversation with a potential client, you need to let him or her talk, gather factual information about the case (including name, telephone number, and e-mail address), convey interest and empathy for the individual's plight, and ask him or her to come in for a consultation. Keep the initial call to less than fifteen minutes.

Do *not* give legal advice over the phone.

If pressed in the initial conversation by the client to evaluate the case, simply say, "It is really difficult to give legal advice based on a five- or ten-minute phone conversation. I think you should schedule an appointment and let us, in a more detailed way, go through the facts in detail so that we can come to some conclusion about the merits of your case (or business transaction)."

If the client insists on going through detailed facts over the phone to try to solicit a legal opinion from you during the initial phone conversation, simply, politely, and with empathy in your voice for the seriousness of the case say, "This sounds pretty serious, and I do not want to misspeak. We like to handle all new client consultations face to face, and I would like to schedule a meeting for you to come into our office. All initial meetings are of no charge to clients, so you have nothing to lose. When would you like to come in?" Do not let a client get you into taking your time in an initial consultation, testing your legal savvy on some issues of law over the phone.

> The purpose of speaking to any potential client on the phone is to schedule an appointment in the office.

If the client has a serious legal issue that requires lawyer involvement, the client should certainly budget the time to come in to see you, share documents with you, and meet with you face to face. Many times, if the potential clients show any resistance to coming into the law office for a free initial consultation, I also add, "You want to see who I am, meet with me, and make sure I am the right fit for you." Last, I will add, "Do not tell me you intend on hiring a lawyer over the telephone—do you?"

These statements and questions convey important information about you to a first-time caller, letting them know that you have been through this in the past and that your policy is what it is: namely, that all new clients need to come in for an initial consultation.

Therefore, the following continuum should be the protocol for all incoming calls:

| Call comes in from potential client. |

| Support staff documents the call. |

| Support staff transfers the call to an available attorney, and in a short call the attorney schedules a meeting with potential client. |

| Attorney meets with client at office (always have a second attorney at the meeting). |

| Engage all necessary postmeeting follow-up with the client. |

In other words, you will increase the probability of getting hired by this potential client significantly if you bring the person into the office. If the person cannot block out an hour of time to come visit you in your office, he or she is not a high-quality prospect.

Also, it is best to have all initial consultations in your office. Make a few, but very few, accommodations to go out to clients' homes or referral sources' offices to initially meet with clients. The previous rule applies: If the potential client does not have an hour of time to come into your office to meet with you in a professional environment, do not hold out great hope that this person is a serious client.

If the client resists meeting you in your office, please remind him or her that in an attorney-client relationship, the client should *want* to meet you and see your office. Tell the person that after the first meeting, a majority of legal work is done through the mail, e-mail, and over the telephone. Remind the person that he or she does not have to meet with you regularly.

Please review Chapter 15 about best practices for new clients and initial meetings. It is critical that you develop a best practices protocol for initial client meetings. Always remember the following:

- Shake hands and look your clients in the eye;
- Introduce yourself as you walk into a meeting;
- Call the client by his or her name;
- Be a good listener;
- Do not assume the client is presold;
- Display your knowledge but do not talk down to the client;
- Sell yourself to the client;
- Speak with confidence;
- Establish credibility by not overpromising;
- Show empathy to the client and the client's situation;
- Emphasize why your law office is different than other law offices (your USP) and why you believe your law office is a good fit for this case; and
- Be personable.

Remember, clients will hire you when they like you, they trust you, and they believe that you can help them.

Keep in mind that during the meeting, you are not asking for a sale. You are there to help the client if possible. You do not want a one-time sale, derived through any sort of trickery, manipulation, or desperation. You want a long-term client and a long-term relationship. As such, keep in mind the following:

- The client's interests must come first, not the law firm and not your own personal interests;
- Keep the promises that you make to the client;
- Clients want to know that you are listening to them and that you are worrying about their matter as much, if not more, than they are; and
- Remember, you can be a client's source of anxiety or the client's source of assurance. You are the expert they have hired. Give the client the peace of mind that you are looking out for his or her best interest all the time.

How can you do it? You need to create a process in writing that you can always go back to in order to check yourself to make sure you are doing all things correctly. The following list of activities is the law office equivalent of the universal lead conversion process.

Follow the universal lead conversion process:[1]

- Engage with the client. Do not assume the client is presold;

---

1. MICHAEL E. GERBER, E-MYTH MASTERY: THE SEVEN ESSENTIAL DISCIPLINES FOR BUILDING A WORLD CLASS COMPANY 316 (HarperCollins 2005).

- Evaluate the initial interview: How is your first impression? Does your support staff greet the client properly? What is the client experience? Do you have a coat closet? Does your staff offer the client a drink—water or coffee?
- Show interest immediately;
- Treat clients with respect. Do not patronize them;
- Explain hard concepts in simple terms; and
- Realize that many clients are smarter than you.

Repeat the emotional message:

- Remind clients that they came to the right place;
- Reinforce your promise to the market (your USP);
- Show your clients that you care about their case through actions and words;
- Put yourself in the shoes of the client and understand his or her pain, hurt, and emotional distress;
- Explain to the client why you think your law office and you are a perfect fit for his or her particular case;

Determine the client's need:

- What does a client really want?
- Does the client really know what he or she wants?
- Are you telling the client what to do, or are you advising the client of his or her choices and risk?
- Listen carefully to the client; when in doubt, the client may ask you, "What would you do if you were in my position?"
- Determine how you can gain a client's confidence that he or she will be making the right choice by hiring you and your law office.
- Ask if the potential client has ever hired an attorney before, and how those experiences went. Find out what the client liked about the past attorney and what went wrong.

Provide a solution:

- Do not sell the client, help the client;
- Provide a roadmap for the solution to the client's case—explain the process of litigation, the documentation, the business closing, and other probable necessities. Explain, as specifically as you can, why your law firm is the best solution, and explain your qualifications and experience;

- Always listen for client feedback carefully and gauge the client's satisfaction or dis-satisfaction and adapt.

Offer your services:

- Have everything ready to sign the client up. Ask the client, "Would you like us to get started today?"
- Be ready to be in second place;
- If the client is not ready to write a check at the first meeting, ask when you can expect a check and signed retainer agreement;
- If the client is vague, ask if he or she would like you to follow up in a week (and do so if the client says yes).

A great lead conversion system in the office has to do with allowing the client to like you, then building trust, and finally demonstrating to the client that you can help him or her.

Give yourself credit—you have invited the client into your office, he or she came, and it is at that point, if the client is a true prospect, that you need to offer your services and believe, in your heart, that you can help this client and add value.

Remember, it is okay to take a pass on a case for reasons set forth in this book. Not every case that comes in the door is a case where you can add value. If you can add value, with experience you will be able to take on the best cases and have a choice of which cases to take.

Chapter 28

Client Fulfillment and Satisfaction

After marketing, developing loyalty from clients, getting the phone to ring, and converting that potential client into an actual client, you must deliver the goods. Client fulfillment and satisfaction is all about *keeping* your marketing promise.[1]

Think about it: Is there anything more hypocritical than law firms talking the talk about how great they operate, how they market their company, and what their USP is—and then be inconsistent with those promises?

You are wasting your time if you try to build a winning law office and engage in the hypocrisy of marketing material that is inconsistent with your deliverables. You must keep your marketing promise.

Exceed Expectations

I have seen the exceed-expectations byline on countless professional service providers' letterheads and marketing materials. Clients are not likely to be impressed with marketing materials that tout the fact that this business exceeds client expectations.

However, it absolutely needs to be a mandate in your law office that you *do* everything you can to exceed client expectations. That does not mean to reduce client expectations so that you can deliver average results and average commitments. It means that you need to surprise the client with the timeliness of your returned telephone calls, first drafts of agreements that you told the client would take three or four days but you deliver in two days, and other similar quick turnarounds on drafts of briefs and other controllable promises that you make.

As lawyers, we cannot and do not give guarantees as to the results of cases, but we certainly can overdeliver on the things that we can control.

---

1. Michael E. Gerber, E-Myth Mastery: The Seven Essential Disciplines for Building a World Class Company 271 (HarperCollins 2005).

You must satisfy the perceived needs of the clients by doing time and time again what they do not even expect of you.

When was the last time you were in a five-star hotel, knowing you were paying a lot of money and seeing the small, subtle things that hoteliers do to exceed your expectations of the hotel experience?

When was the last time you were shocked from a good experience from a repairman who came out to fix the refrigerator or a home appliance? Why were you surprised that they overperformed?

What about certain car dealers who give you a loaner car at no charge while your automobile is being fixed?

What are the things that you can do, that are within your control, to make the experience of working with a lawyer as good as it possibly could be?

Admittedly, some people who come to a lawyer have very troubling situations and facts that need to be sorted through and resolved. Even on the hardest cases, when a client may be crying in your office, you need to have the client leave the office saying that you really made him or her feel better, that the person could see that there is a light at the end of the tunnel, and that the person really does feel that you lifted a tremendous burden off his or her shoulders. That is a great start for the client satisfaction experience.

> Clients are not likely to be impressed with marketing materials that tout the fact that this business exceeds client expectations.

Not all of an attorney's work is enjoyable. Attorneys take clients who have serious problems and try to relieve them of their problems and try to obtain solutions that are fair and just. However, even through the most problematic, painful litigation, as lawyers we need to make the client experience better than clients expect.

Reexamine the best practices discussed in Chapter 15. Incorporate some of the initial consultation issues contained therein into the client satisfaction section of your business plan. In addition, what about the sensory issues that you convey with your appearance and the office's appearance when clients come in to meet? All in all, the measures of success are these:

- How many clients, over time, hire you again and again? for the exact same type of legal work or for a different type of legal work?

- How long do you keep a client (in years), and what is their lifetime value for the client's firm? [2]
- How many referrals to your office do the clients make to their friends and associates?
- Are you retaining your employees on a regular basis? Employees want to be part of successful businesses.
- Is your firm growing each year with respect to profits, employees, and clients? Keep in mind that happy clients mean repeat clients, which means a growing business.
- Are you living your core values every day?

Naming the Relationship Manager

Every client should be connected with an attorney at the law office who is designated as the relationship manager. In the early growth of your firm, you will be the relationship manager for every client. But as you grow, you should have another attorney sit in on every initial client consultation, so, the client will get used to corresponding with attorneys at your office other than you. In fact, anticipate that other attorneys may start to build a rapport with the client, who will see nothing wrong with calling that other attorney first on occasion. You hope that you will still maintain the level of leadership and expertise in the client's eyes that brought the client

> Every client should be connected with an attorney at the law office who is designated as the relationship manager.

originally into your office, and that when faced and confronted with complicated legal issues, the client will still call you first. But nonetheless, some attorney in your law office must be designated the relationship manager for every client.

The duties of the relationship manager are to continue to build and foster that relationship over the life of the client. The relationship manager should watch over the cases as they come into the office from the client and are being handled by other attorneys. The relationship manager should be carbon copied on every piece of correspondence and e-mail that is sent out on the client matter so that the relationship manager follows the case and understands what is going on. The relationship manager is generally a partner or a high-level associate also vested with the responsibility of supervising the case and

---

2. I know it is difficult to calculate the future legal needs of the client, but you can probably realize that each client's value is greater than the client's monthly billing. Keeping that client happy, giving him or her a great client experience will assist you in gaining the client's loyalty and making that client a client for life. Imagine the value of that client over the next twenty-five or thirty years.

making sure that two heads are better than one when weighing in on discretionary decisions on client matters.

As the case ebbs and flows, the relationship manager should always send a signal to the client that he or she is always willing to talk about the case or weigh in on any questions the client might have with respect to the case or transaction.

In between matters for the client, the relationship manager should be calling the client to see how things are going and allow for follow-up questions or concerns in the aftermath at the end of a litigation matter or the closing on a business. Even in matters that appear to be one and done with legal issues, such as a personal injury case or an estate-planning matter, clients are never done with your law office. They are an important connection that you need to continue to cultivate even if you think their legal needs are at a minimum or nonexistent for years to come. Remember, we want the client experience, during and after the hard legal work is completed, to still be endearing, consistent, and caring. What are the specific duties of the relationship manager? The relationship manager should:

- Make sure the client is always getting the mailed newsletters from the firm;
- Make sure the client's e-mail address is on all the e-mail blasts, which includes the electronic newsletter;
- Make sure the client, when engaged in a legal matter in your office, has a good relationship with the support staff and that the support staff is timely with phone calls and delivering information relating to dates and timetables required of a particular case;
- Invite clients out to dinner, lunch, or another outing or event to thank them for past work. Invite clients to social events that may be of interest to their own particular industry;
- Ensure that the entire law office is responsive in returned communication with the clients, including but not limited to telephone calls, e-mails, and letters.

In addition to just managing the relationship, it is the relationship manager's duty to expose the client to additional attorneys in the law firm as the law firm grows. This concept is reiterated in Section 3 of this book, but it cannot be understated that you will not develop a successful business if just you, as the founding partner or the relationship manager, dominate the relationship with the client.

The client needs to understand that the client is hiring the law firm and not the individual attorney. Sometimes the client needs to be reminded of this in a very straightforward fashion. The more you, as a founding partner, and any subsequent relationship manager invite conversations between the client and other lawyers, the more you are doing to enhance the law firm's status with the client and minimize the need for specific attorney involvement, including yours. You can never build a viable, sustaining law firm if it is built on singular personalities that carry the business and client relationships so closely as to put the client relationship at risk if the attorney leaves the firm or stops practicing law. That is why you should always have an additional attorney sitting in on every client meeting in the office and allow a free transfer of information between the client and other attorneys in the law firm. If you have done your job properly as the founding partner, who more likely than not is the main connection between the firm and many of the clients in the office? The clients will start to think of the law firm first as their law firm and will connect with your law firm for many generations to come.

The Client Fulfillment Process

As part of your business plan, the process of client fulfillment needs to be documented. Consider the following best practices:

- Production
  - All projects[3] begin with an internal memorandum that includes a project manager and a relationship manager, an expectation of the finished project, a due date, and an estimate of time needed, if necessary. Set forth facts to make sure they are saved in the system forever so that no facts ever get forgotten from client meetings. These memos are very good to review and refresh your memory between client meetings;
  - Go to the document library to find a good starting document;
  - The attorney will do the drafting of the deliverable;
  - If it is a handwritten markup, the document will go to word processing and an administrative assistant will do the word processing;
  - Everyone involved in preparing the document, between the handwriting of the attorney, the typing of the attorney, and the typing of the administrative assistant, should be charged with a duty to eliminate all grammar and spelling mistakes and typos. The document, along with a cover letter, should be given to another attorney to review; and
  - After the document is reviewed by another attorney, it should be given to the signing attorney for one last review, and then to the client.
- Delivery
  - Delivery should be made either by the project manager (the name that we give to the attorney in charge of a particular case) or by the relationship manager;
  - Consider what other extras you can provide to the client at no additional cost at the time of delivery;

---

3. In a law office, of course, the jobs usually are drafting a brief, a research memo, or a contract of sorts.

- Decide what you can provide over and above the minimum requirement of the document, the filing, or the deliverable at the time of delivery; and
- Always remember to carbon copy the client on all correspondence.

As part of your business plan and every review, you always need to ask yourself, "Is this the best way to do this?"

Part of the client experience involves the internal workings of the office, which ultimately trickles down to client satisfaction. Thus, how the office works must be reviewed time and time again by asking these questions:

Can you

- Increase the quality?
- Reduce production time?
- Reduce overhead waste?
- Increase client awareness?
- Increase the detail of the best practices program?
- Reduce legal fees?

If you can improve on any or all of the foregoing six questions, do it, because in doing so, you will directly improve and heighten client satisfaction and increase market share.

Chapter 29

More Than Profits, You Need
a Winning Culture

Since the discipline of corporate management was invented,[1] almost eighty years ago, the ongoing question has always been "What is the purpose of a corporation?" The answer always was "to maximize shareholder wealth." Not anymore.

It is very difficult to understand the interplay between profits and things that are more important than profits. Make no mistake about it, if your reason for existing is to maximize shareholder wealth, you are limiting the upside of your law firm. In fact, Lencioni calls out law firms and in his study says that this firm did not come across many companies in the category of existing purely for wealth (or they probably did not come to Lencioni's company for consulting) although a number of venture capitalists and law firms he has seen probably fit it.[2] In those companies, it is important for the company owners to be clear to all involved, including employees, what their purpose is for existing. Otherwise, they will waste a lot of time doing meaningless exercises and analytics for nothing.[3]

Contrary to the business school doctrine, Collins and Porras did not find "maximizing shareholder wealth" or "profit maximization" as the dominant driving force or the primary objective in the history of the most successful, visionary companies.[4] Through the history of most of the visionary companies (i.e., long-term successful companies) that Collins and Porras studied, they saw a core ideology or *purpose* that transcended pure economic considerations, and—this is their key point—the companies had core purpose and ideology to a *greater* degree than the lesser-performing companies in their study.[5]

---

1. Peter F. Drucker, The Essential Executive: The Definitive Guide to Getting the Right Things Done 6 (HarperCollins 2006).
2. Patrick Lencioni, The Advantage: Why Organizational Health Trumps Everything Else in Business 89 (Jossey-Bass 2012).
3. *See id.*
4. James C. Collins & Jerry I. Porras, Built to Last: Successful Habits of Visionary Companies 55 (Harper Business 1994).
5. *Id.* at 55.

So how do profits come into play in this discussion?

Profitability is a necessary condition for existence and a means to more important ends, but it is not the end in itself for many of the visionary successful companies.[6] Profits are like oxygen, food, water, and blood for the body. They are not the point of life, but without them there is no life.[7]

You may struggle with this concept for a long time because you may have a hard time believing that profit cannot be the driver for the business to sustain long-term success. This paradigm is set forth succinctly and with clarity in the teachings and doctrines set forth by Peter Drucker. In keeping with the bigger plan and purpose, if your core purpose is to make significant social contributions, note that Drucker indicated that "actually, a company can make a social contribution *only if it is highly profitable*."[8] His supporting explanation is incontrovertible:

> The profit motive and its offspring "maximization of profits" are just as irrelevant to the function, the purpose of the business, and jobs of managing a business.
>
> In fact, the [profit] concept is worse than irrelevant: it does harm. It is a major cause of the misunderstanding of the nature of profit in our society and of the deep seated hostility to profit, which are among the most dangerous diseases of an industrial society. It is largely responsible for the worse mistakes of public policy—in this country as well as Western Europe—which are squarely based on the failure to understand the nature, function, and purpose of business enterprise. And it is in large part responsible for the prevailing belief that there is an inherent contradiction between profit and a company's ability to make a social contribution.[9]

Again, making a profit is not the end; nonetheless, profit is the lifeblood of the enterprise to make a social contribution.

So What Is a Core Purpose or Ideology?

In *Built to Last*, the Collins and Porras textbook on the successful habits of visionary companies, Chapter 3 is dedicated to the vision of companies that are about more than just profits.

---

6. *Id.*
7. *Id.*
8. PETER F. DRUCKER, THE ESSENTIAL DRUCKER: THE BEST OF SIXTY YEARS OF PETER DRUCKER'S ESSENTIAL WRITINGS ON MANAGEMENT 20 (HarperCollins 2001).
9. *Id.* at 19.

It starts with a story about Merck & Company, which was founded by George Merck II, who stated that "we are workers in industry who are genuinely inspired by the ideals of advancement of medical science, and of service to humanity."[10] Fifty-six years later, the then-chief executive officer of Merck, P. Roy Vagelos, reaffirmed the same idealistic mantra: "[A]bove all, let's remember that our business success means victory against disease and help to humankind."[11] Merck invented Mectizan, a drug to cure "river blindness," which is a disease that affects people in developing countries with a parasitic worm that eventually causes painful blindness. Merck knew it was getting into a market of over one million customers who could not afford the product, but he believed that some government agencies or other parties that support countries in the developing world would purchase and distribute the product once it was made available.[12]

Merck was not able to sell the product at all, however, and no one picked it up. As a result, Merck elected to give away the drug *free* to all those who needed it.[13] Merck also involved itself directly into its distribution efforts, all at its own expense, to ensure that the drug did indeed reach millions of people at risk from the disease.

Merck lived its core purpose. The CEO later pointed out that "failure to go forward with the product could have demoralized Merck scientists—scientists working for a company that explicitly viewed itself as 'in the business of preserving and improving human life.'"[14]

Merck's CEO believed at that time that it was the right thing to do, to live up to its core purpose, but it was also good business. He told a story about a medicine that Merck invented, Streptomycin, which was brought to Japan after World War II to eliminate tuberculosis, which was devastating Japanese society. Merck brought it to Japan and did not make any money. But currently Merck is the largest American pharmaceutical company in Japan. The long-term consequences of such actions are not always clear, but altruistic actions always pay off.[15] Merck's belief is that the company never forgets that medicine is for people and not for profit. The profits follow, and if the company's administration and staff always remember their core purpose, profits never fail to appear.[16]

Similarly, even more astonishingly, at the same point where you might be in the history of your law firm, Masaru Ibuka started Sony in the ruins of a defeated and devastated 1945 Japan with seven employees and $1,600 of personal savings. He immediately started making products (many of which failed), but he also did something else remarkable: he codified his ideology for his newfound company and in 1946 created his first prospectus.

---

10. JAMES C. COLLINS & JERRY I. PORRAS, BUILT TO LAST: SUCCESSFUL HABITS OF VISIONARY COMPANIES 47 (Harper Business 1994).

11. *Id.*

12. *Id.*

13. *Id.*

14. *Id.*

15. *Id.*

16. *Id.* at 48.

He wanted to build a firm with the spirit of teamwork and allow his engineers to exercise their hearts' desire of technological capabilities that could bring untold pleasure and benefits to all those involved. He wanted to create a place where engineers could feel the joy of technological innovation and be aware of their mission in society. He wanted all engineers to use technology and production for the reconstruction of Japan and the elevation of the nation's culture, and to be able to apply technology into the life of the general public.[17]

The Sony example is unique in that its founder had enough foresight to document his idealistic sentiments in their founding documents.

Incredible.

So as you study multiple cases of developing the importance of a core purpose, which creates the foundation for the culture of your firm, you need to examine whether you are ready to prepare your core purpose, such as the founder of Sony did in his company's organizational documents, or will you allow your firm to live and breathe for a time before such decisions are made?

There is certainly no one right ideology or core purpose. Be advised that no single item will show up consistently across all of the most successful visionary companies.[18]

- Some companies, such as Johnson & Johnson and Wal-Mart, made their *customers* central to their ideology; others, such as Sony and Ford, did not.
- Some companies, such as HP and Marriott, made concern for their *employees* central to their ideologies; others, such as Nordstrom and Disney, did not.
- Some companies, such as Ford and Disney, made their *products or services* central to their core ideology; others, such as IBM and Citicorp, did not.
- Some companies, such as Sony and Boeing, made audacious *risk taking* central to their ideology; others, such as HP and Nordstrom, did not.
- Some companies, such as Motorola and 3M, made *innovation* central to their ideology; others, such as P&G and American Express, did not.[19]

So what is the conclusion? In short, in the Collins and Porras study, the authors did not find any specific ideological content essential to being a visionary company. Research indicated that the *authenticity* of the ideology and the extent to which a company attains consistent alignment with the ideology and core purpose counts more than the *content* of the ideology.[20]

---

17. *Id.* at 50.
18. *Id.* at 87.
19. *Id.*
20. *Id.*

Why Does Your Law Office Exist?

After the foregoing discussion, your *why* is more than just to make money. I know this becomes a difficult concept to accept, especially in light of the fact that you may be just starting your law office. Many new companies, and probably even as many old companies, have not identified their purpose. This leads to problems.[21]

First, if you do not have a business purpose, your teams do not achieve a sense of collective commitment from their members. Leaders of such businesses want nothing to do with what they see as fluffy metaphysical conversations to provide lip service to nonmoney issues. In those cases, those teams come up with a set of empty promises and a mission statement that will read like countless other empty mission statements.

Second, many businesses do not see the company's reason for existing as having any practical implication for the way the business leaders make decisions to run the organization.[22] Without such a reason, leaders have no goal, no path, and they wind up getting caught up in a series of random pursuits and projects that are not consistent with any purpose whatsoever for existing. It creates confusion for employees. As a result, you should now be convinced of the need for the next exercise. Here is what you need to do.

As set forth with abundant ease in *The Advantage* by Lencioni,[23] start with this question: "How do you contribute to a better world?" Pretty extreme and worldly, wouldn't you say? You are not done. Then ask yourself, "Why?" Then ask, "Why do we do that?" and again, "Why do we do that?" When you come up just shy of the answer, "To make the world a better place," you will know that you are done.[24]

So try this exercise for certain substantive areas of law in which you focus your practice. These are just examples, but as you engage in the exercise, your answers should be your own:

Q: How do we contribute to a better world?

A: By representing individuals in the court system and seeking justice.

Q: Why?

A: Because we want to make sure that individuals who are hurt or harmed on the job are treated fairly and recover for their pain and suffering.

Q: Why?

A: Because life would not be fair if employers provided unsafe working environments for workers.

---

21. Patrick Lencioni, The Advantage: Why Organizational Health Trumps Everything Else in Business 83 (Jossey-Bass 2012).

22. *Id.*

23. *Id.* at 85.

24. *Id.* at 86.

Q: Why?

A: Because then workers would be taken advantage of by employers and their lifestyle and existence would be terrible and regress to sweatshops and unfair labor practices.

Q: Why?

A: Because that is the way I believe the way the world works and I want to make sure that workers' rights are protected.

Let's try this exercise again.

Q: How do you contribute to a better world?

A: By representing small business owners in setting up new businesses and helping them with legal advice.

Q: Why?

A: Because that is what I like to do. I enjoy dealing with small business owners.

Q: Why?

A: Because I connect with them, I appreciate the risks they take in our society, and I believe they contribute to 70% of all the employment in our country.

Q: Why?

A: I believe that supporting small businesses and helping them grow and compete against big businesses is great for our community, our state, and our economy.

Q: Why?

A: As I help small business, more people are employed, more growth comes to our community, and we are helping out with employment and innovation and our community and society.

Let's try this exercise again for criminal defense lawyers.

Q: How do you contribute to a better world?

A: I represent individuals who have been charged with a crime through the court system.

Q: Why?

A: Because many people have not done anything illegal and are charged improperly. Those who have committed a crime are often subject to onerous police and government actions to try to escalate the crime and charge my clients with crimes of egregious conduct, which is wrong.

Q: Why?

A: Everyone has rights, and I want to defend people, especially if they are innocent, and even if they are not innocent, against governmental tyranny and police brutality.

Q: Why?

A: Because in a civil society, courts uphold the rule of law, and I am able to fight for the rights of individuals.

Q: Why?

A: We need to support individuals against governmental tyranny in order to maintain a free and democratic society. Without the work that I do, the government could crush individual freedoms and individual rights.

One last time through the exercise:

Q: How do you contribute to a better world?

A: I help people. Since I am a lawyer, I usually help people with legal issues.

Q: Why?

A: Because that is what I want to do: help people.

Q: Why?

A: Because some people cannot help themselves. Especially in the legal process, you need an attorney to represent you in court or to deal with legal documents.

Q: Why?

A: The world is complex, and I like to help people and I help them any way I can.

Q: Why?

A: Because it makes me feel good.

Q: Why?

A: Because it levels the playing field in society for people who cannot stand up for themselves.

As you can see with the sample exercises, you can talk through most practice groups, go through the exercise, and come up with reasons why you are passionate about what you are doing and why you want to do it. It is critically important that you pursue your goals in a passionate fashion and have, as a guiding foundation, your core purpose.[25]

How Does Your Firm Behave and Act?

How we act and how we behave is a journey of self-analysis that should seem consistent with why you go to work every day in the morning. Certainly, following the path of your core purpose should create clarity on how to behave in a way that is consistent with that purpose. There are various values that come about in a company accidentally, but make

---

25. Note that this discussion is a legal derivation from the system set up in *The Advantage* by Patrick Lencioni when he poses the question, "Why do we exist?" It is certainly a first step to knowing why you go to work in the morning.

no mistake about it, the core values are embedded in the conduct of your top employees, including you.

> Core values are not a matter of convenience. They cannot be extracted from an organization anymore than a human being's conscience can be extracted from his or her person. As a result, they should be used to guide every aspect of an organization from hiring and firing to strategy and performance management.[26]

Also, it is important to remember that there are certain values that do not need to be documented, per se. These are what Lencioni calls permission-to-play values. Those are values such as truthfulness, integrity, and respect for others. All are basic, obvious, necessary values, but your company is not built around those values. They should not even be part of the discussion because a person who even steps through your doorway to be an employee in your office must have those values. To identify core values, Lencioni suggests that you examine your pool of top leaders and employees and ask yourself what it is about them that fits. Obviously, these folks may not have the skill set to be a 100% perfect fit for the character requirements of your law office. Nonetheless, there are certain qualities of the people around you, the people you have worked with in the past, and the people you have corresponded with regularly, that makes them organizationally aligned with your core purpose and beneficial to pursuing your core purpose.

> As you dedicate yourself and your firm to your core purpose and you surround yourself with people who are true to your core values, success becomes not a chance but a certainty.

In addition, examine yourself. What about your makeup and skill sets are necessary for the pursuit of your core purpose?

Some of these values might include:

- Hedgehog determination;[27]
- Commitment to your community;
- Significant commitment to bar association activities and the legal profession as a profession;
- Relentless pursuit of excellence; and
- Blue-collar work ethic.

---

26. Patrick Lencioni, The Advantage: Why Organizational Health Trumps Everything Else in Business 94 (Jossey-Bass 2012).

27. Jim Collins, Good to Great: Why Some Companies Make the Leap . . . and Others Don't (Harper Business 2001).

As you can see, everyone's core values may be different. It is the core values of your business that will identify your behavior and your commitment to your core purpose. Without values, you cannot pursue your core purpose.

Do not lose the definition of what boils down to your core values. Core values are your law firm's essential and enduring tenets—a small set of general guiding principles, not to be confused with specific cultural or operational practices, nor to be compromised for financial gain or short-term expediency.[28] Visionary great companies tend to have only a few core values, usually between three and six. Any more, and those values are not truly core.[29]

In a visionary company, the core values need no rational or external justification. Nor do they sway with the trends and fads of the day. As a result, your core values are never compromised, never changed, and are so fundamental to the business that they will not be changed by the swings of the economy, style, fashion, trends, or that which becomes appealing to the unsuspecting eye. As you dedicate yourself and your firm to your core purpose and you surround yourself with people who are true to your core values, success becomes not a chance but a certainty.

---

28. JAMES C. COLLINS & JERRY I. PORRAS, BUILT TO LAST: SUCCESSFUL HABITS OF VISIONARY COMPANIES 73 (Harper Business 1994).
    29. *Id.* at 74.

Chapter 30

Building a Winning Culture

What could be better than a cultlike culture for your organization? This does not require employees to follow blindly as happened with nefarious individuals such as Jim Jones, David Koresh, or other troubling cult leaders. What you are trying to build is a fervent following for your core ideologies, the reason for which your law firm exists.

With enough culture pulses to the employees,[1] achieved through various correspondence and meetings, the company culture will become ingrained; it will be established, aligned, realigned, reminded, and reestablished in all employees throughout their careers. You need to be careful not to preach your gospel in a manner that turns people off, but it certainly needs to be fervently reminded to them on a regular basis.

The pulse of the message is healthy for the organization, provided in periodic episodes. Remember, first you need to identify your core ideologies and purpose, and then your fundamental values that build toward the purpose. Then consider the following acts as ways to establish and reinvest in your core purpose:

- Make sure you orient your new employees to the firm's core purpose. Make your core purpose clear and any ongoing training or teaching all revolves, first, around who you are as a firm and, second, around the skill sets employees need to be successful in their jobs.
- Ensure that all official training, documents, handbooks, and manuals always reinforce your core purpose. Engage in team-building activities and activities to get people out of the office and have fun together. These events, some with spouses and significant others and some without, should be held to demonstrate, in a real sense, your commitment to people, family, friendships, and teamwork. These can be as easy as a baseball game, bowling outings, company involvement in efforts to help the poor, and other team-related events for the company.

---

1. Verne Harnish, Mastering the Rockefeller Habits: What You Must Do to Increase the Value of Your Growing Firm (Gazelles 2002).

- Understand that a growing firm makes this process easy, but always remember that promotion from within is preferred.
- Give real-time recognition for employees demonstrating the individual building of the company's core purpose.
- Enforce tangible and visible penalties for those who break ideological boundaries.
- Provide celebrations that reinforce successes and other goal-oriented achievements; constant verbal and written emphasis on corporate values, heritage, and a sense of being part of the organization's big plan.
- Have as few rules as possible, but enforce them systematically, without compromise.
- Repeat yourself regularly on core ideologies, and live the firm's core ideologies. Remember, actions and words matter. People will observe both.
- Express your core purpose and core values in meetings. Remember, there is a lot of noise in business. Turn that noise into a rhythm and, in order to keep everyone's attention, change the rhythm around regularly. Say it different ways, give examples of it, tell stories about it, and give real-time recognition to the people who live it.

> Make sure you orient your new employees to the firm's core purpose.

The best example of blending necessary elements for a successful business is the balance and understanding between preserving the core of your business so that it never changes and your core is never compromised, and stimulating progress.[2] The fine balance between keeping what is right about your firm, yet still stimulating progress, achievement, and betterment is the ultimate manner in which to run a company, create excitement, and build a cultlike culture.

Think about it: What better environment can you give a team of lawyers and administrative assistants than to keep them anchored in the core purpose of the business—that is, letting them know exactly where you and the team stand at all times—and yet allow them the freedom to go out and make exciting things happen outside the ordinary tasks of running a business, practicing law, and the daily grind of what we lawyers do. This is critically important to keep an enthusiastic team on your side.

There is no doubt that after practicing law for many years, you will hear stories about your peers, friends, and colleagues leaving the practice of law due to burnout and the components of the practice of law that left them disenchanted and exhausted. All of that will happen to you if you allow the pressure of running a law office grind you down without an enthusiastic team around you. Let the team soar to new areas of the practice of law; let

---

2. JAMES C. COLLINS & JERRY I. PORRAS, BUILT TO LAST: SUCCESSFUL HABITS OF VISIONARY COMPANIES 80 (Harper Business 1994).

team members be engaged in creating the big hairy audacious goals that your office will eventually attain. Stimulate progress, stimulate creative thought, and think about ways to improve the platform on which people work to bring out the best that your organization and the practice of law has to offer.

The conservative response of "That's not the way we do it here," has no place in your business. Instead, when somebody comes up with a unique idea, your first reaction should be "Let's see how we can make that work." Then it is your role to infuse the idea with your years of experience and wisdom, possibly modify the idea, get buy-in from a larger group of people, and then let it fly. These ideas might be about internal operational issues, new marketing ideas, a new approach to your website, an ongoing blog on a practice area that you dominate in your market, or any other new idea that is consistent with your core ideologies and is in furtherance of your unique selling proposition. The business world is full of examples of companies moving into areas of business not necessarily core to their product or services. Those businesses probably put customers or employees as their core purpose or believe in the concept of first getting the right people on the bus and letting the bus go where it may based on the creativity of the people on the bus.

Recall that Johnson & Johnson was a primary supplier of antiseptic gauze and medical items in the early 1890s but then moved into other consumer products such as baby powder and Band-Aids.[3] Similarly, American Express never intended to venture into the financial and travel services industries that it now dominates.[4]

> You will gain credibility with the employees when you recognize a failed process or a substantive area of the law and discard it.

Be convinced of one thing—that you do not know where your firm is headed. So long as you have the right people around you, the services that you offer will develop based on the strength of the people in your office. A business transaction law firm, which attracts a top litigator to complement its transactional practice, may ultimately become a larger litigation firm than a transactional practice based on the strength of one lawyer or a small team of lawyers in the litigation area. A business law firm may have some success at consumer litigation and eventually become a champion of consumer rights in class-action suits. Further, as you try many new things, whether for the internal workings of the business aspects of the office or in substantive areas in the practice of law, some things will work out and some will not. You need to constantly evaluate to see what works. Keep what works and discard the rest.

---

3. *Id.* at 141.
4. *Id.*

Collins and Porras in *Built to Last* calls this the "Darwin theory of evolution applied to visionary companies."[5] If it does not work, end it. If it seems to have legs and is progressing nicely, put more good people on the project or idea and continue to invest time and, if applicable, money to the new process or practice area.

Keep in mind that you will not vet 100% with all of your initiatives. But in a law office, attempting to build a new practice area for the firm helps the firm in multiple ways, including just keeping in-house the outbound referrals of clients in these different practice areas. Again, if the experiment fails, you may need to terminate relationships, retrench the program, and move forward with or without a retooled program.

None of this activity loses credibility with employees when employees see how you navigate the successes and failures of the firm. You will gain credibility with the employees when you recognize a failed process or a substantive area of the law and discard it. Your successes will occur, and your obvious successes will be the achievement of your one- and five-year goals as your employees evaluate the firm's growth. All this helps one important part of employee buy-in, building a cultlike culture whereby people believe in the firm's ability to preserve its core and yet still reach out for progress.

What you need to hire is the right stonecutter—one of Peter Drucker's favorite parables, cited by him as early as 1954.[6] The first stonecutter was asked, "What are you doing?" The first stonecutter's reply was "I am making a living."

The second stonecutter was asked, "What are you doing?" The second stonecutter's reply was "I am doing the best job of stonecutting in the entire country."

The third stonecutter was asked, "What are you doing?" The third stonecutter said with a glimmer in his eye, "I am building a cathedral."

With that said, everyone who adopts your culture and the buy-in of the firm culture must be building a cathedral.

---

5. *Id.* at 148.
6. Kenichi Hirakari, Vital Peter Drucker: 8 Timeless Principles That Will Take Your Company from Great to Greater Loc 136 (Amazon Kindle, 2012).

Chapter 31

Segregating Practice Groups and Management Work

You will continue to grow your law office, and as you have seen in earlier chapters, you will not be able to do it all yourself. Clearly as part of your growth curve, you will need to delegate work to other people who report back to you. Remember, during this delegation process, it is not what you *expect*, it is what you *inspect*. So therefore every task delegated needs to be reviewed, and with good, proper training, employees will begin to assimilate your standards and expectations with their work product and align themselves with your standards and goals.

This is a very positive culture to build, and it is the way to grow and train the people who work with you and around you.

At a certain point in time, you need to start putting people in charge and make them accountable in certain areas of the practice. Remember, the management of the law practice is broken up into two separate areas: the management of the law office, which is the running of the nonlegal work portion of the business; and the practice groups, which are all law-related revenue-generating work.

Law Office Management

As indicated in earlier chapters, your first management person who is not a lawyer will be the bookkeeper, who will eventually morph into the law office manager. In the early stages of the law office's growth, that person has to be in charge of all business functions unrelated to law, including billing, banking, ordering supplies, bill paying, managing the functionality of your computer and billing systems through an IT professional—in short, every function that can be delegated except practicing law.

As the practice grows, the office manager may need assistance with some functions. Some of this work may start migrating to the other top administrative assistants or part-time clerks who are seeking full-time work or to other skilled, competent, and detail-oriented individuals who are not lawyers.

Notwithstanding the potential for adding more personnel in the accounting and practice management group, a talented office manager should be able to manage an office of up to ten or fifteen attorneys with not much help on a regular basis.

Keep in mind that the office manager's busy time is at the end of every month when client bills are being prepared and have to be sent out. Beyond that time, the officer manager's job should be regimented in such a fashion that there are certain days during the week when certain tasks are performed, and there are certain hours in the day when certain tasks are performed on a regular basis. Again, discipline is needed in this role, and you must be in charge of regularly reviewing and auditing this work.

As you continue to grow, you might need more support from your outside accounting firm or tax preparers to systemize your bookkeeping practices in order to minimize the work for the federal tax preparation at the end of the year. The balance between the in-house bookkeeper and the outside accounting firm must be determined by you to see how much your inside bookkeeper can handle on a regular basis.

> The officer manager's job should be regimented in such a fashion that there are certain days during the week when certain tasks are performed, and there are certain hours in the day when certain tasks are performed on a regular basis.

Other human resource duties must be regularly managed because personnel issues will be a constant subcategory of the management of the firm. Proper human resource files need to be kept, vacation schedules need to be kept, and other internal documentation of records need to be kept on all employees, as well as former employees.

As you can imagine, these tasks are all time sensitive, and certain tasks may ultimately be transferred to a top attorney to oversee the office manager in his or her duties of work. Because the human resource function of any business is heavily law driven, it seems fair that another top attorney, possibly a new young partner, should take over the human resource component of the firm from you. Again, in management meetings, you can always get up to speed on what is going on, but that is one function of the office that can be delegated to another attorney to oversee the management thereof from the office manager.

Banking and bill paying, as well as billing and accounts receivable, will always be the core function of the office manager in your office. Remember, your office manager will probably be hired with some financial background and education in that field.

The next area that needs to be delegated to other people in your office is the marketing function. As you can see from the detailed and lengthy Chapter 26, marketing and lead generation are complex and time consuming, and there needs to be a dedicated individual overseeing that function.

Ideally, you would have a person with marketing experience, educated in marketing in college, to manage that function of the business. You may not have that immediately, but an administrative assistant may potentially have some marketing background from college or a previous job and he or she may want to focus on that part of managing the practice. If so, you need to match that administrative assistant with an attorney in the office to oversee the marketing efforts and provide guidance, counsel, and direction. They will make sure the firm's marketing initiative is always in compliance with the code of professional conduct in your jurisdiction and that it ethically and accurately conveys your culture, purpose, and USP.

The next area to consider is technology, which will be your function to oversee for a long period of time because of the expense involved in upgrading technology. The investment of time and money in technology is a capital expenditure that will pay dividends in the future of the firm. It does not have a dollar-for-dollar benefit immediately. It is infrastructure, or as referred to in the past, it is the backbone on which the firm deliverables are built. Depending on your own technology skill set, you may migrate this function to another attorney sooner than other functions of the firm. However, because of the time-consuming nature and ongoing repairs, tweaks, adjustments, and other maintenance required of a sophisticated technology system, you will want to assign another attorney to that type of management and oversight. Remember, that key attorney will be managing the outside IT person and that person's time.

Someday when the firm is large enough, you may need to hire your own inside IT person for this function.

Notwithstanding your assignment of this function to another attorney, significant upgrades, or additional components of the IT budget should be approved by you. These are large dollar investments for your firm and you should always be part of that decision-making process. Therefore, if another attorney is managing the IT process, you would give him or her authority to spend $1,000 or $1,500 to upgrade machines or replace machines without your authority.

Managing Legal Work

As stated in Section 1 of the book, there is no substitute for attorneys managing the legal work of the firm. In fact, for many years you will need to be the overseer of all legal work. The exception to that rule applies if you move your firm into another practice area in which you have no experience and so you have hired an attorney with that experience to manage that area of the law. However, a few sure rules could be relied upon when managing legal work. These rules are explained next.

First Year Out of Law School

During the associate's first year out of law school, you need to proofread every letter, e-mail (if possible), and work product of the new associate. This is important because this new attorney will be anxious in his or her new job and will want to do everything the right way but will have limited experience. Your patience and education during the attorney's first year matters significantly to training this person as to how you like things done for the rest of his or her career. Therefore, the first-year associate's work product, and I mean all of it, needs to be reviewed every day. Now, imagine the level of training that you will have provided in twelve months if you do this consistently. You will have begun to build alignment with the new associate that should last throughout the individual's career. Based on your personality, of course, you will train, teach with great patience, and see that the new associate continues to grow. If the new associate continues to make the same mistakes multiple times, you may need to evaluate whether you have hired the right person.

> During the associate's first year out of law school, you need to proofread every letter, e-mail (if possible), and work product of the new associate.

Further, the new associate should sit in on every meeting you have with clients. The first-year associate should never handle a client meeting by himself or herself without an experienced attorney. All attorneys in the office should be instructed to bring the new first-year associate to as many court hearings, closings, and client meetings as possible (not charging the client, of course). The first-year training is critically important to the new associate. Do not be fooled into thinking that the new associate is fully trained after three, four, or five months. He or she is not. If there are more attorneys in the office, all the better that new associate gets an opportunity to see the styles of as many experienced attorneys as possible.

Two- to Five-Year Associates

Generally speaking, most attorneys believe that they have "figured it out" by the fifth year of practicing law. There is a lot to be gained in the first five years of practicing law, but, even through five years, all discretionary decisions on a case should involve you or the partner in charge of that particular practice area. Further, all difficult client management issues should be handled by a partner-level or senior associate–level person in the law office. Although generally in the law profession a five-year associate has figured a lot out, he or she has *not* figured it all out. There is still a tremendous amount of growth that comes during an attorney's professional path in years 6 through 10.

After the first year, attorneys should be able to send out basic letters and e-mails without review of a partner or you. However, when a letter goes out opining on a conclusion of a law, such letter needs to be reviewed by a higher-level person for its conclusions. Any opinion letter should be tested and run through a partner or senior associate–level attorney.

Court papers, pleadings, and first drafts of agreements should, just in the basic course of best practices, be reviewed by another attorney for grammatical proofing and substantive testing.

Six- to Ten-Year Associates

During the senior associate years, an associate progresses, and his or her conduct should start looking more like partner conduct near the end of this term. He or she should already be advising and helping younger associates, formally or informally mentoring the young attorneys (whether or not in the same practice group), and overall growing in that time period into the fourth tool of the five-tool attorney, namely, helping young associates. As the attorney moves into the latter segment of the senior associate phase, he or she needs to be showing signs of the fifth tool of the five-tool attorney, and that is viewing the practice as a business and managing the business. You will know that your senior associate is moving in the right direction when he or she starts making decisions or adding input in meetings where it is clear that he or she is putting the firm first. When the associate takes that turn in thinking, you have identified partnership-level associates.

Every senior associate should be managing certain functions of the law office both in the practice management area of his or her own practice area and in the law office management of either marketing, IT, finance, or another area of the practice.

All in all, the senior associate should be putting the law office first, and seeing the law office as a business. The senior associate needs to understand the future of the business, be fully adopted into the core purpose and values of the business, and work every day to forward those ideologies of the firm to new associates and support staff.

In conclusion, with respect to the various segments of the law office, whether in the business's management or practice groups, certain attorneys need to start to relieve you of the management of those issues. It will be virtually impossible for you in a small growing law firm to manage all of the business-related items required to run the law office, yet still work *in* the business. Remember, a large reason the practice is growing is because people call to ask for you to work on their cases. You are still a lawyer, and you still practice law. Therefore, you cannot possibly be expected to manage all of these functions of the law office, yet still practice law. Unfortunately, because of our industry, rarely does a business model seem to work where you, the founder of the firm, will stop practicing law before retirement. Therefore, the management of the firm needs to move to people other than you so that you still have hours in the day, Monday through Friday, to roll up your sleeves and do the things you love to do—practice law.

The last issue that needs to be addressed under managing legal work is to determine how many associates you can really be expected to manage.

Between four and five should be the target.

Once your firm gets to involve five or six attorneys (including you), it is at that point in time that you will be ready to elevate one of the associates to partner-level status. Although the associate is not ready for that role—if only because your law practice is growing so fast—and that top associate has not yet been able to demonstrate all five tools of the five-tool attorney, he or she may still be able to manage other young associates and should take on that responsibility.

Keep in mind that if your entire law firm continues to grow by having great associates, but associates are unwilling to adopt all five tools of the five-tool attorney, you probably have the wrong associates to grow the practice as described in this book. As a result, start to look to replace people if you need to grow beyond five or six attorneys.

> You cannot grow beyond five or six attorneys unless you have identified *at least* the first associate to become a five-tool attorney.

You cannot grow beyond five or six attorneys unless you have identified *at least* the first associate to become a five-tool attorney.

Consider these ratios to be advisory. You may be able to create a model where a partner can manage more associates than four or five, depending on the practice group. Depending on the discussion and the way the firm works, that may be so. However, as guidance, as you have your third or fourth associate hired, you need to start seeing signs that one associate will elevate to the necessary level of the full five-tool attorney (i.e., partner).

In light of the progression of attorneys from new associates, to associates, to senior associates, you hope that within ten years of being out of law school, your attorneys are ready to become partners.

Imagine, you took the entrepreneurial risk to start the business years ago, you have built up a successful practice, and now you are about to make someone your partner, which should be exciting, exhilarating, and an indication of the success of your business. Now, what should you expect from that partner?

Chapter 32

The Income Partner

As the firm has grown and your associates have taken on more responsibility, done outstanding legal work, adopted your core purpose and values, been acculturated into your marketing culture, and assisted with both training younger associates and helping manage the business, it is a natural progression for you to start talking to your top associate about becoming a partner in the firm.

In law firms, the term "partner" means many different things to different people depending on the context of discussion. While a partner sounds like a legal relationship between two or more people, if your law office has been incorporated, there really is no legal status given to a partner. However, to the outside world, "partner" means someone who has been elevated to the status of ownership or part of the management team of the law office. Admittedly, the outside world sees that status somewhat incorrectly, but for the purpose of your firm and the development of the firm, partner is an important elevation from senior associate.

It is an exciting time for the senior associate to be elevated to a completely new status of partner and also for you to have someone who is closer to your status in the operation of the business.

Law firms have traditionally used a two-tiered system at the partnership level: a nonequity partner (also known as an income partner) and equity partners or stakeholders (individuals who are actual owners or shareholders in a corporation that operates the law firm). Your senior associates will need to go through the nonequity partner status for one or two years before being offered an opportunity to buy into the company as equity partners.

> Your senior associates will need to go through the nonequity partner status for one or two years before being offered an opportunity to buy into the company as equity partners.

The greatest benefit for the senior associate in becoming an income partner is the ability to hold himself or herself out to the world as a partner for generating business. Large law firms, through their mentoring programs and work assignment funnel, generally start to vet associates through the first four to five years of practicing law to determine which are worthy of partnership. Then, in the next three to five years, the partners will start to invest time, energy, and money into the chosen associate to teach him or her marketing skills.

In contrast, you have been teaching marketing skills as soon as the young associate met the first two requirements of the five-tool attorney: doing exemplary legal work and then meeting all billing goals. Therefore, the chances are very likely that your senior associate will be ready to accelerate the marketing protocol, attract more attention, speak at larger functions, and behave as a partner in order to enhance his or her ability to get referrals and bring in business.

The advantage for you as the founding partner of the business is to have someone, by virtue of the title, who will be responsible for helping run the company and manage people. Further, as that person adapts to working *on* the firm's business, he or she will begin to show signs of being a serious businessperson as well as an attorney. Within a short period of time, you will have that person who will be interested in becoming an equity owner of the business.

Remember, the income partner of the firm is not sharing the profits or equity of the firm. However, when elevating the status of the senior associate to income partner, remember that in that particular year the income partner should be entitled to a significant increase in base salary depending on his or her previous salary increases, probably an amount equal to two or three times his or her previous annual salary increase. This significant increase in salary does not happen every year, but it creates a separation in income between the next ranking senior associate and the income partner. That will reset the base salary of the income partner for the rest of his or her career in your law firm.

The income partner status should be documented properly with clear language and an understanding among the partners that it is not an equity ownership interest in the corporation or other legal entity that operates the law office and that there are no statutory rights bestowed upon the income partner to review the books and records that are otherwise reserved to the shareholders and interest holders of the entity.

Some of the many reports that you have received from the accounting department could be shared with the income partner, however. In addition to the reports that you do share with all the associates (e.g., their billing and new client sign-ups every month) is other information to share with the partner. Also make the income partner aware of the total gross amount of the revenue brought in for the month, total billing monthly, and the sources of your new client referrals and other directional reports that are indicative of which marketing efforts are working, which associates are generating the most new work, and other macro measurables of the firm.

Strictly not available to the income partner would be the balance sheet and cash flow statements of the company, the income statement, operational expenses, employee salaries, including your salary, and other information that is still deemed sensitive and confidential to protect the rights of other people in the office. Also unavailable to the income partner are things that are truly financially sensitive to the owner of the business—you.

There will not be much opposition from the income partner about being denied access to this information because the partner will completely understand that he or she does not have income at risk and that the information in those reports is highly confidential and sensitive.

A Big Decision

Elevating a senior associate to an income partner is a big decision and should not and cannot be taken lightly. In your growing firm, this associate has surpassed the test of time, become internally qualified by meeting the tests of the five-tool attorney, and been invited into the partnership pool. The standards under which this individual is elevated have become the de facto standards going forward and set a precedent for your other associates.

Determine the basic partner-to-associate ratio that you would like established. The higher the ratio, the better for profitability and, believe it or not, firm morale. A firm with three associates for each partner is considered to be in a "sweet spot" for a small law firm.[1] Therefore, the higher ratio (i.e., one partner for every ten associates) is the most profitable ratio, and the lowest ratio (i.e., one partner for every two associates) is still an accepted ratio for small law firms.[2] Even growing law firms having a ratio of 1:1; while not ideal, this ratio is acceptable in the early stages of the firm's growth.

Partnership is a status that every associate wants to achieve, but it is worthless if it is a simple coming-of-age status that everybody achieves and thus starts creating an undesirable ratio of more partners than associates (i.e., an inverse ratio). Then you have a law firm that can accomplish the same goals that you can have with fewer partners and more associates.

Be advised that inverse partner-to-associate ratios create an environment that is just a series of jobs for the partners, not the operation of a real business. Basically, if you have a collection of all partners, whether or not there are a small number of associates, you will either be setting your salaries and draws based on the work and billing that you personally accomplish or equalize the distribution as a hedge against economic misfortunes of one practice group or another. Realistically, attorneys never think that far in advance, and any business model that is full of purportedly equal partners with no associates rarely works in the long run as a business. It is just a placeholder for jobs for the partners.

---

1. Janet Ellen Raasch, *Making Partner—or Not: Is It In, Up or Over in the 21st Century?*, LAW PRACTICE *at* 4.
2. *Id.*

Therefore, it is critically important that the person you elevate into the income partner level is a person who will ultimately be qualified for an offer for equity ownership. Further, when such person meets the income partner status, the partner-to-associate ratio in your firm is acceptable.

Timing matters.

If you roughly followed the pattern set forth herein, your first equity partner will have been your associate for approximately eight to ten years. If you added a new associate every other year, you should have about five associates working with you at the end of ten years. If the senior associate becomes partner, you will be a six-person law firm, with two partners, and that is a very favorable ratio for a relatively new and growing law firm.

Now, if you were to overperform on that growth pattern and have seven or eight associates when the senior associate is elevated to income partner, your ratio would be closer to one partner for every four associates—a better business ratio, to be sure.

The second tier of analysis for this pattern is that although the senior associate is managing and supervising some new associates, your partner-to-associate ratio remains within the optimal ratio for the purposes of supervising legal work.

> Partnership is a status that every associate wants to achieve, but it is worthless if it is a simple coming-of-age status that everybody achieves.

The elevation from senior associate to income partner needs to be done in an honest, open, and forthright manner with the associate. Keep in mind that this position and this invitation into the partnership level is a precursor to having a business partner and an equity partner in your business. Except for the private financial information of the firm, an invitation should include a thorough discussion of your expectations of the income partner's status as an income partner, but also of your expectations of this person *as an equity partner*.

The open discussion about income partner status as a precursor to equity partner status will probably mean a lot to the new income partner and should be seen as a clear statement that this person, in your mind, qualifies to be your business partner. A true equity partner status in a business—whether it be a restaurant, an investment banking firm, a retail store, a body shop, or a small metal-stamping manufacturing business—is that that you will enter into a life relationship for providing for your families together earning income and have a similar work-to-life balance that will be profitable, fulfilling, and rewarding in the long run. This person you have elevated into the income partner status must be aligned with not only your core purpose and core values for the business, but also your values as a person and the way you want to balance your life between work, family, and fun. There is no way that the equity relationship works when one equity partner works sixty hours a week but the other equity partner works twenty hours a week and spends forty additional hours a week on a golf course at dinners, shows, or vacation trips with clients, and takes the position that everybody is putting in the same number of hours.

Does that mean that only the exact same type people can become partners in a business?

Absolutely not. Unmarried individuals could partner up very well with married individuals with families, and stoic, serious personalities can align with gregarious, outgoing personalities, for example, so long as *everyone* follows the necessary requirements of the five-tool attorney and lives the core purpose and core values of the law firm.

Having a variety of personalities in the law office makes work fun, interesting, and enjoyable. Also, there is always more than one way to skin the cat and a variety of approaches and perspectives on the law firm's core purpose and core values makes for creative thinking, creative design, and implementation of the firm's long-term plan. So, while preserving the core purpose, you will have many enjoyable partner meetings as you stimulate growth and progress.

Section 3

The Succession Plan

Chapter 33

The Succession Cycle

At this point, you have grown your business, established a winning culture in your firm, and built systems, checklists, and manuals that allow everyone to succeed. You have created continuity for growth and a system for new hires to understand the culture of the business. Last, you have hired the right people and put those correct people in places to succeed at the firm.

Have you built the business up merely because of your tenacity and great effort—or because you built a great business?

You hope the latter. You have invested your time and money and have developed the systems that through trial and error have established a winning formula for the firm's culture, and the business is now a standalone success. Moreover, you have progressed to being a level 5 leader and have developed a management team around you, currently income partners who now seek to be equity partners (i.e., owners of the business).

The relationship between you and your top management people dramatically changes from a legal standpoint once they become shareholders.[1] You are aligned with respect to the culture and values of the firm. You all hold the legal and business acumen at the same level of importance, and everyone has bought into the requirements that you set forth in your business plan to grow the business and to make a significant impact in your communities. Therefore, other than the legal relationship that changes, the transition from income partner to equity partner should not be dramatic. However, because of the legal implications of being a shareholder in a corporation, the offer, acceptance, and transition must be completely transparent. Also, of course, going forward, the transition from income partner to equity partner must, as a practical matter and under the law, be absolutely transparent.

It bears repeating that the reason why you have a viable standalone business, in which you can sell shares, is because you truly built a business and not just a support network

---

1. Throughout the discussion on ownership of the business entity, the terms "shareholders," "equity partners," and "owners" are used interchangeably. Depending on your business form, there are different ownership names for the equity ownership of the business.

around one or two dynamic attorneys and their personalities. If you watch television and follow the cases that are reported in the media, those cases often have recognizable attorneys representing the litigants. Fortunately, these are mostly high-profile criminal cases, whereby litigants have little concern for cost and hire high-profile attorneys believing that they provide the best representation.

Now imagine a law firm's *name* having that reputation instead of the attorney himself or herself. Imagine the high-profile entity being the law firm's name and not necessarily the work of the individual lawyer. Of course, having well-known high-profile attorneys helps, but many large clients get introduced to large law firms by virtue of a connection with a partner, even though the partner does not handle all the legal work for the client. The law firm's reputation is so good and the firm's name so highly respected that clients are generally pleased to be getting their work done by any attorney in the law firm so long as they have *direct contact* with the partner who introduced them to the firm.

Now translate that culture and identity to the law firm that you have been building. Certainly, the founding partner is no doubt of a higher profile in his or her community and more well known in the circles in which he or she congregates. But note that the sooner the founding partner can introduce additional lawyers to the client, the better it is for the law firm and, in the long run, for the founding partner. In other words, the client needs to be comfortable with the brand of attorneys who work at the firm, and not with just the founding partner. If the hiring partner has considered all the necessary information set forth in this book about hiring the right people and having the right attorneys in place, there should be no problem with another attorney, depending on the individual's skill set and years of experience, working on the client's case and even having client contact. Over time, the main partners in a law office must introduce other senior associates and income partners to the client, and the client needs to know that there is a continuity of service at the law firm for the benefit of the client. Once the founding partner and any other charismatic, dynamic partner subordinate their interest to the firm, the firm has become the business that clients want to hire. This is a critically important element of building a top law firm.

How do you do it?

The first step is always meeting with new clients with another associate attorney in the initial meeting and for the associate attorney to take copious notes at the meeting and learn the senior attorneys' styles with respect to interviewing clients. At the same time, make sure the client knows that if the firm has questions on his or her matter, the associate attorney in the meeting will be calling him or her for the answers. When this happens, the client already knows two names in the law firm that he or she can call upon in an emergency. As bigger clients come in and as skill sets are developed in the law office between particular practice groups—for example, it is only natural that the employment law lawyer will handle employment law issues for the client and a litigation lawyer will handle the litigation issues for the client. The client may still have you, the founding partner, as a relationship manager, but over time, perhaps over many, many years, the client will understand that systems are put in place at the law office to provide the best possible services to the client and that the client will not be dependent on just you, the founding partner, for top-level services.

Another thing that the founding partner should feel comfortable in doing over time is admitting freely to clients that there is another attorney in the office who is better suited to answer their questions on certain specific matters of substantive law. It is actually a firm enhancement for the relationship manager to say to a client, "Let me ask my partner, John, about that copyright question because he handles the intellectual property (IP) legal issues in our office." Then, as a matter of introducing another lawyer to the client, the relationship manager will ask John to call the client and engage him or her in a conversation regarding the facts and issues of the matter. Again, in this way the client is introduced to a further specialty of the firm, and the firm is enhanced with respect to the continuity of services it can provide to the client.

In short, you have successfully grown a business that truly is a business and not just a collection of well-known or popular attorneys, giving you options with respect to transferring or transitioning the law office business to existing attorneys, family members, or an outside law office.

> Make sure the client knows that if the firm has questions on his or her matter, the associate attorney in the meeting will be calling him or her for the answers.

Options

There are basically four ways to consider transferring ownership of your business for purposes of a sale or retirement: sell to colleagues, sell to a third party, liquidate the business and move, or sell to family members.

The first way, as alluded to previously, is the sale to existing employees, specifically, to your key attorneys. This is the best and most obvious way to transfer ownership because, internally speaking, your key attorneys are the best suited to take over your business. On a more macro view, that is the standard law office model. As attorneys come up through the ranks, after certain levels of qualifications and vetting through the alignment process, they become income partners and ultimately have the opportunity to buy in to the business as equity partners.

Unfortunately, in the legal profession there are no employee stock ownership plans (ESOPs) available that are favorable under the federal tax laws such as a qualified ESOP plan. Therefore, the sale needs to be completed on a contractual basis with your qualified senior associates and income partners. The obvious advantages are these:

- The income partner has learned under your tutelage and has grown under your systems, and he or she has adopted your systems and firm culture;
- You have a time period when you can work with the income partners to negotiate a buyout agreement that suits both parties;
- You are able to analyze and vet the funding mechanism for the purchase with the existing income partner;
- You will maintain control and a majority interest during the transition period;
- The purchaser is culturally prequalified through on-the-job training and observation;
- It somewhat ensures, presumptively, that all existing employees will stay in place and no one will lose his or her job during the transition; and
- Sales to existing attorneys lend themselves to a slow selldown, which benefits the business, clients, and you, the founding partner.[2]

The disadvantages may be:

- The funding mechanism for the business purchase;
- An unfavorable earn-out that may come after the sale or partial sale to the income partner;
- Affordability because if you wait too long, it may be prohibitively expensive for the income partner to buy in.

The second option is a sale to a third party. As you may know, the marketability of law offices is very limited in most jurisdictions in the Unites States. This is just a reality, and the transitioning and mergers of law offices and the absorption of law offices into bigger firms is somewhat rare. The larger firms have a mindset of "their type of attorneys," and your smaller law office may not fit into their purported culture. Rarely does the big law firm cash out the owner of the small law firm. A buyout is usually based on the continuity of clients staying with a large law firm and ultimately the firm paying you, the founding member, based on an earn-out of future revenues from those clients.

At the large firm, you may have little or no input as to your billing rate and billing goals, and therefore your clients may see an increase in legal fees for the same attorneys working on their matters. Being realistic, the large law firm does not want to pay you for your law office; the larger law firm believes that the only assets you are bringing over are

---

2. JOHN H. BROWN, HOW TO RUN YOUR BUSINESS SO YOU CAN LEAVE IT IN STYLE, 4TH ED. 96 (Business Enterprise Press 2003).

your clients, and there are no guarantees that the clients will stay with you. The large law office will not pay for your present cash flows because of the unknown nature of the loyalty and portability of your clients. As a result, even the earn-out portion of the buyout from a larger law firm is risky.

This is an important business element that needs to be understood. A law firm, unlike an accounting firm, is not known for having annuity work. The work done by lawyers is generally project based. The only annuity that comes from an attorney's work is derived from doing great work for the client, developing that client loyalty by aligning with their *why*, and relying on that client to come back and hire you for other matters. Somewhat in contrast, accountants have ongoing financial work that needs to be completed and delivered monthly for their clients. If all goes well, the accountant's ongoing work rolls into the following year, and the following year after that, and becomes ongoing annuity of work for them. For that reason, the repeat work from the same client is more reliable for accountants and, as such, calculable, so the purchaser of an accounting practice is more likely to pay a multiple of the cash flows for the accounting practice. The same can be said for certain medical practices and dental practices. Because of the renewal-type of work that dentists provide for their patients, it is repeatable, reliable, and, as such, calculable.

So therefore, the transferability of law offices and the sale of law offices to other larger firms is very unlikely because of the unreliability of the annuity and repeatable work from the firm's clients. This is also true for the corporate work you do for your clients. Although it appears that ongoing business work for corporate clients provides predictable revenue, even this type of repeatable work is not considered annuity work to a prospective buyer.

The third option is the liquidation and migration to another law office. This is a very common transition for a senior lawyer looking to retire with no succession plan in place. The lawyer can take his or her small- or medium-sized law firm, transition the law firm (and thus the clients) to another law office *without* seeking payment for that movement, dissolve the existing law office, and then get paid from the new law office based on the retainage and billing of the dissolving law office's existing clients. These transitions can be very fruitful and successful for the retiring attorney if negotiated properly. Usually, a neutral third-party advisor or a consultant comes in to negotiate for the transitioning law firm.

The best deals can be made for the transitioning retiring attorney if the liquidating law firm has systems in place to keep a continuing flow of young, vibrant clients coming forward. If the existing clients of the liquidating law firm are all elderly businesses, with no succession plan of their own, there is not much value for the purchasing firm. Why adopt the retiring partner's practice and pay very much for the value of the annuity for the existing retiring client base?

The fourth path to leaving your business is transferring the ownership of the law office to your family members, usually your children. Such transfer has a warm, comforting feeling to it with respect to fulfilling a personal goal of keeping the business and family together, and one can view such transition as a way to maintain the financial well-being for younger family members who are unable to earn a comparable income at outside law firms. Further, it will allow you to stay active in your business as an "of counsel" mentor to your children, provide you additional control over your departure date, and provide more control over how much and when you, the founding partner, will get paid for your interest in the business.[3]

Notwithstanding some of the first-blush advantages of such a pleasant transition, it is replete with disadvantages.[4] Those disadvantages may include these:

- There is great potential to create or increase family discord and feelings of unequal treatment among siblings;
- The normal objective of treating all children equally is difficult to achieve because the one child who will eventually run or own the law firm may come at the perceived expense of the others;
- Children usually pay parents with an earn-out over time, not cash up front;
- The founding partner's financial security is normally diminished rather than enhanced because many businesses suffer when they are transferred to family members who either cannot or will not run the business properly; and
- Family dynamics usually diminish the owner's control over the business and its operations rather significantly, thus increasing rather than diminishing the owner's level of personal stress and anxiety.[5]

Passing along a family business to children *and* having the children pay for that equity in the business will add, not reduce, stress for you, the matriarch or patriarch. Now, even in retirement, there will be an implicit responsibility of you to transition a successful business to your children, even if they fail to run it properly and it ultimately fails on their watch. They will not view it as a personal failure; they will view it as "Dad sold us a dying law firm!" Why do it? You built up the business, provided a great lifestyle for you and your spouse, and also provided a wonderful lifestyle for your children. Why put yourself in a position for being responsible for the economic growth of their law firm after you retire? Technically and legally you are not, but emotionally you are.

An even worse idea is to transfer the business to the children and have them pay you out over time based on the success of the law office (i.e., a postclosing earn-out). Time and time again, those earn-out payments fail to come to the retired parent, tensions mount,

3. RICHARD E. JACKIM & PETER G. CHRISTMAN, THE $10 TRILLION OPPORTUNITY 118 (R. Jackim & Company 2005).
4. JOHN H. BROWN, HOW TO RUN YOUR BUSINESS SO YOU CAN LEAVE IT IN STYLE, 4TH ED. 95 (Business Enterprise Press 2003).
5. RICHARD E. JACKIM & PETER G. CHRISTMAN, THE $10 TRILLION OPPORTUNITY 118 (R. Jackim & Company 2005).

family loyalties divide, and ultimately this arrangement does far more harm to the family than good.

Should your children even be working with you?

For many individuals in any profession, starting a business that is owned by the first-generation founder tends to be referred to as a family business without good reason. In the law office model, there is a chance that children or other family members may want to go to law school and want to work in your law office. You need time to think whether that trajectory is consistent with the strategy outlined in this book.

Striving to become the top law firm in your market requires hiring the best people and putting them in places to succeed. Any family member seeking employment in the law office needs to be treated much like any other new hire. In reality, a family member would jump to the front of the line when it comes to law clerking while he or she is in law school and potentially even get preference as a third-year clerk or summer associate. However, these advantages do not mean the family member should automatically and presumptively be hired right out of law school; indeed, *under no circumstances* should the family member be given any management authority in the company as a new associate.

In practical terms, does someone coming right out of law school in their midtwenties have the skill set to leapfrog through the five tools necessary to be an equity partner in the business? What would happen to the morale and culture of the firm if, for example, your family member were given authority over an

> *Under no circumstances* should the family member be given any management authority in the company as a new associate.

attorney who has been practicing law for twenty-five years? As you can see, that would be a nonsensical pattern of growth that would do more harm to the law office than it would do good. However, if a young person who is related to an existing owner of the business comes up through the ranks and works hard, starting from the ground floor and building his or her way up, that young person thereby *enhances* the culture of the firm, the firm's commitment to its culture, and the belief in training and acculturating young people into the values of the firm.

After you consider these ideas regarding family members, specifically children, joining the law firm, the best policy is to make it known very early in the child's admission to law school that he or she will have to work at another law firm or government agency for two years after graduation. That work experience only enhances the ability and skill sets that the family member will bring to your firm if that opportunity arises.

This policy accomplishes two things. First, it takes the pressure off the founding partner, or off the existing partners at the time, from having to have a job that matches the skill sets and career goals of the child. The second benefit is that the child will learn different ways of doing things while managed by other attorneys and partners and so can actually bring something to enhance your firm when he or she joins. As you know, the first few years of practicing law are difficult, and certain missteps by young attorneys are likely to occur. Encouraging law work experience outside your firm is the absolute best policy for children in law school.

What you are attempting to build is not a small family business that will be opened and operated by family members from generation to generation.

Would Walmart be Walmart if Sam Walton just put his family members ahead of everyone else as officers of the corporation? We could discuss that rhetorical question with every successful business in the country. The answer is generally no; these businesses generally grew because they had the best people in the most critical positions during the growth cycle of the company.

Same with you. You need to constantly look to elevate the finest people who are aligned with your values and your culture to carry the company message forward even after your retirement.

This business was never intended to be a small, family-run enterprise. It is intended to be absolutely the finest and best law office in its market, with specific plans to upset the market with its innovative view on delivering client services. When a law firm delivers on those goals, the law firm will undoubtedly grow and continue to expand by virtue of client demands.

Why Sell Off at All?

One obvious consideration that cannot be minimized is the decision to sell equity in the law firm. The purpose behind this book is to do more than just teach a young attorney or group of attorneys how to build a successful law practice. It is also to teach the founding partner how to build a great, successful law practice, but then, through level 5 leadership, not allow it to dissipate upon his or her retirement. The whole premise of this book is to build an enduring, stand-alone business that will continue to grow and transition from generation to generation of leaders. However, a logical conclusion can be made for a completely opposite strategy. Arguably, the founding partner may decide not to sell off equity interest in the law firm at all, but instead just manage the law firm into retirement.

The advantages of that strategy are, of course, that as profits of the business continue to increase, the profits will remain with the founding partner and will not need to be shared with any other equity partners. After all, cynically you could believe that the equity partners who bought in are repaying their loans over the course of three to seven years with profits that would otherwise be the founding partner's profits. Some founding partners have been known to say, "Why should I let them purchase equity in my law firm with *my* profits?"

This question is logical but shortsighted, considering what you are trying to build. The disadvantages of avoiding a sellout and keeping 100% interest in the law firm until the retirement date are many.

First, if it became known to every associate in the law office early on in his or her career that there is no hope for true partnership status or ownership, you greatly increase the chance of highly talented associates leaving the office. They want to eventually own a law office and be in control, and you are thwarting that ability for them by making it known that there is no equity plan in the law office. The probability of disruption and defection by talented, qualified associates is very high.

Second, the question is very shortsighted because if you have, in fact, built up a large, successful law practice and you dissolve it for retirement by allowing it to disintegrate, you allow associates to scatter. This leaves clients to find other law offices, meaning all you have done is built a job for yourself for the last thirty-plus years. You have not built a business because if you had, you would have something to sell. Building a business to provide you a satisfying career and a comfortable lifestyle is an acceptable end in and of itself, of course. No doubt about it, your life's work under such circumstances is not irrelevant, and your colleagues, clients, and family have benefited by your efforts. However, you are losing the opportunity to get real value for the architecture that you have created, known as your law office. Largely for this reason and this reason alone, the ability to obtain value for the infrastructure created for your law office is quite favorable.

> If it became known to every associate in the law office early on in his or her career that there is no hope for true partnership status or ownership, you greatly increase the chance of highly talented associates leaving the office.

Finally, keep in mind everything that was accomplished after your practicing law for thirty or forty years. Clients have become loyal; those same clients may have second-generation management people who also know and rely on your firm, thus giving a greater annuity effect to the services that you provide. You have a well-established set of referral sources. All of those get broken up and taken by the associates if the law office dissipates as associates scatter to other law firms or establish their own small practices. The whole of the law firm that you built that is now in the wind-down stage has had greater value than the sum of its parts. Without the proper transition to your income partners, the value of the whole becomes diminished to zero.

In summary, the value of the sell-off to the income partners over time is twofold. First, it keeps the structure, culture, and architecture of the firm in place to continue to grow and gain market share so that you can leave behind a legacy of a great law firm. Second, it is the only realistic way for you to get value out of the business that you have built. Otherwise, you have been working the last thirty or forty years simply to maintain a job, albeit a great one.

Remember, the goal of this book has always been to show you how to build a winning, successful law firm. It is not to show you how to build the world's greatest job for the founding partner, all to be lost upon the founder's retirement.

This goal should not be understated. It would be a tragedy to spend your entire career building up a law firm only to see it wither away upon your retirement. There are excellent people who have been trained into a system that works, there are clients who have been obtained who would otherwise be without experienced legal counsel, there are contacts that you have developed that are of great value as excellent referral sources that count on your firm, and there is the goodwill of your organization in your community. Your firm, everything you built up, has great value and is greatly needed by your clients, employees, referral sources, and community.

Why throw it all away with retirement?

Probably at this stage, you will have built something that you recognize as bigger and more significant than your job that needs to have an opportunity to be transitioned to the next generation, and then to the next generation, and then in perpetuity. This transitioning can be done only with a good, rock-solid succession plan with a level 5 leader who transitions the firm and its management team with subsequent owners.

Consider all of the factors when allowing the law office to succeed after you retire.

Buy-in and Sell-off Cycle

You will ultimately come to the conclusion that there is a cycle by which the growth of an attorney follows, either with intent or inadvertently, and within a five-year tolerance. This is what you will find:

- *Ages twenty–twenty-nine.* The twenties are the years for education. Attorneys will go through undergrad and law school in their twenties, possibly graduating law school as early as twenty-five; but with some life experiences, career choices, and other educational and career bumps in the road, most lawyers come out of law school in their late twenties. That is no problem and, quite honestly, should be expected. Attorneys coming out of law school later in their twenties have had some other career experiences and opportunities, some real-world business experience, or some other postgraduate work that makes them an even more appealing candidate as an associate for your law office. Keep in mind that as long as your candidate has been doing something, almost anything, through his or her twenties, it is probably positive with respect to the skill sets the candidate needs to be an attorney. Whether candidates are working in the mall or working construction, they are getting real-world experience dealing with people and learning how to talk that particular industry's language. Perhaps they have gone to graduate school for accounting, business administration, advanced degrees in English or the sciences, all of which will make them a better attorney and prepare them for dealing with people over the course of their career.

- *Ages thirty to thirty-nine.* While an attorney is in his or her thirties, the attorney's focus is on honing his or her skill as an attorney. As stated earlier, the cycle to become a partner in a law firm usually covers ten years. So whether you are just starting your own practice at this stage or are an associate looking to join a firm, this period is all about honing your craft. You came out of law school, started your practice, and now in your thirties have an opportunity to become an expert in a practice area.[6] You need to go from good to great in that particular practice area.

- *Ages forty to forty-nine.* When you are in your forties, you want to be a buyer if you are an associate or from a business standpoint building equity if you are building a law firm. Of course, you will have been doing all of those things as you have been growing your practice for the first ten years. In your forties is the time that you pass the threshold of the various ways that typical small law offices fail; it is the time to begin to achieve the value that you desire in your successful law office. For the associates in the law office, the forties are the years that they will want to buy into the practice because they will have established their families, have owned a home for many years, and are now able to undertake a financial commitment necessary to buy into the practice.

- *Ages fifty to fifty-nine.* At this point in time, you need to consider being a seller of your interests. Does it seem too early? Somewhat, but you cannot wait until you are sixty because then your transition period will be shortened. Why would someone buy an interest in your business when you are sixty years old, or older, and may be looking at retiring soon, at which time your clients, systems, and employees will become available (for free) anyway. Selling in your fifties, whether you are the founding partner or a subsequent equity partner, is the ultimate time to act for purposes of maximizing value and continue to build on the culture and the big audacious goals set forth in your business plan.

---

6. Not as defined by the ABA, but as a practical matter, "expert," as used here, means a high-level attorney in a very focused practice area.

After you analyze the buy-in and sell-off cycle for you personally, one way or another, you will be within five years of the above estimations. You may determine that all new attorneys start at twenty-five and that their investment and expertise of the law is between age twenty-six and thirty-five, or you may determine that the sell-off period begins at age fifty-five and should go through age sixty-five. One way or another, you will be within five years of the aforementioned cycle.

That cycle is important on several levels. First, it gives you a forward-looking timetable for the creation of value for the law firm. It gives you a realistic goal—a timetable to put your plan into action, implement your culture, train people, and build your winning law firm.

In addition, when discussed openly in a transparent fashion with your attorneys, the timetable allows the attorneys to know your plan. Senior associates and income partners will not stay with the program if they do not know what the long-term plan is. If they believe there is a plan that includes them and that would include their investment of time and money into a firm that is growing, they will remain in place and support your system.

Last, with the system being in place, it stabilizes nonattorney employees, who realize that everyone's job is not lost when the founding partner retires or quits.

Ownership Enquiries

You hope that with senior associates and income partners, there will be inquiries initiated as to the equity opportunities with the firm. There should be open dialogue as to these opportunities on a regular basis. Keep the dialogue open and be a good listener. When those questions arise, ask your senior associates and income partners what their expectations are and how they would like to see the business transitioned. Are they willing to buy in? Do they expect the equity for free? Do they have a bank that would help finance the purchase? Do they have equity to pledge as collateral for the financing of their purchase? Are they willing to take a deduction on their W-2 income to pay for their equity purchase?

Aside from the whole issue on valuation of the law firm, begin to gather information on the associates' expectations to see if they align with your expectations. Throughout these inquiries, note that this is not a formal negotiation, but a sincere sharing of ideas, so that everyone understands each other's position.

The senior associates and income partners are inquiring because they do enjoy the culture of the law firm, admire what has been built through the firm's architecture, and *want in*. This should all be good news and viewed very positively. Remember, the only people you may be competing against within this negotiation are the associates leaving to start their own law office. That happens quite often in law firms, and that real possibility needs to be considered in your dialogue.

While there are probably many reasons why groups of associates team up to leave a law office—though some may leave individually just for a different job—your real concern is treating everyone fairly and honestly. It is true that the associates may be considering to move outside the office, but they would not engage you in these conversations if that was their preference. Their preferred place to practice law is within your structure and on your platform for a winning law firm. They recognize that the law firm you built is successful and that the infrastructure is in place to continue growing and to continue to be profitable while playing a significant role in your community. All of those inquiries are a positive with respect to an equity plan for the law office.

Chapter 34

What Are You Really Selling?
The Valuation Analysis

If you are lucky enough to have partners willing to buy in, the question becomes, what are you really selling? and, how much will they pay?

A law office does not have much in the way of valuable tangible assets. Used furniture, no doubt you learned when you were shopping for it, does not have a great deal of value, and used computers are virtually obsolete in a little over a year. Many people believe the next generation looking to buy in is purchasing the receivables of the operation. That makes some sense on a certain level because the receivables were earned during a time when you were sole owner. Now in order to share them, somebody should really purchase a share of those receivables. However, that approach is very short-sighted because the receivables are a static number, and the going-concern value for the business is far greater than some portion of the receivables because it considers future cash flow.

Keep in mind for purposes of the discussion on selling off interests of the business to a buy-in partner, we are talking about a stock sale, or interest sale, of the owner's personal stock of the corporation (or interest in a limited liability company) to the buy-in partner. It is important to understand the difference between a stock sale and an asset sale.

As law books explain, when purchasing a business outright, it is preferable for the buyer to purchase the assets of the business and not the stock of the shareholders because then the purchaser is not taking on any of the liabilities of the existing corporation or limited liability company. However, in this case, other than a complete restructuring and moving the assets, client files, libraries, and software into a newly formed entity, law office succession transactions are merely the sale of owners' stock in the corporation to the new buy-in partners. As stated earlier, the true asset values are very low in a law office, and the purchaser is really buying an income statement more so than the balance sheet of the law office. Thus, a sale of stock to the buy-in partner is appropriate. The level of due diligence required by the buy-in partner will be addressed subsequently in this section of the book, but keep in mind that the discussion is on stock sales.

Review of any business valuation book would tell you that in the service business, the value of the business is some multiple of the company's earnings before interest, taxes, depreciation, and amortization (EBITDA) and as such is really a function of cash flows. While this is an accountant-intensive calculation, the conveyance here is that the company is worth some factor of its profitability. If all the cash in the business is being distributed as W-2 income to all the workers, including you, there is no profit and there is nothing to sell. The operation you created was simply a job for you and your coworkers. It is true that everything stated earlier about culture, clients, contacts, referral sources, and continuity of clients has been built up by you throughout the life of a law office and has value, but in reality, if everyone is just living off W-2 income, there is no profit, and as a result there is nothing to sell. If you have W-2 income that is so high that it eliminates any profits and you do not plan on lowering your W-2 income, you again have nothing to sell.

As such, my guess is that your focus on creating profit never mattered much because you have swept the accounts and taken money out of the business accounts either as a draw, as payroll, or as a distribution from the business.

> The true asset values are very low in a law office, and the purchaser is really buying an income statement more so than the balance sheet of the law office. Thus, a sale of stock to the buy-in partner is appropriate.

Since we are talking about a transition period to the law office's new owners, the treatment of your income needs to be analyzed. Take, for example, your law office that exists with you and five other attorneys, whereby each of the attorneys earns $150,000 a year of W-2 income (base salary and all bonuses) totaling $750,000 in payroll, and you pay yourself $250,000 a year in salary, with an additional $150,000 a year as after-tax profits. Therefore, the total attorney payroll is $1,000,000 ($750,000 for the five associates and $250,000 for you), and $150,000 in profit. The total owner's benefit is $400,000: $250,000 in W-2 income and $150,000 in profit distributions.

Shifting around the associates' salary or bonus structure should not be considered as your plan is in place, and it is a good one. It does not need to be changed in any fashion with respect to your associates, even your buy-in income partner.

The focus here is on *your* total compensation package from the organization. You earn a total of $400,000 from the corporation. If you are operating as an S corporation (as previously recommended) or as another flow-through tax entity, such as a limited liability company, you have to pay tax every year on your profit.

If you left payroll as it is, the $150,000 of profit[1] would be the cash flow that you use to determine the value of the company. Now, if you reduce your salary to $200,000, the profit of the company is $200,000—the difference between $400,000 of owner's benefit and your W-2 income of $200,000 adjusted salary. Multiplying the $200,000 of profit by some factor increases the value of the company. Obviously, if you brought your salary down to nothing, the value of the company would be some multiple of $400,000, and you would have greatly enhanced the value of the company, but doing that is not realistic because in an arm's-length transaction, you would not work for free. Your W-2 income has to be reflective of the value you bring to the company as an employee.

One final note on the cash-flow analysis that you perform in anticipation of selling to the buy-in partner. Because you always have to use historical real data for the valuation analysis, you will be using the previous year's data to create a formula to sell to the buy-in partner in year 1. Specifically, if you anticipate the buy-in date to be January 1, you will be using the data from the previous calendar year. This is important to understand because if the law firm is growing, the best-case scenario for the buy-in partner is that in using the previous year's financial data, at the end of the year that the partner buys in, he or she will have realized a profit and benefit because the cash-flow numbers should be better in the buy-in year than the previous year.

What Is Your Correct Salary?

A fundamental question that has to be answered as you try to restate the profit for the company to give the law office value is, how much W-2 income should you earn? It is a time of great objectivity and will be a time of great transparency as you discuss these issues with the buy-in partner. You know what the buy-in partner earns in W-2 income, but he or she does not know what you earn. So, therefore, there is a great deal of sensitivity to how you handle this very fundamental issue. Keep in mind that before this analysis, these issues did not really matter to you much at all, other than in your first meetings with your accountant that dealt with the way to set your salary in a tax-efficient manner. This issue is slightly different, because although you still need to follow the rules of the Internal Revenue Code, the analysis here considers the value you bring to the law office, that is, to the other associates. Factors to consider include these:

- What level of expertise do you have in particular substantive areas of the law?
- How big is that practice group in the law office?

---

1. I refer to the profit from the law office somewhat interchangeably with EBIDTA. Although there is some interest, taxes, and depreciation, in a law office, you will see that the actual dollars out are more meaningful to associates buying in than to an accounting function such as EBITDA.

- How many areas of the law office do you manage?
- Are you the creative force behind various marketing initiatives?
- Are you the problem solver of the miscellaneous issues that come up in the law office?
- Do you make the final decisions on discretionary calls on cases?
- Do you make the final decisions on large technology purchases?
- How many practice groups has your buy-in partner passed you up on?
- How many practice groups do you manage?
- Will you continue to manage the financial aspects of the firm?
- What is the entrepreneurial risk premium (discussed later)?

These are a series of questions that need to be vetted for you to set your W-2 income. Your income needs to be rationally related to the issues set forth above so that when there is a disclosure to the buy-in partner, he or she will understand the disparity in wages, if there is one.

> A critically important factor that will be embedded in your wages that will separate you from the buy-in partner for a long time is the entrepreneurial risk premium that you took by starting the practice, a risk that your buy-in partner never took.

A critically important factor that will be embedded in your wages that will separate you from the buy-in partner for a long time is the entrepreneurial risk premium that you took by starting the practice, a risk that your buy-in partner never took. He or she came to the practice, most likely at least nine or ten years ago, and had a (somewhat) guaranteed W-2 income. This W-2 income is something you did not have when you started the practice, and therefore added to your salary is an entrepreneurial risk premium that should allow you to earn more through your retirement because of the risk that you took in starting the business. You can also factor in all of the systems that were created by you (with others' help, of course) in building the infrastructure for your successful and winning law firm.

When will the entrepreneurial risk premium go away? It may be lessened over time, but it goes away only when you retire—which makes sense. At that point in time, you, the founding partner, will be out of the picture, and the entrepreneurial risk premium will then be distributed to the equity partners.

The entrepreneurial risk premium cannot be tacked on to the profit portion of your distributions and your economic benefits from your law firm. It cannot be done that way because those profits will eventually be distributed to each and every subsequent purchaser of the business and will eventually be purchased away.

Once an objective analysis has been put into your W-2 income versus the buy-in partner's W-2 income, it must pass all of the objectivity tests that go to the fundamental fairness of the following question: "In your capacity as an attorney and partner in the law firm, what should be your proper salary?" Again, if there is a different managing partner, viewing your law office and reviewing the work you do for the law office, someone who acts both as a manager working *on* the business and as an attorney working *in* the business, what is proper salary to pay you? Once that is determined, the remaining portion of the available cash is the profit of the entity that will be worked into the valuation formula.

What Is Your Valuation Formula?

Do not overanalyze or become a victim of paralysis by analysis on the various valuation formulas you can use to value the law practice. The various valuation formulas include the fair market–value analysis, the investment-value analysis, liquidation-value analysis, and a lender's valuation. There are other formulas such as insurable value and hybrids, which do not apply in this case.

The fair market value analysis is defined as a hypothetical price a willing buyer and a willing seller, with mutual knowledge of all relevant facts and not acting under any compulsion, would agree on for the company.[2] The fair market value is usually used in IRS analysis and is distinguished from market value that is a result of an actual sale. The fair market value is a little bit more theoretical, but it is a formula that you will use for your law office as you negotiate with your buy-in partner or partners and that, once consummated, will be the *market value.*

The investment value does not apply, but it is the value of the company to a specific investor for such investor's investment requirements and expectations.[3]

Liquidation value is simply based on the assumption that the business is worth more dead than alive.[4] Liquidation value of the law firm is a de minimis, since you cannot really sell client files, and the value of the library, receivables, and computers and office equipment is de minimis. Sometimes, in a personal injury firm, there may be legal work put into a queue of cases that are transferred to another personal injury law firm. In this instance, the courts would eventually award the liquidating law firm some amount of the settlement and judgment for the work the firm did on the case.

In our fair market approach, you can look at industry rules of thumb (very little exists for small or medium law firms), discounted cash flow, or comparable transaction analysis.[5]

---

2. Richard E. Jackim & Peter G. Christman, The $10 Trillion Opportunity 103 (R. Jackim & Company 2005).
   3. *Id.* at 103.
   4. *Id.*
   5. *Id.*

The best system is a variation of the fair market–value analysis using discounted future cash flows.

Some number, such as profits, needs to be multiplied by a factor to determine the going concern value of the law office. This is a reliable way to discount the future cash flows of the business. First, to determine the profit portion of the formula, please consider an accounting analysis of your financials that would yield the EBITDA. As an alternative, look at the net taxable income and the after-tax income, or simply look at the amount of money you would be able to take out of the business after you adjusted your W-2 income as suggested here. The amount of profit you pull out of the business after your W-2 income will be called *cash-out*.

These various methods of viewing cash flows of the business are all legitimate and are all fair game for your calculation of the going concern value. Note that there is not a real discussion on book value of assets, or asset values (which would include accounts receivable), for reasons set forth above. A law office's value is simply not connected to its assets; rather, it is more finely connected to its cash flows.

> If the purchaser is really trying to calculate the benefits that he or she will receive after investing in the law office, the thing that matters the most to the purchaser is how much cash he or she will get out of the investment.

After you discuss the various methods of calculating your cash flows with your accountant, you will see the potential for understatement or, in some cases, overstatement in the EBITDA calculations, the net taxable income, or the after-tax income of the business. The only thing that is simple enough and ascertainable enough to rely on with your buy-in partner is a cash-out. What else matters? If the purchaser is really trying to calculate the benefits that he or she will receive after investing in the law office, the thing that matters the most to the purchaser is how much cash he or she will get out of the investment. What could be more fundamental and more simple?

So, therefore, if you took a look at the previous year's tax return for the law office, added your W-2 income with the amount in the draws you took out (disregarding the taxable income portion of the tax return for now), you would determine your entire owner's benefits from the business. Then, after adjusting your W-2 income based on the discussion above, you would have your cash-out for the previous year.

Next, no matter what method you use to ascertain your cash flow from the previous year, you then need to multiply that cash flow, or cash-out, by a factor that is reflective of the legal profession. That factor will most likely be somewhere between 4 and 6. The more reliant the law office is on one or very few clients, the lower the factor should be, and therefore the lower the value of the law office. The more diversified the law office clients are (both in industry and a reduced concentration of work from one client), the higher the multiple should be. So, therefore, going back to our earlier example, if the law office had $200,000 in cash-out for the previous year, and you use a factor of 5, the law office's value is $1,000,000. Using a factor of 6, the law office's value is $1,200,000.

As you can see, the interplay between your W-2 income and the owner's total benefits is a driver for the value of the business. If, at the end of the year, there are no profits for the law office, there is nothing to be distributed after reasonable W-2 incomes are paid; then, I would submit, the business has little or no value and no one would really buy in to the practice.

The ideas set forth in this chapter are intended to plant a seed in the young entrepreneur's head about having realistic expectations of W-2 income and profit.

All too often with haphazard and sloppy accounting, a gray area is developed between profit distributions and W-2 income, which is reflective of bad bookkeeping, bad record keeping, and a lack of discipline required by the founding partner to run the accounting department of the law office as a serious business.

Young attorneys, coupled with aggressive accountants, sometimes do the opposite. They will artificially deflate their W-2 income in order to avoid the FICA taxes and take the rest out as profit distribution and just pay ordinary income tax on the profits of the business.[6] While this W-2 income manipulation probably cannot be justified under the Internal Revenue Code, attorneys and aggressive accountants may engage in this technique to save on FICA taxes. Going forward with this suppressed W-2 income, you would increase the value of the business under the calculation formula set forth above, but it is not practical to do so because you, as the founding partner, would not go forward with selling your interests in the business at a largely suppressed W-2 income. Keep in mind the long-term sell-off. Over time, as you sell off interests in the law firm, you will not receive the same profit distribution on a quarterly or annual basis and yet your W-2 income would be artificially suppressed because of the tax play you made early in your career.

Similar to my example above of adjusting your W-2 income to a level that is fairly reflective of what value you bring to the law office compared to the income partners, you need to adjust your W-2 income, possibly upward, pay more FICA tax on that increase, and realize that it is the right way to handle the transition with your buy-in partner.

Early on in the business's development, the disciplines need to be put in place in terms of what is a fair W-2 income and reasonable profit distributions. Your accountant should be involved in these decision-making processes and, for tax-planning and tax-driven reasons, the accountant will weigh in and advise you in terms of what is best for you as the business is in its growth cycle. But make no mistake about it, when the time comes to start selling portions of the business to buy-in partners, it is not about the most efficient

---

6. This strategy is used for S corporations and limited liability companies.

tax planning for you personally; it is about the most realistic way to look at this business and selling interests in the business. It needs to be fair, transparent, and legitimate.

What Does This Valuation Matrix Mean to You?

The valuation matrix set forth above (i.e., determining the cash flows of the firm and multiplying by a factor) means that you are trading future cash flows for present buy-in amounts. If you calculate the profit of the firm at $200,000 a year, for example, and you multiply that cash flow by a multiple of 5, you are basically asking the income partner to pay you in advance for the next five years of profits that the firm will earn. If the firm continues to be successful, in the sixth, seventh, and eighth year (which you hope it will), the buy-in partner has bought in at a great profit and will own that cash flow for the rest of his or her life and the life of the firm.

Moreover, and again with a growing business such as yours, it should be a certainty that the income partner buys in at the year 1 cash flow, but as cash flows increase, he or she gets the benefit of the increase in perpetuity, and you do not. You have lost out on those future cash flows for the present value of five years of cash flows, assuming they are not increasing.

> This valuation model allows you to take money up front from the purchaser, money that you would otherwise earn over the next five years.

Is the income partner paying you for the purchases of the business with your own money? Not at all. The income partner has to find his or her own funding source (discussed later in Chapter 36) in order to buy in, and then he or she has to repay the funding source over the next four, five, or six years.

This valuation model allows you to take money up front from the purchaser, money that you would otherwise earn over the next five years. Moreover, you should invest that money and put it to work for you immediately. If the cash flows from the company are multiplied by 3, you would then determine whether that is a fair price to you because the income partner is purchasing only his or her portion of the business for the cash flows for the next three years. Is that enough money to incentivize you to sell?

What if your valuation model took the cash flows of the business and multiplied the cash flows by a factor of 8, thus greatly increasing the value of the business and, as a result, the purchase price? Certainly, the purchase price would be higher, creating a greater incentive for you to sell. It should seem logical that the higher the purchase price, the longer you extrapolate the cash flows into the future, the greater the incentive is for you to sell and get the highest present value of those cash flows in hand today, taking no risks on the portion of the business that you sold going into the future. Said another way, the higher the purchase price, the greater incentive for you to sell.

Keep in mind that initially you will consider selling only small fractional pieces of the law office, perhaps 5% at first; therefore, you are not really mitigating your risk going forward because you still own 95% of the law firm, and the law firm still needs to be successful because a great deal of your income is derived from the 95% of the income flow that you still own. In addition, the law office still needs to be successful because you will eventually still want to sell the remaining 95% of the law office either to the existing income partner or to income partners who will come in the future to buy you out. This is no time to take your foot off the accelerator to slow down the growth of the law office. While it is true that the valuation formula set forth herein creates a funding mechanism for you to take cash out of the business for the entrepreneurial risk you have taken and the systems and mechanisms that you have created, more importantly, it is also true that the valuation formula has created a succession plan and an exit strategy for you. This allows you to transition the business to the next management team and stay involved during the transition to ensure the stability of client services, systems, and employee satisfaction so that no event occurs to trigger an exodus of clients from the firm.

What Does the Valuation Matrix Mean to the Buy-in Partner?

The valuation formula may mean very little to the buy-in partner if the buy-in partner does not have confidence in the law firm after the preliminary due diligence. Expect the buy-in partner to evaluate the firm on the following criteria:

- The attitude and commitment of the founding partner to stay with the firm and continue to grow it;
- The buy-in partner's and the founding partner's family situations;
- The historical performance of the firm;
- The firm's continued commitment to hiring and developing five-tool attorneys;
- The firm's continued commitment to hiring top-quality legal assistants;
- All the measurables including profitability, revenue, new clients on a monthly basis, and client satisfaction;
- The concentration of the top five clients and the percentage of business they represent to the law firm;
- The firm's continued commitment to update technology;
- The number of malpractice or disciplinary grievances filed against the firm or individual attorneys;
- Federal and state tax compliance;

- The midterm economic outlook and how will it affect the various practice groups of the law firm.

After the buy-in partner analyzes the realistic future of the firm and the subsequent due diligence verification of all of the criteria, then, and only then, the buy-in partner will feel comfortable with supporting the valuation formula.

If you do the math and, for example, the buy-in purchaser pays five times cash flows or, as suggested earlier, five times cash-out, the purchaser stands to achieve a dividend of 20% on his or her investment.

If the buy-in partner buys 10% of the business and the profits of the business were $200,000, yielding a value of the firm of $1,000,000 at a multiple of 5, he or she would pay a purchase price of $100,000 (10% of a $1,000,000 valuation). Then, immediately after closing, if the dividend (or cash-out) from the company in the first year is exactly the same, $200,000, the income partner will receive 10% of that cash-out profit, $20,000. Therefore, for a $100,000 investment into the law firm, the first year's dividend is $20,000, or 20%—not bad. The next year, the purchase price is still fixed because the purchase has been closed at $100,000; but if the firm's profits increase 10% at $220,000, the distribution to the 10% equity partner is $22,000 (10% of the profit), and the return on the equity partner's $100,000 investment is now 22% in the second year. Again, a great rate of return for the equity partner.

Assuming the law office increases in profitability 10% per year, the following chart demonstrates the 10% increase over five years:

Year	Amount of Profit	10% Partner Annual Return
Buy-in year	$200,000	$20,000
End of year 1	$220,000	$22,000
End of year 2	$242,000	$24,200
End of year 3	$266,200	$26,620
End of year 4	$292,820	$29,282
End of year 5	$322,102	$32,210

As you can see, at the end of year 5, with the profit being $322,102, the profit distribution to the income partner will be $32,210. The rate of return on his or her $100,000 investment in year 5 will be 32%. That is only half of the good news.

In addition, using the valuation formula set forth above, the firm's profit at year 5 multiplied by a multiple of 5 yields the value of the law firm to be almost $1,600,000; so now, viewed in a vacuum,[7] the income partner's 10% interest in the company is worth $161,000. All of this makes sense and is a great value for the purchasing income partner, so long as the law firm *continues to grow*.

Whether you consider the 10% increase in cash flow per year too high or too low, give great thought to the additional cash flow to the firm just based on an annual increase of the associates' (and partners') hourly rate of $15 an hour. If the associate is billing *and* collecting on 1,500 hours per year, those hours multiplied by an hourly rate increase of $15 an hour yield an additional $22,500 in cash flow to the firm for that year. If the associate is billing *and* collecting on 1,700 hours per year, those hours times a rate increase of $15 an hour yield an increase in cash flow to the firm of $25,500. Take note, because if the associate's year-end raise happens to be about one-half of the increased cash flow from the hourly billable rate, the rest should fall to cash flow for the firm. There are other increases and expenses that will affect this increased cash flow, such as raises that are given to the administrative assistants and support staff or a potential increase in rent, but by and large, there is a certain amount of increased cash flow for the law firm simply by the increase of the billable hour rate for the next year. Of course, the greatest driver of profit for the firm is good, billable, and collectible legal work on client matters managed by more and more attorneys every year. Every additional attorney added by the firm yields an amount of cash flow equal to the attorney's billable rate, multiplied by the hours the attorney bills and collects on for the year, less the attorney's salary, administrative assistant, and other overhead. There is no question that the main driver in value and increased cash flow is the addition of attorneys into a law office. But do not ever minimize the management of a reasonable (not excessive) increase in the hourly rate for the attorney to assist in the bottom-line cash flows of the law office.

> There is no question that the main driver in value and increased cash flow is the addition of attorneys into a law office.

Last, what better place for the income partner to invest money? The income partner could certainly take his or her money and invest it in stock traded on the New York Stock Exchange, and what do you suppose the rate of return on those stocks is? Moreover, the stocks that he or she would invest in have management teams and policies that are not well known to the average investor. Here, in your case, the income partner is investing in a company at five times the earnings, which will yield a rate of return of 20% for his or her investment; in addition, he or she will have a voice in the management of the company

---

7. The eventual sale of the interests by the purchasing income partner becomes a little bit more complicated, but there is no doubt the income partner purchased a tangible asset that has a value and that eventually, when the income partner is in his or her fifties, he or she will be a "seller" and will be selling into the same type of valuation formula that he or she bought into.

and access to all of its financial records, policy-making decisions, and other proprietary information that you would need to make the best possible investment decision with your money. Moreover, the income partner works in the business to ensure its success. At the end of the analysis, the buy-in formula needs to be a win-win for the selling and founding partner and the purchasing income partner.

Discounts and Premiums

Depending on the experience of the attorney reading this chapter, you need to understand that generally when valuing minority interests in businesses, it is appropriate to take minority and marketability discounts.

Minority discount, or lack-of-control discount, is a discount on a minority interest in a business that is valid because the purchaser does not control the corporation or entity. If the buy-in partner purchased only 10% interest in the business, certainly he or she cannot control the business. As a result, it is traditionally fair that after taking a full valuation of the going-concern value of the business, such minority interests can be discounted by some percentage because of the lack of control connected to that 10% ownership.

Similarly, a marketability discount applies when the 10% interest purchased by the buy-in partner cannot be sold in a secondary market.

Both of these discounts, the control discount and the marketability discount, are generally acceptable ways for valuing closely held minority interests. However, in the instant case, once you start to add additional discounting to the purchase price, you're really just tinkering with the business valuation formula. In fact, the buy-in partner is buying in because he or she has faith in the systems and culture you have built and absolutely will defer to the founding partner's management philosophy and techniques because of the history of success of the firm. The buy-in partner cannot possibly take the position that he or she wants to buy into the founding partner's architecture and then expect a discount for the right to buy in. That seems inconsistent with the dynamic of the buy-in partner's standpoint and the founding partner's position.

Extrapolate the problem further. Eventually, there will be a series of buy-in partners, with each partner possibly maximizing his or her interest to 20% or 25%; as a result, you will have fractionalized ownership and *everyone* will be a minority owner in a closely held business with limited transferability rights. As a result, all of the interests will be discounted—and if that were the case, is that not just an adjustment on the valuation formula?

The inverse argument for the minority and lack of marketability discounts is a control premium for which the founding partner may or may not ever qualify. A control premium is value to a 51% or greater shareholder who maintains the ability to:

- Hire or fire attorneys and managers;
- Establish and change company policy;
- Acquire or sell assets;
- Approve or reject merger plans;
- Determine salaries of employees;
- Control dividend payments and distributions; and
- Liquidate the business.[8]

In all likelihood, even though the sell-off will go slowly and the founding partner will retain more than 50% of the shares for several years, he or she does not want to come across as the controlling shareholder to anyone. The founding partner will continue to be the leader of the firm, but with a well-placed management team. Although the founding partner may legally have the right to exercise the control issues articulated above, he or she will not want to exercise too much authority in the firm but will, rather, participate as a member of the management team. As such, the plan articulated here is not to attach a control premium to the founding partner's interests at the time he or she sells down below 50%. Similar to the position on the unnecessary analysis on minority and marketability discounts, the control premium has little meaning in the law office slow sell-off.

Depending on your conclusion, your valuation formula needs to be either increased or adjusted in some fashion to give consideration to the minority and marketability discounts, as well as to the control premiums. If you concede that eventually all shares being transferred from senior partners to new buy-in partners are all minority interests, all transfers just need to be made at some formula that pleases both the seller and the buyer.

Suffice it to say that the original formula was built upon the founding partner's desire to sell at a multiple of cash flows he or she found appealing, and the buy-in partner (and all partners to follow) agrees that this formula is fair and reasonable.

The Unspoken Dark Side

The most unspoken conversation had among small business owners and among professional service providers such as accountants, lawyers, and insurance professionals is about the false tax advantages of owning your own small business. Too many small business owners tend to want to cheat on their federal and state income tax filings by deducting expenses unrelated to business as if they were ordinary and necessary business expenses. Not only is this conduct illegal, it is completely contrary to the type of business you are

---

8. Richard E. Jackim & Peter G. Christman, The $10 Trillion Opportunity 114 (R. Jackim & Company 2005).

attempting to grow and ultimately transition to your A+ management team. Do not misunderstand: As a business owner, you need to take advantage of every legitimate business deduction you possibly can in a fair and lawful way. But if you grow accustomed to deducting nonbusiness-related expenses such as dinners, entertainment, and personal use of automobiles and gasoline, you are actually taking higher degrees of value out of the business (illegally, I might add), and the whole notion of you disclosing these to your buy-in partner, or losing these illegal benefits in the transition, may be very disconcerting to you. This discussion is raised in this part of the book because all of those practices that you engaged in, if you engaged in them, need to end. Why? Because you are running a real business that follows the law. It makes no sense to continue to pretend that you could sneak out small benefits from the business and hide them from the government and, ultimately, from your partners. That is not the transparency and truthfulness that we are looking for in this transition period.

This issue also comes up, as discussed in later chapters, when trying to merge two small law offices together. The entrepreneurial independence that neither party talks about but does not want to give up usually includes the ability to run personal expenses through the business illegally and take a federal tax deduction for these largely personal expenses.

> Too many small business owners tend to want to cheat on their federal and state income tax filings by deducting expenses unrelated to business as if they were ordinary and necessary business expenses.

If this discussion does not convince you that such conduct is detrimental to the ultimate transition and succession plan of your business, talk to your accountant about the value of the benefits that you are taking out of the business illegally. You will be shocked at the small tax benefit that you are getting on such conduct. Obviously, it is a bad idea to break the law, but it is equally a bad idea for building a law office that is not only the best in its marketplace but also built to transition to the next generation and the next management group.

Chapter 35

The Preliminary Disclosure; Testing Interest

You are probably now at a stage where you are comfortable with the valuation formula, and you believe it is fair for all partners (you and all future parties). Remember, you need to be fair to all partners. Although you could raise the valuation of the company by increasing the figure by which you multiply the cash flows and your very first buy-in partner may agree to it, you need to have a formula that works in the long run and that works for subsequent buyers. Note that the buy-in partner, as a purchaser, will be a seller someday, probably ten years into the future and that as a result, he or she needs to understand the equities of the valuation formula from both sides of the equation, as a buyer and as a seller.

Even from your standpoint, a seller in the entire process, the whole valuation formula will fall apart if it is later determined that you overcharged the first buy-in partner, and now the second, third, and fourth buy-in partners have no interest in purchasing because the business is overvalued.

Expression of Interest

Although, as lawyers you typically would want to have a potential buy-in partner sign a confidentiality agreement to keep the information regarding the finances of the law firm confidential, you can make that determination on your own. However, the buy-in partner should prepare a letter or an e-mail indicating that he or she has a genuine interest in purchasing at a fair market value and that all the information he or she receives will be kept confidential, not copied, and returned to you after the process has been completed. If you have this e-mail or letter, the expression of interest, then you know you have somebody who is sincerely interested in purchasing the business. Also, based on earlier conversations, there has probably been some general understanding about the value of the business, the valuation process, and also the expected rate of return for the buy-in partner. Remember, the expected rate of return at a multiple of five is approximately 20%. The higher the multiple (business valuation), the lower the rate of return for the buy-in partner. The lower the multiple (the lower business valuation), the higher the rate of return for the buy-in partner. Therefore, the buy-in partner needs to be able to see and evaluate for himself or herself the relevant financial information for the company.

Depending on your form of business, the last three years of tax returns are a good place to start, along with a schedule that will readjust or normalize the owner's benefit. The real rebalancing or normalization of these numbers are the numbers of dollars shifting between your W-2 income and the pretax profits of the business. Remember, under your new agreed-upon W-2 income arrangement, you need to demonstrate what the cash-out would have been for the business in the last three years. The cash-out forms the basis for the valuation when multiplied by the negotiated multiple and yields the business valuation.

If you have other financial statements and documents that tie into the tax return, which you should have, these too need to be disclosed to the buy-in partner.

The end result in the first disclosure of information to the buy-in partner is that the buy-in partner feels comfortable that you will be able to deliver on the cash-out of the business as anticipated and that your business valuation is fair and reasonable for the long run.

This first disclosure of financial information to an attorney of the firm who is not an owner is a big event in your life and the life of the law firm. It is deserving of its own discussion, and it cannot be taken lightly. There is a chance that the buy-in partner will reject the whole process and will either decide to maintain the status as an income partner or, eventually, leave the law firm. This is obviously not the optimal solution, but it is a reality.

For that reason, a discussion needs to be had with the buy-in partner in earnest about the buy-in partner's expectations of value and percentage of interest in purchasing.

Initial Percentage Sold

In some businesses, specifically in the medical business, there seems to be a presumption that every partner who comes in buys in as an equal partner. For example, the first partner buying in would presumptively buy in 50% of the business, thus ending with two partners each owning 50% of the business. The third partner coming in would buy a third interest from each of the two existing partners, with an end result of there being three partners owning 33.33% of the business. The fourth partner would then come in and purchases the appropriate percentage interest to yield an end result of four partners each owing 25% of the business. This is a presumption in some industries, but not typical for a law practice.

If you want to sell a large tranche of your ownership, such as 50%, it is certainly accept-able, and as we deal with later in the shareholder agreement section, the governance of a 50/50-owned business could certainly be documented properly in a shareholder agreement.

In law practices, it is more typical to buy into the firm, in small incremental percentages. For example, in a large law firm, a partner may be buying in at a fraction of less than 1%. However, in a small law firm setting, the minimum purchase should be 5%, and no greater than 20% in the first tranche of sale. These numbers are a function of (1) affordability and (2) your desire as the founding partner to convert future cash flows into present dol-lars. Presumably, if you still have faith in the law firm and the systems and mechanisms you put in place for future prosperity, you may not want to sell 20% immediately. Also, the buy-in partner may not be able to afford 20% of the business.

A proposed purchase by the buy-in partner of less than 5% (or even some single-digit amount, depending on your belief in the sustainability of the law office) might be viewed as less than a full commitment into the ownership structure of the business, without a significant financial commitment. An equity purchase of 1% or 2% could be deemed just a cautionary "sticking your toe in the pond" without diving in. At this juncture, your pur-chaser needs to dive in. It does you no good to sell such a fractionally small amount of the firm, yet allow your new equity partner, as required under your Business Corporation Act,[1] to have complete and unfettered access to the books and records of the law firm, with a minimal financial commitment.

> In a small law firm setting, the minimum purchase should be 5%, and no greater than 20% in the first tranche of sale.

The buy-in partner needs to understand the entrepreneurial risk that you took and the reduced risk that the buy-in partner is taking when purchasing into an ongoing concern.

Ideally, any business partner buying into a business that has been already established and is being sold in fractions by the founding partner has the advantage of avoiding all of the start-up risks of a small business. You have heard the statistics before: 33% of small businesses fail in the first and second year, approximately 50% fail by the fifth year, and 66% fail by the tenth year.[2] You have surpassed those statistical stopping points and have improved the buy-in partners' chances of success many times over. Further, as artic-ulated in Chapter 17 as to why so many solo practitioners barely survive, law practices tend to last a little bit longer, but they struggle dramatically in the first five years. Again, a certain level of risk has been taken off the table by you in the sale of the business. As

---

1. Or other statutory authority protecting minority shareholder rights or limited liability company mem-bers' rights, depending on the business.
2. U.S. Small Business Administration, Small Business Facts (2012), http://www.sba.gov/sites/default/files/business-survival.pdf.

a result, and the buy-in partner probably knows this, the buy-in partner is buying into a stable business that has withstood the early dropout rate of small law firms, and he or she wants to be part of a fantastic business culture that is growing and will be profitable in many more years to come.

Due Diligence

After the initial disclosure to the potential buy-in partner, the buy-in partner will presumably feel comfortable that the valuation formulation is accurate and that the financials you delivered under the preliminary disclosure will support the financial analysis of the future cash flows for the law firm. At that point in time, be prepared in any reasonable way to make an unrestricted disclosure to the buy-in partner of all relevant due diligence documents that have a bearing on the past or future performance of a law office. Recall that this whole process needs to be transparent; as a result, you should be prepared to be responsive to the buy-in partner's requests without a hint of or resistance. Expect to produce (or reproduce) the following:

Financial Statements
- Three years of federal tax returns;
- Three years of financial statements;
- Number of new clients monthly and annually;
- Three years of gross billing per month;
- Actual collection revenue per month for three years;
- Any and all growth charts that track actual billing and collecting whether expressed in real numbers or percentages; and
- Monthly bank statements for three years.

Marketing Information
- Any measurables that you have documented on new and potential clients;
- Any charts or grids showing the source of clients and client referrals; and
- Any other documentation or records you have on client conversions on marketing efforts, fees generated from marketing efforts, or repeat work from existing clients.

Human Resources
- Personnel files and internal record keeping on all employees—payroll, bonuses, absenteeism, vacation days.

Client Problems

- Client complaints; and
- Malpractice claims filed and attorney registration grievances filed against the firm or lawyers in the firm.

As may be obvious from previous discussions on the management of the law firm, the buy-in partner may have been instrumental in creating many of these forms for the law office and may already have access to or copies of some of these management reports. Nonetheless, other sensitive information related to employees or finances that were otherwise not available to the buy-in partner should be made available so that he or she recognizes all issues, positive and negative, relating to the law office.

Chapter 36

Financing

After all is said and done with respect to the business valuation, and the buy-in partner has made a commitment to purchase interests in the law office, you have to determine how the purchaser will pay for his or her interests. Based on an earlier hypothetical of a $200,000 cash-out, multiplied by a factor of 5, there is a $1,000,000 valuation, and a 10% acquisition equals a $100,000 purchase price.

Assuming the buy-in partner does not have $100,000 in his or her bank account, he or she will need to be able to finance that purchase in some fashion.

Bank Financing

The most favorable way for you, the seller, to sell to the buy-in partner is for the buy-in partner to get outside bank financing so that he or she can pay you cash and manage the debt repayment on his or her own.

Finding outside financing could be difficult, but not impossible. For example, if the buy-in partner has equity in his or her house or some other asset the partner could pledge, or partially pledge for the loan, that would go a long way for the bank lending the money. In addition, you need to be comfortable with helping to demonstrate to the bank that the cash flows from the business will help, if not fully service, the debt. Many banks will feel comfortable making the loan if the borrower can put 20%–30% of the equity down to you the seller and will amortize the balance over five years.

Initially set aside the tax implications and do the math to test the numbers.

If the partner were to purchase 10% of the law firm with the above hypothetical calculations, he or she would be paying $100,000 for 10% of a $200,000-a-year cash flow business, or $20,000 per year.

It will be reasonable for anyone to expect the purchaser to put 20% down (i.e., $20,000 down) and finance the remaining $80,000 of the purchase. Note that $80,000 financed over a five-year amortization at a 6% interest rate requires a fully amortized monthly debt payment of $1,546. How will that be repaid to the bank?

The buy-in partner will be entitled to 10% of the $200,000 a year from the cash flows of the business if the cash flows do *not* change. Note that 10% of a $200,000 cash flow is $20,000 per year, which equals $1,666 per month—approximately $120 a month more than the monthly debt repayment.

So, as you can see, tax issues aside, the economics of a five-year loan at 80% loan to value is relatively close to the cash flows required from the law firm to repay the loan.

Now consider the tax implications. The buy-in partner should consult his or her accountant or tax advisor on the ability to repay the loan used for financing the buy-in and the associated increase in tax liability for the buy-in partner. The tax advisor will give the buy-in partner various strategies that are specific to his or her total financial picture for anticipating the increased tax liability that comes with being an owner of the law firm.

However, it usually comes down to two methods.

> The most favorable way for you, the seller, to sell to the buy-in partner is for the buy-in partner to get outside bank financing so that he or she can pay you cash and manage the debt repayment on his or her own.

The first is to simply overwithhold on the buy-in partner's W-2 income to accommodate the tax burden the buy-in partner will have because of the K-1 that he or she will receive for the 10% of the profits of the firm. This method is very good because it flattens out the tax burden for the buy-in partner, although it also reduces the partner's day-to-day expendable income because his or her take-home check will be reduced by the increase in the federal and state withholding tax. Similarly, the buy-in partner could engage in making estimated tax payments to the federal and state taxing authorities to prepay the eventual tax debt to the government. Sometimes this increased federal and state withholding tax is offset by the buy-in partner's annual base salary raise in the previous year, thus not materially affecting the buy-in partner's lifestyle.

The second way of making an adjustment for the tax liability associated with the buy-in partner's year-end K-1 liability is simply to stretch out the amortization, if the bank allows, for making the payments directly from the income of the law office. For example, using the above hypothetical, the 10% buy-in partner will expect 10% of the $200,000-per-year cash flow from the law firm, which equals $20,000 per year. Since he or she has to pay tax on approximately $20,000 per year, using an estimated tax rate for federal and state purposes of 35%, the $20,000-per-year cash flow will be reduced to $13,000 per year ($7,000 will be paid to the federal and state taxing authorities through quarterly estimated tax payments), and that, divided by monthly receipts, equals $1,083 per month in after-tax cash flow from the profits of the law office.

The $80,000 loan at 6% amortized over seven years and six months equals a monthly payment of $1,106.02 per month, only $23 more than the after-tax distribution from the law office. So, therefore, by simply stretching out the amortization on the loan two and a half more years in order to accommodate the tax liability on the cash flows, the buy-in partner is able to fully pay the loan in seven and a half years and make the quarterly estimated tax payments.

There are some intangibles. If the interest rates spike and if the loan is at a higher-than-expected interest rate, it becomes less affordable. If interest rates go down, it becomes more affordable. Similarly, depending on the amount of the down payment from the buy-in partner, the debt maintenance can go up or down. Also, a longer amortization period makes the debt maintenance more affordable. A shorter amortization period makes the debt payments harder to make.

What if the buy-in partner does not have 20% to put down?

The buy-in will become very difficult, if not impossible. The buy-in partner will need to have some equity down payment for the purchasing of the law office from some source. Sometimes these purchases are done with home equity lines of credit, and some are done through a bank for the sole purpose of buying into the law office.

Be prepared and do not be naïve if the buy-in partner goes to a bank to finance the purchase. There is a high probability that the bank might ask you to guarantee the debt, since you are the recipient of the money. This is not the most favorable scenario, but it could be a reality. If the bank is new to your firm's progress, you may need to demonstrate for a few years or for a few different buy-in partners that the law office is rock solid and that the cash flows with which to service the debt will continue to come from the law office.

If the bank is your existing banker, the bank officer may feel very comfortable with you and the operation of the law office and, as a result, not require your personal guarantee but may still require a guarantee of the law office to guarantee the debt.

Understand the difference between the law office guaranteeing the debt versus you personally, the founding partner, guaranteeing the debt. In the above hypothetical example, the office should be sufficient to guarantee the debt. Your law office has $200,000 of cash flow in one year, and it should be sufficient to guarantee an $80,000 debt of the buy-in partner amortized either over five or seven and one-half years. In other words, if the buy-in partner were to default, the law office should be able to repay the debt in less than six months. Understand that the debt would be paid with some of the founding partner's cash flow, and there should be language in the shareholder agreement regarding protection and recovery for the founding partner if his or her cash flows are used to repay the debt of the defaulting buy-in partner. Nonetheless, from the bank's perspective, that should be viewed as a very strong guarantee, so long as the bank understands the strength and history of the law firm and the longevity of the law firm.

However, even under that scenario, the bank may request that you, the founding partner, personally guarantee the loan. This situation is not as favorable because although in the early stages of the slow sell-off you may actually still own 90% of the law office (as a result, 90% of the cash flow), in the later years of the slow sell-off you certainly do not want to be personally guaranteeing the loan of the buy-in partner when you then own only 20% or 30% of the law office (and the cash flow). It seems patently unfair that you may not have any control of the company and yet be guaranteeing the debt of a buy-in partner.

The bank will take the position that you are the flow-through beneficiary of the loan and therefore you have, in your bank account, the cash that was lent by the bank to the buy-in partner. While that logic is sound, the loan is really for the buy-in partner to own a portion of the business, and once you are under 50% of the business, you are really no longer in control. For that reason, a guarantee from the law office is certainly better than one from the founding partner.

Also, understand the collateral from the bank's perspective. Without the guarantee, the bank is simply taking a security interest on the partner's shares in the law office, which it cannot really foreclose on because the bank cannot be a shareholder in the law office.[1] The bank, depending on its relationship with the law office—for example, an existing loan for the law office's general line of credit—may require a lien on the assets and receivables of the law office for purposes of the shareholder loan. That would seem completely reasonable and should be supported by the founding partner. Remember, the bank first and foremost views the cash flow of the business as its repayment source of the loan. Second, it will look to the personal assets of the buy-in partner and, ultimately, all of the loan guarantors, including the firm, for the repayment of the loan.

> The bank may require a lien on the assets and receivables of the law office for purposes of the shareholder loan.

In reality, the bank will view this loan as a cash-flow loan, not collateralized by any tangible assets but, in reality, collateralized by receivables of the law office and the cash flow of the law office to the partners. Understand that position when talking to the bank about the loan, and try to facilitate the bank's concerns and needs relating to those collateral issues.

Make no mistake about it—outside bank financing is the best possible financing tool for all involved. First, it allows you to cash out and get paid up front without delay, and you can put the cash to work in your name. Second, bank financing creates an air of responsibility and legitimacy to the obligation for the buy-in partner, who will take the

---

1. MODEL RULES OF PROF'L CONDUCT R. 5.4(d).

obligation seriously. Typically, the buy-in partner will sign his or her own loan documents with respect to the loan and you or the law office may need to guarantee the loan. Once the buy-in partner signs loan documents collateralizing the loan with his or her assets, and probably a second or third position on his or her own house, there becomes a seriousness to the obligation that will, you hope, spur the buy-in partner's activity, interest, and desire to grow the law office.

Seller Financing

Seller financing is not optimal and needs to be avoided to the greatest extent possible. In the seller-financing situation, the exact same math goes into play as articulated above with respect to bank financing, only that you as the seller are also the lender for the purchase. Since you are not receiving any cash up front, you need to be well versed in documenting the loan with a promissory note, a security agreement, an escrow agreement, a financing statement, and probably a subordinate mortgage on the buy-in partner's home. Take a realistic view of the quality of the security of the note and go forward if you are comfortable with continuing to manage the business to pay yourself money that you would have otherwise received had it not been for this purchaser. In other words, you are just repaying the note signed by the buy-in partner with profits that you would otherwise have put in your pocket anyway.

In these cases, since the bank will not make a loan to the borrower (i.e., the buy-in partner) because of his or her lack of assets or lack of credit score, you have a legitimate reason to charge a higher interest rate on the loan that you are making, and doing so would *not* be intentionally exploitative. If the market believes the buy-in partner's application is a risky loan, then you should be compensated with a higher interest rate for such loan. As part of the loan documentation, make sure to hold the buy-in partner's shares in an escrow where, upon default, you will be able to take back the shares. Check your local jurisdiction's laws on the ability to allow the buy-in partner to vote the shares and receive the economic benefits of the shares held in an escrow.

Seller financing is less than optimal because you do not feel as if you receive the "pop" of financial benefits of selling part of the business because it streams to you over time.

The terms and conditions of the promissory note documenting the seller financing are completely negotiable, and you may ask for a shorter amortization or a higher interest rate. Nonetheless, the arrangement needs to be set up in a way that is truly affordable for the buy-in partner; otherwise there will be default, descent, and the whole idea of creating a succession plan will fail when the first buy-in partner fails.

It needs to be a system that works.

Miscellaneous Notes on Financing and the Transition

There are hybrid methods of all of the financing arrangements that can go into the purchase of the law office ownership interests. Certainly, before the buy-in is contemplated, perhaps as much as a year or two in advance, you need to see some demonstration from the income partner that he or she is saving money and has the ability to put the 20% down for the buy-in. Without this indication, it hardly seems reasonable that the person's expression of interest is really genuine.

Also, the buy-in partner may offer to reduce his or her W-2 income in order to help finance the 20% buy-in. Most individuals get accustomed to their W-2 income and live accordingly even if a portion of the income is going to education plans for their children or savings for a new house. Most likely, all the money on their W-2 income is probably spoken for in some fashion.

A few years before the buy-in, it may be necessary to assist the income partner by setting up special accounts in which he or she can deposit a portion of the W-2 or bonus income. Nonetheless, it is a balancing of current dollars with current expenses, in addition to a savings plan, that will allow the income partner to accumulate at least 20% of the anticipated purchase price.

> A system and a mechanism need to be put in place to accommodate a range of financially diverse buy-in partners over your sell-off period.

In some cases, achieving the savings may be much easier than all of the discussions set forth above. The buy-in partner may simply have the money or have significant equity in the house or property that is securing a home equity line of credit, and he or she may simply be able to purchase the law office ownership interests outright using the home equity line of credit. Nonetheless, whether or not the first buy-in partner has this financial ability, the subsequent buy-in partners may not. Therefore, a system and a mechanism need to be put in place to accommodate a range of financially diverse buy-in partners over your sell-off period. Please give these various methods great thought.

As a reality check, do not think that just because you have a new 10% partner, your job running the firm and keeping the law office moving forward has ended. It has not. You will have a higher level of responsibility for the first few buy-in partners because now you will be working hard to justify the wisdom in their buy-in. Before their buy-in, you were able to withstand the ebbs and flows of business personally without much responsibility other than providing for you and your family.

Now, with buy-in partners investing their own money and signing a promissory note for their obligations, the need to succeed is heightened, and so for the first few buy-in partners, or at least for the first five years after the buy-in partners come aboard, you need to continue to press forward and grow the company. It is still your responsibility.

Chapter 37

The Agreement

Once you have reached the valuation formula that is acceptable to you as the seller and to the income partner as the buyer, and sufficient, adequate information has been distributed to the income partner to ascertain the truthfulness and accuracy of the documentation, then the shareholder agreement, or an operating agreement, needs to be drafted and documented between the partners going forward. Of course, this document is highly sensitive and contains information that cannot be left loosely stored in a common location on your server or computer; it needs to be prepared in a fair way in order to document the rights of you as the founding partner, the buy-in partner, and *all* future partners. Depending on your practice-area strength, you may need to hire a lawyer familiar with these types of shareholder agreements to draft this comprehensive document. It is fully understandable that as lawyers accustomed to negotiating a legal document, you may not feel it necessary to hire outside counsel. Nonetheless, it is important that the shareholders executing this agreement are clear on the governing rules and covenants set forth in the document, as well as the future implications of the agreement.

Without an unreasonable level of expectation, these agreements are, on occasion, amended later in the process when certain issues have changed or if issues were missed in the original document, but the agreement does need to be considered a critically important document to set the understanding among the stakeholders.

The intent of the shareholder agreement that you will set forth in the recitals is to:

- Preserve the closely held nature of the firm;
- Assure effective and compatible management;
- Provide for an orderly disposition of shares held by each shareholder either inter vivos or at the shareholder's death;
- Establish procedures to address the resignation or retirement of any stakeholder; and
- Generally summarize the governance of the law office going forward.

The Company Valuation Formula

As discussed in Chapter 34, the company valuation formula needs to be set forth with great particularity in the shareholder agreement. Chapter 34 set forth the series of methods for calculating the company valuation based on a multiple of some cash flow. Cash flow, in that chapter, was defined either by EBITDA, net income, gross income, or cash-out; alternatively, it can be described in any calculable way that your accountant feels comfortable being able to deliver to you annually in an unbiased, completely objective fashion.

Then the cash flow is multiplied by some factor (i.e., a multiple) to yield the company valuation, sometimes known as the going-concern value. This company valuation must be a defined term in the shareholder agreement because it will be used multiple times.

Avoid references to book value of assets or asset value because, as explained earlier, a law office is best valued on its going-concern value or its cash flows. Asset value or the depreciated asset value known as book value grossly understates the value of a law office.

Second, a defined term should be established in the shareholder agreement of a discounted share value, which is some discount off the value of ownership a particular shareholder has in the law office giving effect to a potential bad act of such shareholder. Simply stated, if a shareholder engages in a bad act, the return on his or her ownership of the law office should be discounted by some percentage. The discount should be at least 25%, but no greater than 50%. As an alternative to a pure discount off the company valuation, you might decide that under the bad acts of a shareholder provision, the shareholder should be able to receive back only his or her basis in the shares (i.e., in the amount he or she paid for the shares). This stipulation is usually discouraged because if, in fact, the firm goes through a few bad cash flow years, paying back a bad-acting shareholder his or her basis in the shares might actually be a premium from the true value of the company. Therefore, it is best to use a pure percentage discount from the company valuation.

Restrictions on Transferability

As you will find in most shareholder agreements, buy-sell agreements, or operating agreements for limited liability companies, it is clear that the owners of a business (and you as an attorney giving advice to small businesses) want to retain the closely held nature of the business. In addition, the business partners always want to know who, realistically, will be their partners and fellow shareholders in the business. If there were not strict restrictions on transferability, theoretically an equity stakeholder in a law office can sell his or her shares to another lawyer, someone who is not necessarily an employee of your firm, and so before you are aware of it, you could conceivably have a shareholder you do not know. As a result, most small businesses and your law office will limit the transferability of shares under a sales queue (articulated later) or in some other fashion that works well for the partners.

In general, the transferability restriction in a shareholder agreement will absolutely prohibit the sale to outsiders. However, in this case, the transferability requirements may still require approval from other shareholders, but not more than 50% of the shareholders. Keep in mind that in almost all cases, the significant portion of the original sales will be from the founding partner to new income partners who want to become buy-in partners. Therefore, though it may be somewhat undefined as to who the future buy-in partners may be, a transition line should already be etched in sand and documented in your agreement.

> Most small businesses and your law office will limit the transferability of shares under a sales queue or in some other fashion that works well for the partners.

It will come as no major surprise to any shareholders that there is a sale and disposition schedule set forth in the shareholder agreement that contemplates (1) the founding partner's divestiture of his or her interests in the organization and (2) the ability for the early buy-in partners to get in the sales queue to start sharing their shares at the appropriate time.

Call Options

The company wants to reserve the right to call the shares, that is, to force a repurchase of certain shares owned by shareholders in certain events caused by the shareholder. The law office should have the right to call in the shares from an owner of the law office if the shareholder engages in an involuntary transfer of the shares, if there is a termination of his or her employment other than by death, or if there is a termination of that shareholder's employment by the law office for cause. In all of the foregoing examples, described with more particularity below, the law firm does not want to be engaged in having rogue shareholders who are not actively engaged in the business. Moreover, under the laws in your jurisdiction, a someone who is not a lawyer may not even be able to own shares in a law office. As a result, protections must be put in place in the agreement whereby the law firm, the entity, could call in the shares to protect its interest. In such cases, and under various circumstances, the call price should be determined under the valuation formula or the other discounted valuation formula.

The law office would further want a call option on the shares of the buy-in partner if the buy-in partner defaults on his or her loan to the bank or to the founding partner and the lender takes action on the security agreement of the buy-in partner or the guarantee provided by the law office. The law office will want the ability to call in the buy-in partner's shares if the lender begins to sweep the cash flows of the law office to the detriment of the other partners. Certainly, if the buy-in partner is not making timely payments on his or her loan, and the lender (whether a third-party bank or the founding partner) acts on the guarantee of the law office, the law office should have the right to call in the shares of the buy-in partner, take control of the shares, and pay the buy-in partner for the shares at a discounted valuation formula less the amount of the loan still due and owing on the shares (because the law office will have to pay off the loan). In this case, it should be very clear that the buy-in partner does not receive the benefit of owning his or her shares outside the valuation formula mechanisms and the call option.

This bad conduct would be very disturbing to the law office and create serious problems within the culture of the firm and the relationship among the partners. In addition, language could be drafted in the shareholder agreement to provide a "for cause" termination of the buy-in partner's employment with the law firm.

Put Option

A put option is the ability of an individual holder of shares to put the shares to the entity, obligating the entity to repurchase the shares from the shareholder. This process could be negotiated at length, but you may come to the conclusion that a new buy-in shareholder having a put right is not really taking any risk and

> You want your new buy-in partner to be "all in" and not have the ability to just test the water with respect to the commitment to the law firm.

is completely protected on the downside if the law office struggles financially. As described earlier, you want your new buy-in partner to be "all in" and not have the ability to just test the water with respect to the commitment to the law firm. However, an immediate put option (or call option for the benefit of the firm) is required for any purchase money security interest holders (such as a bank) that may have funded the purchase of the buy-in partner's shares. In order not to violate any rules relating to ownership of the law office, a mechanism has to be put in place through a put, and call, to make sure a shareholder defaulting on a loan to a bank or a lender can be taken out immediately and the shares can be repurchased by the entity or another shareholder.

Sales Queue

Thought needs to be given to the founding partner's long-term sell-off of his or her shares. There may be an overlap period of time when the founding partner still has ownership of shares, and the very first buy-in partner enters into the sell-off stage of his or her career and would also like to begin selling shares. As a result, you need to determine when your recent buy-in shareholders are able to start selling shares in the future. In other words, the founding partner does not want to still own 40% of his or her own shares and then have the first buy-in partner, who bought in ten years ago, selling his or her shares to a new partner. There needs to be set forth an orderly disposition of the interests in a sales queue. There could be a scheduled sell-off using hypothetical shareholders B, C, and D. But without being quite that rigid, your sales-queue limitation could state that no other shareholder could sell shares until you, the founding partner, have sold at least 60%, 70%, or 80% of your shares—or whatever number you feel comfortable with—making sure that the next buy-in shareholder purchases your shares. Then, upon such triggering event, shares are sold to the next buy-in partner pro rata. Keep in mind that one of the benefits of the entire succession plan is for you to be able to sell your shares and for you to get your value out of the entity that you helped build and create.

Involuntary Transfers

There should be a definition in the shareholder agreement for involuntary transfers whereby if a purchase money security holder such as a bank is foreclosing on the shares of the defaulting equity partner (i.e., an involuntary transfer), the law firm needs to be able to repurchase the shares of the defaulting partner. Similarly, if an equity partner is going through a divorce and the spouse is seeking ownership of the shares of the law office, another type of involuntary transfer (the spouse may be an attorney, which is a rightful owner of a law office), the law office needs to have the ability to call in the interest and buy back the shares. In such cases, once the law office is aware of the involuntary transfer (and the rules regarding notice of the involuntary transfer need to be set forth in the agreement), the firm should have a call option to purchase the shares at either the true valuation of the company or a discounted share price.

Upon the Death of a Shareholder

If a shareholder dies, the law office should have the obligation to purchase the shares from the estate. This option is really an *obligation* and not a put right of the estate, nor is it a call option of the law firm. It is an obligation. The law office does not want any spouses or an estate (legally, it cannot) being a shareholder in the law office, and the estate does not want to be a shareholder in the law office.

Thought needs to be given to the funding of the buy-out and whether the law office can afford to buy out the founding partner when the founding partner still owns 60%, 70%, 80%, or 90% of the firm. If that is the case, consideration needs to be given to purchasing life insurance to help as a funding mechanism for the benefit of the law firm and the founding partner.

Similarly, as the law firm grows and has greater value, there could be buy-in partners who own a significant amount of the law office, and so life insurance should be purchased on their lives to create a funding mechanism to buy out the shares if such a shareholder were to die.

There is a tremendous amount of material in articles and books on the various methodologies to draft redemption agreements or cross-purchase agreements in shareholder agreements. Please seek counsel on the nuances that create benefits and disadvantages for each type of agreement.

Termination of Employment Other Than Death

A shareholder of a corporation could still be terminated in his or her capacity as an employee under whatever parameters you create in the shareholder agreement. I previously indicated that such termination might require a 67% vote of the shareholders. In any case,

> Consideration needs to be given to purchasing life insurance to help as a funding mechanism for the benefit of the law firm and the founding partner.

in the event a shareholder's employment is terminated, turn to the shareholder agreement. There should be a discussion and rules set forth in the shareholder agreement identifying the appropriate rights of the law firm and the terminated employee and shareholder with respect to the terminated employee's shares. The company may want to reserve a call right on those shares, or depending on the circumstances under which the shareholder was terminated (either for cause or without cause), the terminated shareholder may have a put right to force the law office to purchase his or her shares. Check with your local jurisdiction's rules and the appropriate legislative acts, but the law firm may consider greatly the thought of having a nonemployee own shares of the law firm, giving that nonemployee, who may be a lawyer, the rights to come in and audit the books and records of the law firm, but doing so without being a lawyer of the law firm.

Also in the agreement, you may give great weight to a terminating partner for cause. You could create your own list of cause activities, but such activities usually include these:

- Acts or conduct detrimental to the reputation of the law firm;

- Conviction of a felony;
- Being charged with a felony;
- Addictions that are reoccurring;
- Loss of a law license;
- Any facts that prove to be true relating to the misappropriation of money;
- Repeated grievances reported to the Attorney Disciplinary Commission;
- Repeated acts of malpractice; and
- Default on a buy-in partner's loan to purchase equity in the firm.

The aforementioned conduct, if resulting in a "for cause" termination, might also result in a discounted valuation formula on the interests owned by the shareholder and reduce the call price buyout on the firm for the terminated shareholder's shares.

Nonsolicitation Duty of Loyalty

A discussion should be had and then rules set forth in the shareholder agreement regarding each shareholder's duty of loyalty. As attorneys, we should all understand our fiduciary duties to fellow owners of the business and our fiduciary duties to the business in our capacity as an officer and even as an employee. However, it is best that you set forth, with great particularity in the shareholder agreement, each person's duty of loyalty to the law office, with respect to practicing law, and even with respect to outside interests. You certainly do not want your partner to open a yogurt franchise in town and be allocating his or her time to the yogurt franchise when that time is best spent in the law office. These concepts need to be discussed and vetted with your future partner before misunderstandings occur and rules are well established. Similarly, attorneys may have other types of licenses, such as insurance licenses and mortgage broker licenses, and may seek to continue to pursue those previous careers in parallel with practicing law. In each case, you need to deny that request because in order to create a great, winning law firm, everyone needs to be focused on the law office 100% of the time, and not be distracted with outside interests. Remember, you and your associates and partners are lawyers, and lawyers only. Any side interests will compromise your time, your USP, and your brand in the market.

While clients can choose whomever they want as their lawyer, you cannot force one law firm or another law firm on your client; contractual limitations need to be set forth in the shareholder agreement stating what is expected of all equity partners from a partnership standpoint. Liquidated damage sections in shareholder agreements may be enforced by the courts so long as they do not hinder a client's rights or the attorney's rights to practice.[1] Violations of the duty of loyalty and the restrictive covenant certainly can trigger a discounted share value when it comes to the law office purchasing back the shares of the departing equity owner. These are critical issues and are controlled, in large part, by state law. Review your state statutes, and get advice on the enforceability of restrictive covenants and liquidated damages in law office shareholder agreements.

Retirement

The shareholder agreement could, and should, also address a reasonable retirement program for the shareholders as they reach a particular age or number of years with the law office. While this is highly negotiable and debatable, it also addresses public policy issues in our country in determining when forced retirement is appropriate. You are really looking out for the best interest of the firm, and although retirement should not be forced, the practice of law has a way of transitioning lawyers in the later years of their career so that they can still add tremendous value to the firm and continue to make reasonable semiretirement income as "of counsel" to the firm. The "of counsel" designation applies to an attorney who will negotiate a salary package that is probably heavily weighted toward bringing in new business and getting paid based on the billable hour. These attorneys balance having the free time they seek to spend vacationing and spending time with their family versus being around the law office part-time to continue to add value to other attorneys. As such, it is difficult to thoroughly document the retirement plan of the equity attorneys in the original shareholder agreement, but it needs to be discussed and expectations need to be expressed early in the process. Whether you actually declare that a specific age or number of years of practice triggers the "of counsel" relationship is up to you, but you and the older attorneys in the office need to discuss retirement issues openly and voluntarily. The issues need to be addressed before a potential involuntary employment termination disrupts the firm.

All in all, the shareholder or operating agreement for the law office is a very important document and cannot be taken lightly. I encourage open dialogue between the founding partner and the buy-in partner to make sure the document is fair and equitable and has room for further dialogue if necessary. Remember, even the Constitution of the United States of America had ten amendments only two years after it was executed.

---

1. Please review your jurisdiction's version of the Model Rules of Professional Conduct, rule 5.6, on the restrictions on the right to practice. Lawyers should not participate in and enter into agreements that restrict the right of a lawyer to practice after the termination of a relationship. The question is whether a liquidated damage section or other sections of the shareholder agreement will limit such lawyer's right to practice. If the provision is determined not to violate rule 5.6, it must meet the requirements of rule 1.5.

Governance and Operations

In the shareholder agreement there needs to be a section on the regular operations and governance of the entity. Check with your local statute to see if there is a closely held business act whereby you can eliminate the board of directors and allow your entity to be run at the shareholder level. If you do have that option, it is advisable to do so, so that the governance is clearly set forth in the shareholder ownership percentages.

Set forth in detail upon the execution of the shareholder agreement the officer positions of the shareholders. If there are only two shareholders, the founding partner will probably be the president and the second buy-in partner will probably be a vice president as well as whatever statutory title is required under your governing act.

There should be a section in the governance section of the operating or shareholder agreement setting forth base salary calculations. In general, 51% of the shareholders should vote on regular base salaries, and a limitation needs to be placed on the founding partner's annual salary increases. It should be 5%, 10%, or limited to a hard dollar amount or in some other fashion to make sure the founding partner does not vote himself or herself so great an increase that the cash-out or profit of the business would be significantly reduced. Since the founding partner will have the 51% vote necessary to control base salary increases, the limitation may be such that the founding partner's salary and year-end bonus increase cannot be an amount greater than the highest base salary and year-end bonus awarded to any other shareholder in the preceding year. This way, the founding partner cannot give himself or herself salary increases and bonuses greater than the highest bonuses given to another shareholder.

Next, certain actions need to be articulated in the shareholder agreement that require either a 51% vote, a 67% vote, or a unanimous vote of the existing shareholders.

Clearly, a unanimous vote of shareholders gives great authority to the minority shareholder. Usually, the only issues reserved for unanimous consent of the shareholder agreement are limiting and controlling ways for the founding partner to get cash out of the business—for example, changing W-2 income for the founding partner or changing year-end bonuses. In addition, if the founding partner owns the building in which the law firm rents its office, the rent needs to be documented in the shareholder agreement so that the founding partner does not just increase the rent to the law office, which would be another way of reducing profits to the law office, in favor of a self-interest payment to the founding shareholder. If there are other ways to favor the founding partner through equipment leases and other related party transactions between the founding partner (or his or her family members) and the law office, all of those need to be disclosed and limited by the modifications allowable in those circumstances.

With respect to actions taken by the entity that require a 67% vote of the shareholders, the shareholder agreement might include:

- Terminating the employment of a shareholder or an officer of the law firm;
- Amending or modifying the shareholder or operating agreement;
- Changing the name of the law office;
- Issuing additional shares of the law office; and
- Authorizing mergers with other law offices.

With respect to actions taken by the law office requiring only a 51% vote of the share-holders, the shareholder agreement might include

- Authorizing mergers with other law offices;
- Pledging assets of the law office for a loan or a line of credit;
- Authorizing the selling of shares;
- Authorizing the distribution of cash to shareholders; and
- Authorizing other actions relating to the ordinary course of business conduct of the law office.

Business Expenses

An honest dialogue needs to be had among the shareholders regarding allowable business expenses, usually for meals and entertainment. As discussed earlier in the chapter, some founding partners may be guilty of having some personal expenses paid for by the company, which is illegal. While some of those items are very clear, sometimes shareholders and small businesses tend to stretch the limitations of acceptability and try to trick each other with respect to how they spend their money on ordinary and necessary business expenses.[2] As a result, it is probably wise to put limitations on how much each equity partner is allowed to spend in furtherance of the business without having to get consent from the other partner. Some law firms allow for a certain amount of business allowance, car and gas expenses, meals and entertainment, that each owner and shareholder can spend on his or her own without consent of the other partner, but *all* of the allowances are subject to Internal Revenue Code limitations. Generally, the abuse happens in the category of meals and entertainment, though realistically it can happen in several categories. It is important that this issue be documented in the shareholder agreement so that going forward, everyone knows what the expectation of each partner is.

Abuses of business expenses have been the triggering event for the failure of many law firms. Be cautious of fraudulent business expenses and how partners vote on legitimate business expenses.

---

2. *See* IRC §162.

Note that when the founding partner is making purchasing decisions about computers, law office equipment, furniture, and décor, he or she is spending money for the benefit of the law office that would otherwise be profit for the law office. These purchases are made for the basic purpose of enhancing the law office and thereby enhancing the client experience, which in turn ultimately grows the law firm.

When the founding partner was the 100% owner of the law firm, he was spending one hundred cents of every dollar that would otherwise go to him. Now, after the slow sell-down, imagine four partners owning 25% each of the law office and making a determination whether one partner's office needs to be redecorated with new, expensive furniture. Of course, that partner who is promoting the redecorating of his or her office would absolutely vote yes to the redecoration because he or she would be spending only a quarter of the law firm profit that would only flow through to that particular partner at 25% and would, therefore, cost that particular partner only twenty-five cents on every dollar spent for the law office on that particular upgrade. This is a slippery slope that business owners need to be careful about once the ownership interest in the law office is fractionalized among many partners. Imagine the large law firms and their decision to decorate a partner's office when that particular partner owns only 1% of the entire law firm. He is spending one cent on the dollar to benefit his office. All of the partners need to institutionalize the concept that spending money for the office should be treated as spending one's own money for the betterment of the law office. If you look at it that way, then only the really necessary items would be purchased, the software and computer technology that provides the best benefit for the law office would be purchased, and items that would translate into a better client experience and better client satisfaction would be purchased, but nothing else extraneous to client satisfaction and a pleasant work environment.

> All of the partners need to institutionalize the concept that spending money for the office should be treated as spending one's own money for the betterment of the law office.

New Client Bonuses

As an associate, the founding partner probably has an incentive plan in place for all fellow associates to generate business and billing hours. Those bonuses, whether paid monthly or annually, are probably a significant portion of the associate's compensation package. As an owner of the business, the equity partner should not expect to be treated as an associate and be incentivized to do the things that an owner would do simply by virtue of his or her status as an owner of the business. For example, working hard and billing hours and trying to develop business and bring in clients for the benefit of the law firm are all things that an owner of a law firm should engage in. As a result, eventually the new client bonuses should phase out or be limited over a period of time.

In the agreement, you can consider ending new client bonuses after a new client has been an existing client for over one year or two years. If the individual stays on as a client of your law firm, then the law firm has done its job with respect to client satisfaction and has earned the right to keep the client, and any attorney commission for acquiring that client should terminate.

In the alternative, you could, probably should, phase out these new client bonuses over time. You could phase them out over three years, four years, or five years, when the buy-in partner's percentage of payment goes away. Again, as an owner of the business, the new equity owner should not need to be incentivized to bring in business, for the incentive should be there already—namely, as being an owner of the business and growing the business in order to sell his or her percentage ownership in ten or fifteen years at a profit. If they are not eliminated, then you have a collection of owners who are driven completely by self-interest and not for the good of the firm. Be aware that these types of concerns can eventually cause great harm to the law office.

Chapter 38

The New Management Team

Notwithstanding your constant attempts to get your associates, income partners, administrative assistants, and office manager to give input on the policies and management issues of the law office, some of these people may disagree. They may believe that the law office is run, not as a democracy where all employees have influence and input into the operations, but as a benevolent monarchy run by the founding partner, a nice person who makes the decisions for the firm.

While most of the attorneys and support staff will probably not understand or believe the level at which you listen to their wants and concerns because that listening helps build trust and culture in the firm, their understanding of the benevolent monarchy may not be far from the truth.

However, now with new equity shareholders in the firm, the firm *does* need to be run differently. Traditionally, law offices called their group of decision makers "partners" and operational decisions are made at partner meetings. What is really happening is the creation of a management team to manage the business of the law office, and part of the business of the law office is managing the legal work within the practice groups. So there are certain elements to building a successful management team that you should be aware of as the practice grows.

Lencioni likens an organization to a family.[1] If the parents' relationship is dysfunctional, the family will be too. Similarly, the leadership team, or the management team, must not be dysfunctional. As a result, you need to understand that it is the founding partner's duty to build a functional, respected leadership team for the law office. Teamwork is not a virtue. It is a choice, and a strategic one.[2]

Remember, the leadership team that you are building—first you, and then your first buy-in partner, as well as other buy-in partners to follow—should become a group of people who are collectively responsible for achieving the core purpose and values of the firm.

---

1. Patrick Lencioni, The Advantage: Why Organizational Health Trumps Everything Else in Business 19 (Jossey-Bass 2012).
2. *Id.* at 21.

Keep in mind that as the firm expands to many partners, there is a point of optimal effectiveness for a management team. Somewhere between four and seven members is optimal. And, of course, in a small law office, they should be shareholders. It would be a true exception to have nonshareholders and nonattorneys on a management team. In large law firms, the CFO, usually not an attorney, sits on the management team. The management of a small firm should be, and always remain, with just the shareholders or equity owners of the entity.

In management meetings, a certain understanding and culture needs to be developed among members of the management team, and the discussion reduced to writing, if necessary, so that all words spoken in management meetings should be candid, unfiltered (or lightly filtered), all with the goal of improving the law office. You have to trust one another and allow each other to voice opinions, direct the conversation into areas that are important to each member of the management team, and listen and hear each other out in an honest and nonjudgmental fashion. Remember, criticism can be constructive when coupled with tact. If one member of the management team has let you down or acted in a fashion inconsistent with the firm's commitment to certain conduct, that needs to be vetted and openly discussed in a management meeting. If the partner at issue does not correct the inappropriate conduct over a period of time, you must look seriously at that partner's commitment to the firm's culture and values; further, notwithstanding the fact that that buy-in partner was elevated to his or her status because of his or her previous commitment to the firm's culture and values, remember that people change, circumstances change, and thus the status of that partner as an employee needs to be reviewed and contemplated for the good of the firm.

> Remember, the leadership team that you are building—first you, and then your first buy-in partner, as well as other buy-in partners to follow—should become a group of people who are collectively responsible for achieving the core purpose and values of the firm.

Notwithstanding certain considerations issued and discussed relating to specific partners, the overall tenor of the meetings needs to be open and honest. Remember, conflict around certain issues should be constructive, not destructive. Having people of different perspectives weighing in on issues, voicing general as well as specific disagreements on a particular subject, is not detrimental to a firm's growth. It is productive when issues get thoroughly vetted, discussed, and corrected.

An important issue needs to be understood and discussed among members of the management team. The management team is not a false front for the benevolent monarch, who claims to take other opinions into consideration. Make no mistake about it, the founding partner probably will still carry a majority of the ownership of the entity in his or her hands and can, as a result, outvote the class of other equity partners so long as the founding partner still owns over 51% of the outstanding shares of the entity.

However, the management team is not intended to be a shill for the founding partner in front of the rest of the organization. The management team is intended to vet issues, all issues, even those that are very difficult, to come to a consensus, and to carry out the charge of the management team in a unified, clear voice.

The management team has to achieve consensus and, subsequently, commitment to the policies of the firm.[3] Be realistic, and be practical. Depending on the size of the firm and the size of the management team, there will be times when you will not get unanimous consent on all issues. When the management team waits for unanimous consent on any issue, the members usually make decisions that are too late and, often, mildly disagreeable to everyone. This tardiness is a recipe for mediocrity and frustration.[4]

Sometimes, the founding partner needs to be at a management meeting simply to break ties if the management team is split on an opinion.

> When a leader knows that everyone on the team has weighed in and provided every possible perspective needed for a fully informed decision, he can then bring a discussion to a clear and unambiguous close and expect team members to rally around the final decision even if they initially disagreed with it.
>
> Some leaders have a hard time believing this. They feel that if they entertain disagreement around a contentious topic, they'll make it less likely that they'll be able to gain commitment. But this is selling their employees short. The truth is very few people in the world are incapable of supporting a decision merely because they had a different idea. Most people are generally reasonable and can rally around an idea that wasn't their own as long as they know that they've had a chance to weigh in.[5]

It is critical in the management meetings, as well as full firm meetings, that everyone has a chance to weigh in and be heard. Employees are smart, and they understand the idea of being part of a larger organization. They just want to be heard, understood, and feel that their opinions matter. As result, through your management meetings, disagreements will occur, conversations and debate will arise, everyone will have a chance to weigh in, and eventually the management team will come to a consensus on what is best for the firm. The founding partner will probably be on the side of the majority, but the founding partner does not always have to be with the majority. After thorough discussion of the topic, rarely will there be anything even close to a 50/50 split on an opinion when everyone in the room keeps the most important rule in mind, namely, that the law office comes first.

---

3. *Id.* at 48.
4. *Id.*
5. *Id.* at 49.

It is important that every team member leaves meetings with clear-cut, active, and specific agreements regarding the decisions. They need to deliver that message to the other associates and administrative assistants in a clear, concise voice. If younger associates and administrative assistants begin consistently detecting a fractionalized management team, whereby certain members do not support the management team's directives, the beginning of the end of the law firm has started. At that point, the management team that is required to build a great law firm does not exist, and the deterioration will begin.

Last, management team members need to be accountable to one another and follow up on commitments, directives, and assignments.

If a team member fails to follow up on those issues and to live the core values and purpose of a law firm, that case needs to be brought up in the open forum of the meetings and not in private.[6]

> If younger associates and administrative assistants begin consistently detecting a fractionalized management team, whereby certain members do not support the management team's directives, the beginning of the end of the law firm has started.

Indeed, when accountability is handled during a meeting, every member of the team receives the message simultaneously and doesn't have to make the same mistake in order to learn the lesson of the person being held accountable. Second, they know that the leader is holding their colleague accountable, which avoids their wondering whether the boss is doing his job. Finally, it serves to reinforce the culture of accountability, which increases the likelihood that team members will do the same for one another.[7]

It is critically important that the new management team and management style be mutually accountable, hold true to company values, and deliver on their promises, in both behaviors and results.

---

6. *Id.* at 63.
7. *Id.*

How Often Should You Meet?

In *Mastering the Rockefeller Habits*,[8] Harnish outlines three sets of fundamental goals in managing a successful enterprise. The first are priorities and the items that you need to work on regularly for the betterment of the firm. The second is data, articulated in Section 2 of the book on reports for management, set forth with more particularity in Chapter 25. The last is rhythm.[9] The connection between meetings and the firm's rhythm is undeniable. Harnish states that until people are mocking you, you are not repeating your message enough.[10]

> To make more than just a lot of noise in your business, you've got to have a rhythm. And the faster you want to go, the faster you've got to pulse. At the heart of executive team performance is a rhythm of tightly run daily, weekly, monthly, quarterly, and annual huddles and meetings—all of which happen as scheduled, without fail with specific agendas.[11]

It is difficult to accept the extent of the meetings suggested by Harnish, including *daily* meetings. Depending on what works best for your firm, the point should be well taken that the firm needs to have a rhythm and a pulse for sending out critical information to the associates and the support staff in a consistent fashion so that everyone is utterly clear on the message and there is no misunderstanding about the priorities in the firm. Are daily meetings necessary? Maybe, maybe not. It depends on the nature of your practice and the speed in which cases and matters are going forward.

There are occasions in a law office, especially in a complicated transaction with a short closing date, where certain members of the transaction team may set aside time early in the morning or at the end of the day to discuss the tasks for that day, the interactions among departments (i.e., show how the various related legal disciplines affected each other that day), and the status reports (i.e., what still needs to be done on certain issues).

It is probably not necessary to hold daily meetings for law office management issues. There are not enough critical data generated daily in a law office that require the review of the data in a meeting. However, I recommend weekly meetings with the management team that should last no more than an hour and have a short agenda including:

- Good news about employee or associate performance;

---

8. VERNE HARNISH, MASTERING THE ROCKEFELLER HABITS: WHAT YOU MUST DO TO INCREASE THE VALUE OF YOUR GROWING FIRM (Gazelles 2002).
9. *Id.* at 83.
10. *Id.*
11. *Id.* at 83.

- Disappointing news about employee or associate performance;
- Any information available on quantifying management reports for the office; and
- Client feedback received in the last week (good and bad).

Oftentimes, some firm-positive recognition needs to be sent out after these meetings based on good performance by an associate or an administrative assistant.

Monthly meetings are advisable for all attorneys. Those meetings are not necessarily designed to discuss cases (there is no sense to discuss a litigation case when a real estate attorney is in the room), but serve, rather, for law office management issues, firm policies, the adherence to those policies, and any fine-tuning of those policies that need to be conveyed to the attorneys. Because the attorneys are the revenue drivers of the law office, some of the management reports and statistical data for the firm should be shared with the associates and income partners so that everyone understands where the firm stands with its measurables. Remember, in attorneys' meetings, certain measurables are not disclosed, such as financial statements and other confidential information that should be disclosed only to stakeholders of the entity.

Certain groups of litigation attorneys can meet weekly, but no less often than monthly, to make sure court calls are covered, discuss strategy on certain cases, and to share information and case management among a group of attorneys. These meetings are case specific, and it is usually very helpful for the attorney managing the cases to share ideas, concerns, and strategies with a group of other litigation attorneys.

At least monthly, just the equity partners (i.e., shareholders) need to meet to discuss the firm's monthly financials and other monetary measurables such as the balance sheet, which includes the bank and loan balances. These meetings, absent any anomalies in the operation of the firm, are usually short, predictable, and if everything is going well for the firm, reassuring.

Reiterate the Message

Management team members need to leave all meetings with a clear understanding of what was accomplished and a directive about what message needs to be sent to the associates and support staff. Again, as Harnish indicates, until your employees are mocking you, you should not feel concerned about stating, restating, and reinforcing the message from the management team. If a six- or twelve-month initiative is started to increase new client sign-ups, that message needs to be sent and resent during the period to make sure everyone is on the same page relating to the initiative. As you look into the objectives and the "to-dos" to improve that part of your practice, all of the related elements need to be aligned, all of the marketing messages consistent, and all of marketing processes followed.

Is a lead conversion system in place and running smoothly? How do attorneys conduct themselves in initial client meetings? What is the sensory package of the law firm when clients come in for the first time?

On the other hand, if the message to the attorneys is to reduce receivables and get clients to pay in thirty days or less, then that message needs to be constantly reinforced; objectives need to be created and set up for not only measurable results but also behaviors of the associates in order to reduce receivables and increase clients payments.

No matter what the objectives that you are trying to accomplish, a plan needs to be put in place by the management team to accomplish those goals, and that plan needs to be overtly communicated and reiterated to everyone involved.

Your communication techniques could be a top-down communication whereby the managing partner or founding partner sends out a weekly e-mail or a memorandum noting how the firm is doing on its objectives and goals. As an alternative, your technique could be to have all members of the management team go out, in a cascading effect, to directly communicate the message to associates and administrative assistants. In fact, it could create an overlapping, cascading effect whereby more than one management team member touches and addresses each individual associate and administrative assistant with respect to the management goals and message. The end result will be that all employees are able to accurately articulate the organization's culture, values, and strategic goals.

In conclusion, the management team members need to speak with one voice, and all members of the management team need to be heard and opinions need to become part of the message being rolled out to the associates and support staff. Not every action or policy will be adopted with a unanimous vote, but all management team personnel must subordinate their own feelings and opinions for the overall consensus of the team. The associates and support staff will receive a clear and concise message that is always consistent with the firm's purpose and values and with the anchors required to execute on its purpose.

Chapter 39

Are You Really Ready to Sell Below 50%? 33%?

There are many wonderful books on retirement and retirement planning, not only for financial planning purposes but also for emotional support and life-change preparation.[1] This chapter is not intended to replace the hours, days, weeks, and months you need to spend learning about the life adjustment of selling off your law firm and the financial and emotional adjustments you will need in your personal life. However, there are some things you need to consider.

First, there are those soft personal issues that you need to explore relating to the significant changes in relationships, your self-interest and ego, and the wind-down of your relevance at the law office.[2] As stated earlier, as a lawyer, you have a very good phase-out role when you contribute to a law office as "of counsel." Although in your shareholder agreement you may have retirement triggering dates or "of counsel" triggering dates, the message here is that there will be a significant change in your relevance to your partners, associates, and clients if, and when, you wind down and sell below 50% interest in your practice and potentially, depending on the language of the shareholder agreement, below 33%. Certainly, when you sell your last share of interest in the law office, your equity stake and voice in the law office will probably end unless you are asked to stay on the management team. Realistically, you may not even want to stay on the management team and have a voice in the firm any longer if you do not have any ownership interest in the entity. However, that is separate and apart from your "of counsel" role with respect to the practice of law.

Preparation is necessary to understand how for thirty or forty years all decisions came to you, the founding partner, to weigh in on and to resolve. If you have established a competent management team, these issues will be minimized or completely eliminated;

---

1. Lee Eisenberg, The Number: What Do You Need for the Rest of Your Life and What Will It Cost? (Free Press 2006).
2. Marshal Goldsmith, Succession: Are You Ready? (Harvard Business Press 2009).

in such case, the major concern here is, will that be as much of a relief as you expected it to be? Arguably, a feeling of irrelevance may set in when you are no longer involved in practicing law and your opinion no longer matters or matters less. Again, balance the perception of irrelevance with respect for the law office management and the practice of law. Of course, you will probably not become immediately irrelevant in the practice of law because you have those years of experience and there is a lot of mentoring to do with young attorneys; as well, discretionary decisions needing your wisdom to resolve will be greatly appreciated.

As you enter the law office at this stage of your sell-off, be prepared to check your ego at the door.

The message that you should be embracing is that this is the time for you to slow down and to do the things that you want to do.[3] As retirement books often indicate, preparing yourself for cruise ships eventually loses its appeal, golfing becomes a burden, beach living gets tedious, and fishing no longer matters. All of the things that we dream about doing in retirement can get old very quickly.

> The soft landing into retirement is largely managed by you and is achieved by the long, slow sell-off of the practice and the changing role that you will have in the practice.

The soft landing into retirement is largely managed by you and is achieved by the long, slow sell-off of the practice and the changing role that you will have in the practice. If your choice is to remain on the treadmill at full speed and, with the click of the switch, jump off into retirement with no time for adjustment and a thoughtful phase-out strategy, it will be devastating. Because of your knowledge of the phaseout and your ability to take advantage of the "of counsel" consultant role in for the law office, you will coordinate a soft landing into retirement.

Letting go is hard to do.[4] As you transition into retirement, there will certainly be some issues that you will need to look out for. Consider these issues:

• Financial security. Are your financials in line, and have you spoken to a financial advisor relating to your investable assets and your lifestyle spending in your retirement? Finances are the highest-ranking concerns for raising the level of anxiety of someone contemplating retirement. Do not take this issue lightly; have your financial situation mathematically analyzed and calculated. We all deserve to know exactly where we stand financially and what we should expect as we wind down and retire. We all know

---

3. GOLDSMITH, SUCCESSION 8.
4. *Id.* at 18.

attorneys have great egos and much confidence, but do not be reliant on your own advice and intuitive feelings over finances going into this final stage of your career and entering your postcareer life. Your financial standing cannot be taken lightly; it needs to be thoroughly analyzed. You need to understand things such as strategies for taking social security, the number of automobiles you will anticipate buying in retirement, and your vacation and travel budget. Will your children be a financial burden, and how much will you budget for such burden? How much can you anticipate earning in your "of counsel" relationship? What are your financial needs—that is, money for the things you absolutely must have, such as a roof over your head, health insurance, and necessary living expenses? What are your wants? travel, second home, or boat? country club membership? All of these things need to be calculated and figured out so that the financial anxiety in retirement is minimized.

- Loss of business perks. It is probably unlikely your law firm has a corporate jet, but even automobile allowances, banquets, parties, dinners, cell phone usage, golf outings, client golf engagements, and out-of-town company retreats are all perks that you need to be prepared to release, both emotionally and financially.

- Loss of status. This may be the most difficult, and people become a few degrees less relevant every year into retirement. Loss of status is real, and it needs to be understood. However, maybe it is never understood until it becomes a reality in your life. Nonetheless, while people may

> The one issue that does seem to get overlooked is the meaning that your life has had in practicing law and contributing to the social good.

no longer seek your legal counsel, which gave you a high degree of status, your life's work and legacy will be that of building the firm as a lasting pillar in the community. Be ready for the loss of power. As a partner in the law firm, you were in the clients' and other attorneys' circle of influence, and people looked to you for problem solving. When you needed administrative work done, you had a team of administrative assistants who did work for you, assisting you with hard problems, easy problems, and everything between. You will no longer wield that stick of power, influence, and authority. Depending on your management team, when your firm was growing, your suggestions became orders and people jumped to execute on those suggestions. That dynamic will be largely gone, but your influence will not.

- Relationships. Like many successful businesspeople, partners in law firms spend an extraordinary amount of time with other partners in the same law firm, with other law firms, and also with clients. It is somewhat surprising, how many of your relationships are business related. Not to minimize how important family relationships are, and these will not change, but it is absolutely true that a majority of your relationships are work related—and those will begin to diminish. Recall that, as noted in the marketing section of this book, it was strongly suggested that you will market to and obtain many clients who are within your age group. Therefore, at this point in your career, many of your clients are also retiring; whether or not they are five or ten years in front of you or behind you, there will be a commonality between you and your clients, who after thirty or forty years of a relationship with your practice have become your friends. As a result, some of those relationships will remain, and more fishing outings, rounds of golf, and dinners with spouses will happen without almost a word about work and legal issues. When those issues do come up, they will be in some happy context, with you and your friends reminiscing about the old cases and transactions that occurred, and in each of these cases the war stories will be delightful to recall.

- Life meaning and social contributions. The one issue that does seem to get overlooked is the meaning that your life has had in practicing law and contributing to the social good. Whether or not you are winning cases for businesses and clients in need, working with the school board or YMCA, running a coat drive, or engaging in other philanthropic endeavors, these are the experiences that have fueled you from project to project and given your life great meaning. That does not need to end in retirement. The biggest mistake about retirement is thinking that the joy of retirement comes from being financially secure and going on cruises, golf junkets, and gardening and that these are the things that will keep you fresh and active. There is a body of authoritative work that suggests that the continued contribution to society, either in sweat equity or with financial support, or even both, continues to give one's life meaning and bring happiness to the retiree. As a result, the phaseout of your practicing law is not the phaseout of your contributions to society. You can continue to do philanthropic work through the law office and through other IRC § 501(c)(3)s in your area that need help and assistance. What about a new undertaking? Start your own IRC § 501(c)(3) to create a platform for the betterment of your favorite social cause. In the end, making a difference is much more important than making a living, or making money.[5]

---

5. *See id.* at 31.

Chapter 40

Fixing the Mature Practice

On occasion, an already existing law office, or a new resulting practice from a combination of various attorneys coming together to form their own law office, reexamines its methodologies and business model only to realize that the law office is not as successful as it could be—for some known or unknown reasons. Sometimes some of the young partners may have a strong opinion why the law office is lacking in the success it deserves. Sometimes the attorneys in the law office, including the partners, are so entrenched in their day-to-day activity, working *in* the business, that they fail to step back to analyze their own systems and efficiencies.

We have frequently seen that as the founding partner matures and starts nearing retirement age, the second generation of attorneys start becoming insecure and start questioning the future of the firm, their jobs, and their careers. Keep in mind that at that time, the second generation of attorneys would be approximately forty years old and starting to think that they may not be as mobile in the job market as they once were. As a result, whether triggered by the senior partners or the next-generation partners, a restart may be in order for the practice to reenergize the firm, the attorneys, and the support staff. As a result, a thorough analysis needs to be made for all of the systems necessary to make the law firm successful. The first place to start is with the execution and completion of the questionnaire for fixing the mature practice by the serious stakeholders in the firm, the partners, and the long-tenured associates, and even key administrative assistants. The questionnaire here sets forth a Q&A for an evaluation of the critical elements of the firm. It asks for answers about clearly objective criteria, many of which will be obtained from reviewing the measurables produced by the partners. What is critical is ascertaining the objective truth from the documentation (such as the measurables that are documented in Chapter 25) provided and then comparing the objective truth to the perceived belief set forth in the questionnaire from the partner. A best-case scenario is the use of this questionnaire, along with a disinterested third-party consultant, to ask the hard follow-up questions to all partners, review and compare the objective measurables, and make a disinterested, objective, assessment of the law office and its deficiencies.

QUESTIONNAIRE: FIXING THE MATURE PRACTICE

DEFINITIONS

Practice Group: A substantive area of the law under which attorneys provide services to clients.

Practice Management: The structure and disciplines necessary to run the business.

1) What are the firm's three (3) strongest Practice Groups, in order of strongest first?

a. _____

b. _____

c. _____

2) Provide the percentage of revenue derived by the firm in each of the above Practice Groups.

a. ____%

b. ____%

c. ____%

3) Rate the following disciplines on a scale from 1 to 5, 5 being the best, on how the firm performs.

Worst   Best

a. All attorneys are committed to providing exemplary legal services and deliver A+ quality work product.   1 2 3 4 5

Comment: _____

_____

If not, specifically who does not? _____

b. All attorneys meet or exceed monthly billing goals.   1 2 3 4 5

Comment: _____

_____

If not, specifically who does not? _____

c. All attorneys uphold their duty to market, be involved in their communities, social organizations, and are active in bar associations.   1 2 3 4 5

Comment: _____

_____

If not, specifically who does not? _____

d. Senior attorneys take the time and are willing to train younger attorneys.

1 2 3 4 5

Comment: _____

_____

If not, specifically who does not? _____

QUESTIONNAIRE: FIXING THE MATURE PRACTICE (continued)

e. All attorneys understand that the law office is a business and want to participate in the operation of the business and be profitable.   Worst   Best

         1 2 3 4 5

    Comment: _____

    _____

    If not, specifically who does not? _____

4) Are any attorneys overpaid?   Yes/No

    If yes, who? _____

5) Who is/are the leader(s) in this firm? _____

    _____

6) Which attorneys add the least value to the firm, and why? _____

    _____

7) Who should be the successor leader in this firm? _____

    _____

8) What is unique about the firm that gives you a competitive edge? _____

    _____

    _____

9) Is there an Operating/Shareholder Agreement?   Yes/No

    a. If no to the above question, is the firm better off not having an agreement?

                         Yes/No

    b. If yes to the above question, is it followed?   Yes/No

10) What are the firm's strengths in Practice Management, in order of strongest first?

    a. _____

    b. _____

    c. _____

11) Who are the best three support staff employees?

    a. _____

    b. _____

    c. _____

12) Who are the support staff persons who add the least value to the firm?

    a. _____

    b. _____

    c. _____

13) What is the pay range for support staff personnel?

    a. Starting wage: $_____

    b. Highest paid: $_____

QUESTIONNAIRE: FIXING THE MATURE PRACTICE (continued)

14) Are any support staff employees overpaid or underpaid?   Yes/No
    If yes, who? _____

15) Describe the benefits package provided to support staff. _____
    _____
    _____

16) Describe the benefits package provided to associate attorneys. _____
    _____
    _____

17) Grade the office manager (head of billing, accounting and banking, etc.) on a scale
    from 1 to 5, with 5 being the best:

		Worst	Best
a.	Competence on billing and accounting software	1 2 3 4 5	
b.	Sending out bills on time	1 2 3 4 5	
c.	Handling irate client calls on billing	1 2 3 4 5	
d.	Accuracy	1 2 3 4 5	
e.	Overall accounting savvy	1 2 3 4 5	
f.	Oversight of cost management of office overhead	1 2 3 4 5	
g.	Managing human resource responsibilities	1 2 3 4 5	
h.	Managing support staff	1 2 3 4 5	
i.	Responsiveness to Partner requests	1 2 3 4 5	
j.	Continually strives to improve office manager skills	1 2 3 4 5	

18) Rate the following disciplines on a scale from 1 to 5, with 5 being the best, on how
    the firm performs.

		Worst	Best
a.	Traditional networking	1 2 3 4 5	
b.	Website management	1 2 3 4 5	
c.	Social media networking	1 2 3 4 5	
d.	The firm's commitment to bar associations and legal profession	1 2 3 4 5	
e.	The firm's commitment to community development	1 2 3 4 5	
f.	Established one-year goals	1 2 3 4 5	
g.	Established five-year goals	1 2 3 4 5	
h.	Client satisfaction and loyalty	1 2 3 4 5	
i.	The firm's commitment to technology	1 2 3 4 5	
j.	The firm's commitment to "best practices" disciplines	1 2 3 4 5	
k.	A method to consider and address client criticism and comments	1 2 3 4 5	
l.	Procedures to incorporate ideas and feedback of clients	1 2 3 4 5	

QUESTIONNAIRE: FIXING THE MATURE PRACTICE (continued)

		Worst	Best
m.	Giving employees (attorneys and support staff) the space and tools to succeed		1 2 3 4 5
n.	Giving "real-time" recognition to attorneys and support staff		1 2 3 4 5
o.	Quality of support staff		1 2 3 4 5
p.	Quality of attorneys		1 2 3 4 5
q.	Billing practices		1 2 3 4 5
r.	Accounts receivable management		1 2 3 4 5
s.	Procedures to incorporate ideas and feedback of employees		1 2 3 4 5
t.	Working in a high-performance environment		1 2 3 4 5
u.	Quality of life (i.e., a balance of work and personal life)		1 2 3 4 5
v.	Mentoring or "buddy" system		1 2 3 4 5

Explain all scores of 2 or less: _____

_____

_____

_____

_____

Explain all scores of 4 or higher: _____

_____

_____

_____

_____

19) Are you willing to work five (5) additional hours per week on marketing? Yes/No

20) How many business lunches do you go on per month?

_____

21) How many after-hours dinners/events do you attend every month?   _____

_____

22) Are you on the board or advising committee of any not-for-profit?   Yes/No

If yes, which one?   _____

23) What bar association activities are you involved in? _____

_____

_____

24) Do you chair a committee?   Yes/No

25) What industry association are you a member of? _____

26) What chamber of commerce or professional networking group are you a member of? _____

QUESTIONNAIRE: FIXING THE MATURE PRACTICE (continued)

27) In your opinion, how many more years will the firm last if disciplines do not improve?

_____

28) What are the three (3) most important problems that the firm needs to fix?

a. _____

b. _____

c. _____

29) Do you have a clear set of business values and purposes?   Yes/No

30) What is the purpose of the firm's existence? _____

_____

31) What are the five (5) most important values for the firm globally, involving client satisfaction, employee satisfaction, profitability, social change or conscience, community involvement, commitment to the legal community, or any other uncompromisable value?

a. _____

b. _____

c. _____

d. _____

e. _____

32) Are there aspects or qualities about the firm that are promoted or advertised but, in all honesty, are not genuinely acted upon or incorporated in the daily operations for the firm? In other words, are there aspect of the firm that would be considered a "false truth"? _____

_____

_____

_____

33) Is there any member of the management team who has not, or will not, adopt the core values or follow-through with the things that are required to continue to grow the firm?   Yes/No

If yes, who? _____

34) For any area in which the firm or individuals are deficient? Are there obstacles that are preventing success that could be corrected? _____

_____

_____

Usually an outside mediator or consultant takes the questionnaire and the report of the measurables and balances the answers to see what consistencies come up regarding the firm's strengths and weaknesses and to see where the outliers exist in partner answers. Once all the partners have time to commit their answers to the questionnaire with some thoughtful analysis, the questionnaires become the talking points for the people, the systems, and culture of the firm and the corrective action needed thereupon.

Therefore, the first place to start is with the revenue-generating employees of the firm—the attorneys.

Five-Tool Attorney

The five-tool attorney requirements never get old, and attorneys never mature beyond the requirements needed to be the five-tool attorney.

First, regarding your attorneys, does the firm have A+ players on the bus? Remember, this is about a mature law firm, and there really is no analysis here on the ramp up for new attorneys. We are assuming all attorneys have been practicing longer than ten years, are experienced in their own practice groups, and could go toe to toe with any of their contemporaries in large firms in a metropolitan area. It is really very difficult to go any further in discussing the future success of the law firm if your attorneys are not A+ players.

Sometimes in small firms, attorneys need to play many roles and be generalists, so even if they have fifteen to twenty-five years of experience, they may not have a concentrated level of experience in one or two practice groups. Remember the discussion on the first tool of the five-tool attorney in Section 1 of the book. If you do not have the right people on the bus, offload them as soon as you determine that changing seats on the bus would be fruitless.

The second tool is meeting and beating billing goals. I am shocked to hear how many senior attorneys, *excellent at their craft*, seem to take billing so lackadaisically and make it so insignificant. Usually these are attorneys who were hired after the firm was established and never became founding partners of a firm. The founding partner always understands and keeps in mind that in the earlier years of running the practice, if he or she did not bill your client, he or she did not get paid, and he or she did not eat. As a result, the founding partners always understand that they need to bill their time in order to get paid.

Some other attorneys, often incredibly skilled, simply do not want to take the time to bill their time contemporaneously when they do their work. There is another type of attorney that sometimes behaves like a new attorney and does not understand or appreciate the value of their services. As a result, such an attorney always underbills, is intimidated by clients, and is afraid to send them a bill for the full time that the attorney worked on the matter. This type of flaw in the attorney's character is usually the result of an insecurity or lack of confidence resulting in the attorney's belief that his or her own work product does not have much value. If the firm has billing goals and the attorney wants to work eighty or ninety hours a week to bill thirty hours a week, that may be acceptable to that attorney, but realistically, that attorney cannot last very long under those circumstances.

In keeping with the theme of meeting billing goals, the mature practice must certainly have some published expectations of billing goals for their attorneys. As part of having a successful practice, and any successful business for that matter, measurables are an absolute necessity for continued motivations for an employee.[1] Attorneys, although with mixed results, want to know where they stand on meeting or beating their billable goal expectations and want a clear set of expectations on all of their performance expectations, but particularly their billing goals. In summary, the mature practice has to ascertain which attorneys are not meeting their billable goals and why they are not. If the attorneys simply refuse to bill clients for their time, that issue needs to be addressed immediately. If the workflow is too light in that particular practice group, marketing has to be intensified or that attorney needs to reinvent himself or herself and provide services in another practice group.

The next analysis of every attorney in the mature practice should be how involved the attorneys are at marketing and civic involvement. For a law firm to flourish all of the attorneys need to be active in their communities and involved in bar association activities to further the growth of the firm. Marketing and civic involvement are the subject matter of Chapter 26, are absolutely required of each individual attorney to further the efforts of the law office, and include traditional law office networking, use of digital media sites such as LinkedIn and Facebook, monthly activities with referral sources, public speaking, and community development. Marketing also relates to an attorney's role as relationship manager for existing clients so that existing clients can be cultivated for additional work.

Many attorneys want to come to the office, put in a hard day's work, go home at the end of the day, and be done with their commitment to the law office. At the mature law office, senior partners are often comfortable resting and relying on lifelong referral sources or clients and are not interested in pushing for new contacts and a broader-based network. You cannot build a winning, growing law firm with that level of buy-in from attorneys. The attorneys are usually complacent. The commitment to make marketing a job requirement may require a seismic shift in culture and conduct by the partners and associates and the law firm in general, but it needs to be made in order to grow the practice.

Partners train young attorneys joining the firm—and generally, senior associates are very good at this—but everyone needs to take the time to train new, young attorneys. We are all charged as professionals to help develop the next generation of professionals, and training and grooming young attorneys is an important part of our duty. Generally, we

---

1. PATRICK LENCIONI, THE THREE SIGNS OF A MISERABLE JOB (Jossey-Bass 2007).

do not see this problem in mature practices. However, as a practical matter, many mature practices tell us they have not had a young attorney in the office for many years. That may need to change.

Last, all associates, especially the senior people in the office, need to accept the principle that the firm comes first. This principle must be ingrained within the law firm's culture. This means, generally, that actions taken at the partner level need to put the firm first, and sometimes individuals need to subordinate their own interest, including financial interest, for the betterment of the firm. Although many of the long-term partners are in the firm to earn a living, increase their own personal net worth, and bring more money home to their families, if they buy into the program set forth in this book, sometimes a short-term step back in income will yield multiple steps forward in long-term company growth and personal income. Every partner needs to treat the law practice as a business, and the business comes first. And, time needs to be invested in growing the law practice, aside from the time practicing law.

> We are all charged as professionals to help develop the next generation of professionals, and training and grooming young attorneys is an important part of our duty.

Support Staff

The next component of quality personnel is an objective look at your support staff and office manager. Remember that attorneys are the revenue-generating employees of the business, and *all* other employees must support the lawyers so they can maximize billable hours.

All administrative assistants need to be paid fairly and at the market rate, but they must keep in mind that small law firms cannot pay for any employee, particularly administrative assistants, based on the expectations of quality. Their pay must be commensurate with their skill set at the time of being hired. Then, in addition, pay increases must be commensurate both with increases in the cost of living and, more important, the additional value the administrative assistant brings to the firm as he or she matures. In other words, it may happen that the administrative assistant's skill set remains limited and so that person's additional value to the firm remains limited, and therefore the person's annual raises should just be consistent with the cost-of-living increases.

In the alternative, if the administrative assistant continues to take on more responsibility, becomes more efficient and is able to help more attorneys, and helps with some of the law office management, that administrative assistant brings more value to the law firm and should be given raises commensurate with his or her value added to the firm.

For example, if the administrative assistant really did not grow in his or her role in the last twelve months and the cost of living increased by 3%, then a 3% annual raise is fair. However, if, during the same twelve-month period, another administrative assistant provided an additional 10% of value to the firm (maybe by just being faster, being more efficient, or taking on additional responsibilities), then that administrative assistant should earn a 13% raise the following year (3% for cost of living and 10% for the added value).

This discussion speaks to the fact that many mature law offices overpay administrative assistants who are no longer interested in increasing their value to the firm, increasing their knowledge and skill set through college classes and seminars to make themselves more efficient and bring more value to the firm. In many cases, we see mature practices grossly overpaying administrative assistants out of loyalty, but not for the betterment of the firm.

The Business Plan

As articulated in Chapter 24, a business plan needs to be built, so that the partners do not guess at the economics of the firm, along with a blueprint for how the firm should be run. With regular, ongoing review, the firm must focus on the shortfalls and improve upon the things that it could do better. It is the blueprint and the architecture for building a winning law firm, no matter what stage of development the law firm is in and no matter how mature the firm is.

Begin by setting goals. One- and five-year goals need to be set, and you also have to create a list of assumptions that you need to meet in order to achieve your goals. Review Chapter 24 on the specifics of goal setting, but focus for the first year on the assumptions that need to be met in order to be successful. These assumptions include, but are not limited to, the proper flow of new clients every month, meeting and beating billing goals, eliminating accounts receivable, providing the right technology and tools for everyone to be successful, and creating a happy work environment.

Next, there needs to be a leader of the firm, possibly from the next generation for the mature firm. Arguably, the firm could be led by a management team, but there needs to be somebody who absolutely takes it upon himself or herself to constantly be working *on* the business, not only *in* it as an attorney. Your firm needs to be led by a leader but managed by a management team. Someone needs to be planning the next improvements for the office, identifying the shortfalls of the office, thinking about the next adjustments of the practice groups for the law office, and being innovative in designing the next wave of marketing for the law office.

The next part of the business plan has to focus on the management team and the systems that you put in place for making the firm efficient, effective, and successful. The management team has to reduce the systems to writing because there needs to be documentation for support staff to follow so that the firm is never reliant on one strong administrative assistant, but can interchangeably move assistants around—especially when minimizing the retraining time and costs associated with turnover—through the use of manuals on which everyone can rely. The management of the firm needs to establish a current document library that is open to the firm, where everyone understands the whereabouts of certain documents and how to find them. The mature practice usually needs an upgrade in technology. Further, certain attorneys, presumably partners, need to be assigned to run certain disciplines of the law office and report to the management team about the functionality of those disciplines.

Next on your business plan, you need to set forth those policies discussed above relating to employees, billing goals, systems for hiring employees, employee review, and overall, getting the right people on the bus and getting them in positions to succeed.

People are the most important component in a law office. The task of hiring and keeping the right people on a team and properly and ethically offloading the wrong people is a discipline in and of itself, and it cannot be taken lightly. This is a difficult process, but it is necessary to turn around a complacent practice.

Marketing and lead generation must be a part of the business plan. Start with the question for each of your practice groups, who is your client? And then once thoroughly analyzed, determine how to find that client and market to them.

> Are we trying to create an environment where everybody looks and acts the same? Absolutely not.

On a secondary level, ask yourself who our referral sources are? Once you determine who your referral sources are, evaluate where they are located and identify who those connectors, mavens, and salespeople are with respect to your practice. Do not assume that your clients from twenty-five years ago are still your core clients. Times change, and disciplines change. Reevaluate your client base and your internal skill sets. Ask yourself what your clients value. Pleasing them after they referred your firm is equally as important as the client satisfaction process for existing clients. As part of marketing and lead generation, you need to have an analysis made of your lead conversion system. You need to specifically have a plan to convert telephone calls, general introductions, and inquiries into clients.

Client fulfillment and satisfaction is a section unto itself in your business plan. Sometimes we refer to this as best practices. Senior attorneys many times mistakenly believe that doing a great job for the client is all the client asks, and as a result you have fulfilled the client's needs and satisfied the client's wants. However, in a winning law firm, it is far greater than that. You need to have systems in place where everyone understands the firm's best practices expectations from the initial meeting and follows up with regard to client communications, client file management, and billing procedures. If you do, you will have a client for life.

Last, perform the exercises in Chapters 29 and 30 to really determine why the firm exists and what the characteristics are of the successful, happy attorneys in the office, and then commit those purposes and core values to writing so everyone understands why the firm exists. Are we trying to create an environment where everybody looks and acts the same? Absolutely not. Diversification is healthy and fun. But two attorneys from completely different backgrounds can align themselves on the same path, enjoying each other's diversified view of life and the firm, and pull together to have the same priorities with respect to the firm's core purpose. Once the core purpose is well defined, an attorney from any background, any political or ethnic persuasion, can get behind the core purpose, and all will have a unified voice as to why they come to work every day.

Opportunities for Improvement

Similar to the steps taken in Section 2 of the book, once the business plan is written, prepared, and signed off on by all partners of the firm (and potentially other stakeholders), the places for improvement need to be looked at as opportunities. Keep in mind that whether the mature practice is in a state of decline or stable, a certain degree of complacency has set in, and some of the items in the business plan need to be addressed immediately as a matter of survival. Like all plans, drivers, and pillars for success, you need to take all of the items in the business plan and grade them A, B, or C. A is for items that need to be addressed immediately, and if they are not fixed and repaired immediately, the firm will further decline to the point of dissolution. B items are items that will begin the process of growing the firm in a successful, upward trajectory. B items may not be addressed immediately, but they need to be addressed if the goal of the management team is firm growth. C items are not priorities at all, but they should be graded as such for the five- and ten-year goals.

Therefore, all of your A items need to be addressed immediately, though you hope there will not be many immediate needs for the firm. The firm certainly needs to address things such as providing the best tools, items for success for the attorneys and support staff, and other items that are pay-to-play requirements to be successful. These might include meeting and exceeding billing goals, collecting on a high percentage of billable work, implementing high work product standards and best practices programs, institutionalizing marketing for all attorneys, and other necessary requirements to be successful. The A- and B-ranked needs of the law firm should be looked at not as deficiencies, though they very well are, but as opportunities for improvement. The lawyers in the firm will be surprised at how many of the administrative assistants and associate attorneys will be delighted to undertake an endeavor to re-create and renew the law firm. Certainly, because additional work will be required in some of these areas, some attorneys and support staff will not buy into the change. Change is difficult for many people who are set in their ways and not interested in restarting when they do not see the immediate benefit for themselves personally. Nonetheless, because of the exercise that the entire management group went through to create the business plan, the benefits will be startling.

Conclusion

It should not be assumed that you cannot teach an old dog new tricks. You can, but it can be difficult. However, if the shareholders in your firm have taken the steps to reenergize its mature practice, the shareholders appear to have recognized a problem and want to fix it. In using a systematic methodology for analyzing the various practice management disciplines required to run a law office, coupled with an analysis of the delivery of high-quality legal services, the management team with the help of a disinterested third-party consultant could cut through the daily noise and grind of running the law office, identify deficiencies and discontinuities of certain systems, and determine where the mature firm needs to focus its attention for success.

Recall, if the mature firm undergoes this process, its ultimate goal will be to survive the retirement of the early founding partners. Otherwise, why go through the process? The founding partners need to buy in and commit to leaving a legacy of the firm behind after they retire. Therefore, as a practical matter, this exercise is generally taken by the second-tier partners who still have ten, fifteen, or twenty years remaining to practice law and want to see the firm grow beyond the subsequent retirement of the founding partners. All in all, it should be a way to reenergize and rejuvenate quality attorneys and further build a winning, successful law firm in their marketplace.

Chapter 41

The Small Firm Merger

Undoubtedly, a young, aggressive, growing law firm will eventually come to the realization that by virtue of its size, it is not large enough to attract middle-market client attention, and such size will hinder the firm's ability to get bigger, more substantial clients. There is some truth that medium- and large-sized businesses do not necessarily want to hire small law firms because in the event an issue breaks bad during a case or during a transaction, the person at the business who hired the lawyer will get blamed for not hiring a large law firm. As a result, in middle-market companies, C suite employees generally want to play it safe and hire a more substantial (i.e., larger) law firm. Some small law firms see this as a limitation to their ability to grow, and, although very confident and competent with their providing of legal services, they seek to merge with other firms simply to add girth to the firm and to increase the breadth of practice groups and legal services they offer to potential clients.

There are also limitations. Taking your firm, which has great culture, energy, vibe, direction, and people, and mixing it with an unknown group of attorneys and support staff could be disastrous to what you have built up. Moreover, even if it is a testing event that fails, it will still set you back several years in the growth of the firm. So, as a result, great thought needs to be given to a merger with another firm.

Purpose

First, examine whether you really want or need to merge with another firm.

There are usually two reasons you seek a merger with another firm.

The first is simply to add skill sets that you do not have. For example, as articulated in the very first section of the book, a group of transactional lawyers who continuously refer litigation cases out of their office to other law offices may want to merge with a commercial litigation firm in order to keep both transactional work and litigation matters in-house. Similarly, attorneys who spend most of their time in court would oftentimes like to have skilled transactional lawyers in-house because once the litigation attorneys do a great job for clients in court, clients want to hire the law office for all of their corporate work. However, many do not understand the dichotomy between transactional lawyers and litigation attorneys and, as a result, ask litigation attorneys to handle transactional matters for them. Moreover, the litigation lawyers may have dynamic personalities and may be very visible in the community and so may get telephone calls regularly on various transactional matters that they do not handle competently. As a result, the safest and best marriage between two groups of attorneys is between transactional lawyers and litigation attorneys.

Second, oftentimes a law firm will find a niche that is outside of the firm's core services, yet because of the physical location of their law office, they receive a steady stream of phone calls from clients on other types of legal matters. A business law firm may get regular calls for traffic and "driving under the influence" (DUI) work, divorce and other domestic disputes, or immigration law. These are all niche services that business transactional lawyers are unqualified to handle and may therefore seek to add that type of expertise to the office. Similarly, transactional lawyers may not have the expertise in federal and state tax analysis and therefore want to merge with a group of lawyers to introduce a higher degree of tax knowledge than presently exists in the firm.

> The starting process for any small firm merger is obtaining a consultant to objectively ascertain the strengths and weakness of both firms.

Further, with respect to merging for the sake of bringing in a new practice group, sometimes an existing firm struggles in one practice group. Until the members of the firm really analyze their strengths and weaknesses, they are unprepared to make a determination that they do, in fact, need a leader or strong partner-level mentor to completely understand the operation of that particular practice group. Different practice groups have different issues: immigration law tends to be very administrative law driven with forms and timing issues, criminal lawyers have their own way of billing and obtaining fees from bonds posted with court, and different practice groups have their own nuances where an experienced lawyer with that knowledge could drive that practice group to greater growth and success.

Another purpose for small firms merging is just simply to get bigger. As stated earlier, sometimes clients just want to hire a larger firm because they begin to recognize that a one- or two-person operation is too small to handle their legal needs, and they need a larger firm with a larger breadth of services. Some of those clients become frustrated with smaller firms because their turnaround time to work starts to slow down, and the turnaround of documents and telephone calls reaches an unacceptable level. At that time, the clients are willing to pay additional fees for better service.

Also, there is a perception that bigger is better in the legal field. As attorneys, you know that is not necessarily true, but it is undeniable that if the perception exists within the client's mind, then that alone is a reason to give consideration for mergers and accelerated growth.

If the merger is geared toward just getting larger for the sake of obtaining bigger clients, an increase in revenue on a per-partner basis is not necessarily the driver. However, the merger of law firms must be looked at closely as a merger of various practice groups to ensure that the clients you are seeking to satisfy will be gaining greater expertise in the practice groups on which they rely. Said another way, an ad hoc system of merging with no goal in mind to increase services in particular practice groups is no plan at all. Further, even if the merger is designed to increase your expertise in particular practice groups, that is a valid and good reason to merge, so long as the end result is a cohesive organization and there is an agreement among the partners that the purpose is true, is just, and will heighten client satisfaction.

The final reason that firms want to merge is to make more money per partner. At first blush, this may not seem like a reasonable plan to justify a merger and assume all of the risks inherent in merging with another firm. However, after your analysis throughout this process and at the conclusion of this chapter, you may determine that a merger can happen with another firm, that the firms' cultures will be enhanced, not diminished. You may believe that because of the synergies brought together among the firms, partners can, in fact, increase their per-partner revenue without compromising their commitment to the community and philanthropic purposes. If you do, that certainly can be a just and fair reason for a merger.

These types of mergers are generally identified when a law firm is referring quite a few cases to other attorneys, cases in which they lose control or take no responsibility for after the referral, which is a loss of revenue for the firm.[1] As a result, your firm, the referring attorneys, could be referring many cases out of the office and losing fees. If those cases were kept in-house, revenue would increase at the firm and, presumptively, earnings per partner would increase.

Process

The starting process for any small firm merger is obtaining a consultant to objectively ascertain the strengths and weakness of both firms, understand the financial strengths and

---

1. *See* MODEL RULES OF PROF'L CONDUCT R. 1.5. There are rules that govern the division of the fee to a client between two or more lawyers not in the same firm. Usually this is done when the fee is a contingency fee and the division is between a referring lawyer and a trial specialist. Remember, in these cases, the fee has to be divided on the proportion of services they rendered and the client must agree to the arrangement.

weaknesses of the firms, interview all partners (and in some cases associates and support staff), and calculate and prepare a report for the proposal for a successor firm that will work culturally and economically well into the future.

The idea that the partners of the two firms can come together, meet around a conference table, and speak freely about their strengths and weaknesses is somewhat idealistic; it can happen, but oftentimes partners in law firms really do not express themselves openly and objectively about these matters. Therefore, the correct starting point is to have all of the partners from both firms complete the following partner questionnaire to evaluate the strengths and weaknesses of the growing law firm, their people, their systems, and their culture. Keep in mind that many of the questions ask for objective information, which can be obtained from financials, payroll information, and management reports. However, it is telling to see how partners perceive these issues and answer the questions that reflect their perception of certain items relating to the firm.

PARTNER QUESTIONNAIRE

THE SMALL FIRM MERGER

DEFINITIONS

Practice Group: A substantive area of the law under which attorneys provide services to clients.

Practice Management: The structure and discipline(s) necessary to run the business.

1) What are your firm's strongest practice areas, in order of strongest first.

   a. _____

   b. _____

   c. _____

2) What type of cases does your firm handle better than the larger firms?

   _____

   _____

3) How many malpractice cases have been filed against your firm in the last ten years?

   _____

   _____

4) How many attorney disciplinary grievances been filed against the firm, or attorneys in the firm, in the last ten years?

   _____

   _____

5) What Practice Groups do you have that are challenges to manage?

   _____

   _____

6) What Practice Groups from the merging firm would your firm keep? Why?

   _____

   _____

7) How concentrated is your practice in your top five (5) clients (and affiliates)? List the top five clients and the percentage of fees that such client represented to the firm.

   a. _____ ____%

   b. _____ ____%

   c. _____ ____%

   d. _____ ____%

   e. _____ ____%

PARTNER QUESTIONNAIRE (continued)

8) After base salaries were paid to all employees and reasonable bonuses paid, how much profit was distributed to partners last year?

_____

_____

9) What is your annual compensation package?
   a. Base salary: $_____
   b. Bonus: $_____
   c. Profit distribution: $_____
   d. Total annual monetary benefit: $_____

10) How much profit (before partner bonuses) did the firm make last year?
    $_____

11) How much does the highest-paid administrative assistant get paid annually?
    $_____

12) What is the starting salary for administrative assistants?
    $_____

13) What is the standard compensation package for a first-year associate?
    a. Base salary: $_____
    b. Annual bonus: $_____
    c. Other bonus opportunities: $_____

14) Do you have a group health care plan?

                                                                    Yes/No

    a. If yes, how much does the firm contribute for the employee? $_____
    b. For the employee's family? $_____

15) Do you have a 401(k) plan?   Yes/No
    a. How much is the employer's annual contribution? $_____
    b. Describe the "safe harbor" provisions: _____

    _____

16) Do you have a high turnover with employees?   Yes/No
    If yes, describe why: _____

    _____

17) Grade your office manager (head of billing, accounting, and banking) on a scale from 1 to 5, with 5 being the best:

                                                                Worst   Best

    a. Competence on your billing and accounting software   1 2 3 4 5
    b. Accuracy   1 2 3 4 5

PARTNER QUESTIONNAIRE (continued)

		Worst	Best
c.	Handling irate client calls on billing		1 2 3 4 5
d.	Responsiveness to Partner requests		1 2 3 4 5
e.	Overall accounting knowledge		1 2 3 4 5
f.	Managing support staff		1 2 3 4 5
g.	Sending out bills on time		1 2 3 4 5

18) What is your billing and accounting software? _____

_____

19) Rate the following disciplines on a scale from 1 to 5, 5 being the best, on how your firm performs.

                                                 Worst   Best

a. All of your attorneys are committed to providing exemplary legal services and delivering A+ quality work product.   1 2 3 4 5

Comment: _____

_____

If not, specifically who does not? _____

b. All of your attorneys meet or exceed monthly billing goals.   1 2 3 4 5

Comment: _____

_____

If not, specifically who does not? _____

c. All of your attorneys are charged with the duty to market the firm, be involved in their communities and social organizations, and are active in bar associations.   1 2 3 4 5

Comment: _____

_____

If not, specifically who does not? _____

d. Your senior attorneys are willing and take the time to train younger attorneys.   1 2 3 4 5

Comment: _____

_____

If not, specifically, who does not? _____

e. All of your attorneys understand that the law office is a business and want to participate in the operation of the business and be profitable.   1 2 3 4 5

Comment: _____

_____

If not, specifically who does not? _____

PARTNER QUESTIONNAIRE (continued)

f. How would you rate your firm's associate requirements or expectations to achieve admission to partnership?   Worst   Best

1 2 3 4 5

Comment: _____

_____

20) Does your firm have documented systems and policies for:
   a. Billing: Yes/No
   b. Managing accounts receivable: Yes/No
   c. Marketing: Yes/No
   d. Digital media marketing: Yes/No
   e. Client communication: Yes/No
   f. Hiring attorneys: Yes/No
   g. Employee handbook: Yes/No
   h. Accounting: Yes/No
   i. Banking: Yes/No

21) In terms of Practice Management, what are your firm's top three (3) strengths, in order?
   a. _____
   b. _____
   c. _____

22) What are your firm's top three (3) weaknesses in Practice Management, in order?
   a. _____
   b. _____
   c. _____

23) Which of the two law firms has better physical office space?

_____

24) Which firm has better technology?

_____

25) Do you have annual partner meetings setting the course for the following year's goals?

_____

26) Do you have a written business plan?   Yes/No

27) What are your annual billing requirements for associates?

_____

_____

28) What is the partnership track for an associate in years? _____

_____

PARTNER QUESTIONNAIRE (continued)

29) How many of your partners should be on the management committee of the merged firm?

_____

_____

30) Is the title partner significant to you? _____

31) What are your marketing requirements for each attorney?

    a. Public speaking? _____

    b. Community involvement? _____

    c. Bar association activities? _____

    d. Chambers of commerce? _____

    e. Trade associations? _____

    f. Monthly networking meetings? _____

    g. Monthly lunches, coffees? _____

    h. Social digital media postings? _____

32) Why do you want your firm to merge? Grade the following on a scale of 1 to 5, with 5 being the highest:

	Lowest Highest
a. Because a bigger firm means we can get larger clients	1 2 3 4 5
b. To make more money	1 2 3 4 5
c. So that clients I used to refer out to other firms stay in-house	1 2 3 4 5
d. To cross-sell existing clients to new practice groups	1 2 3 4 5
e. Just because bigger is better in law firms	1 2 3 4 5
f. We need help in certain practice groups, and the merger would provide that	1 2 3 4 5
g. We need help with our practice management, and the merger would provide that	1 2 3 4 5
h. To become licensed in other states (i.e., expand geographically)	1 2 3 4 5
i. To obtain an expertise that we need	1 2 3 4 5
j. To reenergize our law firm	1 2 3 4 5
k. To increase or diversify the client base	1 2 3 4 5
l. To solidify clients in common with both firms	1 2 3 4 5
m. To enhance the level of sophistication of work through breadth of services	1 2 3 4 5
n. To follow the trend of firms to merge	1 2 3 4 5

PARTNER QUESTIONNAIRE (continued)

o. To correct existing internal weaknesses among staff (e.g., to fill gaps in age
    and experience levels, lack of rainmakers, lack of leadership, etc.)

    Lowest Highest
    1 2 3 4 5

p. To control expenses or cure your existing firm's economic problems

    1 2 3 4 5

33) What is a reasonable age for retirement? _____

34) Should there be a requirement that a partner convert his or her status as a partner
    to "of counsel" at retirement age? _____

    _____

35) What is your firm's mission statement? _____

    _____

36) Do you live it?   _____

37) Do you have one-year, five-year, and ten-year goals?   Yes/No

38) Do you receive status updates on progress toward making them?
    Are they reviewed annually?   Yes/No

39) Does your firm have a "culture?"   Yes/No
    If yes, describe: _____

    _____

40) Why does your firm exist? _____

    _____

41) Is your personal reason for practicing law consistent with the firm's culture and pur-
    pose? _____

    _____

42) Does your firm have a high-energy winning atmosphere?   Yes/No

43) Do you have fun at work?   Yes/No
    Why?   _____

44) Does your firm sponsor firm outings for fun and team building?   Yes/No
    If yes, how many per year? _____

45) Would you best describe your firm as a team or simply as a group of attorneys shar-
    ing space to practice law? _____

    _____

As you can see in the questionnaire, the process starts with brutally honest questions about the attorneys, strengths and weaknesses in the firm, and malpractice cases or attorney disciplinary grievances filed against the firm. It is equally important to know the economics of the firm. How much do the partners make with respect to their base salary and their bonus and profit distributions? These are important issues because you have to immediately look at the high-level income and quality of the attorneys at the office.

The next issue is the quality and skill sets of the office manager, and last the administrative assistants, support staff, and secretaries. It is critically important that you understand the partners' perception of their own firm and the quality of people they have around them in relationship to what the general administrative assistants and attorneys are paid. To state the obvious, it is a difficult starting point when one firm pays the attorneys approximately $175,000 per year and the other firm pays them $90,000 for essentially doing the same type of work. Eventually, that disparity will uncover some shortfalls of one or both of the firms. Similarly with support staff. One firm may pay support staff assistants $14 an hour and the other may pay $30 an hour, and the shortfalls of both of those firms may come to light as you dig into the quality of the workers and the culture of the firm.

> It is critically important that you understand the partners' perception of their own firm and the quality of people they have around them in relationship to what the general administrative assistants and attorneys are paid.

Next, the questions move toward the systems in the firm, including the main systems in the firm regarding the officer manager's role of billing and banking and the attorney's role of marketing. You need to ascertain the commitment the firm has to marketing and the massive department that marketing has become in a successful, growing law firm. Since you know marketing just does not happen on its own, it is important to ascertain which partner or staff member manages and guides the firm with respect to its marketing efforts and who holds the attorneys accountable for their individual marketing plans.

You need to determine if the firms have documented systems and policies on all of these areas, including, but not limited to, client communications, hiring attorneys and support staff, and, of course, their billing and accounts receivable processes. Last, the questionnaire contemplates the analysis of the firm's culture. Taking a positive view, you know that your firm has been led by a founding partner (you) who is culture driven, and the energy in your firm is high. If your firm is run properly, there is a great deal of clarity among the attorneys and support staff as to what your values are and how you execute those values. In most cases, if you are running a successful, winning firm, the firm that you are talking to about a merger does not place as high a priority on culture. In fact, lacking the insight that you have, the other firm might define culture as a general vibe around the office in terms of friendships and the way things work. The other firm members might even think they are even a bit more sophisticated and have a formal mission statement whereby they want to be all things to all people, further illustrating a lack of true direction. The truth of the matter is that this might be the hardest hurdle to get over when it comes to a small firm merger. If the other firm is simply moving forward, perhaps despite itself, it is likely looking for a merger partner to better itself—that is your firm with great direction and a great game plan.

It is critically important that, as you ascertain the strengths and struggles of both firms, the consultant needs to identify the leaders in different categories. As a result, the consultant will make a recommendation in the preliminary Report of Merger, identifying who is best suited to run certain areas of the practice and what systems and culture the postmerger firm will adopt.

The Economics

After a thorough analysis is completed on the strengths and weaknesses of the two firms, and through a deliverable called a Report of Merger prepared by the disinterested third-party consultant, there should be an analysis in the Report of Merger on the proposed postmerger economics of the firm.

Recall, as discussed in Chapter 34 on our valuation formula, the valuation of the two firms will be based on each firm's bottom-line profits. If one firm pays all of its income out in salaries, including base salaries to the firm's partners, and at the end of the year has zero profits, then that firm is bringing no value to the merger and those partners cannot expect an equity ownership in the postmerger entity. In other words, why would the firm that is making a profit share those profits with the partners that are brining no profits to the postmerger entity? They wouldn't. However, if firm A merges with firm B, and firm A credibly produces documentation that it will earn $500,000 in the first postmerger year, and firm B credibly evidences an ability to earn $250,000 in the first postmerger year, then the combined profits of the firm will be $750,000 and two-thirds of the equity ownership of the postmerger firm should belong to the partners in firm A, and one-third of the postmerger firm should belong to the partners in firm B. How firm A allocates its two-thirds ownership of the postmerger entity is up to the firm A partners (but most likely in percentages consistent with firm A's premerger ownership structure), and firm B will allocate its one-third ownership of the postmerger firm based on its discretion (but most likely based on its premerger ownership of firm B).

As you can see, the value that the firms are bringing to the postmerger law firm are directly commensurate with the bottom-line profits of the premerger firms. The valuation analysis for the postmerger firm works exactly like the valuation process when analyzing a sale to other attorneys. It is simply a function of the bottom-line cash flows, net income, EBITDA, or cash-out, depending on your valuation formula. Moreover, whatever formula the two firms use for profit distribution, they need to be equalized (i.e., made the same by recalculating the numbers) for the valuation calculation for the postmerger firm.

As with the sell-off to the income partner, both firms should have a chance to reanalyze their partners' W-2 incomes. If firm B had been operating by just paying its profits out to partners through base salary and bonuses, thus all hitting their W-2 income and leaving no profit behind or being allocated to the partners via IRS form K-1, then, premerger, the partners should be willing to readjust their W-2 income to a level that they would be happy with going forward postmerger and taking the balance out as distributions from the firm. The same analysis and adjustments needed to normalize K-1 income and profit distributions that were done prior to the income partner buy-in can be done to the firm's premerger adjustments to normalize W-2 income.

Another potential sticking point that needs to be vetted by a consultant or by the partners in an open and honest dialogue is the proper W-2 income of partners (and associates) in the postmerger entity. Remember, firm B should not really care (too much) about the W-2 income of the firm A partners so long as their business model is bringing the $500,000 of profits to the postmerger entity. Similarly, firm A should not care about the W-2 income of the firm B partners so long as they are bringing the $250,000 of postmerger income to the partnership. As a result, that dialogue needs to take place prior to the merger so that everyone understands the historical basis for those W-2 salaries. Nonetheless, if there is a significant disparity between partner W-2 incomes, you can still expect some postmerger anxiety or possibly ill will if that issue is not well settled prior to the merger.

As an alternative, lawyers tend to want to equalize all of the partners' W-2 income and then create a bonus system of "eat what you kill" and constantly fight over the referral sources for new clients and who gets credit for those new clients and who benefits economically from those clients. As stated earlier, that is not putting the firm first but instead only drives partners to base their performance and behaviors solely on individual economic benefit. While some of these systems can work, and they can be built to work, please keep in mind that this is a business book on building the most successful and best law firm in its marketplace. Partners need to be incentivized to grow the firm based on their equity in the firm growing and not to be bonused on their everyday necessary behaviors.

Similarly, a simple but not well-thought-out strategy that sometimes works is simply just merging firms, developing a bonus structure for both bringing in new clients and billable hours, and paying out the bonuses to partners just as you would with associates (possibly on a richer scale). At the end of the year, if there is any money left over, it is left to the discretion of the partners to figure out how to distribute the money. Such vague and ambiguous arrangements sometimes work, but more times than not they leave the bottom-tiered partners disgruntled with the ultimate distribution of the profits of the firm.

In contrast, when attorneys know their percentage of the postmerger entity, they will know exactly their income distribution of the profits from the firm.

Distribution of the profits of the firm needs to be handled, just as in a corporation, by the owners of the firm commensurate with their ownership interest in the postmerger firm. This is *not* to say that partners should also not get bonuses. Partners should also be eligible for reasonable bonuses that are either objective criteria-based bonuses built into the shareholder agreement or somewhat subjective and determined by a small compensation committee, usually consisting of three to four partners in a combined composition of the two firms. It is important to note that in partner bonuses, only exceptional and unusual value added by a partner should be recognized in a significant way. Remember, the partners are the owners of the business, and as such, acquiring new clients, meeting and exceeding billing goals, marketing and community involvement, training young associates, and running the business are all in their job description. They should be getting paid their fair wage and their commensurate share of the profits of the business for doing the tasks of the five-tool attorney. Bonuses should be reserved for exceptional and out-of-the-ordinary value added to the business.

> It is important to note that in partner bonuses, only exceptional and unusual value added by a partner should be recognized in a significant way.

These exceptional additions of value could take the form of a year-long project to completely overhaul the social media platforms or the website used by the firm, landing a valuable referral source at a bank or community center, or possibly landing a large client that immediately has significant legal needs and the particular partner has managed client satisfaction to a high level. Similarly, in personal injury firms, there could be a massive verdict awarded to a case tried by one of the partners in the previous calendar year. All of these are exceptional, out-of-the-ordinary course of business value added to the merged firm that should be recognized by the partners over and above the ordinary compensation package for partners. They are equally valuable whether the partner is working *in* the business or working *on* the business.

On the issue of economics, sometimes the reported merger includes a two-year lookback and reconciliation period whereby the parties test whether the representations made premerger have been true postmerger. In other words, through the clients and marketing methodologies of firm A, did the firm really bring in $500,000 of profit, or was it greater? Similarly, did firm B bring in $250,000 or less of profits? In these cases generally, there is a high tolerance for a standard of materiality because it will get a little muddied between who brought in which client and who serviced that client in a successful manner. Generally, the formula is not changed during the two-year "true-up" period if there has not been a major defection of a client or the loss of a major contingency fee case. As a result, try to discourage any sort of postclosing reconciliation and true-up period because they are very difficult, but not impossible, to calculate.

The Report of Merger

After all the analysis is done on the people, processes, and culture, and an analysis is done on the premerger firms' economics, all that information should be distilled into a Report of Merger proposing the structure of the going-forward, postmerger entity. As an attachment to the Report of Merger, you need a postmerger shareholder agreement, but the Report of Merger is a more operational document that ends with a pro forma postmerger salary structure for the partners, associates, and support staff, as well as the anticipated postmerger profitability of the new firm. All of the partners in firm A and firm B need to understand their roles going forward and consent to their roles. In addition, depending on the ownership structure of firm A and the ownership structure of firm B, the Report of Merger will also have a postmerger ownership structure for the new firm. All in all, the Report of Merger should set forth in great detail the changes, if any, to the W-2 income of the employees, the assignments of the head of certain practice groups, and the specific attorneys who will be working in those practice groups.

Further, with respect to all of the practice management items, the Report of Merger will appoint attorneys to chair or head practice management groups such as marketing, finance, social media, technology, and every other area that does not relate to practicing law for the law firm.

Last, among all of those signing the Report of Merger, there will be consensus on the firm's purpose, core values, and foundations on which the firm will be built and its anticipated plan of growth, including, but not limited to, its one-year goals, its five-year goals, and possibly (although not necessary) the firm's ten-year goals.

At the end of the successful merger, you will have built an even larger and greater winning law firm in your marketplace.

Appendix

Additional Forms

ESTATE OPENING CHECKLIST

File Will within 30 days of date of death

DOCUMENTS NEEDED TO OPEN ESTATE

Cover Sheet (County Specific)   ___

Petition for Probate of Will and for Letters of Testamentary   ___

Affidavit as to Copy of Will   ___

Oath and Bond (with or without surety)   ___

Designation of Resident Agent   ___

Acceptance of Office (if executor is a corporation)   ___

Affidavit of Heirship   ___

Order Declaring Heirship   ___

Order Admitting Will to Probate   ___

Waivers of Notice from Heirs to Legatees

(not required, but if not obtained, then see notices section)   ___

NOTICES REQUIRED

Notices to Heirs and Legatees—Will Admitted (within 14 day of order) ___

Notice to Creditors and Unknown Heirs   ___

Death Claim Notice to Known Creditors   ___

ESTATE PLANNING CHECKLIST/INVENTORY

GENERAL INFORMATION

	You:	Spouse:
Date Prepared:	_____	_____
Full Name:	_____	_____
Address:	_____	_____
	_____	_____
E-mail:	_____	_____
S.S. Number:	_____	_____
Occupation:	_____	_____
Business Phone:	_____	_____
Cell Phone:	_____	_____
Citizenship:	_____	_____
Birthdate:	_____	_____
Marital Status:	_____	_____

Accountant Name and Phone Number: _____

Financial Planner Name and Phone Number: _____

FAMILY INFORMATION

Name	Relation	Address (if different than yours)	Birthdate
_____	_____	_____	_____
_____	_____	_____	_____
_____	_____	_____	_____
_____	_____	_____	_____

FINANCIAL INFORMATION

Assets	In Your Name	In Your Spouse's Name	Joint*	Total
Family Home(s)	_____	_____	_____	_____
Other Real Estate	_____	_____	_____	_____
Checking Accounts	_____	_____	_____	_____
Savings & Money Market Accounts	_____	_____	_____	_____
CDs	_____	_____	_____	_____
Marketable Stocks & Bonds	_____	_____	_____	_____
Tax-Exempt Municipal Bonds	_____	_____	_____	_____

ESTATE PLANNING CHECKLIST/INVENTORY (continued)

Limited Partnerships, Oil & Gas Interests	_____	_____	_____
Gems, Precious Metals	_____	_____	_____	_____
Commodities	_____	_____	_____	_____
Business Interest	_____	_____	_____	_____
Life Insurance	_____	_____	_____	_____
Vested Benefits Under Profit-Sharing Plan	_____	_____	_____	_____
Death Benefits Under Pension Plan	_____	_____	_____	_____
IRAs	_____	_____	_____	_____
Valuable Collections, Antiques, Coins, Etc.	_____	_____	_____	
Autos & Other Personal Property	_____	_____	_____	_____
Other Assets	_____	_____	_____	_____
Total Assets	$ _____	_____	_____	_____

Please identify community property, regardless of ownership, by placing a "CP" to the right of the appropriate entry.

LIABILITIES

	Owed by You	Owed by Spouse	Owed Jointly	Total
Loans	_____	_____	_____	_____
Mortgages	_____	_____	_____	_____
Other Debts	_____	_____	_____	_____
Total Liabilities	$ _____	_____	_____	_____

NET WORTH

(Assets minus Liabilities)	$ _____	_____	_____	_____

*If joint owner of obligor is someone other than spouse, please name.

ESTATE PLANNING CHECKLIST/INVENTORY (continued)

BUSINESS INTEREST

List and briefly describe closely held "Business Interests." Please indicate which, if any, of the corporations have secured S corporation status.

_____

_____

_____

_____

_____

_____

_____

_____

_____

LIFE INSURANCE POLICIES

Company Policy Number	Insured Owner	Beneficiary	Death Benefit	Outstanding Loans	Cash Value

TOTALS:

ANNUAL INCOME DATA

	Yours	Spouse	Jointly	Total
Salary (plus bonus, if any)	$ _____	_____	_____	_____
Interest	$ _____	_____	_____	_____
Dividends	$ _____	_____	_____	_____
Income from Business or Profession	$ _____	_____	_____	_____
Other Income	$ _____	_____	_____	_____
Total Income	$ _____	_____	_____	_____

ESTATE PLANNING CHECKLIST/INVENTORY (continued)

ESTATE PLANNING INFORMATION

Trustee—Party who will handle the financial affairs of the trust and make distributions per the document. **Successor Trustee**—Will act as trustee if the primary trustee cannot act.	
Guardian—Party who you designate to take care of your children upon your death. **Successor Guardian**—Will act if the primary guardian cannot act.	
Executor—Party who will distribute your estate according to the terms of the will. **Successor Executor**—Will act if the primary executor cannot act.	
Power of Attorney for Health Care: **Agent**—Will instruct your physician of your wishes regarding life support and health care decisions should you be unable. **Successor Agent**—Will act if the primary agent is unable.	
Power of Attorney for Property: **Agent**—Will handle your financial affairs should you become incapacitated. **Successor Agent**—Will act if the primary agent is unable.	

ESTATE PLANNING CHECKLIST/INVENTORY (continued)

POWER OF ATTORNEY

Power of Attorney for Health Care: Check one of the following statements that most accurately reflects your desire with regard to end-of-life decisions:

_____ I do not want my life to be prolonged nor do I want life-sustaining treatment to be provided or continued if my agent believes the burdens of the treatment outweigh the expected benefits. I want my agent to consider the relief of suffering, the expense involved and the quality as well as the possible extension of my life in making decisions concerning life-sustaining treatment.

_____ I want my life to be prolonged and I want life-sustaining treatment to be provided or continued, unless I am, in the opinion of my attending physician, in accordance with reasonable medical standards at the time of reference, in a state of "permanent unconsciousness" or suffer from an "incurable or irreversible condition" or "terminal condition," as those terms are defined in Section 4-4 of the Illinois Power of Attorney Act. If and when I am in any one of these states or conditions, I want life-sustaining treatment to be withheld or discontinued.

_____ I want my life to be prolonged to the greatest extent possible in accordance with reasonable medical standards without regard to my condition, the chances I have for recovery, or the cost of the procedures.

Check one of the following that accurately reflects your intent with regard to your agent's authority to make anatomical gifts upon your death:

_____ Effective upon my death, my agent has the full power to make an anatomical gift of any organs, tissues, or eyes suitable for transplantation or used for research or education.

_____ I only want to make anatomical gifts of specific organs.

_____ I do not grant my agent authority to make any anatomical gifts.

Power of Attorney for Property: If you do not wish for your agent to have authority to act in any of the following categories, draw a line through the title of the category:

Real estate transactions	Tax matters
Financial institution transactions	Claims and litigation
Stock and bond transactions	Commodity and option transactions
Tangible personal property transactions	Business operations
Safe deposit box transactions	Borrowing transactions
Insurance and annuity transactions	Estate transactions
Social Security, employment, and military service benefits	All other property transactions

ESTATE PLANNING CHECKLIST/INVENTORY (continued)

When should the Power of Attorney for Property begin?

_____ Upon a court determination of my disability or a written determination by my physician that I am incapacitated.

_____ Immediately.

ADDITIONAL INFORMATION

1. Do you or your spouse have a will? If yes, please attach a copy of each will.

2. Have you ever lived in a community property state? (Arizona, California, Idaho, Louisiana, Nevada, New Mexico, Texas, Washington, and Wisconsin). If so, please name: _____

3. Have you or your spouse been married previously? Please furnish us with a copy of any divorce decree or prenuptial agreement.

4. Have you made gifts of more than $14,000 to any person (other than your spouse) in any one year?

    If you have filed a gift tax return, please furnish us with a copy of your most recent return

5. If you own join tenancy property with someone other than your spouse, whose funds were used to purchase it? _____

6. Estimate inheritance, if any. $_____

7. Are you or any member of your immediate family a beneficiary of any trust? _____
    If so, what is the approximate value of the assets of the trust? $_____

8. Special family needs (parent or child support, special education, physical or mental disability): _____

    _____

    Have you set up any trusts for your children? Have you purchased Section 529 plans? What is the value of these assets? _____

9. Do you intend to make any charitable gifts through your estate plan? If so, please provide additional information: _____

    _____

10. Do you wish to provide specific instructions regarding your funeral/burial preferences?

    _____

11. Briefly describe your estate-planning goals:

    _____

    _____

    _____

INITIAL PROBATE CLIENT MEETING CHECKLIST

CERTIFICATES
1. Certified death certificates
2. Car title
3. Veteran's discharge papers
4. Birth certificates of beneficiaries where applicable
5. Death certificates of deceased beneficiaries

FINANCIAL DOCUMENTS
1. Canceled checks and statements
2. Name and address of accountant if returns not available
3. Brokerage statements
4. Certificated securities
5. Interest or dividend checks
6. Bank account statements, passbooks, CDs
7. Annuity, pension, 401(k), IRA statements
8. Life insurance policies
9. Health insurance policy numbers
10. Charge cards
11. Unpaid bills
12. Paid bills to be reimbursed
13. Evidence of liabilities

TAX RETURNS
1. Federal and State 1040s for the past three years
2. Gift tax returns
3. Partnership or corporate returns/minute books/buy-sell agreement/financial statements
4. Federal estate tax returns regarding credit for tax on prior transfers

REAL ESTATE
1. House or apartment keys
2. Deed
3. Title policy
4. Plat of survey
5. Homeowner's insurance policy
6. Real estate tax bill
7. Apartment lease

INITIAL PROBATE CLIENT MEETING CHECKLIST (continued)

ESTATE PLAN
1. Original Will
2. Original Revocable Trust

MISCELLANEOUS
1. Mailbox key
2. Locker key
3. Car keys
4. Safe deposit box key
5. Jewelry and coins
6. Addresses of beneficiaries
7. Social Security numbers of beneficiaries
8. W-9s

DISSOLUTION OF MARRIAGE CHECKLIST

PERSONAL INFORMATION
Full Legal Name

_____

First   Middle   Last

Current Home Address

_____

Street   City   County   State   Zip Code

How long have you lived at this address? _____ years(s) _____ month(s)

City, State and Country of Birth _____

How many minor children, if any, are currently living with you at this address? _____

Citizenship _____ **Date of Birth** ___/___/_____

Social Security Number _____ **Driver's License No.** _____

Home Phone _____

Business Phone _____

Cell Phone _____ **Fax Number** _____

E-mail _____

Occupation _____ **Employer** _____

Business Address

_____

Street   City   County   State   Zip Code

Education _____

Number of this marriage (First, Second, etc.) _____

If previously married, last marriage ended on ___/___/_____

By ☐ Death ☐ Divorce ☐ Invalidity

GENERAL INFORMATION

Date of Marriage ___/___/_____ **Place of Marriage** _____

Number of children born alive of this marriage _____

Date when you and your spouse last resided in the same household
___/___/_____

Previous counsel? ☐ **No** ☐ **Yes—Please provide contact information for the previous attorney and state the reason(s) for seeking new counsel:**

_____

Does your spouse have an attorney? ☐ **No** ☐ **Yes—Please provide contact information for your spouse's attorney:** _____

DISSOLUTION OF MARRIAGE CHECKLIST (continued)

Do you have sufficient financial resources to pay your own legal fees and costs in this case? ☐ No   ☐ Yes

Do you feel that counseling or further counseling, either to preserve the marriage or to aid in adjustment to a divorce, would be helpful? ☐ No   ☐ Yes

Do you feel that your marital problems are irreconcilable? ☐ No   ☐ Yes

Why do you feel that you must institute an action to dissolve your marriage?

_____

_____

How do you feel your spouse has contributed to the marital problems?

_____

_____

Is there any history or pattern of abuse of violence? ☐ **No**   ☐ **Yes—Please describe incident(s) and date(s):** _____

_____

Police contacted?	☐ No ☐ Yes
Pictures taken?	☐ No ☐ Yes
Witnesses or children present?	☐ No ☐ Yes

Is there any history or problem with substance abuse? ☐ No   ☐ Yes

SPOUSE'S PERSONAL INFORMATION
Full Legal Name

_____

First   Middle   Last

Current Home Address

_____

Street   City   County   State   Zip Code

How long have you lived at this address? _____ years(s) _____ month(s)

City, State and Country of Birth _____

How many minor children, if any, are currently living with you at this address? _____

Citizenship   Date of Birth ____/____/_____

Social Security Number _____ **Driver's License No.** _____

Home Phone _____ **Business Phone** _____

Cell Phone _____ **Fax Number** _____

E-mail _____

DISSOLUTION OF MARRIAGE CHECKLIST (continued)

Occupation _____ **Employer** _____
Business Address

_____
Street   City   County   State   Zip Code
Education _____
Number of this marriage (First, Second, etc.) _____
If previously married, last marriage ended on ___/___/_____
By   ☐ Death   ☐ Divorce   ☐ Invalidity

CHILDREN
1. **Children of this marriage**
   Child's Full Name   _____ _____ _____
   Date of Birth   _____ _____ _____
   SSN   _____ _____ _____
   Grade Level   _____ _____ _____
   Name of School Attending   _____ _____ _____
   Living with (provide address
   if different than yours)   _____ _____ _____
   Adopted? Special Needs?   _____ _____ _____
2. **Children NOT of this marriage**
   Child's Full Name   _____ _____ _____
   Date of Birth   _____ _____ _____
   SSN   _____ _____ _____
   Grade Level   _____ _____ _____
   Name of School Attending   _____ _____ _____
   Living with (provide address
   if different than yours)   _____ _____ _____
   Adopted? Special Needs?   _____ _____ _____

DISSOLUTION OF MARRIAGE CHECKLIST (continued)

REAL ESTATE
Marital Residence
Please provide a copy of Deed and Legal Description
Address

_____

Street   City   County   State   Zip Code

Property Tax Number _____

Date Purchased _____

Price $ _____

Down Payment $ _____

Name(s) title in _____

Present Market Value $ _____

Approximate Equity $ _____

Mortgage 1 Balance $ _____

    Payable $ _____ per _____

    To _____

    Mortgage 1 in arrears?   ☐ No ☐ Yes – $

Taxes $ _____

Taxes in arrears?   ☐ No ☐ Yes – $

Insurance $ _____

Insurance included in payment? ☐ No ☐ Yes

Home Equity Loan?   ☐ No ☐ Yes – Describe: _____

Lender _____

Maximum Authorized $ _____

Balance Owed $ _____

Monthly Payment $ _____

Major improvements since property was purchased _____

Other Nonhomestead Real Estate (Vacation Property, Second Home, Vacant Land, Income Property)
Address

_____

Street   City   County   State   Zip Code

Property Tax Number _____

Date Purchased _____

Price $ _____

Down Payment $ _____

Name(s) title in _____

DISSOLUTION OF MARRIAGE CHECKLIST (continued)

Present Market Value $ _____

Approximate Equity $ _____

BANK ACCOUNTS

Bank or Institution _____

Account Type _____

Account No. _____

Name(s) on Account _____

Source of Funds _____

Amount $ _____

Bank or Institution _____

Account Type _____

Account No. _____

Name(s) on Account _____

Source of Funds _____

Amount $ _____

Bank or Institution _____

Account Type _____

Account No. _____

Name(s) on Account _____

Source of Funds _____

Amount $ _____

STOCKS AND BONDS

Company Name/Type of Stock or Bond _____

Number of Shares _____

In Whose Name _____

Source of Funds _____

Present Value $ _____

Company Name/Type of Stock or Bond _____

Number of Shares _____

In Whose Name _____

Source of Funds _____

Present Value $ _____

Company Name/Type of Stock or Bond _____

Number of Shares _____

In Whose Name _____

Source of Funds _____

Present Value $ _____

DISSOLUTION OF MARRIAGE CHECKLIST (continued)

Company Name/Type of Stock or Bond _____

Number of Shares _____

In Whose Name _____

Source of Funds _____

Present Value $ _____

VEHICLES (CARS, TRUCKS, BOATS, SNOWMOBILES, CAMPERS, ETC.)
Vehicle 1

Year, Make, and Model _____

Title Owner(s) _____

Who has possession? _____

Date Purchased _____

Insurance Company _____

Policy Number _____

Lien Holder _____

Balance Owed $_____

Value $ _____

Vehicle 2

Year, Make, and Model _____

Title Owner(s) _____

Who has possession? _____

Date Purchased _____

Insurance Company _____

Policy Number _____

Lien Holder _____

Balance Owed $_____

Value $ _____

Vehicle 3

Year, Make, and Model _____

Title Owner(s) _____

Who has possession? _____

Date Purchased _____

Insurance Company _____

Policy Number _____

Lien Holder _____

Balance Owed $_____

Value $ _____

DISSOLUTION OF MARRIAGE CHECKLIST (continued)

Vehicle 4

Year, Make, and Model _____

Title Owner(s) _____

Who has possession? _____

Date Purchased _____

Insurance Company _____

Policy Number _____

Lien Holder _____

Balance Owed $_____

Value $ _____

RETIREMENT FUNDS AND BENEFITS

Yours

Pension _____

IRA _____

401(k) or other deferred savings _____

Stock Purchase Plans_____

Stock Option Plans _____

Other _____

Spouse's

Pension _____

IRA _____

401(k) or other deferred savings _____

Stock Purchase Plans_____

Stock Option Plans _____

Other _____

LIFE INSURANCE POLICIES

Company _____

Policy Number _____

Cash Value $_____

Loans Insured _____

Owner _____

Beneficiary _____

DISSOLUTION OF MARRIAGE CHECKLIST (continued)

Company _____

Policy Number _____

Cash Value $ _____

Loans Insured _____

Owner _____

Beneficiary _____

Company _____

Policy Number _____

Cash Value $ _____

Loans Insured _____

Owner _____

Beneficiary _____

Company _____

Policy Number _____

Cash Value $ _____

Loans Insured _____

Owner _____

Beneficiary _____

Company _____

Policy Number _____

Cash Value $ _____

Loans Insured _____

Owner _____

Beneficiary _____

Company _____

Policy Number _____

Cash Value $ _____

Loans Insured _____

Owner _____

Beneficiary _____

Company _____

Policy Number _____

Cash Value $ _____

Loans Insured _____

Owner _____

Beneficiary _____

DISSOLUTION OF MARRIAGE CHECKLIST (continued)

PARTNERSHIPS AND OTHER BUSINESS INTERESTS

Name of Company _____ Type of Business _____

Address

_____

Street   City   State   Zip Code

Date Acquired ____/____/_____ Cost of Investment $ _____

Stock Interest $ _____

Approximate Value $ _____

Shareholders/Co-owners _____

INCOME

Yours

Salary $ _____

Interest (taxable) _____

Interest (nontaxable) _____

Dividends _____

Income from Business _____

Other Income $ _____

Total Income $ _____

Spouse's

Salary $ _____

Interest (taxable) _____

Interest (nontaxable) _____

Dividends _____

Income from Business _____

Other Income $ _____

Total Income $ _____

Joint

Salary $ _____

Interest (taxable) _____

Interest (nontaxable) _____

Dividends _____

Income from Business _____

Other Income $ _____

Total Income $ _____

DISSOLUTION OF MARRIAGE CHECKLIST (continued)

Total

Salary $ _____

Interest (taxable) _____

Interest (nontaxable) _____

Dividends _____

Income from Business _____

Other Income $ _____

Total Income $ _____

INSURANCE (HEALTH, DENTAL, DISABILITY, ACCIDENT, LONG-TERM CARE, PROFESSIONAL LIABILITY, ETC.)

Company _____

Policy No./Group No. _____

Type of Insurance _____

Primary Insured _____

Dependent(s) _____

Company _____

Policy No./Group No. _____

Type of Insurance _____

Primary Insured _____

Dependent(s) _____

Company _____

Policy No./Group No. _____

Type of Insurance _____

Primary Insured _____

Dependent(s) _____

Company _____

Policy No./Group No. _____

Type of Insurance _____

Primary Insured _____

Dependent(s) _____

Company _____

Policy No./Group No. _____

Type of Insurance _____

Primary Insured _____

Dependent(s) _____

DISSOLUTION OF MARRIAGE CHECKLIST (continued)

MISCELLANEOUS

Do you and/or your spouse have a safe deposit box?   ☐ No   ☐ Yes

Location _____

Contents _____

Persons with access _____

_____

_____

List any other significant personal property with a value of $1,000 or more:

_____

_____

Contracts?   ☐ No   ☐ Yes—Describe: _____

_____

Patents?   ☐ No   ☐ Yes—Describe: _____

_____

Do you or your spouse have any money or property held by others?

☐ No   ☐ Yes—Describe: _____

_____

Unless described already, was your or your spouse's separate money or property at the time of marriage in excess of $1,000?   ☐ No   ☐ Yes—Describe: _____

_____

Unless described already, was any part of your marriage estate received by you or your spouse by inheritance, gift, or damages resulting from a person injury claim?

☐ No   ☐ Yes—Describe: _____

_____

Type _____

Received by _____

From _____

Date Received _____

DISSOLUTION OF MARRIAGE CHECKLIST (continued)

Are you and/or your spouse beneficiaries under any estate now in probate?
☐ No   ☐ Yes—Describe: _____

_____

Beneficiary _____ Approximate amount involved $ _____
Whose estate? _____
Have you and/or your spouse ever filed for bankruptcy protection?
☐ No   ☐ Yes—Chapter _____
Who filed? _____
Date filed ____/____/_____ Discharged? ☐ No ☐ Yes—Date ____/____/_____

DEBTS AND LIABILITIES
Owed by You
Mortgages `_____
Vehicle Loans _____
Student Loans _____
Other Loans _____
Support _____
Arrearages _____
Credit Cards _____
Outstanding _____
Medical Bills _____
Other Debts _____
Total Liabilities $ _____
Owed by Spouse
Mortgages _____
Vehicle Loans _____
Student Loans _____
Other Loans _____
Support _____
Arrearages _____
Credit Cards _____
Outstanding _____
Medical Bills _____
Other Debts _____
Total Liabilities $ _____

DISSOLUTION OF MARRIAGE CHECKLIST (continued)

Owed Jointly

Mortgages _____

Vehicle Loans _____

Student Loans _____

Other Loans _____

Support _____

Arrearages _____

Credit Cards _____

Outstanding _____

Medical Bills _____

Other Debts _____

Total Liabilities $ _____

Total Owed

Mortgages _____

Vehicle Loans _____

Student Loans _____

Other Loans _____

Support _____

Arrearages _____

Credit Cards _____

Outstanding _____

Medical Bills _____

Other Debts _____

Total Liabilities $ _____

ADDITIONAL INFORMATION

Describe what you consider a fair division of your property and debts.

What items of property do you believe each party should receive?

DISSOLUTION OF MARRIAGE CHECKLIST (continued)

What items of debt do you believe each party should be responsible for?

If you have minor children, how would you like to arrange custody, visitation, and support obligations?

Do you want to change your last name?
☐ No   ☐ Yes _____

NEW COMPANY/INCORPORATION CHECKLIST

OWNER AND OFFICER INFORMATION
Owner/Officer #1

_____   _____   _____ - ____ -_____
Name   Percentage Ownership   Social Security No.

_____   Board/Manager ☐ No ☐ Yes
Officer Positions

Owner/Officer #2

_____   _____   _____ - ____ -_____
Name   Percentage Ownership   Social Security No.

_____   Board/Manager ☐ No ☐ Yes
Officer Positions

Owner/Officer #3

_____   _____   _____ - ____ -_____
Name   Percentage Ownership   Social Security No.

_____   Board/Manager ☐ No ☐ Yes
Officer Positions

Owner/Officer #4

_____   _____   _____ - ____ -_____
Name   Percentage Ownership   Social Security No.

_____   Board/Manager ☐ No ☐ Yes
Officer Positions

NEW COMPANY/INCORPORATION CHECKLIST (continued)

COMPANY INFORMATION

_____ Inc. Ltd. Corp. LLC

Company Name

_____

Assumed Name or D/B/A

_____

Street Address   Phone Number

_____

Suite   City   State   Zip Code

Description of your business:

EMPLOYEE INFORMATION

The Company will have employees other than the owners: ☐ No   ☐ Yes

Number of employees during the first year: _____

Estimated date of first payroll: ____/____/_____

Estimated amount of first payroll: $ _____

OTHER INFORMATION ABOUT YOUR BUSINESS

_____
_____
_____
_____
_____
_____
_____
_____
_____

BUSINESS ACQUISITION: DUE DILIGENCE CHECKLIST[1]

GENERAL INFORMATION

1. Organizational Chart of Company, including parent companies, subsidiaries and other affiliates, percentage ownership, and jurisdiction or organization.

2. List of names and addresses of shareholders, members, directors, trustees, officers, and members of management.

CORPORATE RECORDS

1. Company Records
   a. Charter (Example: Articles or Certificate of Incorporation or Organization)
      i.   Certified copy of the current charter of the Company, including amendments thereto, certified by proper authorities in jurisdiction of Company;
      ii. Bylaws, Partnership Agreement or Operating Agreement, including original and all amendments or restatements;
      iii. Meeting minutes and consents reflecting all actions of the directors, committees of directors, stockholders, managers, members, and partners, including copies of notices of all such meetings when written notices were given;
      iv. Evidence of compliance with publication, filing, and tax requirements; copies of all publications required for the last five years;
      v.   Any other corporate records or material information of Company not described herein that Purchaser would reasonably expect to receive and be privy to in an asset purchase transaction.
   b. List of all states and foreign countries in which the Company, and each active subsidiary of the Company, is authorized or registered to do business or when by reason of its ownership of property or the conduct of its business such registration is necessary.

2. Shareholders/Partners/Members
   a. Capital structure of the Company: subscribed capital; authorized (preapproved) capital; par value of shares, paid in full or in part; current shareholders, partners, members of the Company and their equity holdings, including description of classes or categories of equity; copy of the share register and stock registration or other equity certificates of the Company;
   b. List and copies of any agreements among the shareholders of the Company;
   c. Description and copies of documents relating to any options, warrants, or other rights granter with respect to capital;
   d. All agreements, memoranda, registration statements, prospectuses, or offering

---

1. Gary M. Lawrence, Due Diligence in Business Transactions, Rel. 4 (Law Journals Seminar Press 1997).

BUSINESS ACQUISITION: DUE DILIGENCE CHECKLIST (continued)

circulars relating to sales and securities copies of correspondence with investors and copies of any written proposals for the acquisition of the Company's securities.

3. Management and Control

    a. List of members of the Board of Directors, executive committees, or any other committees with terms of office and background information (biographical information and affiliations);

    b. Description of any remuneration of directors;

    c. List of officers or other persons granter daily management powers and their positions; nature of remuneration and how determined and background information (biographical information and affiliations);

    d. List of persons and entities having powers to represent the Company; list and copies of specific proxies granted by the Company (signatures, specific delegations);

    e. Current statutory auditor(s) of the Company and any auditor(s) (date of appointment, duration of mandate remuneration).

FINANCE

1. List and copies of all documents evidencing borrowing of the Company, including loan and credit agreements, promissory notes debentures, mortgages, lines of credit, agency or commission arrangements, and other evidences of indebtedness.

2. List and copies of bank letter or agreements confirming lines of credit.

3. List and copies of all documents evidencing other material financing arrangements, including industrial development or revenue bonds, sale and lease-back arrangements, installment purchase, etc.

4. List and copies of any pledges, liens, or other security interests and liabilities on any assets of the Company or its affiliates.

5. Description and copies of any documents relating to subsidies, premiums, investments, incentives, tax exemptions, or other grants from national, municipal, or other governmental authorities; description of any undertaking that the Company has made with respect to such subsidies, premiums, tax exemptions, or other grants.

6. List and copies of any commitments of the Company for the benefit of third parties, including loans, guarantees, comfort letters, and/or security interests.

7. Description and copies of documents evidencing any advances or loans made by the Company to its shareholders and/or directors and/or their family members, and vice versa, and any other arrangements made with shareholders and/or directors and their family members.

8. Financial statements (consolidated and consolidating) for the last three full fiscal years (the "Review Period"), with all auditors' reports and certifications related thereto.

BUSINESS ACQUISITION: DUE DILIGENCE CHECKLIST (continued)

9. Work papers supplied to auditors for the last full or partial fiscal year.

10. All management letters and reports from auditors concerning internal accounting control that were received during the Review Period.

11. Interim financial statements for the quarter ended _____, 20____ and the year-to-date period then ended.

12. All filings relating to an election for treatment as a Subchapter S corporation.

13. Financial and business plans and projections for fiscal 20____ and fiscal 20____, including

    a. Sales forecasts in units and dollars of revenue by product;

    b. Cost of sales forecasts by product;

    c. Departmental budges and support operating expenses;

    d. Capital expenditure plans.

14. Lists of all investments, including amounts, maturities yields, credit ratings, etc.

15. Detailed lists of accounts receivable and payable by customer and vendor, with aging.

16. Analysis of inventory, raw material, work in process, and finished goods.

17. Listing of the twenty-five largest customers, with unit sales and dollars of revenue for each of the past three fiscal years and projected for fiscal 20____.

18. Report of sales and contribution margin by product for the last three fiscal years and projected for fiscal 20____.

19. Detailed bills of materials for all current products and as projected for all products currently under development.

20. Complete information relating to any changes in accounting methods or principles during the Review Period or subsequently thereto.

21. Complete information relating to any changes in or disputes with auditors including all correspondence related thereto.

22. Complete information relating to any loss contingencies and/or related provisions or reserves identified for or discussed with auditors.

23. Schedules of royalty payment obligations and of royalties paid and accrued by license and product.

24. All internal management financial and operating reports, including internal audit memos, prepared or reviewed during the Review Period.

25. All external consultant reports commissioned or received during the Review Period or subsequently, including but not limited to reports and analyses of the business and the relevant industries and markets by securities analysts, investment bankers, accountants, and engineers.

26. All reports, if any, relating to market studies and competitive analyses, whether internally or externally generated.

BUSINESS ACQUISITION: DUE DILIGENCE CHECKLIST (continued)

27. Reports and analyses of backlogs.
28. Methods used for accounting for software development expenditures and for software maintenance revenues.

MATERIAL AGREEMENTS

Unless otherwise indicated, "Material" includes any agreement with aggregate revenues or payments equaling or exceeding $10,000.

1. List, description, and copies of all material contracts, understandings, and arrangements between the Company and any present or former affiliates.
2. List and copies of all material contracts, understandings, and arrangements having a term of at least one year, or which cannot be terminated without penalty by notice of less than three months.
3. All agreements or plans for mergers, letters of intent, consolidations, reorganizations, acquisitions, or the purchase or sale of assets or stock involving the Company, or agreements in principle currently in effect, with respect to mergers, consolidations, reorganizations, acquisitions, or the purchase or sale of assets or stock involving the Company.
4. A schedule of the top twenty customers and suppliers of the Company indicating materials and/or services supplied or purchased. Also, copies of any agreements relating to any such customers and suppliers.
5. All contract forms used by the Company as standard service or purchase contracts.
6. All evidences of intercompany debt, if any.
7. All agreements under which any person has registration rights for any securities of the Company or preemptive rights for shares of capital stock of the Company.
8. All agreements, memoranda, registration statements, prospectuses, or offerings circulars relating to sales of securities of the Company, copies of correspondence with investors, and copies of any written proposals for the acquisition of the Company's securities.
9. All agreements entered into by the Company not in the ordinary course of business, including, but not limited to, development, partnership, and joint venture agreements.
10. All insurance policies and policy claims, including or relating to key-man product liability, casualty, liability, title and workers' compensation insurance of the Company, or insurance summaries thereof, and loss summaries for the last five years for general, products, and automobile liability insurance and for workers' compensation insurance and all reservations of rights and denials of coverage received from any insurance carrier relating to pending claims.
11. All marketing, sales, distribution, and franchise agreements.

BUSINESS ACQUISITION: DUE DILIGENCE CHECKLIST (continued)

12. Closing documents, agreements, correspondence, and any other documents pertaining to any material transactions of the Company in the last three years.

13. All lease agreements, nondisturbance agreements, sale and leaseback agreements, installment purchase contracts, consignment agreements, financing leases, licensing and franchise agreements, joint venture agreements, and distributor agreements relating to the business of the Company or to which the Company is a party.

14. All agreements not to compete to which the Company is or was (within the last three years) a party (whether with an individual or another business organization).

15. All confidentiality agreements to which the Company is a party.

16. All material supply or requirements contacts to which the Company is a party.

17. All independent contractor, consulting, commission, agent, service, production, manufacturing, sale, agency, distribution, purchase, marketing, consignment, finder, broker, advertising, and similar contracts to which the Company is a party.

18. Samples of standard form purchase orders, sales agreements, invoices, warranties, and other standard form agreements used by the Company.

19. Documentation relating to contractual indemnification obligations to directors, officers, employees, and others.

20. All other material contracts and arrangements currently in effect or proposed, or that were in effect at any time during the past five years (ten years if termination was disputed and no final judgment was entered by a court of competent jurisdiction), including any agreements containing termination or other provisions triggered by a change of control.

PROCEEDINGS: LITIGATION

1. List and description of all litigation or arbitration involving the Company for the last five years, including claim, amounts, names or counsel, result; same for all pending cases, assessment of likely outcome.

2. List and description of all threatened litigation or arbitration.

3. List of all investigations, inquiries, examinations, administrative proceedings before governmental authorities, whether pending or threatened (to the extent not already disclosed under another item).

4. List and copy of all material judgments or decrees affecting the Company.

5. All correspondence with auditors regarding threatened or pending litigation, assessments, or claims.

6. Correspondence, memoranda, and notes concerning inquiries from or audits by federal, state, or local tax authorities (including deficiency notices, audit, and settlement proposals).

BUSINESS ACQUISITION: DUE DILIGENCE CHECKLIST (continued)

7. All documents relating to inquiries from or investigations by federal, state, or local occupational safety and hazard officials.

8. All documents relating to any claim involving the employment, termination, or inventions of any employee or consultant.

9. All documents relating to inquiries from or investigations by federal or state authorities regarding equal employment law violations.

10. All documents relating to warranty and product liabilities claims (whether or not insured).

11. All documents relating to inquiries from or investigations by federal or state officials regarding product safety matters.

12. All documentation relating to inquiries from or investigations by federal or state environmental officials.

13. All documentation relating to inquiries from or investigations by federal or state authorities regarding antitrust and trade regulation matters.

14. All documentation relating to inquiries from or investigations by any governmental authorities regarding compliance with federal or state securities laws or any other federal, state, or local law, rule, or regulation.

15. All documentation relating to any proceedings or governmental proceeding or investigation involving a significant supplier, distributor, or customer that may have a material impact on the business.

16. All documentation relating to any proceedings or governmental inquiries or investigations concerning import or export regulations.

17. All attorneys' opinion letters to auditors.

18. All attorneys' letters concerning the potential effects of any significant proposed or pending charges in any federal, state, or local law, rule, regulation, or ordinance.

19. Copies of all legal compliance programs implemented or prepared for implementation and a list of any governmental (federal, state, or local) approvals, permits, certificates, registrations, concessions, etc., required in order for the Company to conduct its business.

20. Schedule of fines and penalties incurred arising out of the operation of the business or sale of products.

21. Copies of all invoices received from attorneys during the Review Period and subsequently.

PRODUCTS, MARKETS, APPROVALS

1. Percentage of sales and current year-to-date revenues contributed by each major product for the Review Period and forecasted for the balance of this fiscal year.

BUSINESS ACQUISITION: DUE DILIGENCE CHECKLIST (continued)

2. Literature concerning the corporation's products and major markets.

3. Lists of major competitors in each product category.

4. Product warranties and product literature distributed or to be distributed to the public.

5. Schedules listing, by product, all technical and governmental Approvals (e.g., Underwriter Laboratories, Federal Communications Commission).

6. All documentation relating to regulatory reviews, proceedings, and actions concerning product approvals.

7. List, by product, of the significant national and international standards and protocols supported.

SALES AND MARKETING OPERATIONS

1. List of distributors and other major customers indicating revenues received from each during each of the last three fiscal years and the current year-to-date and forecasted revenues for the balance of the current year.

2. List of all import and export licenses.

3. Principal licenses, permits, and authorizations from U.S. federal, state, or local authorities or any foreign federal, provincial, or local authorities.

4. Advertising copy, marketing literature, and collateral materials.

5. Sales and marketing organization charts.

6. Location and staffing of sales offices.

7. Advertising and promotional programs.

8. Joint marketing and promotion programs.

9. All documentation regarding policies, procedures, and practices relating to customer credit.

10. Press releases.

11. Newspaper and magazine articles and other publicity.

MANUFACTURING AND RELATED OPERATIONS

1. Lists of suppliers and contract manufacturers, with descriptions of items sourced from each of them.

2. Manufacturing organizational chart.

3. Documentation relating to patterns and tooling held by third parties.

4. Plans and analyses relating to alternative sourcing for key components.

5. Disaster recovery plans.

ADMINISTRATIVE OPERATIONS

1. Organizational charts for all administrative functions, including headquarters, treasury, accounting, information services, human resources, legal, etc.

2. General descriptions of principal information services and systems.

3. Human resources, policies, and practices.

BUSINESS ACQUISITION: DUE DILIGENCE CHECKLIST (continued)

PHYSICAL PROPERTIES AND ASSETS

1. Schedule listing all real property owned by Company by location, usage, approximate square footage, ownership status, and adjacent surrounding properties' land use.
2. Title reports for any real property owned and any significant real properties leased.
3. Summary of all leases of personal property greater than $50,000 per year and all real property, including lease terms, rentals, and other payment obligations.
4. Copies of all property insurance policies relating to real property owned or leased by Company.
5. Any zoning restrictions and restrictive covenants significantly limiting the use of any properties.
6. All appraisal reports relating to significant properties.
7. All notices of defaults, breaches, or foreclosures relating to any properties.
8. Plans with respect to any facility closings.
9. Information regarding any construction plans for significant new facilities and data on projected construction costs for such facilities and for any facilities currently under construction.

ENVIRONMENTAL MATTERS

1. General
   a. List and description of all litigation or arbitration proceedings currently involving the Company, including claims, amounts, names of counsel, and assessment of likely outcome.
   b. List and description of all environmental litigation or proceedings currently involving the Company, including claims, amounts, names of counsel, and assessment of likely outcome.
   c. General overview of environmental legislation and requirements in the Company's jurisdiction relating to the Company's activities, including discussion of potential risk areas and liabilities; application of such rules in practice, political climate, and experience with respect to damage claims, etc.; proposed or future legislation.
   d. Organization chart indicating the persons in the Company responsible for permits, contracts with the environmental authorities, reports to the management, follow-ups of applicable legislation, etc.
   e. Copies of policy memoranda, programs, internal procedures, training courses, emergency plans, etc., relating to the environment.
   f. List and provide copies of all environmental studies and audits on real property on which the stores or warehouses operate.

BUSINESS ACQUISITION: DUE DILIGENCE CHECKLIST (continued)

2. Permits and Licenses
    a. List of all environmental permits and licenses required for the Company's activities, including licenses with respect to manufacturing, labeling, and sale of products.
    b. History and current status of Company's compliance with permits and licenses.
    c. Description of procedure for transfer of licenses or permits in event of a stock sale or asset sale.
3. Ownership and Use History
    a. Description of ownership and use history of each parcel of real property and leased property used by the Company in the last ten years.
4. Discharges
    a. Description of the production and storage process and related environmental risks.
    b. Description of any emissions into air or water; wastewater and other discharges; noise pollution; waste produced.
    c. List and copies of any studies, analyses, examination of discharge, and emissions whether produced internally or by external consultants; description of material problems or risks.
    d. Description of removal methods for waste; cleaning methods for discharges and emissions; state of compliance with law.
    e. List and copies of waste removal contracts and any agreements relating to environmental matters (pollution clean-up, etc.).
    f. History of any accidental discharges and results and measures taken to clean up and prevent future occurrences.
    g. Copies of all environmental phase I and II audits of any real property owned by Company.
5. Relations with Authorities
    a. Description of Company's relationship with environmental authorities generally.
    b. Description of obligations of Company to file reports or studies with authorities; copies of reports.
    c. Description of any inquiries, inspections, examinations, investigations, etc., by environmental authorities and results; copies of documentation and correspondence; description of suspensions or withdrawals of any permits or licenses; significant correspondence for the last five years.
    d. Description of any surrounding or adjacent conditions that could give rise to liability for the Company.
    e. Description of insurance arrangements and environmental claims history.

BUSINESS ACQUISITION: DUE DILIGENCE CHECKLIST (continued)

    f.   Description of any injuries or illnesses of personnel, accidents during the last five years, with effect upon environmental matters.

    g.   Copies of documents relating to claims filed from LUST Fund under applicable state statutes.

    h.   Description of any other relevant matters with respect to the environment.

EMPLOYMENT MATTERS

1.   Copy of any internal regulation applicable to the workplace and of any applicable to the workplace and of any applicable collective bargaining agreements.

2.   Copy of standard employment contract for each category of employees, and indication of any difference for individual employees.

3.   Bonus, profit sharing, and deferred compensation plans currently in effect or proposed.

4.   List and copies of all employment contracts.

5.   Certified copies of all agreements that employees have signed, including:

    a.   Confidentiality agreements;

    b.   Invention assignment agreements;

    c.   Conflict or interest declarations;

    d.   Noncompetition agreements.

6.   List and description of all pending or threatened legal actions, claims, charges, grievances, or complaints filed by employees or on behalf of employees, or former employees, and of all such actions of the last three years.

7.   Review and description of significant correspondence with labor and Social Security authorities for the last five years.

8.   List and description of any minutes of meetings of employee bodies within the Company.

9.   Compliance of the Company with laws and regulations concerning:

    a.   Working hours;

    b.   Safety;

    c.   Hygiene;

    d.   Social Security;

    e.   Insurance;

    f.   Transportation.

10. List and copies of any contracts with independent or self-employed consultants.

11. List and copies of any agreements currently in effect between the Company and any former officer, director, or employee.

12. Summary of liability for termination payments to employees.

13. Brochures, information, booklets, pamphlets, policies and procedures manuals, or other written material given to employees or potential employees of the Company to

BUSINESS ACQUISITION: DUE DILIGENCE CHECKLIST (continued)

acquaint them with the Company's business and with services, employment policies and procedures, and compensation and benefits offered to employees.

14. Summary of labor concerns, including whether any strikes are threatened or pending, all current disputes and negotiations, and all Occupational Safety and Health Administration (OSHA) issues and complaints.

15. All correspondence with labor unions and all memoranda regarding communication with such labor unions or union employees.

16. Summary of the history for the last three years of any union negotiations, number of employees, turnover, absentee rates, and distribution.

17. All documents relating to affirmative action programs, if any, that are applicable or have been applied to the Company, whether by court order or voluntarily.

18. All notices to the Pension Benefit Guaranty Corporation (PBGC) concerning reportable events under ERISA, and all documentation of any audits, investigations, or reviews being conducted by the IRS, Department of Labor, or PBGC with respect to any plan and any administrative proceedings in connection therewith.

19. Copies of the most recent actuarial reports concerning all defined benefit pension plans.

20. Copies of all communications regarding withdrawal liabilities under multiemployer pension plans.

21. Copies of the Forms 5500 filed with the Department of Labor for each employee benefit plan (i.e., pension plans, welfare plans) for the last two years.

22. All material documents pertaining to OSHA and the Equal Employment Opportunity Commission (EEOC).

EQUIPMENT

1. List and copy of renting and/or leasing agreements with respect to machinery, equipment, trademarks, or automobiles not owned by the Company.

2. Description of compliance of use of machinery and equipment with applicable laws and regulations, and in particular safety and environmental regulations.

3. List and documents evidencing liens and security interests granted on machinery and equipment.

4. List and copies all documents evidencing ownership of all trucks, automobiles, and equipment owned by the Company.

PERMITS

1. List, description, and copies of all federal, state, and local governmental licenses and permits required for and held by the Company's business as currently conducted or planned (except environmental permits, which are covered in item 11).

2. All reports, notices, fines, certificates, and correspondence, evidencing history of

BUSINESS ACQUISITION: DUE DILIGENCE CHECKLIST (continued)

compliance and noncompliance by the Company of all federal, state, and local gov ernmental licenses, permits, and required filings.

INTELLECTUAL PROPERTY

1. List of U.S. and foreign patents registered and held and applications made or pending by the Company and any applicable expiration dates.
2. List of U.S. and foreign trademarks held and applications made by the Company and any applicable expiration dates.
3. List of U.S. and foreign copyrights held and applications made by the Company and any applicable expiration dates.
4. List and copies of design and model rights held and applications made by the Company.
5. All trade names or assumed business names used by the Company.
6. List and copies of licenses for any form of intellectual property held by or granted by the Company.
7. Description of any pending or threatened infringement claims by or against the Company, and of any such claims for the last five years.
8. Description of any important know-how or trade secrets at the Company's disposal.

TAXES

1. Copies of all tax-sharing and other tax-related agreements.
2. All federal, state, local, and other tax returns and reports filed by or on behalf of the Company, or copies of extensions of time within which to file such reports as have been obtained, for the last three fiscal years and any years prior thereto that remain open and subject to adjustment, audit, or review by the IRS or any state or local taxing authority, and copies of all audit, determination, and other correspondence pertaining thereto, including, but not limited to, levies and liens.
3. All information related to any audit of any tax return or report filed by or on behalf of the Company, whether or not reduced to formal correspondence, for the last five fiscal years and pending audits for any prior periods that could affect the tax liability, credits, or other tax attributes of the Company.
4. For state franchise or similar tax liabilities of the Company, a schedule setting forth, for each state in which such payments were made, the most recent period for which a franchise tax or similar tax payment was made and the date on which such payment is due and payable each year.
5. For personal and real property taxes, a schedule setting forth, for each location in which such payments were made, the most recent period for which such a tax payment was made and the date on which such payment is due and payable each year.
6. A schedule describing any ongoing tax disputes, together with copies of revenue

BUSINESS ACQUISITION: DUE DILIGENCE CHECKLIST (continued)

agents' reports, correspondence, etc., with respect to any pending federal, state, provincial, or similar tax proceedings, with regard to open years or items relating to the Company.

7. Any federal, state, or local tax correspondence in the past three years, including current or pending assessments, reports, proposals, liens, levies, investigations, and/or disputes.

MISCELLANEOUS

1. Copies of all speeches delivered by any officer or director of the Company to trade associations, etc.

2. Copies of all articles from financial or other publications concerning the Company.

3. Copies of master forms of all material relating to the Company distributed to employees generally.

4. A schedule of all insurance covering the Company, its assets and properties, and any of its employees, together with copies of related policies and policy amounts.

5. All customer and independent contractor complaints or demands received within the last twelve months with respect to the Company or the services thereof.

6. All complaints of residents and business establishments near any of the facilities involved in the business of the Company received within the last thirty-six months.

7. All complaints to the Company received within the last twelve months regarding any employee or agent associated with the Company, whether such complaint is by another employee or a person not an employee.

8. All other documents viewed by the officers and directors of the Company as material to the business, financial conditions, or operations of the Company.

9. Internal reports and studies concerning matters that are material to the ongoing business of the Company of the operation or ownership of their real property (whether owned or leased).

CHECKLIST FOR REAL ESTATE CLOSING

GENERAL INFORMATION

Title Commitment Number: _____

Sale Price: $ _____

Contract Closing Date: _____

Attorney Assignment: _____

_____

SELLER'S INFORMATION

Property Addess: _____

Permanent Index No.: _____

Name(s): _____

Address: _____

Telephone No.: _____

SSN(s): _____

SELLER'S REALTOR INFORMATION

Agent Name: _____

Agency Name: _____

Address: _____

Telephone No.: _____

Commission: _____

Amount of Earnest

Money Deposit: $ _____

INFORMATION REGARDING SELLER'S CURRENT MORTGAGE(S)

1. Lender: _____

   Address: _____

   Loan No.:_____

   Telephone No.: _____

   Fax: _____

2. Lender: _____

   Address: _____

   Loan No.:_____

   Telephone No.: _____

   Fax: _____

CHECKLIST FOR REAL ESTATE CLOSING (continued)

If Condominium, name, address, and telephone number of Condominium Association:

_____

_____

_____

(If Condominium, order Certificate of Insurance)

Insurance Co.: _____

Phone No. and Contact: _____

CONDOMINIUM CHECKLIST

	Requested	Received
Bylaws, Declaration, Amendments	_____	_____
Rules & Regulations	_____	_____
Board Meeting Minutes	_____	_____
Budget/Financial Statement	_____	_____
Amount in Reserve	_____	_____
Section 22.1 Disclosures	_____	_____
Paid Assessment Letter	_____	_____
Waiver of Right of First Refusal	_____	_____
Certificate of Insurance	_____	_____
Heating Disclosure	_____	_____
Water Bill	_____	_____

BUYER'S INFORMATION

Name: _____

Address: _____

Marital Status and tenancy in
which they will hold title: _____

INFORMATION REGARDING BUYER'S ATTORNEY

Attorney Name:_____

Firm Name: _____

Address: _____

Telephone No.: _____

Fax:_____

CHECKLIST FOR REAL ESTATE CLOSING (continued)

INFORMATION REGARDING BUYER'S LENDER

Lender Name: _____

Contact Person: _____

Address: _____

_____

_____

Telephone No.: _____

Fax: _____

Loan Amount: $ _____

Loan Number: _____

Endorsements: _____

Information needed to order Certificate of Insurance (for Condo/Townhome Association):

Language to go on Certificate (obtain from Buyer's Lender only):

Buyer's Lender Name: _____

ATIMA Clause: _____

P.O. Box: _____

Buyer's Name: _____

Loan Number: _____

ATTORNEY REVIEW CHECKLIST

Contract Accepted: _____

Purchase Price: $ _____

Initial Earnest Money: $ _____ Held by _____

Additional Earnest Money: $ _____ Due _____

Attorney Review   _____ Extension _____

Inspection Deadline

Mortgage Contingency   _____ Extension _____

Real Estate Tax Proration _____

Property Tax Exemption _____

Closing Date _____

Credits at Closing _____

CHECKLIST FOR REAL ESTATE CLOSING (continued)

DESCRIPTION	DATE SUMBITTED	FOLLOW-UP DATE
Order Title Search	_____	_____
Customer Author. Ltr(s) (if needed)	_____	_____
Order Pay-off Letter I	_____	_____
Order Pay-off Letter II	_____	_____
Order Survey	_____	_____
Condo. Association's Right of 1st Refusal Letter and Letter of Assessment	_____	_____
Condo.'s Certificate of Insurance	_____	_____
Land Trust:		
Letter of Direction	_____	_____
Land Trust:		
Pay Proceeds Letter	_____	_____
Order Municipal Inspection	_____	_____
Prepare Municipal Transfer Tax Documents	_____	_____
Prepare State Transfer Tax Documents	_____	_____
Order Zoning Compliance Certificate	_____	_____
Water Certificate Needed?	_____	_____
Prepare Deed	_____	_____
Prepare Bill of Sale	_____	_____
Prepare ALTA (2 copies)	_____	_____
Prepare Affidavit of Title	_____	_____
Prepare Residential Real Estate Disclosure Report	_____	_____
Power of Attorney	_____	_____
Judgment Affidavit	_____	_____
Well and Septic Test	_____	_____
Agent Commission Letter	_____	_____
Keys/Garage Door Opener	_____	_____
Paid Assessment Letter	_____	_____
HUD-1	_____	_____
Attorney's Fees on HUD-1	_____	_____
Real Estate Tax Bill Payment Receipt	_____	_____
Receipts for Repairs	_____	_____

LETTER OF INTENT TO PURCHASE REAL ESTATE

_____

Attention: _____

_____

_____

Re: Letter of Intent to Purchase the Premises at _____

Dear _____:

    This letter shall constitute a confidential Letter of Intent ("**Letter of Intent**") which shall set forth the terms of our proposed Purchase of Real Estate located at _____ in _____ ("**Premises**"), to which terms the parties hereto shall incorporate and be bound upon the execution and delivery of a definitive and final Purchase Agreement and the receipt of consents required under the Purchase Agreement for the Premises (as defined below). The parties shall work together in good faith to prepare and consummate the Purchase Agreement on the terms set forth herein. For the purposes of this Letter of Intent, Seller shall be _____, (hereinafter "**Seller**"), and the Purchaser shall be _____ (hereinafter "**Purchaser**").

SELLER

Name: _____

Address: _____

PURCHASER

Name: _____

Address: _____

PREMISES/BUILDING

[**OPTIONAL**] Real property and improvements thereon, totaling approximately _____ of total square feet, with an address of _____, _____ and all appurtenant parking (totaling ____ spaces) (the "**Property**" or "**Premises**").

PURCHASE PRICE

Purchaser shall enter into a Purchase Agreement ("**Agreement**") with the Seller to purchase the Premises for a purchase price of _____AND____/100 DOLLARS ($_____).

LETTER OF INTENT TO PURCHASE REAL ESTATE (continued)

EARNEST MONEY

Purchaser shall pay \$_____AND____/100 DOLLARS (\$_____)
as earnest money to Seller upon execution of a final Purchase Agreement for the Premises.

CLOSING DATE

Purchaser shall purchase the Premises from Seller on or before _____ ____,
20___.

DELIVERABLES

Within fifteen (15) days of execution of the Agreement, Seller shall deliver all property reports in its possession, including title commitment, survey, and environmental audits. At closing, Seller shall deliver possession of the Property along with a general warranty deed conveying title free and clear of all liens, claims, and encumbrances.

INSPECTION/DUE DILIGENCE PERIOD

Purchaser shall have a period of _____ (__) days ("**Inspection Period**") from the execution of the Agreement in which to conduct an inspection of the Premises and to obtain municipal entitlements. During the Inspection Period, Purchaser shall have the right to inspect the Premises and perform studies and/or investigations with respect to the Premises, including, without limitation: (i) structural integrity of the building; (ii) structure and condition of the roof; (iii) condition and capacity of the parking lot, electrical system and panel, HVAC system, plumbing, waste, sewer, storm sewer, and other mechanical systems; (iv) third-party appraisal; (v) environmental studies and investigations into regulatory and title conditions; and (vi) other operational matters. Purchaser shall have three (3) one-month options to extend such due diligence period, at no cost to Purchaser.

TAXES

Purchaser shall not be responsible for any property taxes, employment taxes, state sales taxes and any other taxes which have accrued prior to the Closing Date. Real estate taxes shall be prorated as of the Closing Date. Seller will give Purchaser a credit for 100% based on the last ascertainable tax bill. The parties will execute a Re-Proration Agreement at closing agreeing to recalculate the credit postclosing, once the actual tax bill comes out for the tax year at issue. Seller shall indemnify Purchaser for any claim of taxes owed relating back to any period of time prior to the Closing Date.

LETTER OF INTENT TO PURCHASE REAL ESTATE (continued)

ASSIGNABILITY

Purchaser shall have the unilateral right to assign, transfer, or pledge the Agreement and any right, obligation, and/or interest granted therein to a nominee of its choice. Seller shall be prohibited from assigning its responsibilities, duties, rights, benefits, and/or obligations under the Agreement.

SUBJECT TO FINANCING

This Agreement is contingent on Purchaser obtaining financing on or before _____ _____, 20____.

CONTRACT

Upon acceptance by Seller of this Letter of Intent, Purchaser shall cause its legal counsel, _____, to prepare the Agreement for the purchase of the Premises at the agreed upon Purchase Price that incorporates the terms and conditions of this Letter of Intent, which shall include, but in no way be limited to, representations and warranties by Seller for the benefit of Purchaser as to the Premises and Seller's unencumbered right to enter into the Agreement, and which shall otherwise contain terms and conditions as are in form customary for such a real estate purchase transaction for the county and state in which the Premises is located.

CONDITIONS PRECEDENT

Purchaser's obligations to purchase the Premises and to take any other action(s) required to be taken by Purchaser at closing are subject to the satisfaction, among other obligations as may be required of Seller under the Agreement, at or prior to closing, of each of the following conditions (any of which may be waived by Purchaser, in writing, in whole or in part): (i) all of Seller's representations and warranties (see below) in the Agreement shall be true and accurate in all material respects as of the Closing Date as if then made; (ii) all covenants, acts, undertakings, and obligations that Seller is required to perform or to comply with pursuant to this Agreement at or prior to the Closing Date shall have been duly performed and complied with in all material respects; (iii) there not having been issued or in effect any order, decree, or judgment of any court, governmental, or administrative body or agency that makes the consummation of the transactions contemplated by this Agreement violate any applicable law; and (iv) the execution and the delivery of this Agreement and the consummation of the transactions contemplated herein shall have been approved by all regulatory authorities whose approvals are required by all applicable laws, ordinances, rules, regulations, and governmental orders (it being understood and agreed by Purchaser that Seller has not made nor shall be deemed to have made any representation, warranty or covenant with respect to such approvals).

LETTER OF INTENT TO PURCHASE REAL ESTATE (continued)

SELLER REPRESENTATIONS AND WARRANTIES

Seller shall represent and warrant, among other things, the following to Purchaser regarding the Property, if applicable:

A. Authority. Seller has full right, power, and authority to enter into this Contract and to perform all of Seller's obligations hereunder and is duly organized and validly existing and in good standing in its jurisdiction of organization in the State of _____.

B. Leases. The documents constituting the leases identified in the certified Rent Roll that have been delivered (which are in Seller's possession) pursuant to the Agreement are true, correct, and complete copies of all of the leases affecting the property, to the extent the same are in Seller's possession, including any and all amendments or supplements thereto, and guaranties or other security in connection therewith.

C. Employee Obligations. Seller has no employee obligations with respect to the Property which will be binding on Purchaser or give rise to a claim against the Property.

D. Compliance with Laws and Regulations. To Seller's actual knowledge, the Property is presently, and as of closing will be in compliance with all statutes, ordinances, rules, regulations, orders, and requirements (federal, state and local) applicable to or affecting the Property.

E. Litigation. To Seller's knowledge, there is no litigation or proceeding, in law or in equity, and there are no proceedings or governmental investigations before any commission or other administrative authority, pending, or threatened, against the Seller or the Property.

F. No-Lease Defaults. As of the contract date and as of the Closing, the Leases are in full force and effect according to the terms set forth therein, and Seller has received no written notice of default from any tenant thereunder, nor, to Seller's actual knowledge, are any tenants in default under their respective Leases, except as may be disclosed in the Rent Roll. No tenant has paid rent more than ____ (__) month(s) in advance. To Seller's actual knowledge, (i) Seller is not in default of its obligations under any of the Leases, and (ii) no circumstance exists which would, with the giving of notice and the passage of time, constitute a default under the Leases.

G. Condition of Property. Seller is not aware of any material defect with respect to any portion of the Property that Seller, as landlord, is required to maintain pursuant to the leases.

H. Tenant-Related Payments. All brokers' commissions pertaining to the leases have been paid, including any commission that pertains to any option period under any existing lease, and there are no tenant improvement allowances under any of the leases that have not been paid.

LETTER OF INTENT TO PURCHASE REAL ESTATE (continued)

I. Existing Mortgage Loan. Seller is the mortgagor pursuant to the existing mortgage loan from Lender, _____, in the original principal amount of $_____.

J. Environmental. Seller has provided to Purchaser true, correct, and complete copies of all environmental reports relating to the Property that are in Seller's possession or control, and except as disclosed in such environmental reports, Seller has no knowledge of the presence of any material amount of hazardous materials at the Property in violation of any environmental law.

Seller's representations and warranties contained above shall survive the Closing for a period of _____ (_) months.

CONDITIONS OF PREMISES

The Premises shall be delivered to Purchaser in a broom clean, "vanilla box" condition as shall be set forth and further described in the Lease.

MISCELLANEOUS

It is expressly understood and agreed by Purchaser and Seller that this Letter of Intent is not a binding contract between the parties but serves to outline the terms and conditions for discussions regarding a probable Purchase Agreement for the Premises. Neither party shall have any obligation with respect to the other party (except that, after the mutual execution and delivery hereof, Purchaser and Seller shall have the obligation to negotiate in good faith to consummate a Purchase Agreement including the terms set forth herein) until such time as the parties execute and deliver a definitive Purchase Agreement and Seller has consented thereto. Purchaser acknowledges and understands that Seller's consent is required to make any Purchase Agreement lawfully binding.

BROKERAGE COMMISSION

Seller shall pay for all brokerage commissions, if any, on this purchase/sale transaction to _____, at ____% of the Purchase Price.

Upon this Letter of Intent being duly executed by Purchaser and Seller and all contingencies are removed, this executed Letter of Intent shall be used for drafting a Purchase Agreement and shall not be binding on either party until the Purchase Agreement has been duly executed by Purchaser and Seller. Any conflict between the Letter of Intent and the Purchase Agreement shall be controlled by the Purchase Agreement.

LETTER OF INTENT TO PURCHASE REAL ESTATE (continued)

SELLER: PURCHASER:

/s/_____   /s/_____
By: By:
Its: Its:

LETTER OF INTENT TO LEASE

_____

Attention: _____

_____

_____

Re: **Letter of Intent to Lease Retain Premises at** _____

Dear _____:

    This letter shall constitute a confidential Letter of Intent ("**Letter of Intent**") which shall set forth the terms of our proposed Lease Agreement of Retail Space located at _____ in _____ (hereinafter "**Lease**"), to which terms the parties hereto shall incorporate and be bound upon the execution and delivery of a definitive and final Agreement and the receipt of consents required under the Lease for the Premises (as defined below). The parties shall work together in good faith to consummate the Lease on the terms set forth herein. For the purposes of this Letter of Intent, Lessee shall be _____ (hereinafter "**Tenant**"), and the Lessor shall be _____, ___, an Illinois _____ (hereinafter "**Landlord**").

LANDLORD

_____ , an Illinois _____

Attention: _____

_____

_____

TENANT

_____

_____

_____

LEASED PREMISES

Approximately _____ of total rentable square feet, with an address of

_____ , _____.

LETTER OF INTENT TO LEASE (continued)

USE AND EXCLUSIVITY OF PREMISES

To manage and operate a _____ business. There is no exclusivity of use.

COMMENCEMENT DATE

The Lease shall begin, and Tenant shall have access to the Premises beginning the ___ day of _____, 20___.

RENT COMMENCEMENT DATE

The rent commencement date shall be _____ ___, 20___.

TENANT IMPROVEMENT ALLOWANCE

[OPTIONAL] Landlord shall provide Tenant an improvement allowance up to $_____.00.

TERMINATION DATE

On the ___ anniversary of the Commencement Date unless extended or except as otherwise provided in Lease.

INITIAL TERM

The initial term of the Lease shall be for ___ years.

OPTION TO RENEW

Tenant shall have the option to extend the Lease for ___, ___-year terms.

BASE RENT FOR INITIAL TERM

Tenant's Base Rent shall be based on the following Rent Schedule:

LEASE YEAR	MONTHLY RENT
1. _____	$ _____
2. _____	$ _____
3. _____	$ _____
4. _____	$ _____
5. _____	$ _____

LETTER OF INTENT TO LEASE (continued)

RENT DURING OPTION PERIOD

Tenant's Base Rent shall be based on the following Rent Schedule:

LEASE YEAR   MONTHLY RENT

1. _____ $ _____

2. _____ $ _____

3. _____ $ _____

4. _____ $ _____

5. _____ $ _____

SECURITY DEPOSIT

A security deposit equal to ____ month's Base Rent shall be paid to Landlord upon full execution and delivery of the Lease and receipt of Landlord's consent ("**Security Deposit**"). The Security Deposit shall be held to secure the performance of Tenant under the Lease until the termination of the Lease or any Option Term (if any), at which time said Security Deposit shall be refunded to Tenant, if any (less any costs incurred by Landlord due to Tenant's failure to comply with the terms of the Lease). The Security Deposit shall not be used by Tenant to apply to Rent, and shall not be required to be held in an interest-bearing account by Landlord.

COMMON AREA MAINTENANCE CHARGES

Tenant shall pay an additional rent for its proportionate share of Common Area Maintenance (CAM) charges. CAM charges shall be expenses commonly relating to the common area of the Building, including a reasonable management fee, and as set forth in the Lease. Estimates of CAM shall be paid monthly by the Tenant, and reconciled after year-end. The CAM shall be charged pro rata to Tenant's use of rented square footage in building.

UTILITIES

Tenant shall timely pay all charges for all utilities set forth in the Lease including, but not limited to electricity, water, storm water facilities, sanitary sewer, telephone, alarm service, refuse collection, and gas furnished to the Premises.

PROPERTY TAX PRORATION

Tenant shall pay its proportionate share of real property tax. Estimates of property taxes shall be paid monthly by the Tenant and reconciled after year-end.

LETTER OF INTENT TO LEASE (continued)

PROPORTIONATE SHARE

Tenant's proportion share shall be the Tenant's Premises in square feet divided by the total available retail space in Building/Shopping Center. Such proportion share is currently _____ percent (___%).

PERCENTAGE RENT

[OPTIONAL] Tenant shall pay Landlord _____ percent (___%) of Tenant's annual gross sales in excess of the Gross Sales Breakpoint as defined in the Lease.

CONDITION OF PREMISES

The Premises shall be delivered to Tenant in a broom clean, "dark box" condition as shall be set forth and further described in the Lease.

TENANT IMPROVEMENTS

All costs related to tenant improvements, alterations, or modifications to the Premises shall be performed at Tenant's sole expense as described in the Lease. Any improvements to the Premises shall receive Landlord's prior written consent before improvements are commenced, and shall be subject to all the terms of the Lease.

ACCESS

Tenant shall have access to the Premises beginning on the Commencement Date 24 hours a day, 7 days a week, 52 weeks per year.

COMMISSIONS

[OPTIONAL] A leasing commission paid to Landlord's agent, if any, shall be the responsibility of Landlord.

ASSIGNMENTS & SUBLETTING

Tenant shall not sublet or assign the Premises to any third party, related entity, or affiliate to be further defined in the Lease) without Landlord's prior written consent, which consent shall not be unreasonably withheld.

LETTER OF INTENT TO LEASE (continued)

SUBORDINATION/ESTOPPELS

This Lease shall be automatically subordinate to any deed of trust, mortgage, or other security instrument, or any ground lease, master lease, or primary lease that now or subsequently covers all or any part of the Building without any further action or writing of the parties. Upon request of Landlord, Tenant shall execute truthful and accurate estoppels certificates, as more fully set forth in the Lease.

RULES AND REGULATIONS

Tenant shall abide by Landlord's rules and regulations that may change from time to time, as may be deemed necessary by Landlord for the operation of the Building/Shopping Center, including employee parking, and use of the parking lot.

SIGNAGE

All tenant signage shall be approved in advance by the Landlord pursuant to and in accordance with the terms of the Lease, and shall be further subject to all municipal ordinances. Tenant shall pay the cost of removing and installing new signage (including, without limitation, the cost of permits and approvals, design, construction, repairs, and any other costs relating thereto).

GUARANTY

A personal guaranty(s) shall be given by _____ , _____ , and _____ to the benefit of Landlord to guaranty the payment and performance of all provisions, covenants, rent obligations, common area maintenance expenses, late fees, and any other duties and obligations of Tenant, as set forth and further described in the Lease.

MISCELLANEOUS

It is expressly understood and agreed by Landlord and Tenant that this Letter of Intent is not a binding contract between the parties but serves to outline the terms and conditions for discussions regarding a probable Lease of the Premises. Neither party shall have any obligation with respect to the other party (except that, after the mutual execution and delivery hereof, Tenant and Landlord shall have the obligation to negotiate in good faith to consummate a Lease including the terms set forth herein) until such time as the parties execute and deliver a definitive Lease Agreement and Landlord has consented thereto. Tenant acknowledges and understands that Landlord's consent is required to make any Lease lawfully binding.

LETTER OF INTENT TO LEASE (continued)

Upon this Letter of Intent being duly executed by Landlord and Tenant and all contingencies are removed, this executed Letter of Intent shall be used for drafting a Lease and shall not be binding on either party until the Lease has been duly executed by Tenant and Landlord. Any conflict between the Letter of Intent and the Lease shall be controlled by the Lease.

TENANT: LANDLORD:

/s/_____   /s/_____
By: By:
Its: Its:

Index

A

ABA. *See* American Bar Association

Accountability, management team, 400–401

Accountants, 68–69, 80

Accounting department, 219–220

Accounting software, 67, 68–69

Accounts receivable. *See also* Collections
  and billing, 107
  defined, 110
  delegation of, 330
  departmentalization of, 81–84

Accurate bills, client complaints about, 117–118

Added value, for clients, 149

Additional services, marketing, 293–295

Administrative assistants, 217–218, 221, 417–418

ADP, 85

Advertising
  at Lavelle Law Ltd, xxiv–xxv
  billboard, TV, and radio, 287
  direct mail, 280–281
  in Yellow Pages, 278
  Model Code of Professional Conduct on, 132, 206–207
  of legal specialty, 123–124

Advisors, 205–206

Advocates, 205–206

Agreements
  for contract work, 40
  shareholder. *See* Shareholder agreements

Al Knox Award for Ethics in Business, xxvi

American Bar Association (ABA), 9, 58, 123, 154

American Express, 327

Announcement cards, 54

Annual meetings, 260

Apple, 51, 290–291

Applicable law, declining cases due to, 161

ARDC (Attorney Registration and Disciplinary Commission), 49, 119

Art, website, 61

Asset sales, 357–358

Asset value, 386

Associate attorneys
  base salary for, 228–229
  exposing clients to, 344
  management of legal work by, 332–333
  ratio of partners to, 337–338

Attorney Registration and Disciplinary Commission (ARDC), 49, 119

Attorney(s). *See also* specific types
  accounts receivable as responsibility of, 111, 112
  as client advocates, 205–206
  as relationship managers, 311–312
  base salary for, 227–228
  buy-in/sell-off cycle for, 352–354

Attorney(s) (*continued*)

    clients who switch, 159

    compensation incentives for, 228–229

    counselor/advisor roles of, 205–206

    exposing clients to additional, 312–313

    hiring, 199–200, 225

    marketing checklist for, 298–299

    migration of, 36–37

    part-time, 242

    pre-merger questions about, 433

    successful firms vs. successful, 343–344

    year-end reviews for, 243–244

Authenticity, 318

Award for Business Excellence, xxvi

B

Bank accounts, 47–48

Bank financing, for buy-in, 377–378

Banking, 79–80, 330

Bar associations, 9, 58

Base salary

    for attorneys, 227–228

    in shareholder agreements, 393

    of founding partners, 359–360

Best practices for law firms, 165–166

    for client fulfillment, 313

    for estate planning and estate

        administration, 179–180

    for family law cases and divorce

        matters, 180

    for initial meetings with clients, 166

    for litigation cases, 175–176

    for tax cases, 181

    for transactional and commercial real

        estate cases, 178

    on client communication and file

        documentation, 172

Big hairy audacious goals, 257–258

BI Intelligence, 129

Billable rates, 27–28, 98

Billable time

    and research, 58

    incentives based on, 229–230, 231

    tracking, 95–96

Billboards, 287

Billing, 89–91

    and setting hourly rates, 98

    at mature practices, 415–416

    delegation of, 330

    departmentalization of, 80–81

    for flat fee cases, 99–100

    honesty and integrity in, 106

    hourly, 91–92

    hybrid methods of, 103

    software for, 67–68

    tracking time for, 95–96

    value, 103–105

    with contingency fee arrangements,

        100–101

    with monthly retainers, 102

Billing System Form, 96–98

Bill paying, 79–80, 330

Bills

    accurate, 117–118

    client complaints about, 115–116

    detailed, 108

    errors on, 115–116

Bing, 278

Black's Law Dictionary, 57

Blink (Malcolm Gladwell), 156

Boeing, 318

Bonuses

    for attorneys, 228–229

    for support staff, 223

    in small-firm mergers, 435–436

    shareholder agreement on, 395–396

Bookkeeping, 219–220, 330

Book value, 386

Boutique firms, 36

Brafton, 278

Branding, 42, 284–285, 287

Brief writing, 40

BTI Consulting Group, 154–155

Buffett, Warren, 236

Built to Last (James C. Collins and Jerry
    I. Porras), 316–317, 328

Burkin, Alice, 157

Business cards, 54, 138–140

Business expenses, 394–395

Business Leader of the Year, xxvi

Business of the Year, xxv

Business perks, 407

Business plans, 253

    addressing firm improvements in,
        263–264

    and annual firm meetings, 260

    big hairy audacious goals in, 257–258

    components of, 253–254

    five-year, 256

    for mature practices, 418–419

    networking as part of, 276

    one-year, 255

    requirements for employees in, 259

    ten-year, 256–257

    writing, 254–255

Business-related contacts,, 4–6

Business-related responsibilities, of five-
    tool attorneys, 30–31

Buy-in partners

    determining initial percentage to sell to,
        372–373

    due diligence for, 374

    expression of interest by, 371–372

    financing arrangements for, 377

    preliminary disclosure to, 371–372

    savings of, 382

Buy-in/sell-off cycle, 352–354

C

Calendars, electronic, 52

Call options, 387–388

CAM (common area maintenance), 73

Canada, 279

Cash flow analysis, 357–358, 362–363

Cash flow, in valuation formula, 386

Cash-out, 362–363

CDEL (Clinic for the Disabled and Elder
    Law), xxvi

CD-ROM disks, with practice books, 57

Celebrity legal issues, 131

Checklists for law firms, 183–184, 212.
    See also specific checklists

Checks, signing, 220–221

Chicago's Legal Latte (podcast), xxv

Children. *See* Family members

China, 279

Civic involvement

    at Lavelle Law Ltd, xxv–xxvi

    at mature practices, 416

    by five-tool attorneys, 28, 29

    face-to-face networking with, 135–136

Civil matters, specializing in, 127

Claims-made insurance policies, 44

Clerks, 222, 232

Client contact, 201, 225

Client fulfillment, 309

    and exceeding client expectations,
        309–310

    for mature practices, 419

    process for, 313

    relationship managers' role in,
        311–312

Client Intake Form, 89–91, 174

Client letters, 169

Client loyalty, 151–152, 288–289

Client Referrals Form, 293–295

Clients, 147. *See also* Potential clients

Clients (*continued*)
adding value to, 149
as focus of law practice, 147
communication with, 153–154,
154–155
complaints by, 115–116, 375
declining cases from, 159–161
educating, about billing, 113
expectations of, 309–310
incentives based on bringing in,
230–231
initial meetings with, 166, 305–306
marketing additional services to,
293–295
of mature practices, 419
on thirty-day delinquency list, 110–111
questions/comments from delinquent,
112
reliance on single, 201
respecting, 152–153
with existing attorney relationships,
151–152
Client satisfaction, 154–155. *See
also* Client fulfillment
Clinic for the Disabled and Elder Law
(CDEL), xxvi
Code of Civil Procedure, 176
Collateral, for partner buy-in, 380–381
Colleagues
law school, 4–5
selling law firms to, 345–346
Collections, 107–108
and depositing retainer checks,
109–110
and payment plans, 114
by sole practitioners, 200
client complaints about bills, 115–116
creating detailed bills, 108

for clients on thirty-day delinquency
list, 110–111
suing former clients for fees, 119
College students, as administrative
assistants, 218–219
Collins, James C., 235–236, 242, 246,
315, 316–317, 328
Commercial real estate cases, 178
Common area maintenance (CAM), 73
Communication
as leadership skill, 250–251
best practices, 172
of management team's message,
402–403
with clients, 113, 153–154, 154–155
Community development, 283–284. *See
also* Civic involvement
Community, messages about firm in, 275
Complaints, client, 115–116, 375
Computer equipment, 50–52
Concentration, area of, 125–126,
127–128
Concentration (leadership skill), 247–248
Confidentiality
and referral sources, 74, 275
in lawyer-client relationship, 204–205
of financial information, 371
Conflicts of interest, 204–205
Connectors, 273–274
Contact, client, 201, 225
Contact information, disseminating,
283–284
Contacts
business-related, 4–6
of parents, 5–6
personal social, 5
thank-you notes for new, 141–142
Content, website, 62–63, 64, 133

Contingency fee arrangements, 100–101, 103, 119, 160

Contract attorneys, 40–41

Contracts
establishing lawyer-client relationship with, 203
for cases with contingency fees, 101
for legal services, 92
signing of, 109–110

Control premium, 368–369

Cooley, Dick, 236

Cooperative suites, 76

Copy machines, 65–66

Core purpose, 315–316
and client loyalty, 290
and core values of employees, 321–322
and firm culture, 325–326
defined, 316–317
identifying your firm's, 319
of civic involvement, 28
of mature practices, 420
profit maximization as, 315–316

Corporate Law Association, xxiii

Corporations, 37, 85

Counselors, attorney as, 205–206

Courthouses, offices located near, 77–78

Craigslist, 73

Creativity, 326–328

Credit cards, 81–84

Culture. *See* Firm culture

D

Death of shareholders, obligations related to, 389–390

Death plans, 45

Declining cases, 159–161

Delegation, 329
improving firms with, 264–265
of legal work, 331–332

of office management, 329–330

Departmentalizing law office functions, 79–80
banking and bill paying, 79–80
billing and accounts receivable, 80–81
human resources, 85
management of legal work, 88
marketing, 86–87
office management, 87–88
payroll, 84–85
technology-related tasks, 87–88

Depositions, 177–178

Deposits, retainer, 91–92, 109–110

Dictation, 65–66, 216

Digital footprint, 134

Direct mail, 280–281

Disability insurance, 44

Discounted share value, 386

Discounts, 368
lack-of-control/minority, 368–369, 369–370
marketability, 368–369, 369–370

Discrimination (leadership skill), 247–248

Disney, 318

Dissertations, 8

Divorce matters, 180

Documentation
file, 174
of amended billing arrangements, 115
of buy-in. *See* Shareholder agreements

Domain names, 42–43

Drucker, Peter, 147, 269, 272, 316, 328

Due diligence, 374

Duty of loyalty, 391–393

E

Earnings before interest, taxes, depreciation, and amortization (EBITDA), 358

"Easy" cases, 160

"Eat what you kill" bonus structure, 435

EBITDA (earnings before interest, taxes, depreciation, and amortization), 358

Electronic files, 174, 175

Elevator speech, 138

E-mail
  and telephone messages, 59
  communicating with clients via, 51, 158, 172, 173
  dictation of, 66

E-mail blasts, 131–132

Emotionally charged clients, 160

Empathy, 167

Employee recognition, 237–239

Employee retention, 237–239, 243

Employees
  at mature practices, 419
  pay-to-play requirements for, 259
  values of, 321–322
  year-end reviews for, 243

Employee selection
  at successful businesses, 235–236
  importance of, 235–236
  managing process of, 239
  unnecessary limitations in, 242–243

Employer's Tax Guide, 85

E-Myth Mastery (Michael Gerber), 247

Endorsements, 131

Enrolled agents, 181

Entrepreneurial challenges, in law practices, 19

Entrepreneurial personality, 20–21

Entrepreneurial risk, 373–374

Entrepreneurial risk premium, 360–361

Equal partnerships, 372–373

Equipment
  computer, 50–52

copy machines, 65–66

dictation, 65–66

postage meters, 67–68

printers, 52–53

Equity partner(s)
  benefits of taking on, 350–351
  income partners vs., 335–336
  potential. *See* Buy-in partners
  pre-merger questionnaires for, 426–431
  promoting income partners to, 338–339, 343

Errors, on bills, 115–116

Estate administration, 179–180

Estate planning
  best practices for, 179–180
  potential clients for, 269–270
  value billing for, 103

Ethical rules. *See* Model Code of Professional Conduct

Existing attorney relationships, clients with, 151–152

Existing law firms
  migration of attorneys from, 36–37
  office space within, 78

Expectations, clients', 309–310

Expenses, business, 394–395

Experience, 33–34

Explanation of services, 167–168

Expression of interest, by buy-in partner, 371–372

F

Facebook, 9, 130

Face-to-face networking, 135–136
  and asking for business, 145–146
  and marketing, 276
  elevator speech for, 138
  following through in, 144–145
  following up after, 141–142

initial meetings in, 138–140

in law school, 4

marketing mindset for, 136–137

relationship building in, 270–271

researching potential clients/referral sources after, 142–143

with civic involvement, 135–136

Fact-finding questions, 166–167

Faculty members, as mentors, 6–7

Fair market value, 361

Family businesses, 15, 349

Family law cases, 180

Family members

employing, 349

practicing with, 38–39

selling law firms to, 347–348

Fax numbers, 61

Fees, 91, 119

Fee sharing, 206–207, 223

FICA taxes, 37

File documentation, 174

Financial information, sharing

with buy-in partners, 371–372

with income partners, 336–337

Financial security, 406

Financial statements, 374

Financing arrangements for partner buy-in, 377

bank financing, 377–378

savings of buy-in partners in, 382

seller financing, 381–382

Findlaw, 57

Firm culture, 212

at mature practices, 416, 417

building, 325–326

marketing in, 292–293

pre-merger questions about, 433

Firm management, 261–262

creating high-performance environments with, 266–267

improving firms with, 263–264

operating manuals for, 267–268

organizational charts for, 266

reports required for, 261–262

Fit, hiring based on, 239

Five-tool attorneys, 25

business-related responsibilities of, 30–31

in mature practices, 415–416

leadership and training by, 29–30

marketing and civic involvement by, 28

production goals for, 26–27

Five-year business plans, 256

Flat fee cases, 99–100

Fleischman-Hillard, 278

Foonberg, Jay G., xvii, 13

"For cause" termination, 390–391

Ford, Henry, 105

Ford Motor Company, 105, 318

Former clients, suing, 119

Founding partners

determining salary of, 359–360

illegal tax deductions by, 369–370

implications of valuation analysis for, 364–365

in management meetings, 399–400

management by teams vs., 397–398

W-2 income of, 363

Four "S's" model, 21–22

Franchise, law office as, 275

Fraud, billing, 106

Furniture, office, 55–56

G

General Motors, 105

Gerber, Michael, 13, 19, 247

Gladwell, Malcolm, 156–157, 274

Goal(s)
    big hairy audacious, 257–258
    for mature practices, 418
    growth of law firm as, 45–46
    in business plans, 254–255
    production, 26–27
Godaddy.com, 42
Going concern value, 362–363
Good to Great (Jim Collins), 235–236,
        246
Google, 278, 279
Google AdWords, 279–280
Google Alerts, 58
Governance of entity, 393
Gross leases, 73
Growth
    and checklists, 183–184
    and profitability of small firms, 45–46
    and specialization, 124
    elements needed for, 211–212
    of Lavelle Law Ltd, xxiii–xxiv

H
Hard work, 33–34
Harley-Davidson, 290–291
Harnish, Verne, 248, 261–262, 263–264,
        265, 401, 402
High-performance environments,
        266–267
Hiring
    of accountants, 68–69
    of accounting department staff,
        219–220
    of administrative assistants, 217–218
    of attorneys, 199–200, 225
    of clerks, 222
    of support staff, 215–216
Home, office space in, 71–72
Honesty

    and advocating for client, 206
    in billing, 106
    in communication with clients,
        153–154
Hourly billing, 91–92, 98
HP, 318
Human resources, 85, 330–331, 374–375
Hybrid billing methods, 103
Hybrid financing arrangements, 382
Hypothetical questions, 150

I
Ibuka, Masaru, 317
"I Have a Dream" (Martin Luther King,
        Jr.), 291–292
Image, office furniture and, 55–56
Immigration and Naturalization Service,
        227
Incentives
    and employee recognition, 237–239
    for attorneys, 228–229
    for support staff, 223
Income
    and profit, 358–359
    in start-up year, 39–40
    K-1, 378–379, 435
    W-2. *See* W-2 income
Income partners, 335–336
    elevating senior associates to, 337–338
    equity partners vs., 335–336
    ownership enquiries by, 354–355
Incoming call log, 302
Incoming calls, protocol for, 304–305
Incorporation of business entities, 99
Incremental-percentage partnerships,
        373–374
India, 279
Information technology (IT) department,
        87–88

Infousa.com, 280
Initial meetings
    with clients, 166, 305–306
    with potential clients/referral sources,
        138–140
Innovation, 250
Insurance, 43–44, 390
Integrity, 106
Interest, expression of, 371–372
Interest on lawyers trust account.
    See IOLTA
Internal Revenue Code, 359, 394
Internal Revenue Service (IRS), 37, 85,
        181, 182, 227
International Bar Association, 155
Internet searches, for legal services, 129,
        278–279
Interviews, hiring, 241
Introduction (initial client consultation),
        166
Investment value, 361
Involuntary contingency fee arrangements,
        119
Involuntary transfers, 389
IOLTA (interest on lawyers trust account)
    establishing, 48–49
    retainer deposits in, 91–92, 109
    transfers out of, 110
iPhone, 66
IRS. *See* Internal Revenue Service
IT (information technology) department,
        87–88

J
Job sharing, 242–243
John Marshall Law School, xxiii
Johnson & Johnson, 318, 327
Jones, Jim, 325
Jurists Search, 57

K
K-1 income, 378–379, 435
Kennedy, John F., 257
King, Martin Luther, Jr., 291–292
Koresh, David, 325

L
Labor, in law offices, 211–212
Lacey, Robert, 105
Lack-of-control discount, 368–369,
        369–370
Lateral hires, 226, 231–232
Lavelle Law Ltd., xxiii–xxiv
LawCover, 156–157
Law libraries, 56–57
Law practices
    checklists for, 183–184
    clients as focus of, 147
    digital footprint of, 134
    entrepreneurial challenges in, 19
    experience before starting, 33–34
    improving, with firm management,
        263–264
    mature. *See* Mature practices
    naming, 41–42
    obligations of, upon death of
        shareholders, 389–390
    reasons for starting, 13–14
    successful attorneys vs. successful,
        343–344
    time commitment for business activities
        in, 13–14
Law profession, marketplace dynamics,
        265
Law school, 3–4
    bar association activities in, 9
    expanding your network in, 4
    law library of, 56
    publishing writing in, 8–9

Law school (*continued*)
  social media networking in, 9–10
Law school colleagues, networking with, 4–5
Law students. *See* Third-year law students
Lawsuits against former clients, 119
Lawyer-client relationship, 203–204
Lead conversion, 301
  initial meetings with clients, 305–306
  phone calls from potential clients, 301
Leadership, 245–246
  at mature practices, 418
  by five-tool attorneys, 29–30
  firm management vs., 261
  in community organizations, 136
  skills required for, 247–248
Lead generation. *See* Marketing
Legal work
  management of, 88, 331–332
Lencioni, Patrick, 237–239, 239–240, 315, 319, 322, 397
Letterhead, 53–54
Letters, marketing, 280–281
Level 5 leaders, 245–246
Levinson, Wendy, 157
LexisNexis, 56
Liability insurance, 44
Life insurance, 45–46, 390
Lincoln, Abraham, 109
LinkedIn, 9, 130
Liquidation, of law firms, 347–348
Liquidation value, 361
Listening, 140–141, 143
Litigation attorneys
  form books for, 57
  hiring, 227
  in partnerships, 34–35
  preparation for, 34
Litigation cases

and monthly retainers, 102, 103
  best practices for, 175–176
  suing clients for fees in, 120
Local bar associations, 9, 58
Logan, Dave, 113
Logos, 53–54, 284, 285
Loislaw, 57
Loyalty
  client, 151–152, 288–289
  duty of, 391–393

M
Malpractice claims
  and communication with clients, 154, 156–157
  by former clients sued for fees, 119
Malpractice insurance, 43–44
Management meetings
  accountability in, 400–401
  decisions made in, 399–400
  defined, 397
  founding partner's involvement in, 399–400
  frequency of, 401
  tenor of, 398–399
Management teams, 245, 397–398
  creation of high-performance environments by, 266–267
  management by founding partners vs, 397–398
  reinforcing messages from, 402–403
Managing partners, business-related responsibilities of, 31–32
Manuals, operating, 267–268
Marketability discount, 368–369, 369–370
Marketing, 269–270
  and client loyalty, 288–289
  and community development, 283–284

and face-to-face networking, 136–137

and identifying potential clients, 269–270

and messages in community about firm, 275

and public relations, 282

and public speaking, 282–283

and relationship building, 270–271

and understanding values of clients, 271–272

and value of referral sources, 272–273

area of concentration in, 125–126

at mature practices, 416, 419

branding in, 284–285

by five-tool attorneys, 28–29

by sole practitioners, 200–201

delegation of, 330–331

departmentalization of, 86–87

disclosure of information related to, 374–375

in firm culture, 292–293

letterhead as part of, 53

of additional services to existing clients, 293–295

search engine optimization for, 278–279

tracking marketing efforts, 296–299

with billboard, TV, and radio advertising, 287

with direct mail, 280–281

with Yellow Pages advertising, 278

Market value, 361

Marquard, William, 104

Marriott, 318

Martin-Dale Hubble, 155

Mass media advertising, 287

Mastering the Rockefeller Habits (Verne Harnish), 261–262, 401

Mature practices, 409–413

assessing five-tool attorney requirements for, 415–416

assessing support staff of, 417–418

identifying opportunities for improvement in, 420–421

questionnaire for, 409–414

writing business plans for, 418–419

Mavens, 273–274

Maxwell, David, 236

Mectizan, 317–318

Meetings

annual, 260

with clients, 166, 305–306

with management team.

See Management meetings

with potential clients/referral sources, 138–140, 142

Memos, 169

Merck & Company, 317–318

Merck, George, II, 317

Mergers of small firms. *See* Small-firm mergers

Messages

for social media networking, 130

from management teams, 402–403

in community about firm, 275

Microsoft Office Integration Suite, 51

Microsoft Outlook, 51, 131

Microsoft Word, 51, 184, 217

Migration, of attorneys, 36–37

Minority discount, 368–369, 369–370

Mission statements, 212

Model Code of Professional Conduct, 203–204

and organization of law practice, 37

benefits of following, 207–208

on advertising, 123, 132, 206–207

on client advocate role of attorney, 205–206

Model Code of Professional Conduct
(*continued*)
on counselor/advisor role of attorney, 205–206
on fee sharing, 223
on lawyer-client relationship, 203–204
on stealing clients' money, 207
Monthly retainers, 102
Motorola, 318
Murphy, Matt, xxvi

N
Names
domain, 42–43
law firm, 41–42
Networking. *See* Face-to-face networking; Social media networking
Networksolutions.com, 42
New client bonuses, 228–229, 395–396
Newsmakers (television series), xxv
"No charge to client" entries, 108–109, 172
Non-engagement letters, 161–163, 169

O
Occurrence-based insurance policies, 44
"Of counsel" relationship, 392, 405
Offer in Compromise, 182
Office furniture, 55–56
Office management
delegation of, 329–330
departmentalization of, 87–88
Office managers
administrative assistants as, 221
delegating work to, 329–330
responsibilities of, 87–88
Officers, shareholders as, 393
Office space, 71
finding, 72–73

from potential referral sources, 73–74
in cooperative suites, 76
in your home, 71–72
location of, 71, 77–78
retail-type, 75–76
within existing law firms, 78
Office supplies, 54
One-year business plans, 255
Operating accounts, 47–48
Operating agreements. *See* Shareholder agreements
Operating manuals, 267–268
Operations of entity, 393
Organizational charts, 266
Organization (leadership skill), 249–250
Overvaluation of firm, 371–372
Ownership enquiries, 354–355
Ownership, transferring, 345–346

P
Palatine Chamber of Commerce, xxv, xxvi
Palatine Senior Center, xxvi
Palatine Township Board, xxv
Palatine Township Food Pantry, xxv
Parents' contacts, networking with, 5–6
Partnerships, 34–35
Part-time employees, 242–243
Part-time work, mentors from, 7–8
Passion, 20, 21–22
Paychex Payroll Services, 85
Payment plans, 114
PayPal, 84
Payroll department, 84–85
Pay-to-play requirements for employees, 259
Pearce, Alfred, 105
Perks, business, 407
Personal social contacts, 5
Phone calls, from potential clients, 301

Porras, Jerry I., 246, 315, 316–317, 328

Postage meters, 67–68

Potential clients

asking for business from, 145–146

being in second place with, 151–152

following through with, 144–145

following up with, 141–142

identifying, 269–270

initial meetings with, 138–140

phone calls from, 301

researching, 142–143

Potential referral sources

asking for business from, 145–146

being in second place for, 152

following through with, 144–145

following up with, 141–142

initial meetings with, 138–140

office space from, 73–74

researching, 142–143

value of, 272–273

Practice group(s)

adding, with lateral hires, 232

adding, with mergers, 423–425

core purpose exercise for, 319

in cooperative suites, 76

naming firm based on, 41–42

Preliminary disclosure to buy-in partner, 371–372

and determining initial percentage to sell, 372–373

due diligence after, 374

expression of interest after, 371–372

Preliminary legal analysis, 167–168

Premiums

control, 368–369

entrepreneurial risk, 360–361

in valuation analysis, 368–369

Printers, 52–53

Prioritization, 247–248

Production goals, 26–27

Profitability, of small firms, 45–46

Profit(s)

and income, 358–359

in small-firm mergers, 436

maximization of, 315–316

Programming, website development, 62–63

Promissory notes, 115

Publications, 8–9

Public relations, 282

Public speaking, 282–283

Purpose. See Core purpose

Put options, 388

Q

Questionnaire for mature practices, 409–414

QuickBooks, 68

R

Radio advertising, 287

Recognition, employee, 237–239

Reconciliation, bank account, 48, 49, 50

Recruiting, 240–241

Referrals, 144, 278. See also Potential referral sources

Refunds, 50

Relationship building

and asking for sales, 145–146

and marketing, 270–271

and marketing additional services to clients, 295

by relationship managers, 311–312

following up after networking in, 141–142

listening in, 143–144

Relationship managers, 311–312

Relationships

Relationships (*continued*)
  in retirement, 407
  lawyer-client, 203–204
  of clients with existing attorneys,
       151–152
  "of counsel", 392, 405
Repeat business, 289–290
Report of Merger, 434, 437
Reports, for firm management, 261–262
Reputation, 343–345
Research, on potential clients/referral
       sources, 142–143
Residential real estate closings, 100
Respecting clients, 152–153, 272
Retail-type office space, 75–76
Retainer deposits, 91–92, 109–110
Retirement planning, 405–406
Retirement programs, 392–393
Reviews, year-end, 243

S
Salary. *See* Base salary
Salespeople
  attorneys as, 29, 136–138
  referral sources as, 274
Sales queues, 388
Savings, buy-in partner's, 382
Schedule C of Form 1040, 37, 85
Scheduling, 16–17
S corporations, 38
Searchengineland.com, 279
Search engine optimization, 43, 63–65,
       278–279
Selection, employee. *See* Employee
       selection
Self-assessment process, 147–148
Seller financing, for buy-in, 381–382
Selling law firms
  to colleagues, 345–346

  to family members, 347–348
  to third parties, 346–347
Senior associates
  delegation of business-related tasks to,
       30
  elevating, to income partners, 337–338
  management of legal work by, 333–334
  ownership enquiries by, 354–355
Settlement proposals, 101
Shapero v. Kentucky Bar Association
       (1988), 280
Shareholder agreements (operating
       agreements), 385
  call options in, 387–388
  company valuation formulas in, 386
  on business expenses, 394–395
  on duty of loyalty, 391–393
  on governance and operations of entity,
       393
  on involuntary transfers, 389
  on new client bonuses, 395–396
  on obligations of law office upon death
       of shareholders, 389–390
  on retirement programs, 392–393
  on termination of employment other
       than death, 390–391
  put options in, 388
  sales queues in, 388
  transferability restrictions in, 386–388
Shareholders, obligations of law office
       upon death of, 389–390
Sinek, Simon, 288, 289, 291
Size, as driver of mergers, 424–425
Small-firm mergers, 423
  benefits and drawbacks of, 423
  economic implications of, 434–435
  process for creating, 425–430
  reasons for starting, 423–424
  Report of Merger for, 437

Small firms
    profitability of, 45–46
    renting space from, 78
Social contributions, in retirement, 408
Social media networking, 129–130
    and firm's digital footprint, 134
    and marketing, 276
    and rules on advertising legal services,
        132
    at Lavelle Law Ltd, xxv
    consistency of website, 133
    in law school, 9–10
    with e-mail blasts, 131–132
    writing messages for, 130
Society for the Preservation of Human
        Dignity, xxvi
Software, 51
    billing and accounting, 67–68
    dictation, 66–67
    time-keeping, 95–96
    website creation, 64
Sole proprietorships, 37, 85
Solo practitioners
    concerns for, 199
    elevator speeches of, 138
    names of firms for, 42
Sony, 317–318, 318
Speaker phones, 60
Specialization, 123–124
Spirit of Life Award, xxvi
Spouses, practicing with, 38–39
Start with Why (Simon Sinek), 288
State bar associations, 9, 58
State of Illinois Circuit Court of Cook
        County CourtñAnnexed
        Mandatory Arbitration, xxiii
Status, in retirement, 407
Stock sales, 357–358
Stonecutter parable, 328

Streptomycin, 317
Succession planning, 343–344
    and buy-in/sell-off cycle for attorneys,
        352–354
    and successful attorneys vs. successful
        firms, 343–344
    discussing ownership enquiries,
        354–355
    options for, 345–346
    reasons for considering, 350–351
Super Lawyers Magazine, xxvi
Support staff, 215–216
    accounting department, 219–220
    administrative assistants, 217–218
    and time commitment for business
        activities, 16
    banking and bill paying by, 80
    benefits of hiring, 215–216
    clerks, 222
    incentives and bonuses for, 223
    of mature practices, 417–418
    part-time, 242
    pre-merger questions about, 433
    year-end reviews for, 243
Supreme Court Rules, 176
Surveys on the state of the law, 8
Systems
    as barrier to firm growth, 264
    at mature practices, 418
    of successful firms, 212–213
    pre-merger questions about, 433

T
Tax cases, 181
Tax deductions, illegal, 369–370
Taxes
    and bank financing of partner buy-in,
        377–378
    and organization of law practice, 37

Taxes (*continued*)
  and payroll, 84–85
Technology-related tasks
  delegation of, 331–332
  departmentalization of, 87–88
Telephone systems, 59
Television advertising, 287
Tenant reps, 72
Ten-year business plans, 256–257
Termination of employment, 236,
      390–391
"Thank you for retaining us" letters, 169
Thank-you notes, for new contacts,
      141–142
The Advantage (Patrick Lencioni)
      advantage, 237–239, 239–240,
      319
Theft, 49, 50, 207
The Three Laws of Performance (Steve
      Zaffron and Dave Logan)three
      laws, 113
The Tipping Point (Malcolm Gladwell)
      tipping, 274
Third party, selling firm to, 346–347
Third-year law students
  benefits of hiring, 226
  job prospects for, 3–4
  lateral hires vs., 231–232
  management of legal work by, 332–333
Thirty-day delinquency list, 110–111
3M, 318
Time
  billable. *See* Billable time
  for business activities of law practice,
      13–14
  tracking, 95–96
Trade organizations, 270–271, 284
Traditional networking. *See* Face-to-face
      networking

Training
  at mature practices, 416
  by five-tool attorneys, 29–30
  for third-year law students, 231–232
Transactional attorneys
  hiring, 227
  in partnerships, 34–35
Transactional cases, 178
Transferability restrictions, shareholder
      agreement, 386–388
Transfers of ownership, 345–346
Triple net leases, 73
Trust accounts, 50–51
Tumblr, 10
Twitter, 9, 130
Tyler, Tom, 155

U
Unique selling proposition (USP), 147,
      284, 288
United States, influence of Internet in
      purchasing decisions, 279
U.S. Attorney's Office, 227
USP. *See* Unique selling proposition
U.S. Postal Service, 67

V
Vagelos, P. Roy, 317
Valuation analysis
  and drawbacks of overvaluing firm,
      371–372
  and illegal tax deductions by founding
      partners, 369–370
  cash flow in, 357–358
  determining founding partner's salary
      for, 359–360
  discounts and premiums in, 368
  for small-firm merger, 434–435

implications of, for founding partners, 364–365

Valuation formulas, 361–362, 386

Value billing, 103–105

Values

    of clients, 148, 271–272

    of employees, 240–241, 321–322

    of potential referral sources, 274–275

Vendors, networking with, 137–138

Vision, 267

Voicemail, 60

Voting, 393–394

W

W-2 employee, owner as, 84, 85

W-2 income, 37

    and profit, 358, 359

    in small-firm mergers, 435–436

of founding partner, 359–360, 363

    reducing buy-in partner's, 382–383

Walk-ins, 301

Walmart, 104, 318, 350

Walton, Sam, 350

Web.com, 61

Websites, 61–62, 133

Wells Fargo Bank, 236

Westlaw, 56

Wix.com, 61

Y

Year-end reviews, 243

Yellow Pages, 278

Z

Zaffron, Steve, 113

Ziglar, Zig, 21–22